THE RURAL VOTER

THE RURAL VOTER

THE POLITICS OF PLACE
AND THE DISUNITING
OF AMERICA

NICHOLAS F. JACOBS
AND DANIEL M. SHEA

Columbia University Press
New York

Columbia University Press
Publishers Since 1893
New York   Chichester, West Sussex

Library of Congress Cataloging-in-Publication Data
Names: Jacobs, Nicholas F., author. | Shea, Daniel M. author.
Title: The rural voter : the politics of place and the disuniting of America /
Nicholas F. Jacobs and Daniel M. Shea.
Description: New York : Columbia University Press, 2023. |
Includes bibliographical references and index.
Identifiers: LCCN 2023020608 | ISBN 9780231211581 (hardback) |
ISBN 9780231218573 (paperback) | ISBN 9780231558983 (ebook)
Subjects: LCSH: Conservatism—United States. | Right and left (Political
science)—United States | Rural-urban relations—Political aspects—United
States. | Rural population—United States—Attitudes. | Republican Party
(U.S. : 1854–) | Political culture—United States.
Classification: LCC JC573.2.U6 J34 2023 |
DDC 320.5209173/4—dc23/eng/20230606

Cover design: Noah Arlow
Cover image: AP Photo/Charlie Neibergall

The house had gone to bring again
To the midnight sky a sunset glow.
Now the chimney was all of the house that stood,
Like a pistil after the petals go.

The barn opposed across the way,
That would have joined the house in flame
Had it been the will of the wind, was left
To bear forsaken the place's name.

No more it opened with all one end
For teams that came by the stony road
To drum on the floor with scurrying hoofs
And brush the mow with the summer load.

The birds that came to it through the air
At broken windows flew out and in,
Their murmur more like the sigh we sigh
From too much dwelling on what has been.

Yet for them the lilac renewed its leaf,
And the aged elm, though touched with fire;
And the dry pump flung up an awkward arm;
And the fence post carried a strand of wire.

For them there was really nothing sad.
But though they rejoiced in the nest they kept,
One had to be versed in country things
Not to believe the phoebes wept.

—Robert Frost, "The Need of Being Versed in Country Things"

CONTENTS

Preface   ix

INTRODUCTION: TWO AMERICAS   1

1 WHO AND WHAT IS RURAL AMERICA?   23

2 THE DEEP ROOTS OF THE RURAL-URBAN DIVIDE
(1776–1980)   59

3 MANUFACTURING THE MYTH OF "REAL AMERICA"
(1980–PRESENT)   93

4 LISTENING TO RURAL AMERICANS   141

5 DOWN AND OUT IN RURAL AMERICA?   158

6 A WASTELAND OF ALIENATION?   200

7 CLINGING TO THEIR GUNS AND RELIGION?   244

8 IRREDEEMABLY RACIST?   287

9 RADICALIZED BY FOX?   324

10 PULLING IT ALL TOGETHER: FINDING THE
RURAL VOTER   359

11 BRIDGES ACROSS THE RURAL-URBAN DIVIDE   380

Notes   415
Index   453

PREFACE

The idea for this book probably emerged after some pleasantly distracting conversation about maple sap, cider-making, chickens, or the long list of things we needed to do to get ready for winter. Since we met at Colby College in the autumn of 2019, we have spent too much time wasting away the productive hours of our days talking about our little slice of heaven here in rural Maine.

We are a tad unusual for academics in that regard. Our colleagues like to joke that we have "gone native," but both of us have fond connections to rural areas and rural people, even as we have followed our academic careers to different parts of the country than where we grew up. At the end of the day, we wrote a book on rural America because there is much we love and admire about rural life. There is something truly special about rural communities. Sure, living out in the country takes its toll, and our urbane colleagues and students often scratch their heads with wonder as to why we would ever put up with frozen septic tanks, hauling cord wood, the lack of good take-out, all the driving, and, more than anything else, all those Trump voters.

To a point, we have asked ourselves the same things. Why would we live such different lives, and alongside people who seem to have such a different view about what type of leader this country needs? We have lived the rural-urban divide—a divide that took on an even more tragic dimension with the spread of COVID-19. We saw farmers struggle when they were unable to get migrant workers because the border had shut down; we talked with so-called nonessential laborers who had never missed a day of work in their lives; we struggled to make sense of why our neighbors dismissed the severity of the disease as it ripped through places like New York City and then refused to get vaccinated just as the pandemic was wreaking its worst havoc on rural communities. Inevitably, the conversation would pivot to something Trump did, or the idiocy of something Biden said. And yet, where others would end the conversation there, seeing it as nothing more than a cult of personality, naked partisanship, or stubborn irrationality, we suspected something else was going on. We have no desire to make excuses for our neighbors, but in the early days of trying to piece all this together, we quickly realized that the image we had been given of the "rural voter" was not the one standing before us.

No doubt the disconnect had much to do with the pictures of rural America we carried in our heads from growing up alongside rural people. Nick remembers the old dairy farmers at church talking about the days when cows would break free and run down Main Street; but as the suburbs rapidly crept over western Virginia, his mother was having to drive him to the ever-moving hinterlands to pick up hay for their rabbits and find eggs to incubate. Rural Virginia seemed like a lost idea when the last working farm in town was paved over the year after he left for college in Fredericksburg, Virginia, which was booming at the other end of the state's steady march toward suburbanization. Fortunately, Nick feels it will be a long time before someone even thinks about plopping a subdivision in Vassalboro, Maine. Any developer should be scared off by the sounds of his rooster, which starts the day for many of his neighbors on the Priest Hill Road.

Dan was raised in rural upstate New York; his roots were planted deeply in the rocky soil of the northern Catskills. Daily life was in a small town, but escapes to old farms and woodlots to fish and hunt with brothers, cousins, and uncles were recurrent. His dad taught him the grandeur of a twelve-inch native brook trout and his mom, the magic of loons at dusk. A connection to an extended rural family was cemented most weekends when all would gather on "Bowers Hill," just up the road from Roscoe, for big Sunday dinners, tall tales, and family gossip. Over the years, he's moved between a few rural college towns and now spends his leisure time with his wife and kids gardening, tapping maple trees, and fly-fishing in the great woods of northern Maine.

In its rapid disappearance and our constant search to remain connected to the land and its people, we both value what Robert Frost described as the "country things." Of course, the simple interpretation is that there are just things one learns about living in rural parts: felling trees, picking off garden-meddling groundhogs—you know, the fun stuff. But we know that it is much more than that—a mindful disposition about what matters, a careful reflection about nature and its awesome power over us, a commanding sense of stewardship for the land and the people who call it home. Frost wrote the poem three years after the U.S. Census announced that for the first time, a majority of Americans lived in urban areas. Would they, he wondered, learn the same lessons living a city life? Would they develop the sense of humility and love of place that keeps us grounded and oriented to larger purposes?

And then, we wonder, could one ever imagine finding such sentiments in a campaign speech by Donald Trump, a man who made his career paving over the country things we hold dear and commercializing on his urbane pride? Humble, frugal, and outward-looking—if that is what rural means to us, why did so many of our rural neighbors see *this* guy as their salvation? Worse still, that is surely not the image we got from all the news reports and flyover commentary in the aftermath of 2016. Rural people were mad, loud, primed for a rebellion. Maybe they no longer valued the country things. J. D. Vance told us of their homes being ripped apart by drug addiction and job loss, communities in disarray. Others pointed to all those whites in the countryside who hated immigrants and wanted to keep them out of the country. Maybe Thomas Frank was prophetic when he told us about how the yokels had been hoodwinked in Kansas when Republicans stormed into power by stoking fears of abortion, same-sex marriage, and women working outside the home!

At every step of this long journey, we have been more than ready to confront the grim reality that the rural America of our past and our mythology has disappeared and that, in its place, we have come to live alongside people chronically depressed, irredeemably racist, and culturally backward.

But that is not what we discovered in writing this book. The country things are still to be found in rural America. But you need to know where to look.

In writing this book, we have benefited in untold ways from the hundreds of conversations we have had with our students, colleagues, and friends. Nick would not be thinking much about rural politics if not for the warm friendship he developed with the displaced rural Montanan Kal Munis at the University of Virginia. Their early musings on place and rural identity were fervently criticized and ultimately encouraged by several scholars, especially: Kathy Cramer, Lynn Sanders, Justin Kirkland, Nick Winter, and Sid Milkis.

Not far from Dan's mind at every step of this process was an admonition from his mother, Rosemary Bowers Shea, stretching back twenty years or so. Not long after he had completed his doctorate and written a few books, they were riding in the backroads of Delaware County on a fair spring day. As they bent around a curve, yet another dilapidated farmhouse came into view, rife with burn barrels, rusty lawn furniture, junked cars, and outbuildings pitched to the side. Dan muddled, half under his breath, "What slobs. . . . Can't they clean up that mess?" In a beat, Rosemary's head shot around. "Who the hell do you think you are? Those are your people, Danny. That's where you come from and don't you forget it." They rode home in silence, and he never did.

But the seeds of those early lessons and mentors could blossom into the much larger work presented here only with strong support from our Colby College community. The President's Office and the Provost of the college provided tremendous financial support, and the Rural Voter Survey would simply not have been possible without David Greene and Margaret McFadden's commitment to research at our small liberal arts college. Our Diamond Hall colleagues have endured hundreds of small distractions as we crossed the hallway between our two offices on a near daily basis these last two years. We are thankful for not only their patience but also their support as they have shown a genuine curiosity about our work: Tizoc Chavez, Nazlı Konya, Sandy Maisel, Lindsay Mayka, Carrie LeVan, Joe Reisert, Ken Rodman, and Jen Yoder.

The Goldfarb Center for Public Affairs at Colby College offered us financial support and, under the leadership of former director Kimberly Flowers, enabled us to speak and engage with rural voters across the country.

The research would not have been possible without the tireless support of our student researchers. From the start, Claudia Miner, now pursuing a Ph.D. of her own, crunched data and helped lead other research assistants. A small team of ambitious Colby undergraduates joined us as we sketched out the first few questions of the Rural Voter Survey: Ellie Batchelder, Emily Glass, Olivia Greif, Emma MacCallum, Will Short, and Maddie Wehr. As you will soon read, we pulled together one of the largest historic election/census data sets ever created, and that massive undertaking would not have happened but for the hard work of Brooklyn Clark, Nicole Huebner, and Azalea Yunus. An array of research support came from Ben Dixon, Linh Dinh, George Fitzgerald, Eleanor Goldman, Joe Grassi, Amir Jiru, Margo Kenyon, Natasha Rimalovski, Caroline Scarola, Dov Shore, Maddie Silano, and Lily Yustein. Mandie Lisco and Sabrina Jiang had the "pleasure" of coding open-ended questions from more than ten thousand respondents, for which we are eternally grateful.

And, of course, we have been unable to talk about much else but rural politics these last few years, and we owe a debt of gratitude to our friends—fellow scholars and neighbors—who contributed to our thinking: Richard Burke, Emile Lester, Anthony Sparacino, and our many neighbors in Vassalboro and Mt. Vernon.

We are deeply indebted to Kal Munis, as well as Zoe Nemerever and Sam Hayes, for reading the manuscript in its entirety and offering honest and insightful comments on each chapter. Three anonymous reviewers commissioned by Columbia University Press also gave keen and careful and attention to our work.

It has been a pleasure to work with Stephen Wesley and the entire team at Columbia University Press. Stephen has been an enthusiastic supporter of this project from the time we pitched it, and he is a committed partner in our effort to make rigorous scholarship accessible to a wider public audience.

If our friends and colleagues think we constantly talk to each other about rural politics, they have no idea what our wives go through on a daily basis. Rachel Jacobs and Christine Gatto-Shea are not only deeply supportive and patient partners, they are keen observers of rural politics in their own right. Not a single good idea you read in this book has not been subject to some eyebrow raising across the dinner table on their part.

And finally, there are our children—the most important reason we call rural Maine home and seek to better understand it. Sometimes academic work can feel a bit detached from the concerns of everyday people. We sincerely hope this book can play some small part in preserving what we love and value in rural life so our children can pass it along (even if they leave us and move to the big city).

Nick would like to dedicate this to his kids—the future caretakers of the Jacobs homestead: Benjamin and Anderson.

Dan would like to dedicate his efforts to his mother, Rosemary, who remained a proud fern picker's kid all her life.

THE RURAL VOTER

INTRODUCTION

Two Americas

Sometimes it feels as if we live and work in two different countries. The drive into Waterville, Maine, home of Colby College, is just twenty-five minutes for each of us. On the road, we pass familiar sights: kids at bus stops, hay fields, maple groves, duck blinds, a tractor here or there, junk cars. In Waterville, there is, as our students remark, a glimmer of "civilization"—stores, restaurants, new EV charging stations, construction everywhere, especially in the "revitalization" of downtown.

In the small village of Vassalboro, you know summer has arrived when American flags can be seen hanging from every telephone pole in town. Near Mount Vernon, the farm stands are open and the first cut of hay lies drying in the sun. One of us lives right down the road from a defunct wool mill, so old that it had made uniforms for Union soldiers and where, every Saturday, a handful of farmers meet on the green out front to sell fresh veggies and talk of winter on the horizon. The other lives in the Belgrade Lakes region—the land of pointed firs and granite shorelines—an ancient summer retreat for Bostonians looking to escape the heat for two weeks of serenity out on the pond.

And then there are the Trump flags. Hung next to Old Glory on porches, draped over tents at the farmers markets, fixed to the backs of pickup trucks, sometimes alongside Confederate flags, even though we're six hundred miles from Gettysburg. And the bumper stickers:

"MAKE LIBERALS CRY AGAIN." "TRUMP: NO MORE BULLSHIT." "KEEP AMERICA GREAT." Bright red MAGA hats sit on dashboards. Up the road, one farmer put up a new cattle barn, but before the siding went on in November 2020, he emblazoned TRUMP 2020 on the paneling. Homemade billboards are spread out across front lawns and seem to hold up the sides of old sheds: "DON'T BLAME ME, I VOTED FOR TRUMP." "LET'S GO BRANDON!" And then, as you cross the bridge into town, they all disappear.

Driving through rural America, you would think there is nothing more important in our lives than Donald Trump. You may guess that we are obsessed, and plenty of images could confirm your suspicion that rural America is pissed off. You may have read that rural America is anxious about immigrants. You may have listened to economists tell you that rural America is falling behind and doesn't know how—or want—to catch up. You may be sitting there thinking, "Of course they voted for Trump and watch Fox News incessantly. What else are they to do? It's so boring out there."

But when we talk to our neighbors, it is hard to believe that someone like Donald Trump could be so popular. Sure, when looking at vote returns it's very clear: Trump ruled over rural America in 2016 and 2020. But why is that true? An ethically challenged businessman who seems to caricature the glitz and glamor of jet-setting Manhattan luxury—how on earth did he become the voice of rural America? Sure, there are racists, homophobes, sexists—the deplorables—out here in the countryside, but they are everywhere in America. Can that really explain why rural America is so supportive of Trump and Republican candidates down the ballot?

We do not ask these questions just because we are rural residents. As social scientists, we also find these images ironic because both of our rural communities, by any objective measure, are doing better than the grizzly old town of Waterville. Median incomes are higher, the schools are better rated, home vacancy is practically nonexistent, drug crimes are lower. And while Waterville has a Republican presence, Donald Trump's luster loses its sheen once you enter town. In this urban hamlet, he netted just 35 percent of the vote in 2020.

The intensity of Republican partisanship and the ubiquity of Trump support in rural America has become a basic fact in contemporary American politics—a common talking point among pundits since the 2016 presidential election. In the days after Trump's shocking victory, analysts learned the correct pronunciation of sparsely populated counties in western Michigan and central Pennsylvania. Producers scrambled to get the inside perspective from recovering country dwellers who could speak to the bigotry, desperation, and collapse of communities primed for Trump's harsh rhetoric and nativist appeals. Collectively, we have learned much about how the other half—actually, the other fifth—lives, and the rural-urban divide is now one of the most important ways for making sense of the country's intense partisan acrimony. We have seen countless stories of Appalachia in disarray. Pills, closed mines and factories, and crumbling infrastructure left communities primed for the anger and populist message of someone like Trump. Media portray rural voters as desperate. Left-leaning writers talk about how Republicans can distract simpletons in rural Kansas with tales of the abortion doctor gone rampant and teachers peddling critical race theory. Racist, backward-looking, uneducated, and poor—in retrospect, they say, it seems obvious how Trump could take hold in these places.

From our perspective, the picture painted by these memoirs and journalism is, at best, simplistic and more often just plain wrong. It is undeniably true that rural America supports Trump, as true as it is that Republican candidates have courted rural voters and brought them into the party fold over the last forty years. Whether they are Republican, Democrat, journalist, or campaign strategist, everyone seems to look to the hinterland and say, "There's the real America. Of course Republicans are going to do well there. It's simple."

But while rural life may be, at times, simple, its politics is anything but. We are told that rural America's support for Trump exists simply because voters there are whiter, older, and less likely to have a college degree. One perspective is that there is nothing special per se about ruralness. The rural-urban divide is just another part of America's racial, ethnic, and generational divide.[1] And yet, white rural Americans behave differently than whites living in urban and suburban places; they do not share the same universe of opinions, even if they voted for the same Republican. Even nonwhite residents of rural places seem to have a different relationship with government than racial and ethnic minorities living elsewhere. On closer examination, ruralness is not, in fact, reducible to whiteness. Geography matters.

Likewise, rural America is undeniably poor, and the economic livelihood of many rural communities has withered with globalization, free trade, and the move to an information-centered economy. But rural America is not all poor. There is a middle class, and there are even deep pockets of wealth. One story that's often told is that the downtrodden and economically dislocated are enraged, ready to embrace Trump and other firebrand Republicans.[2] But even if rural America is poorer, and therefore more likely to vote for populist candidates, its citizens are not that much poorer than those in other parts of America, which are also suffering economically. Income inequality plagues all of America, and over the last forty years, it has increased the most in urban areas, not the countryside.[3] If you had to choose, would you rather be poor in Hannibal, Missouri, or on the streets of San Francisco? Why are only some of the poor drawn to Trump? And why are those doing just fine in rural areas voting for him, too?

Maybe it's the quality of public services in rural communities? Sure, some schools in rural America are closing, but shiny new regional education campuses are springing up in many communities. Has government turned its back to rural Americans? Rural America is older and sicker, but it also receives a disproportionate share of government funding to shore up its health care system. Nearly one in four nonelderly rural residents is on Medicaid.[4] Even if politicians like to yell that they are not getting their fair share, many are quick to point out that rural residents are no more or less deprived than their fellow Americans living elsewhere.[5] Are there really two Americas—a rural America and an urban America—or is it all just a picture in our heads?

Getting this story right matters. These days, when sharp partisan leanings are added to the mix, objective assessments can become, well, muddled. The best route is to rise above gut feelings, snapshots, and narrow assessments and test where our assumptions are backed by any shred of evidence. That is what we present to you in the following pages. Over the past three years, we have pulled together one of the most comprehensive and data-driven accounts of rural politics that exists. We created one of the largest historical data sets on voting patterns in the United States going all the way back to 1800. We combine these statistics with centuries-old census reports and other leading economic and community data, providing an unparalleled look at what has taken place in rural America. Next, we scoured existing surveys all the way back to 1936 and conducted three of our own polls; the Rural Voter Survey project boasts more than ten thousand survey-interviews with rural voters and four thousand with nonrural residents. It is fair to say that our conclusions rely on the culmination of more hard data than any other work on the dynamics of rural politics. It is why our story is different than the one you have heard.

SO THE STORY GOES

Turn on the TV on election night, and you would be hard-pressed to argue that there is not a deep and widening chasm in America. You know the maps: the vast field of red crossing the heartland and wrapping around the pockets of deep blue. It certainly looks like two Americas. But has it always been this way?

And at first glance, you would be right. When it comes to recent voting trends, rural America is solidly red, and yet the rural-urban divide has not always been central to American politics. Rural America has traditionally divided its loyalties. In 1936, four years into Franklin D. Roosevelt's New Deal, rural areas in the Upper Midwest enthusiastically endorsed the Democratic president. In the same election, rural areas in the Northeast gave his opponent, the Republican Alf Landon, equally large margins. For more than a hundred years, the most rural parts of the region were solidly Democratic—while most rural areas outside the South during the same time were either a partisan mix or heavily Republican. And it was only fifty years ago, during the 1970s, that some of the most progressive members of Congress hailed from rural areas. In 1972, the Democratic Party's nominee for the presidency was arguably one of the most liberal candidates in its history. Our students are stunned to learn that George McGovern was from South Dakota.

That is not what the American political landscape looks like today. Even though the 2016 presidential election was a nail-biter, in most parts of the country, it wasn't even close. Hillary Clinton won 199 counties by 60 percent or more, and Donald Trump won a staggering 2,035 counties by an equally steep margin. Most voters lived in "sorted" communities, where their neighbors primarily voted one way.[6] Only one of every three rural voters cast a ballot for Hillary Clinton, and the more rural the community, the worse she performed. Just 25 percent of rural voters living in the least sparsely populated parts of the country voted for the Democrat.[7]

What seemed lopsided in 2016 proved to be just the start. Four years later, in Tennessee, for example, Trump boosted his support by 21 percent in the towns and rural counties outside the state's big cities. The same thing happened in Michigan. There, some 5.5 million voters went to the polls—the highest percentage of eligible voters in sixty years. Turnout in urban Democratic strongholds was robust, but in the rural areas, Trump's margin of victory was enormous. In nearly all the counties north of Grand Rapids, Trump garnered at least 70 percent of the vote. In many of these areas, he topped 80 percent.

The same dynamic has played out across the country. Turnout in metropolitan areas was high enough to push Biden over the finish line, but the margins netted by Trump in rural areas were unprecedented—and it spread down the ballot. In Iowa, Democratic Rep. Abby Finkenauer came to office in the 2018 Blue Wave, but in 2020, she lost her reelection, likely due to Trump's huge margin in her district, which went from fifteen points over Clinton in 2016 to twenty-one points over Biden. In North Carolina, Trump offset Democratic gains in urban areas by building on already impressive numbers in one rural county after another. In Columbus County, for example, he netted an additional twenty-four hundred votes beyond his 2016 returns.[8] There are many ways to define "rural," a topic taken up in the next chapter, but in places with fewer than five hundred residents per square mile, Biden received just 26 percent of the vote, on average.[9]

The hemorrhaging of Democratic votes in rural areas affects nearly every aspect of American government. According to one analysis, in 2006, congressional voters in rural areas roughly split their votes between Republican and Democratic candidates. By 2022, Republicans claimed a whopping 68 percent.[10] The transformation of governorships and state legislatures has been equally dramatic. When Ronald Reagan trounced Jimmy Carter in 1980, Democrats controlled twenty-nine state legislatures. Republicans had only fifteen, and the other six chambers were split. After the 2020 election, that figure was nearly reversed: Republicans controlled thirty state legislatures compared with the Democrats' eighteen.[11] Overall, about 54 percent of state legislators are Republican, but the gap is vast in states with the largest rural populations. In many of these states, the ratio of Republican to Democratic state legislators is upward of four to one, and the few Democratic legislators always come from the urban areas of the state. Competitive general election contests in rural areas have evaporated. GOP candidates often run unopposed. As to the number of Democratic state legislators from rural districts in any state? Let's just say they could hold a convention in a phone booth.

But why did this happen? The image is clear, but the story of how we got here is not. And while there has been no shortage of offhand theories for the emergence of this unprecedented and destabilizing divide, most fall flat when subjected to some basic facts.

Of course, one character looms large in current explanations of the rural-urban divide: Donald Trump. By far the most common way to think about the rural-urban divide in popular media is to lean into the idea that something about Trump made him irresistibly popular in rural areas. Nobody really understood rural voters before Trump, they say. Want to do well in rural America, they ask? Act like Trump. Thousands of Election Day postmortem interviews in the heartland showed how Trump's brash personality resonated in hardscrabble rural America. As one rural voter summed it up, "Trump, he didn't take no crap."[12] Although initially critical of Trump when promoting his book *Hillbilly Elegy*—a best-selling account of poverty in rural Appalachia—J. D. Vance later embraced Trump and his persona when running for Senate in Ohio: "[Vance] learned that rural Ohioans voted for Trump not because he was wealthy or famous but because he was fighting for them."[13] *Politico* put it best: Trump's election was the "revenge of the rural voter."[14] So the story goes: without Trump, the rural-urban divide disappears.

Except that the current rural-urban divide had been widening for decades well before Donald Trump. As we will discuss in much greater depth, rural support for Democrats at all levels of government—from the presidency to the state legislature to local school boards—has fallen each year since 1980. Yes, rural America did not seem to have the same enthusiasm for Mitt Romney in 2012; there were no massive rallies and no flags draped over tractors. But Romney still clobbered Barack Obama in rural areas, as did John McCain in 2008.[15] No presidential candidate has performed better in rural America than Trump, certainly; but when put into historical perspective, the increase in rural support for Republicans from 2012 to 2016 was not unusually high or unexpected given the decades-long trends in rural partisanship. Trump may just have been the right guy at the right time, and the rural-urban divide may be just as much about love for Trump as it is about hatred for Democrats. Take Trump away, and the rural-urban divide remains huge.

The rural-urban divide has deep historical roots. But some reduce it to differences in the types of people who live in rural areas—what social scientists call a "composition effect." The rise of rabid Republican partisanship among rural voters is nothing more than a growing concentration of the type of person in rural areas.[16] We know that rural voters, on the whole, are older, more likely to be white, and less likely to hold a college degree. Regardless of where someone lives, if they are white, they are more likely to vote for Republicans. If they are older, it is more likely they will vote Republican. Ipso facto, rural America is more likely to swing Republican. It has nothing to do with being rural and everything to do with the fact that rural people are more likely to have certain demographic profiles. Brushing aside the issue of the rapidity of the change, many assume it is not geography that matters but, rather, the type of person living out there. Cue one of the country's foremost demographers, William Frey, who chalked up the Trump-Clinton divide in rural areas this way: "It's a cultural-generational gap. There's a different view of the country among the White, older age group than among the more diverse, younger age group."[17] So the story goes: it does not matter where you live, just who you are.

Except that these demographic gaps are not the same in rural and nonrural areas. No doubt there are important differences in the ways that various demographic groups vote. Consider, for example, one of the largest demographic gaps that has emerged in the last few decades: the Democratic Party's sizable and growing advantage among young voters. In 2020, 61 percent of voters below the age of twenty-nine supported President Biden. Voters above the age of forty-five were more likely to cast their ticket for Trump.[18] But those are national averages, which are insensitive to where these voters are. In rural areas, a majority of young voters under the age of twenty-nine voted for Trump. Because rural voters, and rural youth, make up a smaller proportion of the electorate, their enthusiastic support gets drowned out by young urban voters when one is calculating national averages. Still, the simple fact remains that young rural voters are different from young voters elsewhere. It would be a mistake, and politically neglectful, to simply say that young voters are Democrats. As it turns out, it does depend on where you live.

To be fair, many explanations have tried to account for these geographic differences and tease out the different amalgams of demographics and geography. One such common explanation is that rural areas have simply suffered more from broken policies and trends in the larger economy. So the story goes: rural communities are reeling from economic dislocation. Just take a drive in rural parts, and you'll see the mothballed factories and decaying downtowns. The collapse of civic life in rural towns, which have been ravaged by unemployment, drug addiction, and despair, has fed a sense of hopelessness. There's nothing left, nothing on which to build a sense of community and optimism.

So the story goes, with the withering of communities and the decline of good jobs, rural residents have been drawn into far-right talk radio, internet conspiracy theories, and, of course, Fox News. There's nothing else going on—certainly no local news—so they are glued to Tucker Carlson. Ah, yes, there it is: now we know why so many would support such a scoundrel as Donald Trump. The nation's economic engine churns in metropolitan areas, but rural areas have been left behind. Less sympathetically, Hillary Clinton endorsed this idea as an explanation for her loss in 2016, saying, "If you look at the map of the United States, there is all that red in the middle, places where Trump won. What that map doesn't show you is that I won the places that own two thirds of America's gross domestic product. . . . I won the places that are optimistic, diverse, dynamic, moving forward."[19]

Except that more Trump voters live in those moving-forward places than all of rural America combined. Most poor people in the United States live outside rural America. So do most gun owners and evangelicals. One study suggests that there are five times as many viewers of *Fox News* living outside rural America as viewers who live within it.[20] Rural America is not an economic powerhouse, but neither does it have a monopoly on economic problems confronting all Americans. Thousands of rural residents hunger for community, and thousands feel the same while living in big cities or the suburbs. Globalization has fundamentally altered the economic landscape of the United States, and yet, more blue-collar jobs left urban and suburban areas than rural areas. In short, these types of analyses turn a blind eye to the fact that large swaths of urban areas are also suffering from the same structural changes in the American economy and that though rural America is small, the political divides by class, income, and culture are big. Those divides may sometimes seem clearer when mapped onto rural and urban areas, but they are not confined to any one segment of America.

There is another, related explanation. It says that starting in the 1980s, savvy GOP operatives somehow convinced rural residents to shift their attention from harmful economic policies to cross-cutting cultural grievances, especially abortion and gay marriage. It was a way for Republican leaders to have their cake and eat it, too. They could maintain laissez-faire economic policies while also bolstering their support among working-class voters in flyover country. The leading volume along these lines was Thomas Frank's 2004 book, *What's the Matter with Kansas?* "While earlier forms of fiscal conservatism emphasize fiscal sobriety," Frank writes, "the backlash [in rural parts of the country] mobilized voters with explosive social issues." Moreover, "cultural anger is marshaled to achieve economic ends."[21] So when we watch Arkansas Governor Sarah Huckabee Sanders's GOP response to Joe Biden's State of the Union address in 2023—bashing Democrats for their "wokeness," gender identity issues, and critical race theory—it made sense. Why promote an economic, jobs-centered agenda when you have cultural wedge issues? The poor rural saps have been hoodwinked, so we are told.

Setting aside the assumption that "rational" voters should prioritize economic issues over guns, abortion, and other related issues, on close inspection, we find no discernable difference between the potency of cultural wedge issues based on geography. A study by the Pew Research Center, for example, found no gap between urban, suburban, and rural votes when it comes to attitudes on abortion.[22] Conservative values, as we will show later, are no more or less extreme in rural communities than elsewhere. That is to say, Huckabee Sanders's message resonated with conservatives on Staten Island as much as with those in rural Kansas. Saying that Republican voter priorities have shifted in rural America is not the same as saying they have developed unique voting priorities—just because they are more likely, on the whole, to vote for GOP candidates.

Whatever the story, we have long suspected that the tales we have been told countless times about rural voters are wrong. As much as visiting journalists, academics, and the native sons want to dive deep and expose the inner workings of rural life, most just echo broader developments in American politics. The fact is that *all* Americans—urban and rural—are socializing with their neighbors less. "Bowling alone" is a feature of American society, not just rural life. Technologies have disrupted employment patterns and traditional communities in the old neighborhoods of the sprawling metropolis as much as they have in the tiny village. Local newspapers are closing across the country, and fewer Americans are going to church each Sunday. There is less prestige for those who work with their hands in both small towns and big cities.

So if the stories we have been told about rural America don't hold up to scrutiny, what is happening? Yes, some of it is attributable to Trump, and some of the divide has to do with the fact that rural America overwhelmingly white and more likely to be blue collar and older. But there is something much more foundational to America's geographic divisions, and our failure to come to grips with it is leading to disastrous consequences.

SHARED DESTINY IN RURAL AMERICA

Rural voters are different. But it is not because they are angrier than city dwellers, or struggling more to make ends meet, or particularly hyped up on social issues. It is not because rural communities are predominantly white. It is not just because that they are more conservative, or naturally predisposed to distrust the government or dislike immigrants. Rural Americans are different because they see themselves as different. Fewer things matter more for the average rural voter than the fact that they live in a rural community. And, increasingly, ruralness matters more and more each election year.

Rural Americans see themselves as a group—a group on the defensive, ready to come together and preserve what makes their rural community unique. The challenges confronting rural areas may not be all that special, but the way rural Americans think about these challenges is. Rich and poor, college-educated and high school dropouts—in rural America, there is still the belief that hard work overcomes most obstacles. At the same time, rural Americans are bound in tight communities. Those who are wealthy see poverty in their community regularly and care about how the group as a whole is doing, not just themselves. They know the story of how past policies to "fix" their communities played out (free trade will lift all boats, and broadband internet is coming soon . . .) and are collectively suspicious about the attempt to modernize country living to move them "forward." Rural Americans feel devalued, stereotyped, degraded, and misunderstood. Most are not farmers chewing on a straw of hay. Most do not attend church. And fewer still would describe their community as backward, broken, or barren. Rural Americans love rural America, warts and all. Talk to someone living out there in the country, and before you ask them how they will vote, ask them what they think about where they live. You'll discover a remarkable and unflinching sense of place.

That sense of place helps rural Americans form that collective, group identity. They identify with their place, and their place is rural. And, for these Americans, this sense of place is foundational to how they understand politics. Even though there have always been rural voters, only recently have rural voters nationwide come to foreground their understanding of politics in this belief that they are a distinctive people. That itself is a consequence of a dramatic racial, economic, and cultural realignment. Rooted in geography, this rural identity means that residents of rural America have developed a distinct sense of belonging or group cohesion. Rural identity has become so powerful that regardless of how much money they make, their age, or even their education, rural Americans overwhelmingly vote together. For this segment of the American electorate, the fundamental variables that should determine their voting patterns just do not matter as much. Ruralness is what matters instead.

Individuals are members of many communities and groups. To a certain extent, ruralness is like other important identities we use to make sense of American politics, such as class, race, and gender.[23] In a way similar to how individuals relate to one another based on the color of their skin, their profession, or their sexual orientation, individuals also relate to their neighbors and those who live around them.

Rural Americans are not the only group to so identify. For decades, social scientists have been exploring the pull of group identities for particular demographics—a pull so strong that it is more than just a warm fuzzy feeling of group attachment but, rather, a sense of "linked fate."[24] This concept implies a sense of connectedness, a cohesion among marginalized group members, whereby individuals see their own prospects for success or fulfillment as dependent on the entire group's success or failure. It doesn't matter whether I am personally better off— it only matters if the group as a whole is better off. Understandably, given the United States' history of slavery and violence toward ethnic minorities, research in this area has focused on the development of these attitudes among racial and ethnic groups and, to a lesser extent, women.[25]

The evidence is clear: linked fate is a powerful lens through which these groups see the world.

We take elements of this line of thinking but, for the first time, put "place" at the center. We are all members of places, just as we all have a household income, a race, or any other group identifier that social scientists like to combine us in. But not all of us link our home with our politics. Not all of us use our connection to place as a way to make sense of how the economy is changing, or what a particular candidate running for office might say. By "place," we are interested in more than just someone's physical mailing address. Rather, for some people, a place can become something that one's life is invested in—a deep, personal attachment to the spaces where they work, play, and live and that matter for their own sense of personal fulfillment.[26]

This collective sense of place draws rural residents together, especially when animated by stories of mistreatment or unfairness. Much in the same way that Kathy Cramer noticed rural Wisconsinites making sense of politics through their own "rural consciousness," we, too, see a place-specific narrative of how rural voters make sense of problems in their day-to-day lives. For Cramer, the overarching idea was resentment. Rural voters "used identities rooted in place and class . . . to structure the causal stories they told to each other," which manifested in hostile attitudes toward urban areas, government bureaucracies, and universities.[27] Rural resentment is why angry politicians like Scott Walker and even Donald Trump captured the passions of rural voters. "The people I listened to felt like they were on the short end of the stick," Cramer wrote about her travels in rural Wisconsin. "They felt they were not getting their fair share of power, resources or respect. They said that the big decisions that regulated and affected their lives were made far away in the cities. They felt that no one was listening to their own ideas about how things should be done or what needed attention. . . . Onto this terrain trod Trump . . . [and] for people who were feeling ignored, disrespected and overlooked by the urban elite, the Trump campaign had a strong appeal."[28]

We owe a debt of gratitude for these pioneering insights. Resentment, as you will read in what follows, figures prominently in our account of rural America's political economy. Resentment is a useful construct when trying to make sense of otherwise paradoxical voting habits or attitudes toward government spending – why, for instance, someone that might benefit from Obamacare may vote for a candidate pledging to repeal it. But we argue that resentment is just one pathway through which rural residents use their sense of place—one that is highly politicized or context-dependent. It is no wonder that we see resentful attitudes in 2016 or 2020—or, as Cramer observed, during the rise of Scott Walker as governor of Wisconsin. In each of these electoral contexts, eager politicians exploited rural communities' sense of mistreatment and channeled it to their own political agendas, which denigrated the government in the process.[29] Resentment was there, and it was a major force in elevating Republican candidates not just to the White House but in House, Senate, and state-level races as well.[30]

But there are other aspects to this sense of place that are not necessarily tied to resentment, and a sense of place can matter even when there is no antigovernment message. For example, when it comes to policies, such as gun control, rural Americans think differently about the issue than do gun owners in nonrural America. Seen from fifty thousand feet, it seems like there is nothing separating the gun owner over there from the gun owner over here, especially when each casts their ballot for the same candidate. But the reasons they give are different, and for rural Americans, those reasons are grounded in the specific characteristics of what makes rural living special and distinct.

Some people have a sense of place, and others do not. Most academics we talk to do not. Most grew up in one part of the country, left for graduate school, and then probably moved two or three times on their way to their current professorship. Many will grow accustomed to their new community, quirkiness and all, but they will not feel personally invested in the success of their adopted home. Most will probably move again. They are, comparatively speaking, disconnected from the places where they live, even if they like the tangible aspects of their community: the schools, the scenery, the family next door.

And people outside rural America surely have a sense of place. You can see it when Packers fans in their cheese hats fill up Lambeau Field on a frigid December afternoon. Ever met anyone from South Boston? They surely have a sense of place. Big-city neighborhoods certainly have a distinct feel, and the residents cherish that connection. When they travel abroad, most Americans return with a newfound appreciation for our big cars, roomy refrigerators, and expansive view of personal space. There is, after all, no place quite like home.

But that sense of place does not matter when it comes to making political decisions, especially when it comes down to whom to vote for. It is only when that sense of place becomes politically animated that we see it start to count, and see that group identities begin to structure how entire swaths of people vote, even when the individual factors that make up their other identities would suggest otherwise.

The emergence of the rural voter demonstrates how widespread this sense of place has become, but in this way, the type of rural politics we see is different from the place-oriented politics that has long animated American history. Rural politics used to mean a variant of local politics. It was different from town to town, region to region, state to state. As the scholar of local politics V. O. Key Jr. once wrote, "The size of their populations and the magnitude of their operations make many of our states quite as important political units as many of the independent nations of the world."[31] The issues that brought voters to the polls in Delaware County, New York, were different from what sold newspapers on the hilltops of Mesa County, Colorado. Rural meant local. But American politics has nationalized, and rural America is a part of that transformation.[32]

Today, rural voters are a monumental force on a national scale, and although a sense of place reminds us of the particular and the distinctive, it matters because millions of voters in all parts of rural America are drawing on the same ideas. Local issues have become second in importance to the national fights that pit all of rural America against the rest—the others, who live over there in big cities and the sprawling suburbs. Rural America as a whole feels neglected and disrespected. As a result, the rural-urban divide has become a part of our national political conversation because rural Americans have developed a nationalized sense of place.

OUR APPROACH

Through talking about our work for several years, we know that the rural-urban divide is not just a statistical phenomenon. It also sits at the heart of our deepest, most perplexing, most polarizing debates about what Americans owe to one another. Getting it right matters. It matters more than most other forces—particularly because of the way geography physically separates us into different camps, and because key governmental institutions are shaped by geography. And because it is so easy to divide people by place, when most people talk about our geographic divide, they not only simplify the causes of it but amplify just how divided we are.

It is too easy for politicians on both sides to exploit the geographic divisions that benefit them at the ballot box and overlook the common stories and problems we need to understand to heal this country's political wounds. Faulty geographic comparisons also reinforce the idea that rural voters are just "wrong" about the basic facts and vote against their self-interest when they are clearly the ones "falling behind." News coverage, we will show, is apt to paint rural voters as politically extreme and prone to conspiracy theories, when that captures barely a sliver of the populace. Much of our book is simply an attempt to get people to think about geography the right way—that it is not all about the demographic composition of different areas, and that different areas are, in and of themselves, unique and important to understand.

The truth is, both rural and urban America need each other. Nobody with any real power seems to deny the fundamental goodness of healing this country's racial divide or defends gender inequality, even if they have divergent opinions on how to reconcile differences. But when it comes to the gulf between rural and urban America, it's not just politicians who seem willing to throw their hands in the air and give up; our neighbors seem ready to cut ties and abandon one another, too.

Once we recognize that rural people make sense of politics through their shared affinity for rural community, we give them a voice. And nowhere do we need to hear everyone's voice—unfiltered by the Twitter pundits or drive-by journalists—than when it comes to building a multiracial, inclusive democracy.

To be clear, there is no place in our theory for political radicalization or ideological extremism. There is anger and distrust—but we would be mistaken to boil this nuanced story into a simple one of rage and rebellion. We know that image exists and turn to recent work in the social sciences to explain why the pictures in our heads about rural voters are dominated by the most extreme elements living in rural America—the rabble-rousers who make up a tiny percentage of their communities and who actually do not share in many aspects of this shared fate.[33] We see the flags and we read the signs—every day—and even we had to pause and remind ourselves occasionally that rural voters, like most Americans, are much more reserved and cautious in their political behavior than headlines suggest.

A degree of despair and resentment exists, certainly, but we also found rural Americans who were happy about the way things were going—a far cry from the common portrait of rural folks as helpless, unable to escape their collapsing towns. We see a rural America that takes pride in a distinct way of life, emphasizing values of hard work, individualism, and localism. Conspiracy theories about child sex rings, anger over immigration, traditional gender stereotypes—they are out there, for sure, and there is no escaping prejudicial and stereotypical beliefs about racial minorities. There is an ugly side to rural politics. But these attitudes are not confined to rural areas.

We were pulled to this project because, as political scientists and also rural residents, we sensed that the emerging narratives were missing a lot. We knew more rigorous methods—historical, survey-based empirical models—could help. We spent years building one of the largest historical election data sets on rural politics that exists so we could distinguish our modern divide from the past. We also conducted three of the largest surveys of rural voters in recent memory—maybe even in history. In surveying nearly ten thousand rural voters from across the country, we asked them how their schools were doing, how often they prayed, what they thought about people like Anthony Fauci and the mysterious Q-Anon. We asked them how America is doing and whether their kids will be able to continue living in the town in which they grew up. If given the chance, would they actually want to leave rural life behind? We asked them questions about race, immigration, and gender roles. They told us how often they got together with their neighbors and how they received their news. They described their communities and what made them special places to live. They told us who they voted for and why.

We conducted the first poll before the 2020 presidential election, administered the second in the spring of 2021, and finished with a third in the spring of 2022, after Joe Biden had been in office more than a year. We compared their responses with those of more than four thousand nonrural Americans, from the suburbs to the nation's largest cities. We did not confine our analysis to the hinterlands and search out stories of desperation and desire, as has been the case in many popular recent works. As tragic and important as these instances may be, anecdotes and personal narratives get us only so far. They are limited perspectives, championing stories that make a splash and will sell more books. Especially important for us, almost all existing work fails to consider rural America as a whole. The fact that we can even write about something as vast as rural America—not just the South or Appalachia or Kansas—suggests a massive change in American politics needing a comprehensive approach.

This two-part analysis informs the entirety of the book. First, our argument is grounded in an understanding of political development. It hinges on the fact that there is a defined, accepted group identity, which has developed over time. There cannot be a shared fate if there is no identifiable group, and those groups must develop from something.

At one level, in the case of rural residents, the development of a rural identity seems straightforward. The rural identity is legendary, a point of pride for centuries. Rural residents live in the heartland, after all, where you find "real America." They are the salt of the earth, filled with old-fashioned country wisdom—the goodness of America. When things get crazy, we look to the country. The founders celebrated rural life because it imped freedom and equality, and it was not England. "Our government will remain virtuous for many centuries," said Thomas Jefferson, "as long as they are chiefly agricultural."

But to what extent have rural residents considered themselves linked to an identifiable group compared with Americans living in suburban or urban areas? As it turns out, this is a much more recent phenomenon than even we expected. American history is filled with stories of farmers' protests and agrarian revolts, and until the 1920s, most Americans were rural Americans. However, larger social, economic, and political forces prevented the emergence of a politicized rural identity until much later.

The data lead us to the 1980s as the tipping point in the transformation of rural partisanship, and we zero in on the political forces that shaped that decade. It is then that rural identity took on its national shape, because that is when rural Americans—regardless of region—came to be viewed as marginalized and threatened, a distinctive "other." Rural Americans have felt the pressures of urbanization and change for decades. Historically, though, all these pressures have been interpreted through local or regional understandings of economic and social duress. Mill towns shutting up shop in the New England countryside were unrelated to the consolidation of family farms in the Midwest; fighting off suburban sprawl in California was of little concern to rural communities in the mid-Atlantic, who would welcome a little more development in the face of declining populations. And the South was always the outlier in any story of rural political development: maintaining white supremacy mattered more than anything else, even at the expense of economic development. But since the 1980s, these local concerns have morphed into a shared, or nationalized, group identity. Just as American politics, in general, has nationalized, so, too, have rural residents expanded their sense of what "rural" means in modern America.

Voting patterns and historical evidence—including dozens of never-before-analyzed polls from major news outlets—show that a rural identity has become vastly more pronounced in the last forty years, well before Trump took to the stage. Even so, we have heard only half the story of why this identity—so easy to witness in election returns—has become so central to national politics. Do rural Americans vote as a distinctive, pivotal bloc? Absolutely. Why do they do that? Answering that requires a different approach.

An easy, go-to explanation is that geography has become a fault line in contemporary American politics, because these other forces—education, race, class—fall neatly on the urban and rural spectrum. Rural America is less educated. Outside the South and parts of the West, rural America basically means white. There are no high-tech start-ups next to grain silos; it's next to impossible to get an Uber in Vassalboro, Maine. Likewise, it would take a full-length volume and then some to adequately chart the role of race and class in American politics. The intersection of the two has been recurrent; ethnic and racial oppression is often centered on economic injustices. Furthermore, merely suggesting that race and class are foundational elements in our politics does not imply that other forces are unimportant. Religious divides have, at the same time, been critically important. All these forces exist in rural America—so much so that it is tough sometimes to see anything particular about rural areas beyond the fact that there is just more of one thing there than others.

And yet, our evidence shows that the changes in rural partisanship came about because ruralness has become a distinctly salient identity on its own. So, for example, while education remains important, education *and* ruralness leads to something else. Race *and* ruralness is different than just saying whites vote one way and nonwhites vote another way. Ruralness takes on greater importance among those who have a well-defined attachment to a particular locale or who clearly recognize the distinguishing attributes of their rural communities. Given the general tendency in most polls to take the individual as the unit of analysis and aggregate upward in nationally representative samples, contextual differences are often drowned out by the vast amount of placelessness that many Americans experience.[34] Most people may not think about what it means to be a member of a suburb, where a plurality of Americans actually live, and whether they should vote as a member of that community. Place may appear, on average, politically meaningless, so researchers do not account for it.[35] As such, while a Georgia Democrat may be different than a Massachusetts Democrat in terms of the issues they care about, they nevertheless often register as the same when considered in national survey samples.[36]

The Rural Voter Survey allows us to probe alternative explanations and to account for place. In the end, we present the results of a large multivariate model that attempts to sort out all these factors. The data are clear and support our primary contention that there is something unique going on in rural America. Regardless of where they live, voters have felt tectonic swings threaten themselves and their community. As we will reveal, the key here is not that the marginalization is accurate or that the changes are any worse than elsewhere. In some ways, rural communities are doing better than their urban and suburban counterparts. Rather, the difference it makes in our politics is because there is a full-bodied and growing perception that ever-greater forces are amassing and that the reservoir of resistance will soon run dry.

We approach this undertaking as scholars who have taken great pains to better understand the forces that make rural America different and how those growing differences are threatening the social and political fabric of the United States. We also write as rural residents who find much value in the ways of living that our neighbors are trying to protect. We take great care not to excuse or evaluate the beliefs we find objectionable—particularly those that seem to cut short the promise of a healthy, vibrant multiracial democracy. We take seriously, though, the idea that politics is about persuasion, a lesson that many commentators and elites have forgotten. Doing that hard work of persuasion means meeting people where they are, and for rural residents, that means meeting them in their place.

1

WHO AND WHAT IS RURAL AMERICA?

I f you were to close your eyes and conjure images of rural America in the twenty-first century, it might be a bit unpleasant. You could imagine towns and villages wrecked by drug addiction and crime. Residents would be worn out, tired, lacking any sort of entrepreneurial spirit, tuned out to the latest headlines—unless they heard it on Fox News. There would be withering factories and schools. It would be a cultural wasteland, where fashion trends lag a decade (or two) behind the rest of America; flannel, though, is making a big comeback. Population would be declining across the board, especially in the remotest communities. Everyone would own guns, and Christian, patriarchal values would be rigid and sweeping. Single-parent households would be much more common than in the rest of the country, and there would be little racial or ethnic diversity that make up the pictures in our heads.

But for others, rural America might inspire a different picture. An optimist could imagine pretty farms and vacant lands; healthy men and women breathing in fresh air, enjoying a relaxed and picturesque lifestyle. Communities would come together at thriving churches on Sundays, praying and singing as one. Others would simply meet at the town dump every Saturday to exchange gossip and the latest tip. Football would be ubiquitous (think Friday night games!), and country music would stream from the dashboards of pickup trucks.

But when you open your eyes and look at the data, all these assumptions—both good and bad—would be mostly wrong. Consider, for instance, that 22 percent of rural residents are people of color. Rural Indigenous, Asian, and Latino groups are growing fastest, but there are also modest population gains among Black Americans. Non-Hispanic white groups are actually experiencing the slowest growth in rural America.[1] To the surprise of many, only about 6 percent of rural Americans are involved in farming, and, in fact, manufacturing is a more substantial source of employment in rural than in urban areas.[2] In recent years, overdose death rates in urban areas matched or exceeded those in rural communities; drugs are a problem, but not any worse in the countryside.[3] Rural residents are certainly not stuck in their trucks obsessing over conservative talk radio; one study found very little difference in news consumption habits between people in rural areas and those living elsewhere.[4] The favorite sport in rural areas is not actually football but, rather, baseball. In fact, love for professional football is much more pronounced in urban areas than in rural communities.[5] Rural residents are not, on the whole, more fit because of access to outdoor spaces; instead, they are much more likely to be obese and sick.[6]

Why do we get so much wrong about rural life? For many, knee-jerk assumptions spring from pop culture stereotypes, something we will explore in depth in chapter 7. We draw on the material given to us by Hollywood producers, flyby journalists, and our own deep sense of history. "People's longing for small towns is an understandable fantasy," noted one observer. "Small towns seem like slower, saner havens in an overly connected, frenetic world, places where a blackberry is an ingredient in jam."[7] Or it may be because many urban and suburban residents can't get their heads around why rural voters would back Donald Trump. Surely it must have been the grim realities of rural life that pushed those poor people to the extremes, they think: yes, yes, it must be economic desperation, community collapse and cultural decay!

But another explanation for these misperceptions is that detailed, data-based accounts of rural America are scarce. In the wake of

Trump's upset victory in 2016, visits to rural communities by journalists became a small cottage industry. But that did not mean we got an accurate, complete picture of what was going on there. *Columbia Journalism Review* contributor David Uberti made the following observation in 2017:

> Virtually all national outlets have run some version, and likely multiple versions, of a story taking the temperature of Trump country, be it a hard-on-its-luck coal town in Appalachia or a hollowed-out manufacturing hub in the upper Midwest. . . . The pieces focus heavily on the white working class, a group portrayed as struggling to come to grips with its dimming economic fortunes and diminished social dominance in a multicultural and post-industrial America. . . . While some stories have offered insight into these communities' affinity for a billionaire with authoritarian tendencies, much of the coverage feels like checking a box: *We sent a reporter to explore the heart of American darkness.* Such drive-by attempts signal that the national media isn't grappling with its mistakes in any sustained way.[8]

This does not mean that data alone solve the problem. Where there are data, interpretations can be sloppy. Geographic comparisons are often misleading, and at the most fundamental level, it is hard to even agree on what "rural" means. Multiple measures exist, and few precisely define it in their accounts. Confederate flags, meth, junk cars . . . obviously that is "Trump Country." American flags, community picnics, hardworking farmers . . . that is "Real America." All those things exist throughout America, though, not just in rural places. This is a problem, because if we are unable to define what exactly rural America is, then how can we make sense of the rural-urban divide? At best, we have detailed snapshots of how specific rural communities across the United States are doing at the moment; at our worst, we have overgeneralized from these small case studies and missed the big picture of how rural America, as a whole, has developed into a distinct political identity that is different from urban areas and even Republican-leaning suburbs. Nobody has captured both the forests and the trees, so to speak. This is a problem of bad definitions and measures—something we seek to correct in this chapter.

We focus on two challenges inherent in research on rural politics and political geography more generally. Each of these challenges limits our ability to make sense of the current rural-urban divide and to really explain why it has widened (or if it even exists in the first place!).

The first problem deals with our inability to make historical comparisons, given that our understanding of what "rural" means changes over time. We call this the problem of the "shifting baseline," and to overcome it, we describe a unique measure for identifying rural communities, which we rely on throughout the book. We compare this measure with others, such as population density, which, although commonly used in research on rural politics, is problematic in attempts to distinguish rural from nonrural areas. This is one reason, we argue, that our perspective on rural politics diverges from other accounts, but we are convinced that it offers major advantages.

Still, even with more accurate measures of rurality, we have to make decisions about what, exactly, to compare over time. There is a so-called rural America, but that big, national community is made up of many small ones. In the second part of the book, we zero in on individual-level measures based on our survey results. That is, we will assess each respondent's "ruralness" based on answers to key questions.

But what are we to do when exploring the past—especially before surveys were used? What is the best way to combine rural people together into different, politically meaningful groups? Most rural Americans live in or outside small towns, but those towns may not actually have the local school their children attend or a grocery store where residents gather to share local news. Much of American politics takes place at the state level, but does such a thing as a "rural state" exist? What about counties? Not only do counties vary in population size, but some counties are bigger in landmass than entire states. In many states, counties are pretty meaningless—somewhat arbitrary lines on the map that were drawn centuries ago to give some structure to the administration of local tax courts. Louisiana does not have counties but parishes. Alaska uses boroughs, and throughout New England towns are the primary unit of local governance. But as we will argue, when making comparisons between groups of people—rural and urban, for example—it is always best to use the smallest geographic unit possible. And since we want to better understand voting behaviors over time, there is no better unit for understanding rural partisanship than the county.

Both of these measurement challenges—establishing a baseline and the right group to compare—matter because they change our understanding of where rural people actually live and vote. It is the necessary initial step in figuring out rural America's larger influence on American politics. Why do 20 percent of American voters matter so much? Most point to the overrepresentation of rural people in our governing institutions. While we support aspects of that thinking, we argue that something else is ultimately at work. The rural-urban divide is not just about institutions; it is about politics—how people in those communities think about their broader place in American society and who can best represent their interests.

While this chapter introduces these problems, it will take the entire book to accurately sort out how they fit together into our larger argument about the importance of place and place-based identities in the rural-urban divide. Ultimately, we argue that the current rural-urban divide is a new, unprecedented phenomenon—one that is particularly responsive to recent developments in modern American partisanship and specific issues that exploit a sense that some places are just not as important as others.

We do not use the term "unprecedented" lightly. One of the most complicated parts of our research has been figuring out just how new all this is, because at one point in American history, rural America was just that: America. Settlers and adventurers, fleeing Europe for gold or from persecution, encountered a vast new continent—not empty, of course, but sparse—unspoiled, pastoral, the land of Arcadia. First Nations people developed complex relationships with the land and, as folklore and historical reality make clear, helped ensure the survival of the colonists, unprepared and unfamiliar with nature's bounty. By the Revolutionary

War, hundreds of towns and hamlets dotted the present-day eastern third of the United States.

The country's foundation as a rural society has guided the development of American culture and politics for nearly three centuries. Ruralness has long been a central feature of the American ethos: the revolutionary spirit of independence and the strong sense of civic idealism that brought people to this strange land. Thomas Jefferson, the patron saint of American liberty, recognized that the "cultivators of the earth are the most valuable citizens. They are the most vigorous, the most independent, the most virtuous, and they are tied to their country and wedded to its liberty and interests by the most lasting bands."[9] Of course, at the time of the Revolution, 90 percent of Americans made their livelihoods as farmers. If one was to be a man of the people, to praise democracy and self-rule, one had to praise the rural way of life.

Today, the United States is an urban nation, as is every other industrialized democracy in the world. And the story of this country is also the story of urbanization. The glitz and glamor of the American metropolis is where fortunes are to be made. True liberty is not in the heartland's oppressive small town—the "world of groceries and sermons," the "dull and repetitive lifestyle," where people "tired of drudging and sleeping and dying," as Sinclair Lewis wrote in his condemning novel *Main Street*.[10] No, cities are the hubs of culture, where museums display the relics of the country's rural past as memorials to a generation that sacrificed good hygiene and indoor plumbing so their children could move away and live a better life. Cities are learned places, home to the most massive and elite universities. They are rich, places where multinational corporations set up shop. People bike there or take the subway: the new servants of the Earth. Cities are vibrant, youthful, diverse, and, above all, progressive. There is where you find the new microbreweries and niche distilleries, theaters showing foreign movies, and Whole Foods. Sure, there is the "inner-city," easy to overlook when constructing a grand narrative about where the action is in American life. "Cities and metropolitan areas are the engines of economic prosperity and social transformation in the United States," as Bruce Katz and Jennifer Bradley argue in their book, *The Metropolitan Revolution*.[11] This is what Hillary Clinton was referring to when she declared that the future of the Democratic Party was in the places that are "optimistic, diverse, dynamic, moving forward."[12]

Even with all the change, though, rural America has not disappeared. It has just become difficult to find. Its history has become mythologized—perverted by Hollywood productions that either idealize or ridicule rural life. In the late 1970s, you could watch *The Little House on the Prairie* on Mondays and end the week catching up with *The Dukes of Hazzard*. Rural life has also become grossly simplified. Most individuals living in rural America, do not, in fact, farm, as previously noted. And beginning in the 1950s, factories left the big cities and abandoned the old railway yards of the largest cities. They were just too expensive. Today, what little manufacturing exists in the United States is found alongside massive interstate highways in the countryside, where rents are cheap, labor is nonunionized, and small-town governments award massive tax benefits to attract better-paying jobs.[13] Rural America is not a monolith. Dig into "flyover country," and you will find that some places are doing just fine.

But more important than the myths and simplifications of the rural story, it is hard to fully come to grips with rural America either currently or historically because the topic presents a whole host of data problems. Data are the way we make accurate comparisons between urban and rural America and within the rural communities that interest us. Data confirm and refute the narratives and stylized accounts of authors who may drive by or visit small-town life for a brief moment. Data help us overcome our own biases as residents of rural communities, and data inform our historical arguments about the changing political allegiances of rural peoples and the unification of rural partisanship. Data help us better understand what is new and what is old and when the transformation began. And data help us parse through competing explanations and narratives that, while tantalizing, may mischaracterize how millions of rural voters actually participate in politics and make their voices heard.

MEASUREMENT MATTERS:
SHIFTING BASELINES AND RURAL "BLOCKS"

Believe it or not, the main data problem we confront in studying rural America is that defining "rural" is hard. In 1776, the great urban center of Philadelphia, the global capital of colonial America, stood at forty thousand—about half the capacity of the current city's football stadium. So, the first problem confronting us is that rural, as a concept and a measure, is highly relational. Not until the late 1800s was the word "rural" even commonly used to describe places, because it was simply the normal way of life.[14] But as America and the world industrialized, and as towns morphed into cities and then metropolises, rural places became distinct in relation to other types of places. Is America less rural today than it was two hundred years ago? Yes. How much so? Well, it depends on whether you think Philadelphia was urban back then in the same way it is now.

As noted earlier, we call this first issue the problem of the shifting baseline. The United States has grown in size, from just about 3.9 million persons in 1790, when the first census was taken, to 329 million in 2020. Even some rural communities today would have eclipsed the "mobs of great cities" that Jefferson bemoaned. The town of Vassalboro, Maine, where one of us lives, is just slightly smaller than the Richmond, Virginia, of 1776—the largest city in Jefferson's home state. But compared with other areas in the United States today, it would be a mistake to think of Vassalboro as anything other than rural and the Richmond of 1776 as anything but urban. Both, however, are roughly the same size—just two hundred years apart.

The problem of the shifting baseline is especially problematic for making comparisons over time. What it means to be a partisan does not change. Voting for a Democrat in 1820 registers the same as voting for a Democrat in 1920 and then 2020. But what it means to be rural—or, for that matter, urban—does change. It changes every year as the population grows and as the relationship between rural and urban areas shift. And so, if we are to claim that the partisan fissures between rural and urban areas are growing, we need a measure of ruralness that goes back in time and accounts for this shifting baseline for what makes a community "rural."

Our historical measure of ruralness is sensitive to the changing relations between rural and urban America over time. We can track, with detailed precision, the changing loyalties of voters in these distinct communities, and the patterns we find are unequivocal. Given our measure, we can further bracket these trends by region and zero in on the moments of political change that explain contemporary divisions. That will be our focus for the bulk of this chapter and the next two. We hold that our current political moment is as much the product of historical forces as it is any of the bumper stickers or slogans of recent presidential campaigns. We will demonstrate that point with data, not anecdotes.

Now, it would be great if we could go back in time and survey the millions of people who have called rural America home since the beginning of the United States. We could use our measure of ruralness and sum up all the differences between them that may account for differences between rural and urban areas. Alas, those data do not exist. Today, we are inundated with precise data and multiple surveys of the American electorate. Watching vote returns on election night, you will see analysts zoom into neighborhoods—precincts—to report turnout statistics, past results, and voter registration data. You will hear the pundits reference exit polls in particular precincts, where individuals tell pollsters how they voted, what they do for a living, and much else. But even just twenty years ago, it would have been impossible to find these data. You may find how a small town or neighborhood voted in 1980 but certainly not in 1880. And there were no generalizable exit polls, even in the mid-twentieth century. Even Dixville Notch, New Hampshire, which takes pride in being the first municipality to report its presidential election returns, started that tradition only in 1960.

Since we do not have individual data, we have to use aggregate data— or what is generally called grouped data. It is our only option. But we know that comparing groups can lead to some pretty faulty comparisons. In calling some groups "rural," we may sometimes lump together people who are very different but share a common place. In doing so, we may fall into what Hans Rosling calls the "gap instinct"—the "basic urge to divide things into two distinct groups, with nothing but an empty gap in between."[15]

We know that rural New York is not rural Arizona. An upstate New York orchardist would feel very out of place on an Arizona ranch, even if it would make for entertaining reality TV (at least for rural viewers)! In the eastern third of the United States, it is not uncommon to find densely packed towns and small cities of several hundred residents surrounded by woods, farms, and backcountry roads. This is a function of old patterns of industrialization, which brought people together in dense "urban" locales but where sprawling suburbs never materialized because the town stopped prospering. Conversely, in the Southwest, urban areas are on the rise. The fastest-growing cities are taking over former ranchlands. Here the line between urban and rural is stark.

Elsewhere throughout the United States, thousands of people live in neatly manicured planned communities in "the country." For example, in Loudoun County, Virginia—the richest county in the United States—old horse stables and Christmas tree farms are being cut down for low-density subdivisions, named "The Hamlets of Blue Ridge," "Orchards at Round Hill," and "Fawn Meadow." But these homes are replacing farmland, and their new owners commute into Washington, D.C., and its surrounding edge cities. Are they really rural or just pretending? And yet, we know that these rural residents have more in common with one another than with residents of big cities—the subject of many, rather cliched, reality shows. Rural is different from urban.

There are steps we can take to mitigate the risks of drawing faulty comparisons using group-based data, especially when making dichotomous comparisons. The trick is to pick up on what rural Americans actually hold in common while respecting rural America's vast geographic diversity, rich history, and the different ways of living found there. We need to get as granular as possible and group people in ways that maximize the likelihood that what distinguishes them is, in fact, their residence in a rural community.

At its most basic level, ruralness means not urban. Residents may travel to urban areas once in a while for work or pleasure, but the main way they experience life is outside the city center. Rural areas do not have the amenities that dense residential patterns make affordable, services that many—in fact most—Americans may take for granted: sewers, public water, a local bus line, or broadband internet.

In defining ruralness in the negative—what it is not as opposed to what it is—we are not pulling an academic sleight of hand. In finding rural America by first identifying urban areas and their immediate outlying areas, we are opening up our understanding of ruralness to encompass the vast diversity of rural ways of living in the United States. In fact, rural America is much more complex and varied than modern cityscapes, and especially the suburbs. About the same number of Americans live in the largest one hundred U.S. cities—from New York City (population 8.5 million) to Birmingham, Alabama (pop. 212,000)—as do in rural communities. Both NYC and Birmingham have vibrant downtowns, home to major international and national businesses. They have museums, cafes, public parks, zoos, and sports teams. Public hospitals and private medical insurance companies employ thousands of residents, and universities and colleges bring thousands more highly educated families into town on a daily basis. Yes, New York City is in a league of its own—a global center of finance and culture. But the average lifelong Manhattanite would find Birmingham more familiar than the daily routines and comforts of nearby Mechanicville, New York (pop. 5,196), or McMullen, Alabama (pop. 10). They may visit the cute B&B, but given the choice, they would much rather prefer to live in a city, not a rural community.[16]

Rural America, in contrast, has a complex range of lifestyles. In upper New England, on the borders with Canada, you are likely to find hamlets where French is still the dominant language of exchange and families have hauled timber from the same forests for generations—some still doing it with horses. In the Southeast, rural America is far more diverse than even some of the largest U.S. cities, and it is increasingly diversifying in terms of race, ethnicity, and language. Yes, you can pass by tobacco barns and cotton fields, but the Southeast is actually the last bastion of American manufacturing—the final resting place of bygone industries that left the Northeast and Midwest a century ago.

In the rural West, life and livelihood seem to revolve around the region's most precious commodity: water. And there, rural communities are suffering the brunt of climate change—losing the ability to survive as a result. Rural westerners' relationship with the government is like nowhere else in the country; nearly half of all land in the West, including vast swaths used for ranching, is owned and managed by federal agencies. In the East, a four-hundred-acre farm is massive, but in the West, four hundred acres is a lawn. Ranches are not even noteworthy until they blast beyond twenty thousand acres. Elsewhere throughout the region, national borders are a chimera, as the international rural economy, dependent on migrant labor, brings people from all over North America together with the changing seasons and harvests. No two areas in rural America are alike.

Once we realize the complexity in rural America and the relative similarity in urban America, we can shift our measurement strategy to reflect this reality. Of course, we are not the first to make this realization. For almost two hundred years, the U.S. Census has taken a similar approach, mainly because the historical development of the United States meant that it made more sense to identify urban areas first; these used to be the special areas, where a minority of Americans lived. The process has periodically changed, with significant revisions taking place alongside drastic technological developments in mapmaking and satellite imagery. But the logic has remained the same.

The census identifies urban areas by first carving up the entire United States into small units called "blocks." These bear a striking resemblance to the city blocks that you may walk, because these small units are defined by visible and mappable features such as roads, railroad tracks, and streams. They are also the building blocks for every other geographic unit used in the United States—from school district borders, to counties, to states. The United States is made up of more than eight million blocks, none of which overlaps. They are the smallest units for measuring population used by the census.

The emphasis here is on visible borders. Because blocks are drawn using the visible and mappable features of a locale's terrain—natural and manmade—cartographers, and now advanced geographic information system computing, can determine the amount of area the block covers. Some blocks are larger than others, given the scarcity of mappable features. What borders exist in the middle of the desert? As you can imagine—especially in urban areas—some blocks are small in terms of the land area they cover.

Once every square inch of the United States is placed into one of these blocks, the census determines how many people live within each block's borders, and that is the block's population density. A small block with a few families—think of your average suburb—may be as dense as a large block with many families. Block density is a function of geographic size and total population; the 117 individuals living in just twenty-six square meters in Camden, New Jersey, was the densest block in the 2020. Conversely, many blocks in the West do not even have a single individual living in them.

Once block density is calculated, two population thresholds are used to determine whether the people living there are "urban." The first pass identifies blocks that are very dense: one thousand people per square mile. To be sure, very few blocks have that many people, but very few blocks are a square mile in size; some are just a few square meters. Over 242 million Americans live in blocks exceeding these thresholds, and although there is considerable variation, all are considered urban.

The second pass uses a slightly lower threshold—five hundred persons per square mile—which identifies blocks that may have landscapes that limit the number of persons living in it but that nevertheless are urban. Features such as public parks, parking garages, or commercial centers with few apartments may limit the number of households, even if they are part of an urban area's larger residential footprint. Another 18 million Americans are in these blocks.

Finally, the Census Bureau considers places where even fewer people may live in measurable blocks, including areas such as airports or harbors, where no people may live but which otherwise may be clearly urban. These usually contain just a few people, but they help to map the spread of an urban area's geographic scope. Taken together, these three passes account for the vast majority of Americans who live in urbanized blocks, which then make up urban tracts, urban neighborhoods, urban cities, and so on.

MEASUREMENT MATTERS: FROM BLOCKS TO COUNTIES TO RURAL VOTERS

There are alternative approaches to measuring the rural-urban continuum, including a variety of measures used by the U.S. federal government.[17] The Office of Management and Budget inside the White House classifies areas into metro and nonmetro areas and then assigns counties to one of these two broad classifications, since counties—not blocks—are usually the smallest unit from which important economic and budgetary data are collected.[18] Over in the Department of Agriculture, statisticians have developed another way of measuring ruralness: taking census tracts (a bunch of blocks grouped in a politically meaningful way, such as town or neighborhood) and assigning them a level of interconnectedness between those blocks and urban centers. The "Rural-Urban Commuting Area" distinguishes between rural areas based on what percentage of the population commutes to small urbanized towns like Pittsboro, North Carolina (population 4,287) and communities in which a large percentage of residents commute to larger towns, such as the smaller hamlets in neighboring Randolph County, North Carolina—home to the more sizable city of Asheboro (pop. 25,012).[19] Still other government agencies, research organizations, and scholarly studies may choose to adopt another measure of ruralness, such as "Urban Influence Codes," micropolitan statistical areas, or the most straightforward of them all: county-level population density measures.

There are as many measures for identifying rural areas as there are reasons someone may need to know where rural America is. Commuting patterns matter for highway planners, and influence codes could mean a lot to a media market strategist. For us, the advantage of the block approach is unparalleled because it allows us to think about the politics of rural America historically—as it has developed throughout time, and how those developments have tracked with our political system. In other words, the measure thrives on its consistency; the process of categorizing blocks into urban areas has stayed more or less the same. As such, whether we are interested in 1820 or 2020, we can then take the block-level measure of urbanicity and use it to calculate the ruralness of larger units, such as counties. We can then calculate the percentage of each county's residents who live in urbanized blocks. This gives us a continuous measure, where some counties are mostly rural and some are mostly urban.

That continuum of rural counties produces a map like the one in figure 1.1. The darkest-shaded counties are the most rural places in America—counties where less than 25 percent of the population lives in urbanized census blocks. This includes 699 counties where not one of those 5.2 million residents lives in a dense, urbanized census block. On the other side, the counties most lightly shaded are where more than 90 percent of the county population lives in urbanized blocks. Even though some residents live outside urban blocks—in lower-density neighborhoods—the county as a whole is still predominantly urbanized. In 30 counties, where 11.3 million Americans call home, not a single resident lives in a block of fewer than five hundred persons per square mile. It is completely urbanized.

But why rely on counties? Good question. Ultimately, we put so much effort into distinguishing rural from nonrural counties because the "county" is the smallest unit that has consistently reported important political statistics since elections were first held in this country. If we did not care about electoral politics—if we were interested just in government policies—we might use a different measure of ruralness. But we care about politics, and in the United States, you cannot get historic elections data at a level smaller than the county.

To be sure, this measure is used by statisticians at the Census Bureau but few other social scientists. For one, it is more difficult to compute than the ready-packaged "urban-rural" codes provided by other government agencies. And, largely for ease of data access, scholars often turn to county-level population density measures, which take the total number of persons living in a county and divide it by the total number of square miles in that county. In contrast, we compute density at the smallest scale possible and then build up. This method considers where people in a county actually live and how closely they live together, even if the county is very large.

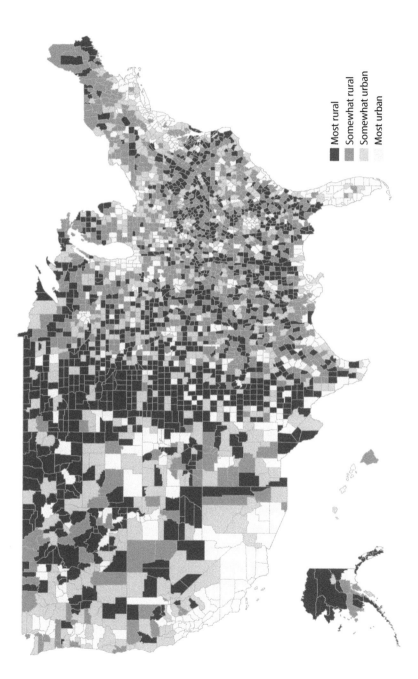

FIGURE 1.1 Map of rural America, 2020

Note: Map displays the average percentage ruralness for each county in the United States. Percentages of county population living in nonurban census blocks are as follows. Most rural counties: 75–100 percent; somewhat rural counties: 50–74.99 percent; and somewhat urban counties: 25–49.99 percent. The most urban counties are where 0–24.99 percent of the population lives in a nonurban census block (or where 75.01–100 percent of residents live in urban blocks).

Most rural
Somewhat rural
Somewhat urban
Most urban

There is a big difference between working up (blocks to counties) versus working down (just starting with county-level density estimates). For instance, let us consider San Bernardino County in Southern California. In figure 1.1, you can identify it as the massive four-sided polygon with a small protrusion in the lower-left corner of the county. This is the largest county in the United States, and at twenty thousand square miles is almost the size of West Virginia; its population is actually larger than that state's, housing over 2.18 million people. In the far western edge, the county seat of San Bernardino City bumps up against Greater Los Angeles City. It is an urban locale, without a doubt.

But in the far eastern part of the county, the terrain quickly gives way to treacherous deserts and mountain passes. For that reason, some 88 percent of San Bernardino County residents live in just 8.6 percent of its total land area. This has enormous implications for understanding the county's level of ruralness. If we first calculate population density at the county level, we get a measure of about one hundred persons per square mile—about half as dense as Kanawha County, West Virginia, where the state capital of Charleston is located. But using our measure, which first considers how many blocks are urban, we identify San Bernardino residents as among the most urban in America. Fully 95 percent of residents in that county live in places properly measured as urbanized. This is not rural America, despite the county's relative low county-level population density.

The example of San Bernardino is not cherry-picked. As figure 1.2 shows, it is endemic to most research that relies on the more straightforward but grossly oversimplified measures of county-level (or even state-level!) population density. Our measure of ruralness, which builds up from census blocks, is graphed along the x axis (the bottom measure). It ranges from 0 percent of the county population living in rural (nonurban) blocks to 100 percent of the county population. Along the y axis (on the left) is the measure of a county's population density.[20] It is clear that the line slopes downward, suggesting a negative relationship between county-level population density and our measure of ruralness. This makes sense; as population density decreases, so does the percentage of the population living in urban census blocks. But notice how

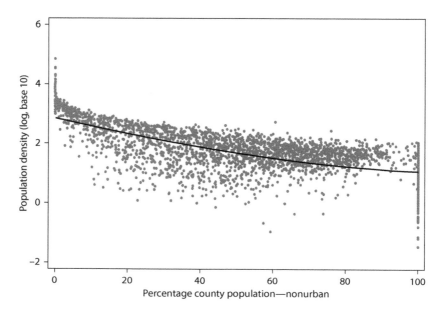

FIGURE 1.2 Relationship between population density and percentage ruralness, by county

Note: Figure plots each U.S. county in 2020 based on its population density (persons per square mile) and the percentage of county residents who reside in nonurban census blocks—the measure of ruralness introduced in this chapter.

weak the relationship is—how scattered the data points are along the line; the greater the scatter, the more the variance. In some counties, no residents live in an urban block. These are the data points on the far right of the figure; notice the cluster that moves up and down. And yet, using population density as the measure (the *y* axis), we see that some of these counties are as "dense" as counties where nearly everyone lives in an urban block (high on the scale). In reality, the actual ruralness and urbanness of these places differ while the population density does not! In much of rural America, county-level density varies because the geographic size of American counties varies, even though the same percentage of the population lives in rural areas.

Let us give you a brief example. Mathews County, Virginia, is located on the Chesapeake Bay. It's geographically tiny, boasting just eighty-six square miles. There are about eighty-eight hundred residents in Mathews County, meaning roughly one hundred people per square mile, which would seem rather high. But when we drop down to the block level, we find that none of these residents lives in an urban area. We suspect the residents of the county would agree with this assessment: regardless of the ratio of residents per square mile, Mathews County is rural. On our scale it would be on the far right, but on the density measure, it may be somewhere in the middle. In short, population density measures would make sense only if the geographic sizes of counties were more or less the same.

There is an advantage in using multiple measures of ruralness. We are not arguing that ours is the best—just the best for our purpose. Since our goal is to make valid historical comparisons between rural and urban America, and not necessarily find every single rural American living in the United States at a single moment, county-level figures prove remarkably flexible. Once we calculate the proportion of each county's population that lives in an urban block in every census, we can categorize those counties by their levels of ruralness and urbanness.

This conclusion is open to interpretation. We define any county as rural if fewer than half the county's residents live in urbanized blocks (any of the three density thresholds described earlier). This captures 1,881 U.S. counties as of 2020, the latest year for which we have census data. We then measure any county where more than 90 percent of the population lives in urbanized tracts as "very urban." This includes 251 counties, which today capture over 55 percent of the American population. In between, we identify those counties where more than half the population lives in urbanized blocks but where a sizable portion (up to 40 percent) still lives outside urban areas; these counties are mixed, usually containing sizeable cities, but large swaths of rural areas.

Endemic to any type of grouped data, we recognize that our measure does not capture every single rural person living in the country—just those rural residents living in majority-rural counties. Consider, for example, Wabash County, Indiana. By our measure, it is about as close to being rural as a county can be without actually being rural as we define it: 50.1 percent of its population lives in census blocks with urbanized levels of population density. Most Wabash residents living in these urbanized blocks call the city of Wabash home—a decent-sized community of about ten thousand people—the first town to be fully lit by electricity (or so it claims). Wabash City, by our measure, is not rural, and neither are the smaller towns that dot Wabash County: North Manchester, Largo, and La Fontaine. Collectively, a bare majority of the county population lives in those urbanized areas, which means that the county as a whole is not a rural county. We are not saying it is the most urban place in America; it just falls out of our analysis for measuring rural politics over time.

Now, though we say Wabash County is more urban than rural, our measure groups the fifteen thousand residents of Wabash who do, in fact, live in rural census blocks within a nonrural county. And we do this for all the rural residents who live in nonrural counties nationwide. In 2020, this amounts to almost 18 million Americans—and it is why our population percentages are slightly different from other estimates of rural America that you may find, including those we calculate using a survey of rural residents later in this book.

The decision to measure ruralness this way has trade-offs, but we think it is a conservative trade-off; it biases our results against us. We want to count every rural resident everywhere, including those who live right up against urban centers and urban voters. But we cannot, because there is no way of matching their votes with their rural locations once we go back a few years. Today, given widely reported election data at the precinct level, we can (and others have) done just that.[21] The result is that some rural residents will be grouped in urban counties and some urbanized residents will be grouped in overwhelmingly rural counties. On average, though, these groupings represent each county's dominant geography.

In general, and as figure 1.3 makes clear, this trade-off makes no discernible difference in our analysis. Since the early 1800s, the percentage of residents living in predominantly rural communities has fallen. The first time a majority of the American population lived outside rural counties was in 1920. And beginning in the late 1960s, the share of the population living in fully urbanized communities has come to eclipse the number of Americans living in lower-density suburbs.

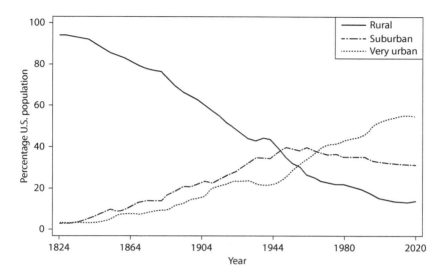

FIGURE 1.3 Rural, suburban, and urban populations in the United States since 1824

Note: Figure illustrates the changing proportion of the American population residing in rural counties (0–50 percent of the population living in urban census blocks), suburban counties (50.1–90 percent of the population living in urban blocks), and very urban counties (more than 90 percent of residents live in an urban block).

The measure has good face validity and matches the broader narrative of demographic change in the United States.[22]

MEASURING RURAL VOTING PATTERNS IN THE PAST

In an ideal world, we would want to find out what percentage of each census block voted for the major presidential candidates in each year. But census blocks are not political units; they are a demographer's tool. Local elections boards do not need to report election returns by block level, nor would they—they are politically meaningless. Does anyone even know the block they live in?

In politics, counties mean something, because the county is the main unit by which elections—federal, state, and local—have been administered throughout American history. As a result, we can track how each county votes through time. It is only at the county level that you can find out how the one hundred thirty men of Patrick County, Virginia, voted in 1800 (they all voted for Thomas Jefferson, by the way).

That said, it is also true that these data are difficult to find. It took a team of a half-dozen undergraduate research assistants over two summers to collect county-level data on presidential vote share and county-level ruralness going back to 1800. (Don't fret. Maine during the summer is gorgeous, even if you're stuck indoors tabulating ancient ballot reports.) Thanks to the work of tireless historians, archivists, and many election officers and Secretary of State offices, we pulled it together. We took decennial population estimates and interpolated new county-level estimates of the rural population for election years that took place between censuses. We then merged it all into what is arguably one of the largest U.S. aggregate election data sets ever created, boasting nearly two hundred thousand observations.[23]

Although we can go back to the start, there is a good reason to pick up the long-term trends in presidential elections beginning in 1824. Prior to that year, a large number of states still selected their slates to the Electoral College by voting in the state legislature.[24] The idea that a state's population would show up on Election Day and cast ballots was preposterous when Washington was first elected president. And even in communities that did have such a thing as a popular vote, electors were not beholden to the state's choice. In fact, most counties did not even report their election returns for federal offices until the turn of the nineteenth century.[25] It is also the case that prior to 1824, such a small sliver of the American population voted that it would be misleading to categorize the political elite of most counties as decidedly urban or rural. And since we know that so few Americans, even eligible voters—white property-owning men—were characterized as urban at this time, we pick up our analysis when the data become more reliable and consistently reported.

Figure 1.4 reflects how three counties voted over the last two hundred years and across fifty presidential elections. As most others do, we

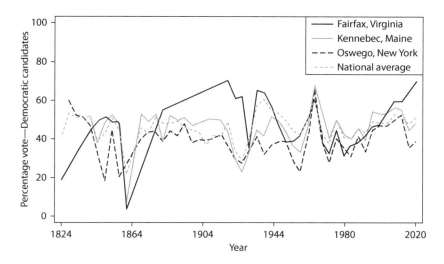

FIGURE 1.4 Vote share for Democratic Party, three counties in the United States since 1824

Note: Figure plots the percentage of ballots cast for the Democratic candidate in each presidential election between 1824 and 2020 in three counties, and the national vote share for the Democratic candidate throughout the country (solid black line).

map partisan trends by referring only to the Democratic Party, since historically it predates the emergence of the Republican Party by a good fifty years; and since we live in a political system dominated by two major parties, we can see larger trends in the electorate by plotting just one of the two.

The story our data tell comports with so much of what we already know. Fairfax County—a comfortable suburb of Washington, D.C.—was once considered the deep South, so much so that it bucked the national Democratic Party candidate in 1860, Stephen A. Douglas, to vote for the secessionist sympathizer, John C. Breckinridge. But throughout the twentieth century, except when the Catholic New Yorker Al Smith was the candidate for president in 1924, Fairfax County was the bastion of southern support for the Democratic Party. Today, it is highly urbanized and staunchly Democratic.

In comparison, in Oswego, New York—a modest-sized community on the edge of Lake Ontario—we see the transition of a Republican stronghold into a battleground county. Even in 1936, when Franklin D. Roosevelt set a new record for the national vote, Oswego residents remained steadfast Republicans. That is what upstate New Yorkers did! Today, it ebbs and flows. Support is mixed, loyalties are up in the air, and voters respond to the candidates on the ballot, particularly Trump in 2016. Likewise, as Maine goes, so goes the nation. In our home county, Kennebec, Maine, vote shares closely track the national average. In 1964, when Lyndon Johnson swept the national vote for president, Mainers went with it. But when certain Democratic candidates faltered nationwide—Jimmy Carter in 1980, for instance—Kennebec County residents turned their backs on them, too.

It is common in American politics to leave the story there. Knowing the vote share for presidential candidates tells us all we need to know about partisanship in that county. That is how Bill Bishop, in his widely read study of American polarization, *The Big Sort*, measures the country's growing geographic divide. Counties where the margin of victory for a presidential candidates was more than twenty points, he claims, are "landslide" counties—places where "people who live alike, think alike, and vote alike."[26]

Although useful, we argue that you can take it one step further. For one, the average margin of victory in a county changes each year, not just because there are more Republicans or more Democrats living there but because the Republican or Democrat running for office is different each election. Support for presidential candidates is one part party loyalty, another part candidate. As such, we care not only about margins of victory in a given year but how county-level partisanship differs from the national average in that year. For example, in 1984, when Ronald Reagan won every state except Minnesota and Washington, D.C., margins of victory across thousands of counties were at the landslide level. But that was not because we were more geographically polarized in 1984 than other years; Walter Mondale was a dull candidate, and Reagan was atypically popular.

What we need to do is find the places that were unusually more Republican than normal, even when the Republican was incredibly popular. Figure 1.5 considers the same three counties as before but measures

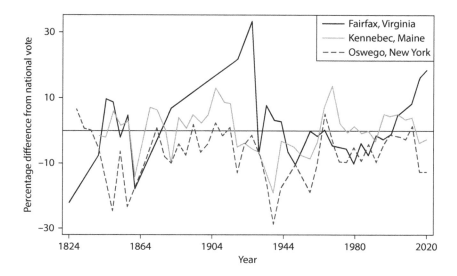

FIGURE 1.5 Difference in vote share for Democratic Party, three counties in the United States since 1824

Note: Figure plots the percentage of ballots cast for the Democratic candidate in each presidential election between 1824 and 2020 in three counties, as it relates to the national vote share for the Democratic candidate. Points above the horizontal line (0) indicate that the Democratic candidate overperformed in the county in that year (did better there than nationally), while negative values indicate that the Democratic candidate underperformed in the county in that year (did worse there than nationally).

how different they were from the national average. If we consider each county's presidential vote share and subtract it from the national average, we get a better idea of how voters in those places relate to the rest of the country—even if, as a whole, they ended up voting like almost everyone everywhere else in the country. If the difference between the percentage of voters who voted Democratic compared with the total national Democratic vote is negative, there were fewer Democratic votes in that county than we might expect, given the popularity of the Democratic candidate that year. Visually, the county's line falls below the horizontal line, which denotes a difference of zero. Calculated that way, we can see that in Oswego and Fairfax, voters underperformed for the Democratic candidate in 1984; Mondale was even more unpopular there than he was nationwide (and he was unpopular!). Kennebec, Maine—per usual—voted right in line with the national average, even though voters there supported Reagan by twenty points; it would be disingenuous to stay it was a Republican bastion, because voters, there, supported Reagan as much as they did elsewhere.

In looking at county-level differences in vote share instead of just outcome, we can begin to see interesting patterns that national swings in candidate popularity may overlook. In the case of Reagan's 1984 win, we can see that while support for the incumbent president was high everywhere save Minnesota and D.C., it was particularly high in some places. Armed with our other set of data, we can figure out if those places were overwhelmingly rural.

All in all, our new measure of county ruralness, combined with our collection on presidential data, gives us the first in-depth national measure of partisanship in rural America since the early decades of the nineteenth century. As we detail in the next two chapters, which focus on the ebbs and flows and rural partisanship, our data unequivocally support our contention that what American politics is going through is unprecedented. It is an empirically based fact, supported by arduous data collection efforts, innovative measurement strategies, and detailed methodological reporting.

HOW RURAL POLITICS SHAPES
AMERICA TODAY

Our measure of ruralness enables us to go back in time and make accurate comparisons between rural and urban areas, even when most of America was rural. It also helps us sort out geographic differences in modern America when survey data are nonexistent or irrelevant to the analysis.

By our measure, only about 20 percent of Americans live in a rural community. It is reasonable to ask, "Why go to all this trouble to overcome shifting baselines and adjust for election-to-election swings in candidate popularity when such a small fraction of the American population lives in these types of places?" In fact, you may be wondering, "Is it not the case that our historical data suggest that rural America is becoming less significant each and every year?"

One reason to care, floated by many, is that despite their small number, rural voters are important because they have an inflated level of influence in governing institutions. Rural politics is about geography, and geography is embedded in every major American political institution, from the local town hall all the way to the White House.[27] Who votes for whom, which areas get what, which government is in charge: these are questions about place, and rural voters exist in very particular places. You cannot understand America's political institutions or any election without making sense of the ways that geography transforms various outcomes. As Jowei Chen and Jonathan Rodden have pointed out, the simple facts of human geography—urban areas are dense—mean that geographic schemes of representation will create inefficiencies in how votes are distributed—and that is before partisans get their hands on electoral maps to gerrymander them even more.[28] As a result, the nationalization and consistency of the rural vote reverberate throughout national politics with a louder-than-expected voice.

Those facts understandably drives resentment in urban areas. Overrepresentation of rural places seems unfair in our modern political culture. For example, following the death of the late Supreme Court justice Ruth Bader Ginsberg, Nate Silver was left with little else to predict except the following: "Here's what I do know: the Senate is an enormous problem for Democrats given the current political coalitions, in which Democrats are dominant in cities while Republicans triumph in rural areas. And because the Senate is responsible for confirming Supreme Court picks, that means the Supreme Court is a huge problem for Democrats too."[29]

The Supreme Court is already antidemocratic, in that citizens do not vote for the justices who make important decisions on their behalf. It is reasonable to see it as even less democratic in giving only some people—allegedly, rural voters—greater control over its appointments. Of course, there is a legitimacy crisis confronting our institutions, and, as it seems, rural power—not its weakness—is at the core. Writing on the one-year anniversary of the January 6th Capitol insurrection, Osita Nwanevu placed the blame for the extremism at the feet of these unequal institutions, which give "rural voters in sparsely populated states in the middle of the country [more] power than the rest of the electorate." Those institutions, he writes, "helped produce that violent outburst by building a sense of entitlement to power within America's conservative minority."[30]

But just how large is the rural advantage? No doubt, you have read arguments very similar to the ones noted earlier, but what do the data have to say about the ways in which rural voices get channeled into our politics? For starters, you actually need data on ruralness, which is easier said than done.

It turns out that once you take pains to standardize shifting baselines and figure out exactly where rural voters are in this great big country, you get a different story about the rural advantage in American politics. For instance, in talking about the Senate or the Electoral College, academics are as quick as pundits to point to statistics like the one we chart in figure 1.6.[31] There are plenty of ways to make sense of the unequal distribution of power in the Senate, but a favorite is to consider the percent of the U.S. population that is needed to create a theoretical majority in the Senate.[32] After 1960, with the introduction of Alaska as the fiftieth state, that would mean calculating what percentage of Americans reside in the least-populous twenty-five states, each of which would send two senators, creating a fifty-seat majority (assuming unified government). That is the solid black line in the figure, which has hovered between 16 and 19 percent since 1900. If there were no malapportionment, that line would be at 50 percent; that is, if geography did not matter, it would take 50 percent of the population, living in the twenty-five smallest states, to get 50 percent of the voting power. The reality, though, is pretty skewed. Today, only 17 percent of Americans live in states controlling 50 percent of the power in the U.S. Senate. Using this exact calculation, the *New York Times* concluded, "The Rural Vote's Disproportionate Slice of Power" . . . It's "As American as Apple Pie."[33]

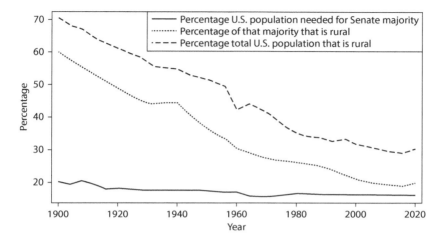

FIGURE 1.6 Voting advantage in the U.S. Senate for rural areas (1900–2020)

Note: Figure plots three trends between 1900 and 2020. The solid line represents the percentage of the American population represented by the group of smallest states needed to construct a majority in the U.S. Senate (over 50 percent of votes in the chamber). The dashed line indicates the percentage of residents living within that group of states (the fictional majority) who live in rural communities in those states. The tightly dashed line represents the percentage of the American population living in rural communities nationwide.

But what are we really doing when we take something like the U.S. Senate or the Electoral College—whose disproportionality stems from the equal representation of states? One thing we are not doing is measuring ruralness.

We love to use small states as a proxy for ruralness. It's easy. Wyoming: small, rural, disproportionate! But Rhode Island is small and overwhelmingly urban. So, too, are Hawaii and Delaware—all three are overrepresented in the Senate, and all are predominantly composed of urban residents. Nevada also. Really, Nevada is urban, with all that space, endless deserts? Yes. As we have tried to make clear throughout this chapter, if what we care about is ruralness, then what we need to think about is exactly that: the percentage of residents living in urban areas—and in the case of Nevada, that percentage is high, even if much of the land in Nevada is rural.

So, if we want to think about how rural America influences American politics and tie it to an institutional advantage in the Senate, we need a way of measuring what percentage of that theoretical minority (the 17 percent who can get a majority) actually live in rural areas within each state. That is the dashed gray line in figure 1.6. Moreover, we need to compare it with the actual percentage of rural residents living in the United States at any one time. That is the dotted black line. The gap between those two lines is the rural over-representation gap in the U.S. Senate.

Once we go to all that trouble, you will notice that there is indeed a gap between how rural areas are represented and how they should be represented, strictly speaking. If you were to take a look at the nearly 49 million Americans it would take to make the smallest Senate majority possible, 30 percent of them would live in rural areas. That's higher than their actual representation in the American population throughout the twentieth and early twenty-first centuries, but only by about 10 points on average. That means rural residents have a bit more weight, a bit more say, in the Senate.

And yet, while that weight is disproportionate, is it really what is driving the massive and growing gap between rural and urban areas? Once you recognize that so-called small states are not a rural monolith and begin to consider who lives there, it turns out that rural areas have more power than a strictly proportional system would allow—but they do not have a majority of power in these states. Not by a long shot.

An illustration may help. On any lists of the states that are part of the Senate "problem" just described, you will find Utah. With only 3.4 million residents, it is simply unfair that they have the same say in the Senate as Texas, New York, California, and other large states. Given the massive size of the state, some eighty-five thousand square miles (ranked thirteenth overall), it has a very low population density (ranked forty-first). So, as the story goes, Utah and all its residents are gumming up the democratic works. But are rural voters the problem? According to our data, some 90 percent of Utahns live in urban or suburban areas. Just 10 percent live in rural areas.

In fact, a majority of rural residents live in states that are under-represented in the Senate. Most rural people do not have the power they should, and most of the people living in that fictional Senate majority live outside rural areas. Roughly 64 percent of Montanans live outside rural areas. And in those small states, about half are Democrats! How does that build "a sense of entitlement to power"? You can blame the undemocratic nature of the Senate on the constitutional framers, but bear in mind that rural America has not been able to capture a majority of the Senate since the 1950s. And considering a long view of twentieth-century politics, it is clear that some of the most progressive moments in American politics have taken place when rural areas actually held most of the power in institutions, such as the Senate and Electoral College.

The same difficulties exist when trying to make sense of policies: who gets more and who gets less. One possibility is that these institutional advantages lead to very real differences in how the federal government spends its money—sending more than it should to rural areas while wealthier urban centers wallow in disrepair. Again, this presupposes some measurement choices, not only, in this case, about measuring federal dollars and cents but in allocating them to different geographies. Consider, for example, the data Paul Krugman—a Nobel-winning economist—uses to support his argument that "rural America is heavily subsidized by urban America."[34]

Analysts, including Krugman, often use a measure known as a "balance of payment" to describe how much money the federal government redistributes to various places.[35] The advantage is that balance of payments data can easily account for differences in population size between different places—a per capita balance, indicating how much money the federal government spends in a place for every person living there.

At first glance, it may seem that the more difficult measurement task is figuring out where the trillions of dollars of federal spending actually go. But with advances in data transparency and federal budgeting guidelines, we have a decent understanding of where money is actually spent in the United States and how much each person in each state "receives" on average. Of course, as an average, very few citizens actually receive that much, since this includes all the money that goes to universities for research, shipbuilders for defense contracts, employees in the federal government, Medicare payments to hospitals, and so forth. Still, take all the money sent to a state, divide it by its population, and that is what becomes the per capita federal balance of payments, listed along the *y* axis (left side) of figure 1.7.

But just because we can measure it does not mean we have captured the underlying concept we care about. Existing balance of payments data are problematic for making geographic comparisons between urban and rural areas because they are calculated only at the state level. And this is likely to remain the case, since it is nearly impossible to allocate some federal receipts to counties or towns (e.g., the corporate income tax). However, millions of rural residents live in "urban states"

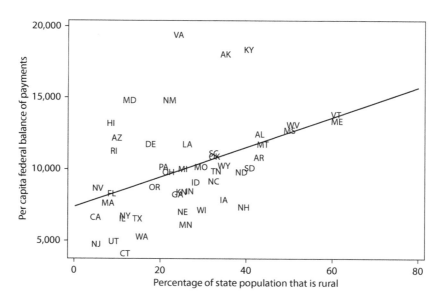

FIGURE 1.7 State-level balances of payments and states' ruralness, 2020

Note: Figure plots each state in 2020 by the percentage of its population living in rural communities and the amount of money each state received from the federal government in FY2020, divided by the state's total population— the state's per capita federal balance of payments.

and vice versa. Some 59 percent of Kentucky residents (near the top in figure 1.7), for example, live in nonrural areas. Moreover, much federal investment in, say, highways or mass transit cannot be allocated across different types of geographies. And residential patterns and federal spending are also complicated within states. Virginia residents, for example, receive back nearly three times as much from the federal government as they send. But we know that the billions of dollars coming from the government are not going to the 25 percent of Virginia residents living in rural areas. That spending is for the thousands of contractors in northern Virginia and the thousands of sailors in the state's southeast. Virginia may be an exceptional case, but it is demonstrable proof that states are poor units for confirming "facts" about rural-urban distribution in the United States.

Perhaps most problematic is that some trends can suggest a rural-urban gulf when in reality those trends do not exist. Sure, on average, as our replication of the balance of payments analysis shows, the more rural a state, the more its residents, on average, receive in federal money. But is that really due to ruralness? We have good reason to doubt it. There are many states with sizable rural populations that receive much less on average than more urban states; most of the states receiving the highest are not rural by any stretch of the imagination. Some are, and this creates the illusion of a trend. Most are not, and this suggests that something else is driving the differences between Maine, let's say, and California. In fact, we could draw a better trend line by looking at the percentage of each state's residents that are over the age of 65, or the percentage of residents who are military veterans. So is it a rural advantage—or the fact that rural areas are more likely to have older residents, or that more rural states have a higher percentage of military veterans, or even something else? By now, you know this to be a problem of comparing large geographies that have lots of variation within them (that gap instinct problem), and while the distribution of government monies between urban and rural areas is part of the widening geographic divisions facing this country—and one we will spend some time sorting through in later chapters—at least we can begin from the same premise and acknowledge that the answer to those questions is much more complex than commonly thought. At the very least, it requires us to be very attentive to our measurement choices.

RECONSIDERING THE URBAN-RURAL DIVIDE

There is a rural-urban divide in the contemporary United States. Plenty of analysts and scholars less attentive to the particular difficulties of geographic data can point to the growing chasm and have offered up plenty of reasons for why it exists and why it matters.

We have spent this chapter discussing some methodological problems that often accompany these types of arguments. Some of them relate most clearly to historical comparisons, and the challenge of understanding changes in rural politics as the very definition of what constitutes "rural" changes over time. Some of the problems are endemic to political geography, and the fact that the geographic units we care about—counties, states, even countries—are often poor representations of the individual-specific attributes that motivate our analysis. And still other issues relate to some of the smaller but no less profound challenges that accompany our current thinking about rural life in the United States: that rural America is much smaller than we may often realize and that rural residents do not always live in the places we tend to group under the banner of "rural America."

Ultimately, the reason we stress these geographic facts here is because our understanding of rural politics is very different from what you usually find. In the first case, our understanding of the "facts" suggests that arguments about the changing nature of rural politics are not what many believe. For example, the overrepresentation of rural areas in the U.S. Senate and Electoral College is exaggerated. Or, simply put, rural areas' representation has not fundamentally changed, even as the evidence for a growing rural-urban divide has.

This is not to suggest that institutions do not matter. But there is a reason we do not emphasize institutional disparities in this book. Sure, you can find many examples of a so-called rural bias in this country's history. It is well known that Thomas Jefferson was able to position the nation's capital on the swampy, undeveloped shores of the Potomac River in northern Virginia—instead of the then urban centers of Philadelphia or New York—in exchange for backing Hamilton's economic scheme. State capitals, too, are often located in rural areas. The rural bias has been massive in state legislatures as well. Before industrialization, many state senate districts were counties, leading to dramatic population disparities. Cook County, for instance, would have the same say in the Illinois State Senate as would Shelby County. Before the Supreme Court mandated population equality in state legislative representation, one state house district might have two thousand residents, but the neighboring one might boast ten thousand. In many states, redistricting rarely occurred, even though population shifts were dramatic.[36] Before the 1960s, for instance, the Tennessee state legislature had not undertaken a reapportionment process since the turn of the century. Maryland had not done so since the Civil War!

Fast-forward to today, and you can make the argument that we still live in the shadow of these early decisions. Given the concentration of Democratic voters in urban areas, the overall partisan balance in legislatures often does not match statewide voter preferences. For instance, from 2012 to 2016, Michigan voters cast more than 50 percent of their ballots for Democratic legislative candidates. That translated into 44 percent in the state house, 31 percent in the state senate, and just 35 percent in the U.S. House of Representatives.[37] Moreover, there have always been imbalances in an array of policy areas, called "small-state minimums." Because of formulas set by Congress, less-populated states and communities (including urban ones!) get a disproportionate share of federal education aid, for instance.[38] Transportation aid is another area where small states net a disproportionate share based both on population and miles of roads.[39]

And yet, rural areas have always had these types of advantages. They are over two hundred thirty years old. And that is what leads us to our second, more foundational conclusion: our deepening crisis between rural and urban America is not just the work of old institutions; rather, it is because rural America has undergone a dramatic transformation in its politics over the last four decades. The real power behind the rural vote is political, not institutional. It is because rural America votes as a homogeneous block, and it has done so with increasing consistency since 1980. Institutions explain a lot about American politics, but that does not explain why rural America now votes as a monolithic force come Election Day and why its vote overwhelmingly favors the modern Republican Party.

There is something more fundamental about this conclusion than simply making sense of who wins and loses on Election Day. At the risk of overstating the importance of our work, we assert that rural voters are not like any other segment of the American electorate. Other groups are important and essential to understand beyond some academic insistence for the truth. Black Americans, women, the youth vote, evangelical Christians: all are important, have their own history, and matter beyond the horse race of any campaign cycle. But none of these voting blocs is currently as disruptive and more central to recent developments in American partisanship than rural voters.

The speed and magnitude of the change stems from the fact that rural voters are unique because their politics, attitudes, beliefs, and behaviors are shaped by a sense of place. Yes, rural areas are different from urban areas, and that is part of the story. Yes, rural areas have some institutional advantages, and that matters, too. But what really makes the difference is the fact that rural people, unlike any other group in American politics, think about politics through a geographically based worldview. It has given rise to a national voting bloc, which matters beyond its massive size, given the fact that electoral institutions overrepresent sparsely populated areas. It also matters because that sense of place is a very strange idea for many of the people who purport to know something about rural voters, which has led to a great deal of erroneous thinking about how best to bridge the rural-urban divide.

But if the rural-urban divide threatens this country's future—which we believe it does—then the first step at bridging that divide is understanding what that divide actually is. That requires good data—historically rich, as detailed as possible, and from multiple perspectives. That is what this book offers, which is why, in the final analysis, we are confident that such bridges can be built.

2

THE DEEP ROOTS OF THE
RURAL-URBAN DIVIDE (1776–1980)

Politicians and pundits describe America in many ways. There is a red America and a blue America; some Americans are more educated, others work with their hands; there is an America for whites and an America for everyone else. Americans, it is fair to say, are divided.

Americans are also physically divided. They live in different communities and call different places home. For the first one hundred years of American history, it was common to introduce oneself by the state from which they came (and were likely born). Even after the Civil War made clear that this was, indeed, a single, unified country, it was common to use the plural form when discussing "these United States."[1] And every four years, we still witness plenty of evidence of how geography shapes American politics: the divisions between red and blue are physically embodied in Election Day maps, showing that Democrats and Republicans not only vote differently, they live differently as well.

Divides are nothing new in American politics, and some, such as those that exploit racial prejudice, are woven into the very foundation of the country. So, if American politics has always had a "rural voter," why all the hubbub now? As we showed in chapter 1, the percentage of American voters coming from rural places is declining. It would seem that they are becoming less important to understand, not more.

And yet, despite becoming less representative of Americans in general, rural voters have become more influential in American politics, particularly presidential politics. Some of this, as we explored in the last chapter, is a result of our electoral institutions. The Electoral College and Senate give rural voters a disproportionate say in presidential contests and legislative deliberations. Still, the small representational advantages we identified pale in comparison to the massive sway the rural vote seems to have on the country's politics. Institutions matter, and institutional reform may be needed so that Americans can rebuild trust in government. But institutions are not the root of the problem.

Indeed, these institutional problems take for granted the idea that there is such a thing as a rural voter in the first place. Again, at the time many of these institutions were created—when the Constitution was written—all voters were essentially rural voters. Something else has had to change for rural voters to have gained the outsized influence they now have. In short, the rural voter had to be created. And as we detail in this chapter, drawing on our extensive historical elections data, it took nearly two centuries for rural voters to finally become a powerful electoral coalition.

The rural voter, we argue, is a new and unprecedented phenomenon in American politics—and it is a powerfully divisive force because of those institutional and political advantages given, unintentionally, to rural America. Rural Americans have come to see themselves as the "real America"—a separate community rooted in their geographic distinctiveness and ways of living. Although there have always been rural voters, rural areas across the United States have often voted differently from one another. There was no set pattern, or uniformity, to the rural vote. Throughout most of the country's history, sectional divides—the North versus the South, for example—hindered the formation of a potential rural vote. The rural-urban divide never really existed, because rural America itself remained deeply divided. For nearly two hundred years, both major political parties found support in rural America at the same time, as they tapped into what made rural places different from one another. Rural voters were progressive, they were conservative; they supported free trade and protectionism; they were on both sides of the Civil War; they were never the singular political force they are today.

Those distinctions within rural America no longer matter in American politics. Place is still important. Geography still matters. In fact, even in our globalized age, place remains surprisingly important. But place is no longer local or regional. The places that matter in our politics have become nationalized. Rural America has become just that: unified. This chapter explores the seeds of that change—a maturation two hundred years in the making. The next chapter explores the solidification of a rural voter and the forces that prevented it, and which we detail next, quickly eroded.

THE RURAL-URBAN DIVIDE: ROOTED IN THE FOUNDATION (1760-1824)

Geography has always been one of the critical fault lines in American politics. It is often overlooked. Unknown by most, the American Constitution was actually born from a very early rural-urban split that fractured the nation in the aftermath of the Revolutionary War. We often think of the protests led by Daniel Shays and his followers as a catalyst for the Constitutional Convention because the "rebellion" demonstrated the weaknesses of the national government under the Articles of Confederation. However, the centrality of geography-based politics to this moment is too often lost. As rural America would experience time and again, the end of war led to plummeting prices for agricultural commodities. The fact that the war had left a physical scar on the rural countryside made the transition even more difficult. Moreover, money, especially specie or "hard money" (silver and gold coin), became scarce following the revolution, as a booming commercial economy in the coastal cities led to a volatile political and social situation in the hinterlands that lasted nearly a decade. The hardest hit were small farmers, and because they had little or no hard money with which to pay their debts and newly imposed taxes, farm foreclosures skyrocketed. As one farmer, "Plough Jogger," lamented to his fellow citizens, "I have been greatly abused, have been obliged to do more than my part in the war, been loaded with class rates, town rates, province rates, Continental rates, and all rates . . . been pulled and hauled by sheriffs, constables, and collectors, and had my cattle sold for less than they were worth. . . . The great men are going to get all we have and I think it is time for us to rise and put a stop to it, and have no more courts, nor sheriffs, nor collectors nor lawyers."[2]

Such testimonials were greeted with little sympathy in Boston. Benjamin Lincoln, who eventually led the army to put down Shays's Rebellion, complained to George Washington of his "indolent and improvident" neighbors, who had "diverted from, their usual industry and economy . . . [to] idleness and sloth."[3]

This first "populist movement" in American politics was fueled by rural discontent, and eventually it succeeded in taking over most state legislatures, which issued stay laws that halted foreclosures and tender laws that allowed farmers to use agricultural products (rather than hard money) to help pay loans to merchants and bankers in the country's growing commercial, urban centers. But not in Massachusetts. With its deep roots in Puritan Congregationalism and the rule of church elders, Boston politics was the longtime exception to New England town-hall-style democracy. Many of the country's pseudo-aristocratic families claim pedigree in the "Boston Brahmins"—the Adamses, Coolidges, Delanos—and those are just from the first four letters of the alphabet. Under control of this "idling class," many of whom made their wealth in the rents and sale of lands in the far northern reaches of the state in what is present-day Maine, the legislature resisted farmers' demands.[4]

Instead of helping small farmers, the Massachusetts government levied heavy taxes to pay off the state's wartime debts, with most of the money going to wealthy business owners in Boston. The outcome was an insurrection by Shays and his followers. The event pushed the political and business elite to seek structural changes that would head off similar rebellions and galvanized the cause favoring a constitutional convention, which would create a national government that could regulate commerce and protect commercial, urban interests. Importantly, this was not so much about class as it was about geography, given that most of the rebels who joined Shays were the wealthiest taxpayers, albeit in rural Massachusetts, where the agrarian economies had failed to recover. They rebelled to protect the interest of a specific area in the growing United States—their homes, farms, and, importantly, rural communities. It is instructive that when James Madison made his oft-cited pitch for an extended republic in "Federalist No. 10," he singled out the slate of changes advocated by the farmers in western Massachusetts as one of the "improper or wicked projects" that would be curtailed.

The Constitution did not settle the debate so much as shift the terrain on which the battles between urban and rural were waged. It is a wonder that there was a fight at all, since so much of the American populace lived in the rural countryside. The war of independence removed the boundaries that the British Empire had placed on the colonists at the end of the French and Indian War (1763), which fueled a wave of westward expansion that would come to define the American experience for nearly a century. If life was too stifling in your hometown, all you had to do was get up and leave—find untilled land on the wide frontier and call it your own! So common was this idea in the land of liberty that democracy and landownership were fused together; and by landownership, we do not simply mean a house in the suburbs but land that could support and raise a family. Some contended at the time that democracy was possible only in a republic supported by an agrarian people.

Nevertheless, the American Constitution, in creating a more centralized and powerful federal government, had larger ambitions than a country of yeoman farmers on the frontier. This debate was personified by the two leading characters in George Washington's cabinet: Alexander Hamilton, Secretary of the Treasury, and Thomas Jefferson, Secretary of State. Jefferson believed that America's future lay in small, agriculturally based communities. He was deeply suspicious of cities, having spent more than a decade in Europe. In a letter to his friend James Madison, he opined, "I think our governments will remain virtuous for many centuries; as long as they are chiefly agricultural. . . . When they get piled upon one another in large cities, as in Europe, they will become corrupt as in Europe." Moreover, "I view the great cities as pestilential to the morals, the health and the liberties of man."[5]

Hamilton, on the other hand, thought the future lay in the development of vibrant urban centers based on a strong manufacturing sector. He advanced an ambitious, expensive economic plan designed to boost the fortunes of the growing urban class. To pay for his scheme, he persuaded Washington (who was originally opposed to the idea) to back an excise tax on distilled spirits—whiskey—the primary way in which farmers in the Appalachian foothills could deliver their crop to markets back east. The move actually taxed small farmers at a higher rate than large producers, and all were forced to pay in cash. The so-called Whiskey Rebellion soon fomented a mob of nearly seven thousand, who marched on Pittsburgh determined to raze the American "Sodom" and loot the homes of its merchant elite who lived in the growing urban center.[6] It is instructive that the only time in American history when a president donned a military uniform as commander and chief was Washington when he headed west with some twelve thousand federal militia troops to put down the protests of angry farmers and rural laborers. The mob had dissipated by the time Washington arrived, and the excise tax stayed in effect—that is, until Jefferson and his fellow Republicans repealed it in 1802.

But such rage paled in comparison with reaction to another of Washington's decisions—the 1794 Jay Treaty. The war had left thousands of British troops stationed on the American frontier in a disputed boundary war. While the British agreed to give up several of their most important forts in the contested borderland, they did so for a heavy price. American traders were expected to honor Britain as the "most-favored nation" in establishing trade agreements—a policy that would hamstring trade with the French, raise prices on imported goods, and subject American agricultural commodities to competition with the entirety of the British Empire. "The boldest act they ever ventured on to undermine the Constitution," Jefferson wrote, was the impetus for the first party war between Hamilton and Washington's Federalists and the new Jeffersonian Republicans.[7] At that point, Jefferson and his fellow Virginian, James Madison, had succeeded in organizing a burgeoning "republican movement"—a nationwide counter-protest to nationalizing, industrializing, and urbanizing plans Hamilton proposed. In response to the Jay

Treaty and the discord flamed by Jefferson, hundreds of rural communities burned effigies of Jay and denounced Washington as a closet king! As one historian wrote, the anger arising from the Jay Treaty, particularly from rural communities, "transformed the Republican movement into a Republican party."[8]

Jefferson and the Democratic-Republican Party won the debate in 1800, and over the next century, the Hamiltonian forces of commercialism and industrialization would have to fight their battles in a political culture that celebrated the myth of yeoman democracy that Jefferson so eloquently painted for the young country. Tremendous resources and countless lives were spent to "venerate the plow" and establish a country of smallholders, each with their stake in local community life.[9] Ironically, it was not in Jefferson's southern homeland where that vision was most realized but, rather, in the north and western territories. With the purchase of the Louisiana Territory from France—an act so important to the future of rural America that Jefferson even bent his principled interpretation of the Constitution to make it possible—the area to be brought under cultivation and democratic self-government doubled overnight. At the same time, southern planters and slave owners consolidated their wealth and even began to describe themselves as akin to British feudal barons. The South was no longer the land of the free-spirited farmer but of class, privilege, and unequal wealth.

While the South was, and would remain (even after the Civil War), a bastion of antidemocracy, it is about at this time that we can begin making sense of the political divide between urban and rural America. Although in 1820, just over 3 percent of Americans lived in what we define as an urban locale (see chapter 1) and just 3 percent lived in something a little less than that ("suburban"), we are still able to make sense of the vote count difference between these types of communities because there was widespread expansion of voting rights. In other words, prior to the 1820s, it is impossible to make sense of the rural-urban vote split because the vote as we think of it today—one person, one ballot—did not exist in most places. Depending on how you count, at least fourteen states had constitutional or statutory restrictions on suffrage for adult white males. But by the 1820s, "local authorities did little to prevent the exercise of the suffrage franchise by almost any member of the adult male population." Indeed, "the United States was already a functioning mass democracy for white males and in many states substantially had been for some considerable time before the rise to political prominence of Andrew Jackson."[10]

As figure 2.1 illustrates, at this point in American political development, we can get a sense of how rural people voted because they were, in fact, voting. Using the measurement strategy we described in the previous chapter, we illustrate the gap between urban and rural voters by measuring how much these two areas over- or underperformed for the Democratic Party based on the total percentage of the vote received by the Democratic presidential candidate every four years. We measure support for the Democratic Party because it is the oldest political party in the country; Republicans did not run a candidate until 1856—four

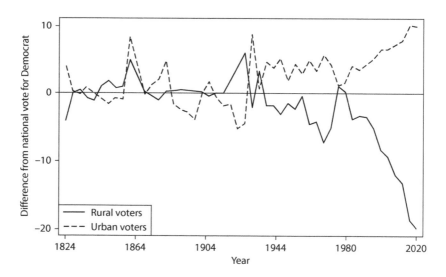

FIGURE 2.1 The rural-urban vote in American political history (1824–2020)

Note: Figure illustrates the percentage of votes cast in urban and rural counties between 1824 and 2020 for the Democratic candidate in that election and subtracts it from the Democratic candidate's national vote share. Points below the horizontal line (0) indicate that the Democratic candidate did worse in rural or urban counties than nationally; points above the horizontal line indicate that the Democratic candidate did better in rural or urban counties than nationally.

years before the Republican Abraham Lincoln took the White House. Recall, too, that "urban" and "rural" are not mutually exclusive categories. Both areas can under- or overperform in a given year if a sizable enough percentage of "suburban" voters vote for or against the Democratic candidate, respectively.

THE EARLY REPUBLIC, THE CIVIL WAR, AND AGRARIAN UNREST (1824-1912)

As we begin our analysis, we can clearly see that the geographic division between Hamilton and Jefferson had largely dissipated by the 1820s. Much of this has to do with the fact that there was no strong, formal opposition to Jefferson's Democratic-Republican Party after the so-called Revolution of 1800, which elevated Jefferson to the presidency. But with time, the existence of two societies within a single country produced an untenable, hostile struggle between the North and the South. This was not, however, a divide between urban and rural America, as many are tempted to see it. Even on the eve of the American Civil War, 68 percent of the northern population lived in decidedly rural communities. The South was much more rural than the North—only 8 percent of the South's population lived in urban or suburban counties—but this is a difference of degree, not type. The Civil War was a war fought between two rural, agricultural countries, even if one side did hold a massive advantage in manufacturing capacities and was quickly urbanizing. It was a sectional conflict between two regions—two regions that Jefferson thought would remain united in their steadfast commitment to liberty because of their smallholding tendencies.

In fact, as figure 2.2 illustrates, rural areas were often on different sides of the partisan aisle, depending on the region of the country. Prior to the Civil War, the rural Midwest was a bastion of Democratic support. During the war, the fiercest opponents to Lincoln and his Republican Party came from these rural areas, whose populace feared what an influx of newly freed Black farmers would do to the agrarian economy that

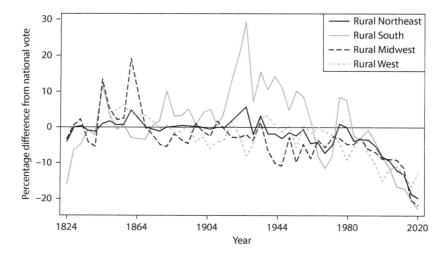

FIGURE 2.2 Sectionalism and rural politics (1824–2020)

Note: Figure illustrates the percentage of rural votes cast in four regions of the United States between 1824 and 2020 for the Democratic candidate in that election and subtracts it from the Democratic candidate's national vote share. Points below the horizontal line (o) indicate that the Democratic candidate did worse in rural counties in that region than nationally; points above the horizontal line indicate that the Democratic candidate did better in rural counties in that region than nationally.

supported, at that time, exclusively white rural communities. In the aftermath of the Civil War, the rural South became synonymous with the Democratic Party. No Democrat would have captured the presidency if not for the lock-tight grip that an all-white, exclusionary Democratic Party had on the South, and its rural areas in particular. Important to our story, sectionalism—the divides between different regions of the United States—is more important than the rural-urban divide within those regions—at least until the 1980s.

These data give us new insights into the complicated relationship between geography and politics and the tension between rural and urban America that has been roiling the nation since the beginning. It helps explain why the first real rural moment in American politics—the "Populist Movement"—failed to translate into meaningful political change.

The seeds of a nationalized rural political movement were planted in the soil of economic anxieties following the Civil War. On the one hand, in the decades after the war, there was a dramatic expansion of rural America, particularly in the Great Plains. Agricultural production soared; yields from commodities like wheat and cotton doubled from 1870 to 1900.[11] The population in agricultural areas grew quickly, as immigrants arriving on the Eastern Seaboard moved west for cheap land, facilitated by new government investments and programs: the Homestead Act, agricultural extension schools, and the transcontinental railroad.

On the other hand, the Industrial Revolution brought about the first wave of modern globalization, which fueled the growth of urban centers as it weakened the resiliency of rural economies. Growing imports of agricultural commodities from Europe and other parts of the world kept farm prices low. White farmers in the South confronted mounting labor costs with the end of slavery, and Black farmers across the country confronted an array of obstacles. European imports like cotton flooded the market. Droughts were common. Industrialization in cities pulled rural folk away in search of consistent work and a better life. Interest rates were high, and there was a shortage of credit. Most significantly, the monopolistic ownership of railroads and grain elevators led to crippling commodity shipping costs.

Infused with a sense of indignant furor against what David Danom has called "markets, middlemen, and money," American agriculturalists organized themselves into a broad-based movement to reform the political and economic system that was leaving them behind.[12] The Patrons of Husbandry (also called the "Grange") was launched in 1870. On July 4, 1873, the group published the "Farmers Declaration of Independence" as a protest against railroad monopolies, low credit, and high interest rates. A network of regionally based Farmer's Alliance organizations sprang up in 1875, including The Colored Farmers' National Alliance and Cooperative Union, which offered Black farmers in the South some economic and political clout. For example, they joined forces with the white Farmers' Alliance in opposing a move by Louisiana to tax the production of cottonseed oil, an extremely valuable crop for tenant farmers.[13]

The agrarian-dominated Greenback Party followed, with the goal of increasing the amount of money in circulation in an effort to lower the cost of credit to farmers. A decade later, the firebrand Kansas activist Mary Elizabeth Lease helped launch the People's Party (also called the "Populist Party"), pushing many of the same issues. Her oft-repeated line was that farmers should "raise less corn and more hell." The platform called for a progressive income tax, the abolition of national banks, the direct election of senators, and government regulation of railroads, telegraphs, and telephones. The party took aim at the country's rigged financial system, which produced what was dubbed two great classes of Americans: "tramps and millionaires."[14] To a large extent, this rural protest was the foundation for American progressivism, especially in breaking down class, gender, and racial barriers.[15] The Populist Party constituted the first national social movement dedicated to transforming the country's constitutional commitments, building a national state, and even tackling the most vexing issue in American history: white supremacy.[16]

Ultimately, the Populists were unsuccessful. A rural voter—progressive, egalitarian, and unafraid of national government—never materialized. Our evidence is not just of historical significance; it confirms our contention that rural voters had to be created. They do not just exist and find all the same issues in common, as the Populist movement earnestly sought to do. Drawing on the language of the common man, these "plain people" had all the makings of a successful social revolt. The Populists not only tapped into America's egalitarian, frontier spirit but also wedded their cause to the traditional virtues of rural life. As Frederick Jackson Turner, perhaps the preeminent scholar of American politics of the day, argued, the distinctiveness of the American spirit—the grit, determination, and ingenuity that he believed were at the heart of American culture and politics—was nourished first and foremost in rural communities and their continual spread into the frontier. Updating Jefferson for the modern age, Turner and other luminaries of the age rooted America's unique character in the settlement of untamed regions and successive waves of settlements. "[E]ach frontier did indeed furnish a new opportunity, a gate of escape from the bondage of the past; and freshness, and confidence, and scorn of older society, impatience of its restraints and its ideas, and indifference to its lessons, have accompanied the frontier."[17] Rural America, again, was defined as simply that: America. Urbanism was the deviant culture.

A rural voter, nevertheless, failed to materialize even as a grassroots political movement sought to cultivate one in a culture still primed to consider the virtues of small-town agrarian life. The Populist movement failed to translate into national political action. In the rural Midwest, agrarian anger turned farmers—and a majority of the population— against the Democratic Party, including in 1896, the year the Populist-in-name-only candidate, William Jennings Bryan, headed the Democratic ticket. Bryan was a fusion candidate, named because he picked and chose among a hodgepodge list of populist policies and slogans to advance his career. But Bryan's candidacy, though wrapped in indignant furor and his advocacy for the free coinage of silver, never embraced the full cause of the Populist protest and the farmer's plight. As a result, in some rural areas, Bryan did better than Grover Cleveland (the Democratic candidate in 1892), but in other areas, he did much worse. In the agricultural Midwest, the heart of the Populist movement, Bryan lost more states than he won. Although several of the farmer-centered organizations were able to play a role in state and local politics, neither of the major national parties was able to harness a "rural vote."

Again, as our data show, a national rural political movement never materialized because even in 1896—thirty-one years after the end of the Civil War—the country was still deeply divided between North and South, East and West. As Elizabeth Saunders has summarized, "the chance for a bottom-up, farmer-labor coalition led by a sympathetic populist president was lost in 1896."[18] Regional politics sold the Populist movement upriver.

The Grange and the Populist Party had initially eschewed organized political parties altogether, viewing them, rightly so, as a formidable obstacle to their quest for economic justice nationwide.[19] Nevertheless, throughout the South, the Republican Party still bore the label of Lincoln, the Union, war-time devastation, and Reconstruction. No Republican, however much on the side of the farmer, would have captured voters still reeling from the emotional and physical scars of the Civil War. Even "lily white" Republicans, who played to the South's deep racial animosities, failed to gain traction as a viable alternative to the Democrats.[20]

Sectionalism was not confined to the South. The Republican Party owed its success to "waving the bloody shirt," kindling memories of a disastrous war, and labeling the Democrats as the party of "Rum, Romanism, and Rebellion." Bryan's plot to coin silver, they argued, was nothing more than an effort to hamstring Northern industry—which implied even more revenge for the Civil War![21]

In truth, even without Bryan, both parties reinforced the ethnic, racial, and regional differences of the American electorate. Farmers were everywhere in the United States, and although the Populists sought to translate the celebration of rural life into a cohesive voting bloc, they failed to overcome two cleavages in American history perhaps more enduring than even the rural-urban divide: region and race.

RURAL POLITICS IN THE AFTERMATH OF POPULISM (1896–1932)

Bryan's failed candidacies (he ran again in 1900 and once more in 1904) represent the ironic high tide of rural politics for nearly a century. Bryan did not win, and he co-opted much of the Populist vision; and yet, that was the best rural America could do in a party system deeply divided along racial and sectional lines. Not until the 1980s would rural culture, society, and values play such a prominent role in American electoral politics. Urban America still might be the deviant way of life, but it was new, exciting, modern . . . progressive. Rural America was quickly being lost to another era.

If the Populist movement of the late 1800s imagined an empowered, self-determined rural movement of farmers, laborers, and white and Black Americans, the turn of the twentieth century brought about a tidal wave of changes that sapped rural America of its energy and importance in national affairs.

First, rural America at the turn of the twentieth century succumbed to a type of cultural fascination—not as a serious interest within American politics but something to be gawked at or emulated during summer vacation. The Country Life Movement was a half-baked, insincere effort to celebrate what the Populists had seen as a pure, virtuous form of American democracy. Central to the movement was the role played by Theodore Roosevelt. Like Jefferson a century earlier, Roosevelt held that agrarian life lay at the heart of the American experience. According to one account, Roosevelt believed the farmer represented the best hope for perpetuating a "mighty breed of men." Rural Americans were "law-abiding, intelligent, energetic, and deeply devoted to the family and private property."[22] In 1907, Roosevelt established the Commission on Country Life with the aim of identifying ways to make rural places more attractive to those who might otherwise migrate to the cites. Even then, concerns about the youth brain-drain were intense. As noted by one of the country's leading sociologists at the time, Edward Alsworth Ross, the departure of young people from rural communities left them little more than "fished-out ponds populated chiefly by bullheads and suckers."[23]

The goals of the Country Life Movement were to preserve rural lifestyles and bolster the economic prospects of country residents. Most important, however, the energy behind the movement came not from rural residents themselves but, instead, from urban reformers like Roosevelt. Harkening back to America's creation myth—or, at the very, least notions of simpler times—elites fashioned that agrarian values might calm the waters of the Industrial Revolution. Many of the retreats, camps, and estates in the Adirondack Mountains, Western Pennsylvania, Maine, and elsewhere for urban economic elite sprang up at roughly the same time.

Country life—pastoral and idyllic—was acceptable only up to a point. For urban elites and progressives, country life was to be recovered in bits in pieces. In 1925, the nation—particularly urban progressives— read in awe the spectacle that was engulfing the small town of Dayton, Tennessee. There, John Scopes, a high school science teacher, had taught his students various principles of evolution in direct defiance of state law.

To "rescue" Scopes, the newly founded American Civil Liberties Union—representing modern, cosmopolitan, urbane culture—sent one of the nation's star lawyers, Clarence Darrow. Representing the state, creationism, and traditionalism, the personification of rural America . . . William Jennings Bryan, the three-time presidential candidate.

Bryan scoffed at the idea of humans evolving from apes, but he primarily rooted his defense of Scopes in the political debate that had divided rural and urban America from the start. Arguing that local school districts should have control over their own curricula, Bryan gave the traditional rural answer. He insisted that Scopes threatened the democratic control of public education, while Darrow countered that Scopes had the right to teach the truth no matter what the public wanted.[24] Urban elites piled on. It was backward, hayseed fundamentalism against science and modernity. A Princeton biologist told a *New York Times* reporter that Bryan's argument "would be amusing if it were not so pathetic."[25] All in all, the trial and media coverage reflected a growing geo-cultural divide—a riff laid bare in the aftermath of the first rural revolt.

These cultural divides were exacerbated by the growing economic divide between urban and rural America. The beginning of the twentieth century proved to be an exhilarating decade for upper- and middle-class urban Americans, especially following World War I during the Roaring Twenties. For urban Americans, the decade ushered in unprecedented growth and prosperity, but it brought changes that upended rural communities. America's entry into World War I, too, forever changed the dynamic between the urban and rural economy and the federal government's relationship with small-scale agricultural communities—at that point, the backbone of rural life in America. Although it would take another sixty years to fully play out, wartime industry fueled the historic movement of Black Americans out of the rural South and into the Northern metropolis, forever changing the demographics of rural America. The First Great Migration would from there on make rural politics largely inseparable from white politics.[26]

By most accounts, the war was not popular in rural America. A large number of German immigrants were living in the Midwest, leading to bitter disputes and divisions. In addition, there was also general unease with entanglement in European conflicts, and many worried that war would accelerate the drain of youth to industrial urban areas. Having seen the cities of Europe, would returning soldiers embrace austere life on the farm? There was also understanding that while many rural men would be drafted and sent abroad, those left would have to feed not only Americans but allies abroad. As suggested by one scholar, "During the long debate that preceded American entry into the war, midwestern and southern farmers had been unenthusiastic at best."[27]

The war disrupted not only rural society but the rural economy as well. In many ways, the economic struggles of the 1910s and 1920s were extensions of the problems the Populists had identified a generation earlier. War accentuated the dilemmas that rural communities confronted between a demand for local control on the one hand and the desire for more government oversight on the other. During the war, for instance, prices for farm goods soared. Seeing dollar signs in their future, most farmers took out hefty mortgages to finance expansions and increase production, all with the encouragement of the U.S. government. But wars come to an end, and prices plummeted as trenches in Europe were replaced with farmland. As before, rural communities once again were in debt to faraway creditors in the major cities.

Congress also passed a series of measures that led to unprecedented control of local agricultural practices. Some farmers, but not others, were granted licenses to produce certain crops—and prices were controlled. The enforcers of these new regulations were county agents, who would sometimes play an oversized role in community affairs, including serving on the local draft board, an especially unpopular group. During times of war, a heavy hand may be expected, and many farmers prospered because of the price supports. But the country agents and their rules and regulations spurred bitterness and antipathy toward a distant federal government.

The extent to which rural Americans' relationship with the government changed as a result of war cannot be overstated. Consider that to increase production during the war, the United States began observing Daylight Saving Time (DST) in 1917. This did not go over well in rural America. "On dairy operations, farm families were forced to milk their cows at unreasonable hours, since cows would not observe DST, but creamery truck drivers would."[28] The change pushed farm kids to do their morning chores in the darkness before heading to school. If nothing else, DST was a not-so-subtle reminder that the clout in American politics had shifted to urban centers.

Finally, at the same time that the divide between urban and rural America was growing, the sectional and racial lines that hindered the Populists' dream of building a national rural movement became more fully entrenched at the beginning of the twentieth century—the nadir of racial relations in the United States, as it is commonly called.[29]

Rural identity may have become slightly nationalized, but it was a stereotype drawn up by urban reformers, who harbored deep concerns about immigration, urban slums, and even a degenerate white bloodline. The effort to eradicate hookworm in the rural South accelerated after conscripts for World War I proved to be far from desirable.[30] One of the more grotesque manifestations of the belief in the superiority of the Anglo-Saxon race were the so-called Better Babies and Fitter Families contests, common in farm communities during this period. Prizes were awarded based on physical characteristics and attractiveness. Several state fairs held "Fitter Families for Future Firesides" competitions from 1920 to 1940. As noted in one account, "These contests encouraged families to reimagine their histories as pedigrees subject to scientific analysis and control, while appealing to a deeply rooted sense of nostalgia for the rural family as the nation became increasingly urban, as rural children left farms, and as the culture of the Roaring Twenties challenged 'traditional values.'"[31]

All this built into the Klan movement in the 1920s. In the years following Reconstruction, the Ku Klux Klan had essentially disappeared. In 1915, and after seeing G. H. Griffith's film *Birth of a Nation*, "Colonel" William Joseph Simmons of rural Georgia resurrected the Klan, this time setting sights on Catholics, Jews, immigrants from southern and eastern Europe, as well as Blacks. The new Klan advocated Christian fundamentalism and devoted patriotism and, of course white, Anglo-Saxon supremacy. "The Klan was entirely mainstream in its enthusiastic support of eugenics."[32] They railed against industrialists, intellectuals, bootleggers, and the excesses of urban life and high culture. The movement was a celebration of traditional agrarian life.

The Klan was astonishingly popular, with a membership approaching six million nationwide. Members of the so-called invisible empire captured public office in cities, towns, and villages across the country—from Portland, Maine, to Portland, Oregon.[33] The electoral success of Klan-backed candidates skyrocketed in states like Indiana, Oklahoma, Oregon, Colorado, and Texas.[34] Oregon is singled out in Linda Gordon's work as "arguably the most racist place outside the southern states, possibly even of all the states."[35] From 1922 to 1932, a majority of the state's elected officials were Klansmen.

As for the precise geographic distribution of the Klan in the 1920s, there is no question that the movement had a firm grip in many of the nation's larger cities. In all, some sixteen senators, dozens of U.S. representatives, eleven governors, and thousands of state and local officials came to power as openly Klan supporters. Detroit, Los Angeles, and many other large cities had Klan mayors. Nevertheless, it appears, as with the Prohibition movement, that there was heavy support in rural areas. The widespread support for the KKK was indicative of traditional, "rural" anxieties. As Hiram Evans, the Imperial Wizard of the Ku Klux Klan, said in 1926, "we are a movement of the plain people, very weak in the matter of culture, intellectual support, and trained leadership." For example, during this period, Indiana, Ohio, and Texas had roughly three times the Klan membership as New Jersey, Michigan, and New York,[36] even though their populations were smaller.

Virginia Commonwealth University recently created a map of places in the United States that had a high level of Klan support, drawn from newspapers sponsored by or sympathetic to the Klan during the 1920s.[37] It's a blunt instrument, to be sure, but even a cursory look reveals the popularity of the Klan in the small towns and rural hamlets—from Rolla, Missouri, to Bunker Hill, Kansas; Pulaski, Tennessee; Oil City, Pennsylvania; and West Oneonta, New York. This is consistent with an assessment conducted at the time by the sociologist John Mecklin, who found that the Klan drew its members chiefly from the "descendants of the old American stock living in the villages and small towns of those sections of the country where the old stock has been least disturbed by immigration, on the one hand, and the disruptive effect of industrialism, on the other." As to the root cause of Klan support in these areas, Mecklin offers a direct assessment: "A psychological need for escape from the drabness of village and small town life plays no small part in the appeal of the modern Klan.[38]" Another scholar a few years later wrote that the rise of the Klan sprang from the "numerous reaction of the original American stock against the insidious subjugation of foreign blood." He further noted, "The Klan literally is once more the embattled American farmer and artisan, coordinated into a disciplined and growing army, and launched upon a definite crusade for Americanism!"[39]

Adding to the sense of foreboding for rural residents, the 1920 Census reported that for the first time in U.S. history, more Americans were living in urban areas (defined by more than twenty-five hundred residents) than in rural communities. It was not only that a threshold had been crossed, but so had the pace of change. Only three decades earlier, just 28 percent of Americans lived in urban areas. All parts of America were growing, but the population of urban areas was increasing 50 percent faster than in rural communities. That is, for every two residents who moved to or were born into a rural community, three were added to urban America's population. The migration of existing rural residents to urban areas was also brisk, roughly 11 million between 1870 and 1920.

But again, these rural pressures failed to translate into enduring political movement. Like the end of the nineteenth century, the foundation for a widespread rural political coalition was there. And like the end of the nineteenth century, sectionalism, traditional partisan alliances, and racial divisions prevented the emergence of a full-scale rural vote.

To be clear, that was not just the result of the Democratic Party's lock on power in the American South. It is true that in some rural communities, particularly in the West and Northeast, rural voters were far less Democratic than average—sometimes the least Democratic in the entire country. Nearly four in every five rural New Englanders cast a vote for the Republican, Coolidge, in 1924! But these voting patterns were not consistent over time. Over 42 percent of rural New Englanders, for instance, jumped on the bandwagon for Roosevelt's 1932 victory, and even more (46 percent) supported him in 1936. So, although the rural South remained a bastion of Democratic support, other rural communities were apt to support Democratic presidential candidates a number of times during the early twentieth century.

In sum, this era marked another political nonstarter for the rural bloc. Although rural America suffered a common cultural and economic fate, its partisanship never wavered. Both parties fought their fight, not over rural and urban voters but between regions, ethnicities, and industry. Although it may seem that rural America—represented as it was by both parties—may have retained its influence in American politics, rural issues were second in importance to debates over prohibition, industrialization, immigration, and the general size of government.

As if to vividly dramatize the end of rural America's prominence, Bryan unexpectedly died five days after the Scopes Monkey Trial ended. He won the jury, to the cheers of many rural Americans. But in an obituary, the journalist and author H. L. Mencken wrote the following in the *Baltimore Evening Sun*:

> Bryan was a vulgar and common man, a cad undiluted.... He preferred the company of rustic ignoramuses. It was hard to believe, watching him at Dayton, that he had traveled, that he had been received in civilized societies, that he had been a high officer of state. He seemed only a poor clod like those around him, deluded by a childish theology, full of an almost pathological hatred of all learning, all human dignity, all beauty, all fine and noble things. He was a peasant come home to the dung-pile. Imagine a gentleman, and you have imagined everything that he was not.[40]

That could be one of the most acerbic obituaries ever written by a mainstream writer about a prominent political figure. But what it says about elite perceptions of rural communities—and the "rustic ignoramuses"— that Bryan defended throughout his life, and about his populist appeal in America's heartland, is a testament to the changed status of rural America on the eve of the New Deal.

THE NEW DEAL AND THE RURAL REALIGNMENT
THAT WASN'T (1932-1960)

In a 1922 paper titled "The American Intellectual Frontier," John Dewey described what we might now refer to as tribal impulses brought on by rapid changes. And the 1920s and 1930s were filled with rapid change. In rural America, Dewey argues, "attachment to stability and homogeneity of thought and belief seem essential in the midst of practical heterogeneity, fuss and unsettlement."[41] Other writers during the period noted an emerging breach between the "metropolis and the countryside," caused by "envy and resentment of the farming population."[42] And yet, this anger and resentment did not translate into a significant voting bloc. There were growing anxieties in rural America, but neither party was able to harness that umbrage on Election Day for most of the twentieth century. Despite massive economic, social—or even, perhaps, psychological—upheaval, rural voters never came to form such a bloc.

The reasons are multifaceted. For one, the Democratic Party was composed of two very different factions. Consider the 1924 Democratic National Convention. About half the delegates supported Al Smith, then governor of New York, and the other half backed William Gibbs McAdoo, the former secretary of the Treasury. Smith was popular with urban, mostly Northeastern voters—a New Yorker through and through. But McAdoo was the darling of the prohibitionists and was a Christian fundamentalist who espoused strong nativist sentiments; he was the most aggressive member of Woodrow Wilson's administration in seeking to re-segregate government offices, including in the North.[43] Southerners and Klan supporters were anxious to keep Smith, a Catholic, off the ticket, and because of a two-thirds voting requirement, the convention was deadlocked for days.

On the one hundred third ballot, a compromise was reached, and delegates selected John W. Davis, a member of Congress from West Virginia. Davis was conservative—opposed to women's suffrage, for instance—but he was also against Prohibition, a position supported by the urban wing of the party. Likely due to sheer exhaustion among delegates, Davis became the consensus candidate, but the negotiations between the southern/nativist wing of the party and the urban/western wing would keep a large part of rural America in the Democratic fold; it would keep the other part out.

Less than a decade after Bryan's death and the failure to reinvigorate a national rural movement, yet another Democratic politician had another chance to pull together rural voters into a durable, powerful coalition: Franklin D. Roosevelt. Many of Roosevelt's policies helped bind rural voters to the New Deal coalition for more than a generation. His ability to smooth divisions between urban, labor-centered progressives and southern segregationists was as masterful as it was unfortunate. That Roosevelt was willing to turn a blind eye to Jim Crow to cement the winning coalition is a stain on this record. It was not a seamless alliance, however, as evidenced by the "conservative coalition" of Republicans and southern Democrats, but this Faustian bargain generally worked.[44]

In many ways, FDR was an unexpected leader for the next wave of rural indignation. A self-proclaimed tree farmer, Roosevelt was, in truth, about as close to American nobility as has ever existed in the land of the free. Yet, he shared the traditional Jeffersonian-Democratic vision of rural life and rural values as being distinctively American. He found peace in the rural retreat of Warm Springs, Georgia, where he convalesced there so often during his time as president that it was called the "Little White House."

More than just having an affinity for rural ways, Roosevelt understood that in a country gripped by a global economic depression, there was poverty throughout the nation—but rural poverty was in a class of its own. At the time of FDR's inauguration, one in three farmers had lost their land, and the price on some commodities, including corn, had dropped by 75 percent from the decade prior. Farmers were growing more and making less. The situation was particularly devastating in the South. As Lorena Hickock—an investigator for one of FDR's many new creations, the Federal Emergency Relief Administration—would testify, the rural South was a "situation where half-starved Whites and Blacks struggle in competition for less to eat than my dog gets at home, for the privilege of living in huts that are infinitely less comfortable than his kennel."[45]

The Southwest was also barreling toward catastrophe. Following the Civil War, the federal government passed a series of statutes designed to draw residents to the region: the Homestead Act of 1862, the Kincaid Act of 1904, and the Enlarged Homestead Act of 1909. The result was a massive influx of new farmers and settlers. At first, the region seemed an agricultural Promised Land; the untilled soil and periods of copious rain pushed up crops from the ground nearly overnight. Yields were massive, and big money was being made. But it was a semiarid landscape, and some worried the rain might slow. It helped that many still held to the nineteenth century adage that "rain follows the plow." In an 1881 book, *The Great Valleys and Prairies of Nebraska and the Northwest*, the journalist and land speculator Charles Dana Wilber popularized the phrase: "God speed the plow. . . . By this wonderful provision, which is only man's mastery over nature, the clouds are dispensing copious rains. . . . [The plow] is the instrument which separates civilization from savagery; and converts a desert into a farm or garden. . . . To be more concise, *Rain follows the plow*."[46] That is, many believed rain could be created—that the climate would be altered—by cultivation. The region swelled with settlers, and eastern speculators and bankers were pleased to give hefty loans for land and new machinery.

But the rain stopped. By the 1930s, a literal dark cloud appeared on the horizon; the region entered into a historic drought. Cultivation did not create more rain but, instead, stripped the topsoil of key nutrients, leaving few of the indigenous grasses to hold the soil. The result, as we know, was the Dust Bowl—a vast stretch of land from northern Texas to Colorado, Kansas, and the Oklahoma Panhandle. So-called black blizzards would engulf towns for days. By 1935, it was estimated that some 34 million acres of farmland were rendered useless, and another 125 million acres—an area nearly the size of Texas—was rapidly losing its topsoil.

On top of that, the drought was coupled with plummeting commodities prices. Bankers were desperate to collect on their loans, and in 1933 alone, upward of two hundred thousand family farms were fore-closed, a disproportionate number in the Southwest.[47] The Promised Land had become a wasteland of despair. This led to one of the largest migrations of rural residents in U.S. history, as "Okies" and others in the region headed to the Garden of Eden—that is, California—for a fresh start.

Roosevelt's personal attentiveness to the problems of rural economy and society, coupled with his Democratic Party's traditional stronghold in the South, meant that the New Deal would fundamentally alter rural America. In his first term alone, FDR and congressional Democrats pioneered new forms for managing crop prices by paying farmers not to farm. Indeed, of any New Deal program, none was perhaps more cen-tralizing and dependent on federal authority than the new regulations for stabilizing crop prices. It was struck down as unconstitutional gov-ernment overreach in 1936, but revised parts of it were upheld in 1938, with similar effects.

The new Farm Credit Administration was established, which became, for the first time in many parts of rural America, a consistent and reliable system of financing for crops and farm mortgages. The Farm Bankruptcy Act prohibited full foreclosure or repossession of farms for five years as long as the farmer could make rental payments; this act was also struck down by the courts. The New Deal's Resettlement Agency simply bought up defunct farms and gave loans for farmers to move to more fertile ground. The Shelterbelt Project, created by an executive order, fought wind erosion by marshaling farmers, Civilian Conserva-tion Corps employees, and Works Progress Administration workers to plant over two hundred million trees in a belt running from Bismarck, North Dakota, to Amarillo, Texas. As noted in one account, "the Shelterbelt Project remains one of the great environmental success stories of our time."[48] And in what was arguably the most visible change to rural America, the New Deal—through projects such as the Tennes-see Valley Authority and the Rural Electrification Administration—brought electricity to a part of the country in which nine out of ten residents lacked power. When Roosevelt died in 1945, 90 percent of rural Americans had electricity in their homes.[49]

After his visit to the region, and during a fireside chat on September 6, 1936, FDR addressed the plight of farmer:

> I saw drought devastation in nine states. I talked with families who had lost their wheat crop, lost their corn crop, lost their livestock, lost the water in their well, lost their garden and come through to the end of the summer without one dollar of cash resources, facing a winter without feed or food—facing a planting season without seed to put in the ground.
>
> I shall never forget the fields of wheat so blasted by heat that they cannot be harvested. I shall never forget field after field of corn stunted, earless and stripped of leaves, for what the sun left the grasshoppers took. I saw brown pastures which would not keep a cow on fifty acres.[50]

Bryan and the Populists may have bespoke the challenges of rural life during the Industrial Revolution, but Roosevelt and the New Deal put money where their mouths were. Rural voters paid back with votes. As our data show, rural America coalesced around Roosevelt and the Democratic Party during his first election in 1932 and maintained their support in 1936. A whopping 71 percent of rural voters in the South backed FDR in 1936. Even in the traditionally Republican strongholds of the rural Northeast, nearly half of rural voters cast a ballot for FDR. If anyone were to take a guess as to whether the Democrats' investments in rural America were paying their political dividends, it would seem like no other time in American political history was as ripe for a rural political revolution.

And yet, as we have seen throughout this chapter, rural America remained divided. The gains made by the Democratic Party were short-lived. By 1940, rural voters in the Midwest and mid-Atlantic states had returned to the Republican Party. Nearly 20 percent of voters turned against Roosevelt after having voted for him and his policies four years earlier. The "rural" advantage that Democrats enjoyed was really just a southern advantage—particularly in the deep southern states of Louisiana, Alabama, Arkansas, and Texas. There, support for the Democratic coalition never wavered, but it would be a mistake to interpret the party's electoral successes, overall, as a revolution in rural voting.

That's because, for one thing, Democrats were already the party of the rural South prior to FDR and the New Deal. In 1924, nearly 60 percent of rural Southerners cast their ballot for the Democratic ticket—in a year when the Democratic candidate, the very forgettable John Davis, got just 29 percent of all ballots cast nationwide. (A third party candidate, Robert La Follette, netted 17 percent of the vote that year.)

Second, it is difficult to disentangle the number of reasons that support among rural Southerners remained extraordinarily high. It is possible that the agricultural stabilization programs and electrification successes brought new voters into the Democratic fold. But, as Ira Katznelson and many others have long noted, Democratic policy successes were tied to welfare policies that reinforced Jim Crow segregation and widened the wealth gap between whites and Blacks—especially those who still made their living from the land.[51]

Finally, if we are to consider rural voters as a whole—the percentage of the rural vote won by Democrats during FDR's twelve-year presidency—it was in rural America where he was actually least popular after his first election. He averaged 59 percent of the rural vote in 1936, 53 percent in 1940, and 50 percent in 1944—anywhere between six and nine points below urban votes. There was a rural-urban divide during this decade, but for the Democratic Party, it split in favor of urban areas!

More evidence against the so-called rural realignment thesis is that Democrats were popular throughout the South, but their support was always weakest in rural areas in the South (figure 2.3). Although a majority of states in the South would continue to support Democratic candidates throughout the mid-twentieth century, they did so because the Democrats were relatively more popular in suburban and urban communities throughout the South than they were in rural parts. This point is still more obscured by noting that 1952 was the last year the rural South constituted a majority of all votes cast in the South (suburban, urban, and rural combined). By the time we witness a genuine rural realignment nationwide in 1980, rural voters made up just 46 percent of the southern vote. The South has a lot of rural imagery but throughout the twentieth century, it simply had fewer and fewer rural people.

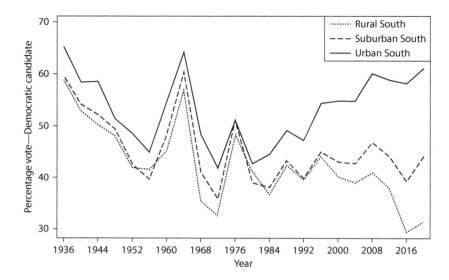

FIGURE 2.3 Geographic realignment within the southern states (1936–2020)

Note: Figure illustrates the percentage of votes cast in rural, suburban, and urban counties between 1936 and 2020 for the Democratic candidate in that election.

That is within the South. Compared with the rest of rural America, rural Southerners were more Democratic than just about anywhere else. Returning to the long trajectory we illustrated in figure 2.1, the Democratic Party after the New Deal was mildly competitive in rural parts— slightly less than the national average and much less so than in the South. While Democrats did not have a rural advantage thanks to the New Deal, neither was rural America the Republican stronghold it is today.

THE GREAT AGRICULTURAL TRANSITION (1960–1980)

No region more typifies the aforementioned sort of partisan ambivalence than the Midwest. And to a large extent, the partisan voting patterns in rural communities through Illinois, Iowa, Michigan, and Wisconsin represent the two-faced nature of rural life and rural communities outside the South during the postwar period. Whereas the rural South remained overwhelmingly poor and dependent on traditional small-scale farming, rural communities throughout the Midwest underwent a transformation akin to how the Industrial Revolution changed urban America. Small, diversified farms where families harvested multiple crops and raised a diverse range of livestock were transformed into "specialized" enterprises. Capital investments in large machinery replaced the traditional value of simple family and neighborly labor. In fact, throughout the Midwest, industrial enterprises in rural areas—businesses such as meatpacking, food processing, and ethanol refinement—outpaced industrial growth in urban areas throughout the postwar period.[52] Rural areas as a whole lost nearly a quarter of their overall population, as communities suffered the first of many repeated brain drains to the cities: first with the GI bill and soldiers returning from Europe, then with the expansion of universities and the baby boom of the 1960s, and once more with the farm crisis of the 1970s and 1980s, which saw further farm consolidation and foreclosures.[53]

As we have repeatedly stressed throughout this book, rural politics and rural America is not the same as agricultural politics and life on the farm. Nevertheless, it is impossible to understand the development of a rural political movement without accounting for "the Great Agricultural Transition." As the sociologists Linda Lobao and Katherine Meyer define it, "The exodus of Americans from farming is one of the most dramatic changes in the U.S. economy and society in the past century." More than that, however, among those remaining in rural areas, the transformation is most evident in the fact that "most farms have become marginal production units that cannot fully employ or sustain families. To survive in farming, families take off-farm jobs. Almost 90 percent of farmers' household income now comes from non-farm sources."[54] The change in the way agriculture is practiced fundamentally altered rural life, primarily because it has exacerbated inequality in rural communities between those who barely survived and those who created farming industrial empires. Ragtag family farms would often border massive agribusinesses, where the actual owner never tilled an acre or meet a hog. Adding fuel to the fire, in many rural communities, local farmers overextended themselves by investing in land, machinery, and chemical fertilizers—investments that made farming an unsustainable financial risk.[55]

Scholars continue to debate the political ramifications of these changes. Although many Americans may think of agricultural industrialization and corporatism as a "Republican" or "conservative" policy, this has really just been a convenient storyline for advocates in the "eat local" or "slow food" movements.[56] The truth is, as Nathan Rosenberg and Bryce Stucki write, "Republicans and Democrats, alike, have supported laws that favor corporate agriculture, which continue to drive small farmers out of business and depopulate the countryside."[57] We should not be surprised that in the first wave of agricultural consolidation after World War II and through the 1970s, if the architects of those policies—Democratic politicians, administrators, and New Deal programs—bore the brunt of rural America's revenge. In truth, some of this change sprang from policy, while other pieces were based on demographic shifts as rural America grew older and relatively less educated. And some of it was undoubtedly cultural and centered on issues of race and immigration.

Our data do show that memories of the New Deal certainly faded fast outside the South. Lyndon Johnson's Great Society, which also promised to end rural poverty as we knew it, was a nonstarter in solidifying a rural political movement. Unlike Roosevelt, Johnson was from rural America—born in the family farmhouse in Stonewall, Texas. He experienced rural poverty first hand. Although urban poverty and urban renewal dominated public debate over the Great Society and continue to be the focus of our historical memories of the era, Johnson prioritized rural development issues from the moment he became president. The centerpiece of his legislative agenda—the 1964 Economic Opportunity Act—had special provisions for rural communities in nearly every title of the law. It included provisions for a Youth Conservation Corps (Johnson had served as head of the New Deal's National Youth

Administration in Texas), gave increased federal funding to areas suffering from rural depopulation, and backed about one-fifth of rural homes with new federal loan guarantees. It took nearly a hundred years, but Johnson finally achieved the Populist movement's promise of using the federal government as a lender of last resort for rural land purchase and agricultural development.[58]

The bitter irony of Johnson's presidency and the Great Society is that no president in American history has wanted to use government more to improve the livelihood of rural Americans than the rural Texan, Johnson. But no president was more fully repudiated by rural Americans than Johnson. The election year 1968 was the low water mark for Democratic support in rural America up to that point. While Johnson chose not to run for reelection, his policies and his brand of liberalism were on the ballot. Even the rural South—the bastion of Democratic Party support—bolted the party and championed the cause of the third-party segregationist candidate, George Wallace. But throughout the country, even where Wallace was not on the ticket, rural voters turned against the Democratic Party, which was unfairly characterized as the party of urban elites, metropolitan development, and, of course, Black ghettos and crime. America was quickly changing—a transformation that was not especially welcome in the American heartland.

But rural America would continue to flirt with Democratic candidates. In local races and in choosing senators, they were less eager—especially in the South—to abandon their traditional party loyalties. In 1976, with the peanut farmer Jimmy Carter at the top of the ticket, the urban-rural divide in Democratic vote share disappeared. It would be the last time, however, that rural America bent toward the Democratic candidate. As we explore in the next chapter and throughout the remainder of the book, the 1980s witnessed the convergence of political, economic, and social forces that had been working toward the consolidation of a rural voting bloc for nearly a century. It would take the right set of issues (race and economic anxieties), the right politician (Ronald Reagan), and the right cultural buttons ("hard work," "family values," "real America") to pull these voters into a coherent bloc.

RURAL POLITICS AT THE DAWN
OF A CONSERVATIVE REVOLUTION

On a crisp, clear spring day in late April 1964, Lyndon Johnson launched his "unconditional war on poverty." Rather than kicking off the ambitious, sprawling federal program from the White House Rose Garden, or from any number of urban centers across the country, Johnson traveled to tiny villages and hamlets in Appalachia. His first stop was Inez, Kentucky, where he went to the ramshackle house owned by Tommy Fletcher, a former coal miner in his thirties. Fletcher and his wife were parents of eight children. There is an iconic picture of that meeting. From there the entourage moved from one poverty-stricken rural community to the next, where Johnson talked about hardship, desperation, and the failings of business and government. A few months earlier, *Life* magazine sent a reporter and photographer to the same region, later publishing a stunning account. The twelve-page spread opened with the following: "In a lonely valley in eastern Kentucky, in the heart of the mountainous region called Appalachia, live an impoverished people whose plight has long been ignored by affluent America. Their homes are shacks without plumbing or sanitation. Their landscape is a man-made desolation of corrugated hills and hollows laced with polluted streams. The people, themselves often disease-ridden and unschooled are without jobs and even without hope. . . . President Johnson, who has declared 'unconditional war on poverty in America,' has singled out Appalachia as a major target.'"[59]

And it was not simply a photo op or media stunt for Johnson. Perhaps more so than any other twentieth-century president, Johnson understood rural poverty. He had lived it, and he had represented it while in Congress. With the First Lady by his side, Johnson connected with the men, women, and children he met during that fourteen-hour tour—and on each of the days during his five-state trip. In very real ways, Johnson was simply following the lead of FDR. Roosevelt's efforts to lift up rural residents during the depths of the Depression were even more explicit and sustained. As we have said, he put federal money where his mouth was.

So we are left with a quandary. Roosevelt and Johnson were two of the most effective policy leaders in the twentieth century, and both were able to rally their party behind changes that made a meaningful difference in the lives of rural residents. These were not merely symbolic gestures like many of those pushed by politicians of both parties during the era; rather, they were concrete shifts that changed the lives of those spread across the small towns and villages of America.

Why, then, were rural voters lukewarm, at best, about these two presidents—and about the Democratic Party that endorsed their ambitious plans? As we note earlier, after his first win, support for FDR in rural areas decreased in each of his subsequent elections. For all of his aggressive, meaningful policy moves to help rural America, FDR's vote share among this group declined. We do not know how Johnson would have stacked up against Richard Nixon in 1968, but we certainly know that rural voters turned against his vice president, Hubert Humphrey, and the Democratic agenda. It's a safe bet that Johnson would have been trounced in rural areas.

There is little public opinion data to help guide our assessment of Roosevelt, but our best guess is that while some rural voters may have benefited from federal policies and government outlays, these moves also challenged the broadly held conviction in rural America of local autonomy. As with all elements of FDR's New Deal, the locus of control shifted to the national government. Roosevelt's scheme centered on a top-down approach—using Washington expertise and federal money to save rural communities. In many respects, it worked, but it was also seen by some as federal encroachment; and, to be sure, maybe New Deal rural policies are not as successful as we often think. The rural backlash in the 1930s echoed the concerns about overreaching, unsympathetic federal agents during World War I. Again, some farmers benefited from Wilson's programs, but many balked at the role of outside authorities, who did not understand the complexities of rural life.

For Johnson, one part of the explanation is rather simple and unfortunate. Beyond the growing cultural divide, touched on earlier, Johnson's support in rural America tanked due to his support for civil rights, the growing unrest in urban centers, and the "law and order" message of Republicans, especially Nixon. Here, too, there are echoes of the 1920s. This was especially true in the rural South. This issue—the historic omnipotence of rural attitudes toward race—will be taken up in chapter 8.

States' rights, home rule, and local control have been powerful themes in rural politics for more than a century, rearing their head most recently during the COVID-19 pandemic. Reagan, a key character in the next chapter, burst on the national political scene after delivering a televised speech in the waning days of the 1964 election, a somewhat desperate move to help Republican Barry Goldwater gain some traction. Reagan had been a strong New Deal Democrat but had undergone a conversion because of what he saw as the burgeoning size of the federal government and growing federal intrusion in the lives of Americans. Given that most politicians had not yet come to understand the potential of a rural voting bloc, that Reagan would dedicate a large portion of the speech to the injustices aimed at rural Americans was exceptional. "In this vote-harvesting time, they use terms like the 'Great Society,' or as we were told a few days ago by the President, we must accept a greater government activity in the affairs of the people. . . . Well, I, for one, resent it when a representative of the people refers to you and me, the free men and women of this country, as 'the masses.'"[60]

It was an audacious move. At the time, there was no clear indication that making an overt pitch to rural voters would yield dividends for Republicans. In many parts of the country, especially the Upper Midwest, farmers and other rural residents remained tied to the Democratic New Deal coalition. Minnesota and Michigan, for example, stuck with Hubert Humphrey in 1968. Perhaps Reagan understood then, sixteen years before his successful run for the presidency, that by linking concerns about federal incursions into racial and other cultural and economic grievances, the GOP could define a powerful, potent rural identity—a topic taken up in the next chapter.

3

MANUFACTURING THE MYTH
OF "REAL AMERICA" (1980–PRESENT)

Dubois is a small town of about seven thousand located in the rolling hills and farm fields of western Pennsylvania. It's rural, and in Pennsylvania, that means conservative; as James Carvel once quipped, "Pennsylvania is Philadelphia and Pittsburgh, with Alabama in between." So there was little doubt that Donald Trump would win the place, and he did handedly in both 2016 and 2020. But something different is happening in Dubois and in the thousands of small towns and back roads across the country. Something unprecedented. In the summer of 2021, in midst of the COVID-19 pandemic, a man living across the street from a Methodist church in a relatively affluent section of the town erected a huge flag in front of his house emblazoned with the words, "Fuck Biden." It caused a stir, especially among the church elders, but the owner refused to back down. After months of pressure, the flag was changed to, "Joe and the Ho got to Go."[1]

A few months earlier, author Michael Sokolove spent time driving around rural Pennsylvania—his trek leading to a story in the *New York Times*.[2] He had long conversations with voters in reliably Republican areas, places where the last Democratic presidential candidate to win was Lyndon Johnson in 1964 when he romped Barry Goldwater. Trump had won these areas with ease in 2016, and everyone knew he would do so again. Biden/Harris yard signs were few and far between, but pickup trucks with Trump/MAGA banners on makeshift polls were common, almost pat. Still, there was something strange here, even in a place that traditionally voted Republican—an intensity of conservative energy that seemed out of place for a bellwether state. In Duryea, a hamlet in the eastern part, another sign caught the visitor's eye; "I'll smoke weed with Willie, but I'll never vote Democratic again!"[3]

What unfolded on election day in 2020 stunned even the most seasoned observers. Biden won the state by a whisker, due in large measure to higher turnout in the urban corners. But in the rural counties, the places where Sokolove traveled, Trump's margins were massive. In Clearfield County, where Dubois is located, Jimmy Carter prevailed in 1976, but it had leaned right ever since; Reagan got 54 percent in 1980, and Bush secured 58 percent in 2000. By 2020, Trump would net an eye-popping 74 percent. In Susquehanna County, located in the northeast part of the state, Trump beat Clinton by a bigger margin than any presidential candidate in the past six decades. In 2020, he got 70 percent. In neighboring Bradford County, it was 72 percent, and farther west, in Tioga County, it was 75 percent. In Porter County, still farther to the west, Trump netted a staggering 80 percent of the general election vote.[4]

David Byler points out that Trump actually made inroads in a number of metropolitan areas in 2020, especially Miami and Los Angeles. But it was in the rural villages and hamlets where the numbers were truly impressive. Writing about Pennsylvania, for instance, Byler notes, "Trump's gains in Philadelphia and Pittsburgh were notable, but he gained most of his new votes in the many smaller metros, towns and rural counties that dot the rest of the state. These communities shifted away from the Democrats in 2016, and helped keep the race close for Trump in 2020."[5] In Tennessee, Trump boosted his support by 21 percent in the towns and rural counties outside the state's big cities. In North Carolina, Trump offset Democratic gains in urban areas by building on already impressive numbers in one rural county after another. In Columbus County, for example, he netted an additional 3 percent votes beyond his 2016 returns, helping him win North Carolina by the smallest of margins.

And these victories extend beyond Trump. The process has played out across the country, in state after state, and it has played out "down-ballot" in races for Senate, the House, and even local offices. Rural voters not only come out to support Trump; their votes for all Republican Party candidates is overwhelming and historically unprecedented.

Elections turn on the arrangement of different electoral blocs over time. As we discussed in the previous chapter, these blocs, or factions, shaped American politics for nearly a century, largely in the absence of a rural bloc. The Solid South, dedicated in service to Jim Crow, ended the realigning potential of a national agrarian movement in the nineteenth century. Since the turn of the century, there had been the New Deal coalition and the Yankee Republicans and near iron-clad support among business types for GOP candidates—and many other coalitions, large and small.

Our concern in this chapter is with the rural bloc—simply put, that there is now one on which to write. For much of American history, conflicting electoral forces were as common in rural areas as in suburban and urban communities. This might help explain the unpredictable, sometimes seemingly erratic nature of geographically based voting throughout much of American history.[6] But something has happened in rural communities in the last few decades; the old cross-cutting pressures that once kept rural America separate now simply pale in comparison to a distinct sense of rural identity—a collective sense of economic anxiety and grievance, anger over cultural stereotyping, a loss of community, and belief that too many have given up on the values of hard work. Growing social divisions foster political tribalism; as election returns make clear, for many residents, to be rural has meant that they need to vote Republican.[7] Moreover, it is all self-reinforcing. Social scientists have found that when people sort themselves politically, and when their cultural and political affiliations begin to overlap, resentment and anger toward the outside group grow. The battle of us "over here" and them "over there" becomes intense.[8]

Rural voters are not "rural voters" just because they come from the same place or share characteristics with other blocs that make up the ever-shifting fabric of American politics. Rural voters have the power they do because they have developed an identity centered on place and a shared destiny. As we will show next, the rural-urban divide has a long shadow in public opinion and political developments, which has shaped the last several decades of American politics. Although rural voters seldom drew attention from professional pollsters or political scientists, we dive into older surveys to reveal these important shifts in attitudes, including those that distinguish rural Republicans from Republicans more generally. We also show that the cultivation of this rural identity was part of a deliberate strategy on the part of elected officials within the Republican Party. Moreover, Democrats' ambivalence about their performance in rural America is not a new phenomenon; for decades, the Democratic Party has struggled to react to the GOP's growing dominance in rural communities throughout the country, as traditional regional or state loyalties succumbed to this new, national message about rural America.

Ultimately, it is because of that ubiquitous, nationalized identity that rural voters can leverage their relatively small voting power into big electoral shifts. It is why they vote so overwhelmingly for Trump and continue to express their political unanimity down-ballot. It is why the rural voter is not just the Trump voter and why they will continue to remain a potent force in national politics even without him at the top of the ticket. There may be something special about Trump's popularity in rural America—his over-the-top urbaneness had a certain potency when he crisscrossed the countryside. And, as we will test with greater precision in chapter 10, certain aspects of Trump's candidacy were especially attuned to rural attitudes and predispositions.

And yet, viewing this transformation in a deeper historical context, it is also clear that the rural voter is not a consequence of Donald Trump, nor was it an inevitable development. Although we see rural-urban divides in other industrialized countries, particularly in Europe, the rural voter in the United States is fully a product of this country's unique history and political travails. Nowhere is that more paramount than in the shifting loyalties of the American South and the reaction to the towering successes the civil rights movement reached during the 1960s and early 1970s.

It is a complicated story, but we see two larger trajectories in the creation of the rural voter. The first has to do with the transformation of American conservatism and Republican Party politics in the aftermath of the sixties.[9] Rural America is unique in many ways, but it was not immune to one of the most pivotal decades in American history: what Hugh Heclo calls America's "cosmic crack up."[10] The growing importance of moral issues in national politics and the political energy that pulled evangelical Christians into mainstream Republican Party politics also helped the GOP in rural areas, where large percentages of Christian voters responded with enthusiasm. The political blowback against Vietnam made patriotism a political issue and, together with the politics of race, multiculturalism, and political correctness, cemented the Republican Party's position as the party of conservatism.

Those changes would have made a difference in rural America just as they made a difference in suburban and urban America. They would have led to a more ideologically homogeneous Republican Party and created a vicious cycle of polarizing conflicts around race, culture, and identity.[11] However, we argue that the rural-urban divide would not be a part—or as large a part—of our national political conflict without something else. The new conservatism, while important, is insufficient for explaining the rise of the rural voter.

Something else also happened. Although it has often worked in tandem with the change in Republican partisanship on a national scale, rural partisanship is a distinct development. There was no single trigger, no solitary focusing event or skilled operative. And it is fair to say that while it was mostly a top-down process, with conservative elites looking to harness an increasingly malleable group of voters, there were also bottom-up pressures. The same elites and political officials working to transform the Republican Party set their sights on rural voters and communities for extra attention. Their narratives about hard work had special currency in communities where blue-collar workers made up the largest percentage of the working population, where good jobs were harder and harder to find, and where residents were least likely to want to leave. The politics of race and civil rights play out differently in places where few ethnic or racial minorities live. And Ronald Reagan's skillful cultivation of distrust toward government was amplified in the countryside—in towns and communities long skeptical of outside expertise.

Debates within the GOP also portend the rise of a different type of conservatism that would finally come to the fore with Trump's candidacy but which had started to transform rural partisanship in the previous decades. While there was a conservative ascendancy, debates within the GOP over free trade and America's global military presence brought more rural voters into the fold, even as they represented a divergence from formerly mainstream Republican positions. As we will discuss, the GOP's unfailing message about American military might and patriotic duty may have galvanized millions of new voters, but it was not especially potent in rural America. At the same time, a subset of conservative leaders—none more important than Pat Buchanan—were weary of overextending the United States' global military presence and overlooking the consequences of free trade. Well before Trump uttered the words "America First," Buchanan challenged Republican Party elites to place "America First—and Second, and Third."[12] With elite consensus largely solidified on these core issues, rural voters felt left out—that is, until a certain candidate recognized the latent power of that message.

Our point is to show that a rural-urban split did not emerge just because there happened to be more conservatives or Republicans in rural communities willing to embrace the new conservativism of a post-sixties era. Rather, Republicans crafted their message to elevate rural communities and rural ways of life. Ultimately, the myth of "real America" became synonymous with rural America; that it was possible to find the idealized version of traditional families, breadwinning men, God-fearing Christians, and local democracy only outside the hustle and bustle of big-city life, and even away from the suburbs—long idealized as the American dream. The Rural Voter Survey makes the culmination of this historical development clear. When we asked whether you are more likely to find real America in small towns and rural communities than in big cities, 80 percent of rural voters agreed. A full 66 percent of suburban and urban voters did, too!

It is a political myth, of course, that you can only find real America in rural America. But like all political myths, it serves its purpose well. It has drawn rural America into the Republican Party over the last four decades, well before Donald Trump decided to sully his oxfords by stepping out of Manhattan and into the far-far-far outer boroughs.

FIGHTING ABORTION, AMNESTY, AND ACID: THE POLITICS OF CONSERVATION REACTION SINCE 1960

Rural politics is part of a broader transformation in American politics: a conservative counterrevolution that emerged in the wake of progressivism's high-water mark in the 1960s. As Robert Novak, one of Washington's leading reporters throughout that tumultuous decade, described, it was at this time that the GOP crafted itself into a home for those disillusioned with "abortion, amnesty, and acid."[13]

The focus of this book is on rural America's unique attributes, but it would be a mistake to think that Republican ascendency in rural areas could have happened without the dramatic rise of partisan polarization, the increasing toxicity of the country's culture wars, or the timeless challenge that is this country's attempt to build a multiracial democracy.

We have been clear that rural politics cannot be understood simply as the sum of its demographic parts, namely: old, Christian, blue collar, white. But you would leave out a large part of the story if you did not include it in the equation. The fact that the Republican Party outperforms the Democrats among whites nearly two to one does increase their vote share in rural America; the fact that the GOP is increasingly seen as the party of "traditional family values," does matter in communities where nearly four in ten residents say they are "born again Christians," the highest of anywhere in the United States. Even if a minority of the country's evangelicals live in rural America (75 percent of evangelicals live outside rural America), they still are a part of the fabric of rural America.

Nevertheless, that basic fact of electoral geography—that rural America has been declining as a part of the electorate since the turn of the twentieth century—was not lost on politicians in the 1960s and '70s. For savvy political elites like Richard Nixon, the future of the Republican Party was not in rural America but, rather, the suburbs. After World War II, the electoral weight of the suburbs mushroomed, and the rise of the civil rights movement created tensions within the Democratic Party that became untenable. In 1969, the journalist and historian Kevin Phillips penned *The Emerging Republican Majority*, in which he outlined the slow, steady movement of the South away from the Democrats.[14] The old order, based on the New Deal coalition, was coming to an end. And yet, for the Republicans to move beyond their historic base in the Northeast and the business class, they needed a strategy to draw support from the thousands of new suburban communities dotting the South and West: the Sunbelt. Instead of attracting blue-collar votes by shifting the party's probusiness, small-government appeals, Phillips argued that racial and cultural cues would do the trick. Recall, a greater percentage of Republicans than Democrats in Congress supported the 1964 Civil Rights Act, so Phillips's strategy represented a major change in tactics that would draw a clear line on those issues. While the book was not particularly popular in academic circles or with the general public, it is hard to overstate the importance of Phillips's thesis in GOP campaign war rooms. Most agree that Phillips ordained the so-called southern strategy that helped Republican presidential candidates overcome a national party registration deficit.[15] The goal, argued Phillips, should be to pit racial and ethnic groups against one another and capitalize on the resentments that followed. "The whole secret of politics is knowing who hates who."[16]

There is no doubt that Nixon's law and order message tapped latent racial animus among many white voters, and certainly his steadfast defense of traditional family values had broad appeal among the same group. But in the 1968 election, Nixon charted a centrist path between Hubert Humphrey and George Wallace, and he was certainly not the darling of evangelical Christians. Two years later, during the midterms, he attempted to mobilize voters against the antiwar Democrats and against civil rights activists. His vice president, Spiro Agnew, took the lead. "It's time to rip away the rhetoric and divide on authentic lines," he thundered.[17] America was dividing into two camps, and the Nixon team pushed supporters to see political Democrats as the enemy, poised to decimate the country they loved.[18]

In the short term, the strategy failed; Republicans lost twelve House seats and continued to find themselves in a near-permanent minority in Congress, given the Democrats' monopoly control of the South. According to one account, Nixon pulled himself back to the center after the election.[19] During his administration, he ushered in a host of changes that would raise the eyebrows of today's hardline conservatives— including greater federal control of public lands, an array of new environmental regulations, and improved relations with China.

Mostly, for our concerns, Nixon was not particularly skillful at connecting with rural voters. He performed worse in rural areas in 1972 than four years earlier. He talked about the "silent majority," which resonated in the heartland, and Nixon sometimes harkened back to his presuburban Whittier, California. But he was not rural in manner, nor was he willing to sport any sort of "country style." The idea of Nixon donning cowboy boots, driving a pickup truck, or marching out to a duck blind at 5:00 A.M. for a photo op was inconceivable. To paraphrase Willy Sutton's line as to why he robbed banks, Nixon went where the votes were: the suburbs, the new battleground in American politics. His style and pitch were aimed at the blue-collar and southern whites who had fled to suburbia and beltway communities in the wake of the Supreme Court's prointegration decision in *Brown v. Board of Education* and subsequent cases requiring school busing. "Running up big margins in the suburbs helped [Nixon and other] Republicans neutralize the Democratic Party's advantage in the cities."[20]

While the seeds of grievance may have been planted during the 1960s, during Nixon's presidency, the rural vote was still considered fickle. An excerpt in *The Almanac of American Politics* put the matter this way: "[During most of the twentieth century,] rural America could be called the least predictable of the nation's demographic or geographic blocs. Unlike the cities, which for decades had voted overwhelmingly Democratic in federal elections, rural voters were willing to split ballots and make quick partisan turnarounds. . . . Country values, with their emphasis on self-reliance and social conservatism, often worked to the political advantage of Republicans. But that was offset, at least in some rural areas, by a sense of unease with the economic status quo."[21]

While Nixon's presidency ended in disgrace and ushered in new, massive Democratic majorities, modern conservatism's reaction lost little steam—and it had plenty to react against. The 1960s are remembered rightfully as a critical decade in redefining America's social contract with government, especially around civil rights. But as Shep Melnick reminds us, "The second half of the 1960s may have been a wild time, but the programs that emerged now seem rather tame. Conversely, the allegedly conservative 1970s produced many of the policies that liberals are now most determined to defend"—and which conservatives continue to rail against: expansion of food stamps on disability insurance; the Special Supplemental Nutrition Program for Women, Infants, and Children (WIC); age discrimination prohibition; affirmative action; the Clean Air, Clean Water, and Endangered Species Acts; campaign finance reform; and the creation of the Occupational Safety and Health Administration and the Equal Employment Opportunity Commission . . . not to mention two of the most contentious advances in civil rights: national abortion access (*Roe v. Wade*, 1973) and Title IX of the Education Amendments of 1972 banning gender discrimination.[22]

A decade after Nixon's first win and in response to these landmark policy developments, the conservative reaction had reached such momentum that it pulled modern progressivism from its twentieth-century high pedestal. For many—on the left and on the right—we are still living in the shadow of its greatest advocate, Ronald Reagan. Prior to Reagan, the Republican Party flailed as a conservative party—embracing aspects of Great Society reform and promising better management of the national administrative state, not its deconstruction. Reagan, who cut his political teeth stumping for Barry Goldwater's 1964 presidential run, delivered the same line throughout his career: government expansion would lead to a dependent society; military weakness or détente was the path toward Soviet domination. Real America had to be defended with strong, forceful leadership.

Reagan's real gift was rhetorical—to make new, heterodox economic theories sound old; to challenge the federal government's powers without diminishing the broad support many Americans still felt toward the New Deal; to inspire while also sowing the seeds of distrust. He recognized that the cultural battles fought during the 1960s—on feminism, racial equality, and immigration—were not over. Particularly in reaction to *Roe v. Wade*, a new force in American politics was brewing in the form of an organized evangelical movement that was unafraid to pursue its agenda in politics.[23] The Supreme Court handed down *Roe v. Wade* in 1973, but abortion politics in the 1970s did not fall neatly along partisan lines. In perhaps the leading work on the politics of abortion up to and shortly after *Roe*, Linda Greenhouse and Reva Siegel demonstrate that Republicans in Congress supported abortion rights at about the same level as did Democrats.[24] Later, grassroots organizations, such as those led by Phyllis Schlafly and Jerry Falwell, helped to stoke a culture war that animated evangelical voters across the country. It would be particularly potent in the South and the suburbs. In concert with those grassroots organizers, Reagan folded this nascent voting bloc into the Republican Party, where they would remain a powerful constituency.

The rise of the evangelical conservatives in electoral politics coincided with concerns about a nation adrift, and it found fertile ground outside urban areas. Evangelicalism has been an important part of American culture since the nineteenth century, but it did not congeal behind one party until the late 1970s. *Brown*, the banning of prayer in public schools, the revocation of religious tax exemption status for segregated religious schools, and the forced busing of many public schools in the 1970s teed up the political mobilization of white conservative Christians.[25] Reagan's opponent, the incumbent President Jimmy Carter, was a born again Christian; he talked of Christian values and referenced biblical passages on the campaign trail, but he also endorsed progressive aspects of the Baptist tradition, like confronting human rights abuses abroad, racial inequality in the United States, and closing gaps in social welfare programs.

By the end of Carter's term, a fissure had grown between conservative and liberal evangelicals—which grew into a canyon with the explosion of television-based Christian ministries in the 1980s. As noted by James Guth, the Christian right emerged during the malaise of the Vietnam and Watergate eras and was further invigorated by the *Brown* decision, but the tipping point was the mushrooming popularity of a new breed of "electric church" ministries willing to capitalize on trigger issues.[26] Television evangelists like Falwell, Pat Robertson, Jim Bakker, Oral Roberts, and Rex Humbard cultivated vast audiences on hundreds of radio and local television stations. They fermented a potent mix of cultural, economic, and political grievances to drive membership—and, of course, to solicit contributions. Movement on the Equal Rights Amendment and gay rights, as well as federal protections around abortion, stirred fundamentalists to fight, as Guth put it, the "secularization of public policy."[27]

Conservative operatives understood the emerging power of this group and worked diligently to merge ranks. In 1979, Gary Jarmin of the American Conservative Union commented, "the beauty of it is that we don't have to organize these voters. They already have their own television networks, publications, schools, meeting places, and respected leaders."[28] Endorsements, score cards, and sermons on the virtues of some candidates and the perils of others became common by the early 1980s. Economic insecurities, foreign policy threats, and a sense of decline merged with a culture war over ERA, gay rights, pornography, drug use, school prayer, and especially abortion. In 1978, following the assassination of San Francisco mayor George Moscone and Harvey Milk, the first openly gay man elected in California, Falwell preached that "the wrath that is falling upon the city is of divine origin." And that "the liberal churches are not only the enemy of God, but the enemy of the nation."[29] The religious right began pushing a new version of us-versus-them politics. "What right wing extremists once said about communist subversives, Falwell and his brethren now said about liberals—and do so from their pulpits."[30]

Evangelical voters switched in mass from the Carter brand to the Falwell model. And once the bond was forged, white evangelical Christians became Republican—solidly Republican.

Reagan and the new right also fused this culture war to larger issues about what it meant to be a proud American. Campaigning for president, Reagan was a harsh critic of the so-called Vietnam syndrome—the belief that America's failure in Southeast Asia was the product of hubris and a lesson about the limits of military strength. Reagan forcefully rejected this line, which led to the most significant peacetime military buildups in American history and, among other things, the rapid invasion of Grenada in October 1983. In the shadow of Jimmy Carter's failed military move to free the 52 American diplomats being held hostage in Iran in the spring of 1980, and within days of the bombing of a Marine headquarters in Lebanon that killed 241, the quick rout in Grenada reassured many of the righteousness and might of America's military, boosting Reagan's approval ratings throughout the country and making the Republican Party the party of proud patriots, American greatness.[31] A CBS/*New York Times* poll taken in the final few days of Reagan's administration showed that 93 percent of Americans (96 percent of rural Americans!) approved of the outgoing president's relations with the Soviet Union.[32]

However, it may be an overstatement to suggest that Reagan's foreign policy was especially popular in rural areas. With regard to the hijacking of TWA flight 847—another instance of American hostages in the Middle East—rural residents were the least likely to want to see military action in retribution for the crisis; only 21 percent of them wanted to "take military action to punish the people" responsible, compared with nearly four in ten urban residents.[33] And throughout the decade, support for increasing military spending was lowest in rural areas, according to the Chicago Council on Foreign Relations' biennial poll (fielded by the Gallup organization).[34] Suburban voters consistently favored Reagan's more aggressive foreign policy stances more than rural voters, even after accounting for partisanship.[35]

While rural voters may have been less enthusiastic about a growing role for America's military overseas, one fact remained clear at the end of the decade. It used to be the case that politics stopped at the water's edge. In the aftermath of Vietnam, foreign policy was fair game. What it meant to be patriotic was politically contested and embroiled in the deepening partisan divisions that would continue to grow into the new millennium.

"REAL AMERICA" AND THE CREATION
OF THE RURAL VOTER

These explosive social issues around patriotism and Christian morals transformed American politics. By raising the specter of massive cultural decay the idea of nation in decline, the nationalization of rural culture and politics was set in motion, in part, by conservative organizations that mobilized at a national scale.[36]

Rural identity was also carefully and deliberately braided into the messaging of a more conservative Republican Party. The discourse of "roots," "small-town values," and, above all else, "real America," is now so commonly associated with rural life and rural people that we tend to overlook how it was politically constructed. Republicans, in other words, now own those labels or traits, seizing them in the service of a conservative movement. That was not an inevitable or foreordained development.[37]

The evidence, though, is clear. Going back to Reagan's first major public address in 1964—what scholars and even the president's former aides simply refer to as "The Speech"—the values of rural life, particularly farming—the most bucolic of rural activities—were used to advance the larger goals of Reagan's conservative vision for all Americans. Farmers and rural people were "responsible," they epitomized "thrift and hard work." Above all, though, they were the clearest example of the danger posed by government run amok. To Reagan and all his listeners, farmers were under assault. They offered a simple but powerful story of a bureaucracy out of control ("There's now one [bureaucrat in the Department of Agriculture] for every 30 farms in the United States," Reagan tallied). Rural communities were politically powerful for Reagan's message because, as he saw it, they were politically helpless: "The wheat farmers voted against a wheat program. The government passed it anyway." And they faced an existential crisis: government will "imprison farmers who wouldn't keep books as prescribed by the federal government," it will "seize farms through condemnation and resell them to other individuals." For the millions of Americans detached from rural life and who may never even have visited a farm, the image of the small, helpless family farmer in service to the suited-up federal agent was a powerful, unequivocal image in support of Reagan's conservative philosophy.[38]

By the time he announced his third run for the presidency in 1979, Reagan knew that rapid cultural, economic, and political upheavals of the preceding decades had left a swath of Americans desperate for a return to America's roots. It is telling that shortly after announcing his bid for the presidency, Reagan traveled to rural Mississippi to hold the first rally of the campaign. It was held just seven miles from Philadelphia, Mississippi, the place where three civil rights activists were murdered in 1964 during Freedom Summer. As noted by one commentator, Reagan's lines were "a dog whistle fully understood by the white people in attendance who embraced the conservative former California governor and actor as a political hero straight from central casting."[39]

Reagan, the "Great Communicator," was skillful at linking grievances with an argument about the ineptitude and indifference of the federal government. He also tapped into a nostalgia of more traditional times and blamed government for its demise. His "Morning in America" reelection theme hit all the right chords; stability, consistency, and connections to the past oozed from his speeches and commercials. And so, too, did rural themes. His lead television ad portrayed small-town life—rife with newspaper boys on bikes, picket fences, tractors, and white faces, lots of white faces—harkened voters to a simpler time.

As we document in figure 3.1, relying on survey data collected since the 1970s from the General Social Survey (GSS) at the University of Chicago, these antigovernment messages (and government's many scandals) resonated through large swaths of the American public.[40] Taking the percentage of individuals in each community who had a favorable opinion of each institution, and subtracting the percentage that had an unfavorable opinion, we can see the precipitous decline in trust affecting government institutions. Only the Supreme Court squeaks out a positive net rating in urban America. To our point, though, trust in government institutions has plummeted throughout the country.

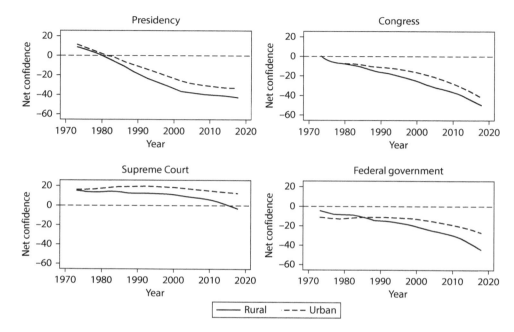

FIGURE 3.1 Confidence in government institutions in rural and urban America since 1970

Note: Using data from the General Social Survey (GSS), we identify respondents from rural areas (counties having no towns of 10,000 or more people) and urban areas (central city of 112 largest metropolitan statistical area). We then subtract the percentage of respondents who had a "great deal of confidence" from those who had "hardly any" to calculate a net confidence score. Points above the horizontal line (0) indicate that more people did than did not have confidence in the institution, while points below the horizontal line indicate that more people lacked confidence. Individual, poststratification weights are applied when creating rural and urban group estimates.

And, it has been a particularly dramatic decline in rural America. At the start of these developments, rural America had a higher net rating for the federal government, in general, than urban America; now it is considerably less.

In a strict objective analysis, it seems odd that rural areas may have responded so positively to Reagan's message. His own policies seemed to confirm and reinforce the system he denounced. For example, although subsidies for ailing farms skyrocketed during the Reagan years (by 1986, nearly 3 percent of the federal budget was going into agricultural subsidies[41]), the highest-grossing farms, the top 2 percent, received 15 percent of all the benefits.[42] Reagan was an avid defender of free trade, and in the speech he used to launch his 1980 campaign, he crafted an image of what would eventually become the North American Free Trade Agreement. But NAFTA and other free-trade agreements were political nonstarters in most rural communities.

Nevertheless, Reagan's message had power in the countryside. As Ross Benes explains in his 2021 book, *Rural Rebellion*—a thoughtful memoir of his early life in Brainerd, Nebraska, population 421—the transformation of rural Nebraskan politics is defined by the shift from a tempered and pragmatic view toward government to its present-day reactionary stance. "There is," Benes writes, "no single bullet that stripped Nebraska of its political moderation."[43] But a hefty section of the book explores the growing disdain for "big government." Writing of his coming-of-political-age period, Benes's disdain for government was palpable:

> My distaste for big government came out in full force during high school when Congress passed an energy bill intended to phase out incandescent light bulbs. . . . I raised my hand in home economics class and stood up near the warm steel radiator in the back of the classroom to rant to my fellow classmates about how the government's regulation of light bulbs was a harbinger that would be followed by more oppressive rules. . . . The liberals in government would force us to drive fuel-efficient Priuses and eat vegetarian. Light bulbs were just the beginning, I tell you what![44]

Benes's friends and neighbors brushed aside, like water off a duck's back, how federal budget deficits tended to grow faster during Republican administrations and that small towns like Brainerd receive an outsized share of public funds—or that rural services, like road and school construction, carried a heavy price tag, leading to subsidies by urban residents. It didn't matter. "Government was an onerous set of rules . . . the nanny that paid lazy people for being lazy."[45]

Benes's community expressed special ire about the bailout of bankers and automakers during the Great Recession and toward Obamacare—especially the contraceptive coverage mandate. But a generation earlier, and for rural residents a bit farther west, "government bureaucrats" often meant the Bureau of Land Management (BLM). The story of public land acquisition and regulation in the American West is fascinating, nuanced, and long. For our concerns, it is enough to note that there have always been competing interests for the land—from ranchers looking for vast acreage to graze cattle, to loggers and miners hoping to extract resources to turn a profit and fuel the nation's industry, to conservationists hoping to stave off the type of exploitation that ravaged lands in the East before regulations. By the time Ronald Reagan was given the keys to the White House, the size of the federal government's landholdings had grown to more than 640 million acres—roughly 25 percent of the nation's landmass. A vast majority of those lands were located west of the Mississippi. Today, in Wyoming, Idaho, Utah, Oregon, California, and Alaska, upward of 50 percent of the land is owned and controlled by the federal government. Topping the list is Nevada, with 80 percent. Nearly all (95 percent) is overseen by various agencies and bureaus under the Department of the Interior. The largest single entity is the BLM, created in 1946.

In 1976, and as part of the growing environmental movement, Congress passed the Federal Land Policy and Management Act. The act's goal was to dramatically broaden federal land regulations. A premium was put on protecting natural, cultural, and historical resources and protecting threatened lands and species. It was a conservation-centered move, a win for environmentalists. The BLM was placed at the helm to create new rules and regulations, and by 1977, a massive survey of all federal holdings on pieces of more than five thousand acres was implemented.

The Sagebrush Rebellion was born nearly overnight. Throughout the West, cattle ranchers, mining operators, loggers, and a large swath of residents accustomed to using federal lands with little oversight railed against tighter federal control. Big government became synonymous with BLM agents. Washington bureaucrats and environmental activists were telling westerners how they could use vast stretches of land in their state; it was federal colonialism, plain and simple. According to one account, "To critics, it locked-in the 'absentee landlord' relationship Washington had with much of the West."[46] In the 1960s, Reagan exploited the memory of the small family farm the Depression had wiped out; now, nearly two decades later, he had the real-time image of hard-scrabbling ranchers oppressed by overzealous government agents.

Soon large numbers of state and federal politicians from western states—entire boards of county commissioners—had joined forces demanding an end to the new BLM regulations. The move to transfer federal lands to state control intensified. Nevada, Utah, New Mexico, Wyoming, and Washington passed laws laying claim to BLM lands within their boundaries.[47] At the federal level, the Utah senator Republican Orrin Hatch introduced a bill that would have allowed state land commissions to take over some 600 million acres of public lands nationwide. Hatch, along with Senators Barry Goldwater of Arizona and Ted Stevens of Alaska, headed up the League for the Advancement of States Equal Rights, the largest and most influential rebel organization.[48]

As quickly as the rebellion emerged, it ended. In an August 1980 campaign speech in Salt Lake City, then candidate Reagan told the crowd, "I happen to be one who cheers and supports the Sagebrush Rebellion. Count me in as a rebel."[49] Then Reagan won. Once in office, he and his Secretary of Interior, James Watt, dramatically slowed the BLM review process. There was less to rebel against. And it also helped the rebel cause that the Senate switched to Republican control after the 1980 election, in large measure because several rural Democrats were sent packing. At the top of the list was Frank Church of Idaho, who was beat by Republican challenger Steven Symms, a vocal member of the rebellion. It is hard to say with certainty if land management policies were at the heart of Church's defeat. Still, his loss, along with the departure of Birch Bayh of Indiana, Warren Magnuson of Washington, George McGovern of South Dakota, and John Culver of Iowa, was a vivid sign that rural voters were moving to the Republican ranks. (Church was the last Democrat to represent Idaho in the Senate.)

BUCHANAN, CLINTON, AND NAFTA

Despite the ambiguous consequences of Reagan's actual policies, the branding worked. Years after he launched onto the scene, Republicans had made the image of "real" versus "other" America a major part of their national message. In 1992, the chair of the Republican National Committee proclaimed to a national television audience that "we are America [and] those other people are not." The former speaker of the House, Newt Gingrich, described Democrats as "the enemy of normal Americans."

Of course, there was nothing especially different between urban and rural communities on many of these issues (and, as we will discuss in later chapters, the gap today is not as wide as is commonly believed). As Mo Fiorina has pointed out, there is scant evidence that a culture war raged in the minds of most Americans during the late twentieth century, regardless of where they lived.[50] Results from the GSS confirm that changes in attitudes on a host of so-called culture war issues have become more consensual even as the fires were stoked. From sexual liberation to women's rights, attitudes have liberalized in both urban and rural America (figure 3.2). More importantly, we know from basic demographic statistics that Republicans would not have won if these beliefs and attitudes were found only in rural America. There simply are not that many rural people in the country!

Even though the real differences between urban and rural America were not as great as many claimed, savvy politicians knew that in creating such a divide, they could reap the rewards at the ballot box. Few were more skilled at recognizing the potential of this divisive strategy in rural America than Pat Buchanan. He was a communications adviser to Richard Nixon during his 1968 and 1972 presidential campaigns and a member of Nixon's administration in the second term. Buchanan rose to national fame as a conservative newspaper columnist and radio/television commentator in the early 1980s. Long stints on CNN and PBS offered a platform for his views, which cemented the real America rhetoric in the mainstream. By 1985, he had joined the Reagan administration as the White House communications director. By 1990, with Reagan gone and George H. W. Bush in the White House, Buchanan

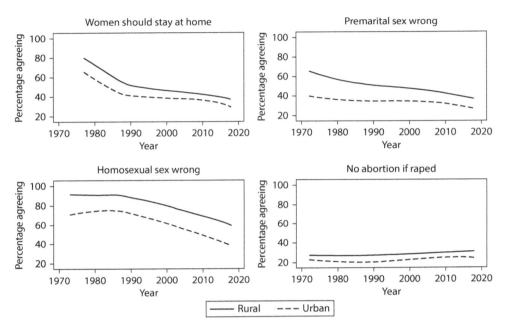

FIGURE 3.2 Culture war issues in rural, suburban, and urban America since the 1970s

Note: Using data from the General Social Survey (GSS), we identify respondents from rural areas (counties having no towns of 10,000 or more people) and urban areas (central city of 112 largest Metropolitan statistical area). We then calculate the percent of respondents in those two communities agreeing with the following questions: (1) "It is much better for everyone involved if the man is the achiever outside the home and the woman takes care of the home and family"; (2) "It is always wrong f if a man and woman have sex relations before marriage" (3); "sexual relations between two adults of the same sex" is always wrong; (4) "it should be possible for a pregnant woman to obtain a legal abortion if she became pregnant as a result of rape." Individual, poststratification weights are applied when creating rural and urban group estimates.

began voicing frustrations that the GOP had become too centrist in its policy positions. "The greatest vacuum in American politics is to the right of Ronald Reagan," he once remarked.[51]

A "draft Buchanan" movement emerged when George H.W. Bush backtracked on his "read my lips: no new taxes" pledge in 1991. Running against a sitting president is a Sisyphean task, especially when he is riding high in the polls in the wake of an easy military victory (the Persian Gulf War). So although Buchanan never really stood a chance of snatching the nomination from Bush, his vociferous criticism of the Republican establishment nevertheless had long-lasting appeal. He understood the potency of the culture war and his antielitist message, as he railed against immigration, free trade, multiculturalism, and gay rights. He painted mainstream Republicans as out of touch as Democrats. He condemned Bush's liberal foreign policy doctrines: "Should the United States be required to carry indefinitely the full burden of defending rich and prosperous allies who take America's generosity for granted as they invade our markets?" he asked at a 1992 campaign rally.[52] At a San Diego campaign stop, he called for the government to build a wall—a two-hundred-mile-long physical boundary between the United States and Mexico.[53] One of the attack ads Buchanan used against Bush in Georgia featured scenes of scantily clothed gay Black men from a PBS documentary, *Tongues Untied*. The film is about the intersection of homophobia and racism and was subsidized by the National Endowment for the Arts. The director, Marlon Riggs, said the aim of the film was to "shatter the nation's brutalizing silence on matters of sexual and racial difference."[54] Buchanan's ad told viewers, "the Bush administration has invested our tax dollars in pornographic and blasphemous art too shocking to show. This so-called art has glorified homosexuality, exploited children and perverted the image of Jesus Christ. Even after good people protested, Bush continued to fund this kind of art."[55]

At the onset of the race, Buchanan drew a surprisingly high level of enthusiasm, but the establishment wing of the GOP, while on the ropes, was still dominant. Buchanan netted just 37 percent of the New Hampshire vote, signaling that his chances for the nomination were slim. But he refused to withdraw. He received 23 percent of the GOP primary votes when it was all said and done, but in several states, that figure jumped to nearly one-third. Buchanan eventually endorsed Bush and in return was granted a prime-time speaking slot at the GOP convention in Houston later that summer.

It is difficult to tell with certainty the weight of Buchanan's candidacy on rural attitudes and voting trends. A county-by-county analysis of his support during that first run (he would throw his hat in two additional times) suggests he did somewhat better in rural parts, but the pattern is not universal, nor is it overwhelming. A few reporters and pundits offered speculation about how Buchanan's campaign resonated in the countryside. Writing of the pending Arizona primary vote, the reporter David Rogers of the *Wall Street Journal* suggested that Buchanan "commands a strong base in the state's rural counties."[56] A few years later, David Brooks, then of the *Wall Street Journal*, wrote that Buchanan "paints modern politics as a replay of the Scopes trial, when rural simple folk led by William Jennings Bryan confronted urban liberals."[57] Some of the media polls taken in the lead-up to the 1992 Republican nomination suggest that about a quarter of rural Republicans supported Buchanan's insurgency, whereas just 10 percent of urban Republicans felt similarly.[58] But snapshots also hint that Buchanan's support was strong in large urban areas and its suburbs. Interestingly, the KKK leader David Duke's numbers were three times higher in urban than in rural America.[59]

Even though Buchanan's run may not have directly transformed the voting allegiances of rural voters, new right activists like Buchanan continued to ruffle the feathers of the establishment. Beating the drum of cultural grievance and economic populism, they hammered thorny issues for mainstream conservatives, especially abortion, immigration, and free trade. Buchanan showed that these issues could captivate a national audience. In a fiery, bombastic convention speech, he laid out the culture war as a battle for the soul of America. It was "as critical to the kind of nation we will one day be as was the Cold War itself." This was a "religious war" that pitted the GOP against a Democratic Party "that supported abortion, radical feminism and the 'homosexual rights movement.'"[60]

Most importantly, by fusing cultural and economic issues, Buchanan helped craft an image of real America on the ropes. His idea was to summon public outrage over everything from busing to un-Christian art and tie it to economic elitism. Pitted against the real Americans, Thomas Frank would later write, were the urban elite: "the high-taxing, government-spending, latte-drinking, sushi-eating, Volvo-driving, *New York Times*-reading, Hollywood-loving, left-wing freak show."[61] Regional differences faded away, and stories told about rural America painted them as one, singular group of people. Not only that, Republicans came to view rural America as the symbol of a plain, peculiarly American people. Many of the issues Buchanan ran on were to become Trump's issues, or, as Buchanan himself would opine during the first summer of Trump's presidency, "The ideas made it, but I didn't."[62]

In short order, mainstream journalists bought into the idea that rural voters represented the heart of the American electorate. In 2008, Gerald Seib wrote a piece on the four groups of voters whom he believed would likely decide the presidential election. Rural voters were one of the groups, of course. "Rural and small-town voters are the best indicators of whether a candidate is connecting with the values of Middle America."[63] Even some prominent Democratic strategists and pundits began to equate rural America with real America. Peter Hart told the audience, "They are America. . . . If you can speak to [rural voters], then you relate to the rest of America."[64] It did not seem to matter that rural voters make up just one-fifth of the electorate or that they were demographically distinct from the rest of the country. They represented something fundamental about what most Americans valued; they were wrong. The myth of real America was born.

In truth, very little research, analysis, or punditry was fixed on how Buchanan's candidacy, or any other candidate, played in rural parts. We know that by 2000, Buchanan's final run for the White House, his numbers had solidified in rural America: nearly 8 percent of rural voters said they preferred Buchanan in a match-up between Vice President Al Gore and George W. Bush—double the percentage of nonrural voters.[65] Rural Republicans were nearly two times more likely than their urban counterparts to say Buchanan made them feel hopeful and proud.[66] Half of rural respondents believed the nation's moral climate had gotten worse since 1992, and an even larger percentage of rural residents believed immigration should be decreased. Fully three in four rural residents believed the government was getting too strong. Even though rural residents did not completely line up in support of every one of Buchanan's positions, there was something about his candidacy that drew segments of the rural voting population together. In an *Esquire* piece entitled "When Pat Buchanan Tried to Make America Great Again," published after Trump's victories throughout the countryside, Sam Tanenhaus made a telling observation: while pundits seized on the cultural war piece of Buchanan's candidacy, perhaps it was a harbinger of something more—about who we are and what we believe. Could it have been a "raw message, a shout from a distant shore, that even now many seem unable to hear. Our delicate moral antennae are attuned to the faintest dog whistle, but they filter out the deeper rumbles through which democracy makes its urgent claims."[67]

So there is more to the story than cultural wedge issues and the emerging narrative of rural as the locus of real America. Yes, Buchanan doubled down on many cultural issues, but he criticized mainstream Republican leaders for their elitist stances, particularly on free trade and foreign policy. In his 1998 book, *The Great Betrayal: How American Sovereignty and Social Justice Are Being Sacrificed to the Gods of the Global Economy*, Buchanan railed against the "transnational elites" who were responsible for the decline of blue-collar jobs, for "broken homes, uprooted families, vanished dreams, delinquency, vandalism, crime."[68] The book begins by highlighting a rural southern community gone asunder when the local Fruit of the Loom plant closed and sent its jobs to Mexico.

Buchanan was referring to Bill Clinton, certainly, but also free-trade Republicans like George W. Bush, Newt Gingrich, and even Ronald Reagan. A trade deal with Mexico, Canada, and the United States was pushed by Reagan in 1980, and a formalized arrangement was negotiated by Bush. Eventually, NAFTA narrowly won bipartisan ratification during Clinton's first term. In the House, some 132 Republicans joined 102 Democrats, and in the Senate, 34 Republicans teamed up with 27 Democrats to secure the deal. Clinton hailed the agreement as the creator of jobs and prosperity:

> The only way we can recover the fortunes of the middle class in this country so that people who work harder and smarter can at least prosper more, the only way we can pass on the American Dream of the last 40 years to our children and their children for the next 40 is to adapt to the changes which are occurring. . . . NAFTA is a debate about whether we will embrace these changes and create the jobs of tomorrow, or try to resist these changes, hoping we can preserve the economic structures of yesterday. . . . I believe that NAFTA will create 200, 000 American jobs in the first two years of its effect.[69]

But it was a controversial move right from the start and a harbinger of tough times for some. A few months earlier, Ross Perot, who had challenged Clinton and Bush in 1992, said the deal would lead to a "great sucking sound" of jobs being sent to Mexico and Canada.

As to the precise effect of NAFTA on rural America, we know that exports of some agricultural commodities grew; between 1993 and 2017, U.S. agricultural sales to Mexico and Canada jumped from $8.9 billion to $38 billion.[70] Large farm operations made a lot of money, and rural American consumers, like the rest of Americans, saw declining prices on many goods. But the prices for other commodities produced by rural economies declined. Not long after the trade barriers were removed, for example, Canadian cattle ranchers flooded the American market with beef, and prices plummeted. The number of small-scale farms actually declined during this period, as large-scale agribusinesses seemed better positioned to capitalize on open borders. The NAFTA champions, both Democrat and Republican, said the deal would benefit small farmers, but between 1998 and 2018, one in every ten small U.S. farms disappeared; nearly 243,330 small U.S. farms were lost.[71] Dena Hoff, a grain and livestock farmer in eastern Montana, commented, "NAFTA was going to be so wonderful for American agriculture. Everyone was going to make money, because there were going to be all these exports. . . . There was going to be prosperity for all three countries. But of course the opposite happened."[72]

Likely an even greater consequence of NAFTA was its displacement of small-scale manufacturing—the economic mainstay of many rural communities. The deal was a boon for large-sector manufacturing, especially corporations able to move segments of their operation to Mexico, where labor costs were lower and environmental regulations less cumbersome. But localized manufacturing—the small tool and die shops, appliances factories, textile mills, food-processing plants, and paper manufacturers—that had dotted the rural American landscape since the Industrial Revolution were caught in the crosswinds. Products like gym shoes, T-shirts, lawnmowers, handbags, car tires, tools, and toothpaste were cheaper to make elsewhere. Sometimes suddenly, other times by dribs and drabs, small factories began to close. Within a decade after NAFTA was adopted, more than seven-hundred thousand U.S. manufacturing jobs were lost, and the wages for the jobs that remained declined.[73] Union shops were the first to go.

The Danville River Mill in Danville, Virginia, is a case in point. Opened in 1882, four generations of local families had worked at the textile mill, and by the time Clinton was preaching about the need to embrace change, some sixty-five hundred employees were operating at the seven sites. Two years later, the mill began laying off employees, and by 2001, all the jobs were gone.

In 1968, more than 1.4 million Americans made clothing, many in small and medium-sized towns. By the end of the century, that figure had dropped by 50 percent.[74] Today, you pick up a pack of socks or a sweatshirt at the local Walmart for a few bucks, but your neighbor who used to work at the mill across town is either out of a job or working in a service industry making less money with no benefits.

Maytag began building washing machines in Newton, Iowa, in 1883. The small city prospered as the company grew into a global brand. When NAFTA was ratified, upward of four thousand area residents held good jobs at the plant, representing 20 percent of the town's population. Newton was proud to be the "Washing Machine Capital of the World." Like so many of the small industrial towns scattered throughout America, it served up the American dream. "With its 30 churches, its cozy downtown, and its Midwestern passion for high school football, Newton [was] right out of Central Casting: a storybook small town."[75] But within a few years, the plant started to downsize as more and more appliances and their components were manufactured in Mexico. By 2007, the factory closed entirely. It was "a nightmare," said Mike Duffus, who had put in thirty-four years at the plant. "Most of the people would say that if you were to cut them, they would bleed blue—Maytag blue."[76]

Any American who is not familiar with a NAFTA ghost town has likely not driven past the gas stations and fast food franchises at the interstate off-ramp. Decaying downtowns in rural parts are as ubiquitous as are the megastores, Taco Bells, and Pizza Huts on the outskirts. Find that bend in the river at the apex of downtown, and you'll find brick or concrete structures that once fueled the town's economy. All was not golden in 1970s small-town America, not by a long shot, but ask any old-timer, and she'll say her town was once alive. Kids raced through high school because you needed the degree to start working at the factory. They stayed because there was a steady job, fair wages, and a bright future. Some of these communities, the lucky ones, have filled corners of these brick buildings with niche shops, dentist offices, and apartments, but in most communities, the old factory stands as an ever-present reminder that "the bright future," "exciting change," and the "promise of prosperity" had passed them by. The transnational elites, as Buchanan called them, were wrong.

For these reasons, Bill Clinton had a complicated relationship with rural voters. While a bit muddled by the presence of a strong third-party candidate, Ross Perot, his performance among rural voters in both 1992 and 1996 was better than his immediate successors—Al Gore, John Kerry, and Barak Obama.[77] He had deep rural roots, and his vote share in the small towns and villages in the South was likely boosted by a perceived connection to a rural way of life. But like other so-called new Democrats, Clinton staked his liberal credentials on social issues like abortion and environmental protections while also courting corporate America. Gun control is wildly unpopular in rural America, a topic taken up in chapter 7, and many rural residents never got over Clinton's backing of the Brady Bill—a move that mandated federal background checks for the purchase of handguns and rifles.

Under Clinton's watch, the Environmental Protection Agency and other federal offices began to implement what many rural residents saw as radical environmental schemes, highlighted by the near complete shutdown of logging in the Pacific Northwest to protect the spotted owl.[78] Livelihoods and communities were being sacrificed at the altar of environmental extremists. Reflecting on growing up in the 1990s in southwestern Washington, Democratic Rep. Marie Gluesenkamp Perez, who stunned observers by narrowly winning a rural seat in the 2022 midterms, suggests, "People had trouble feeding their families. That indignity cast a really long shadow. People felt like they were being told they couldn't work."[79]

Perhaps most significantly, while Republicans before him had primed the pump, Clinton unleashed a new economy centered on emerging technologies and open trade. There is no denying that the economy soared during his tenure. As Hillary Clinton would say two decades later, "What didn't you like, the peace or the prosperity?"[80] The change may have been necessary and inevitable, and it is also fair to say that many of the small towns are showing signs of adaptation—as we will chart in subsequent chapters. But for a generation of rural Americans, NAFTA left them blind-sighted. And the ripple caused by free trade would propagate through families and communities for generations.

BARACK OBAMA, THE TEA PARTY, AND THE NEW RURAL-URBAN DIVIDE

When it came time to replace George W. Bush, it was impossible to deny that the "two Americas" rhetoric had captured the Republican Party. Both during the campaign for the presidency, which pitted John McCain against Barack Obama, and during Obama's eight years as president, the rural-urban divide took on its modern-day form. The Buchanan-esque wing of the GOP found a new standard-bearer, who not only bespoke a real America in the heartland rhetoric but embodied it with her folksy, salt-of-the-earth, proud-outsiderism: Sarah Palin. While the culture wars galvanized conservative voters throughout the country, Palin's nomination as the Republican Party's vice presidential candidate crystalized the image of rural America as Republicans' America, solidifying rural voters' growing and steadfast support for Republican candidates, and paving the way for Trump's election.

Although the election of Trump in 2016 would really drive a wedge into the geographic divide gripping the American party system, the largest changes unfolded during Obama's presidency, as historic patterns of rural support for Democratic candidates imploded down-ballot in races for the Senate and state legislatures. Knowing what we know about rural voters' positions on cultural issues—abortion, guns, LGBTQIA+ rights—it is fair to say that political fighting over rural voters was closer than we may believe in retrospect. But President Obama was not fully committed to voter outreach to rural areas; and without a doubt, his race played a major part in the reaction to his presidency, which was mired by birther conspiracism that elevated Donald Trump into a formidable political opponent.

To say that Barack Obama was a different type of candidate would be a vast understatement. He had only modest experience in politics, and very little of it was in Washington, D.C. He was a lawyer, professor, and self-described community organizer. His early family life was complicated. Obama is biracial, and there is that unique name: Barack Hussein Obama. It was different, hard to pronounce at first; and the middle name became controversial considering that at the time, we were at war with Saddam Hussein in Iraq. According to a *Time* article in February 2008, it was deemed contentious to even say Obama's middle name. At the Oscars in 2008, host Jon Stewart joked by saying, "Barack Hussein Obama running today is like a 1940s candidate named Gaydolph Titler." Obama was also different in another way. He was the first successful Democratic presidential candidate in the post–World War II era, except for John Kennedy, who did not hail from a rural area; Harry Truman, Lyndon Johnson, Jimmy Carter, Bill Clinton—all of them stressed their rural, especially southern, bona fides to get elected. Even FDR played the role of gentleman farmer, but Obama was a proud, unabashed city dweller.

It is hard to imagine a presidential candidate who better represented America's increasingly complex, diverse society than the senator from Illinois. And, bucking an age-old tradition in our politics, Obama made no pretense of having rural roots. An *Esquire* piece following the election offered that he was the first truly urban president: "He is the only American president in recent history to seem unembarrassed about claiming a personal residence in a major American city."[81] For many, this difference—the break from the mold—was at the heart of Obama's appeal. He represented change, a new direction, a new America. His message of transformation was particularly potent for younger voters; they preferred him over John McCain by 68 percent to 30 percent— the highest share of the youth vote obtained by any candidate since exit polls began reporting results according to age in 1976.[82] Still, early in his campaign, before the nominees were even finalized, there were signs that Obama may have been able to close the rural-urban gap: 40 percent of rural residents, according to a May CBS/*New York Times* poll, were ready to support him as president, while McCain polled around 52 percent (and that was during the week of the Jeremiah Wright news story!).[83] Race mattered, for sure, but it did not make him a lost cause even in "real America."

In fact, during that first campaign for the White House, Obama made overtures to rural voters, and it is doubtful that he would have been able to wrestle the nomination away from Hillary Clinton if not for his win in the Iowa Caucus, one of the more rural battlegrounds in the Democratic nomination calendar. He pledged to pull together a "rural summit," with the aim of proposing concrete policy changes in the first one hundred days, and he talked at length about fundamental changes in farm and rural policy. On Election Day, Obama improved Democratic performance in rural areas by two points over John Kerry's 2004 performance: to 40.9 percent. But in key battleground states, the increase, by some estimates, was between 8 and 12 percent, an important shift for the overall outcome.[84]

Obama won a majority of the rural vote in rural Nebraska and Indiana, for example, outperforming Kerry, according to our measure of rural partisanship, by ten points. And there was notable variation across rural regions of the country (unlike today). Unexpectedly, given the larger proportion of Black voters in the rural South, Obama's performance in rural communities in that region was the lowest, around 36 percent of the total vote. In the rural Northeast, he actually captured a majority. The key, suggested Anna Greenberg, a Democratic pollster, was that "Obama was able to peel off the more conservative-leaning voters who just don't place as high a priority on social issues like gay marriage and abortion."[85] As noted by Samantha Bauman, a drugstore clerk in Moberly, Missouri (pop. 13, 878), "With this election, I've kind of started to think that Democrats are not as wrong as I usually like to think."[86]

Of course, each election is unique, and W. Bush's historically low popularity, coupled with the most calamitous economic recession experienced in decades, made 2008 Obama's to lose. The precipitous decline of Democratic vote share in the countryside slowed, but it is the exception that proves the rule. More telling is the strong signal GOP officials sent to rural America with the selection of Sarah Palin as John McCain's running mate.

If Obama was typecast to represent the diversifying American electorate, Palin was the GOP's response to cash in on their long-term cultivation of the real America myth. Palin was the living embodiment of the Republican Party's small-town fetish. At a campaign stop in North Carolina, she summed up the party's position: "We believe that the best of America is in these small towns that we get to visit and these wonderful little pockets of what I call the real America, being here with all of you hard-working, very patriotic, very pro-America areas of this great nation." McCain stated that rural western Pennsylvania "is the most patriotic, most God-loving part of America." And the constant spoof of Palin as a dim-witted backwoods woman served her well among her desired constituents, as it infuriated urban liberals—proof that she represented a vision of America lampooned by viewers of *Saturday Night Live*, who never dared to step out into real America.

According to one poll of rural voters in September that year, half the respondents said they were more likely to support John McCain because Palin was on the ticket. As to why she had developed such favor in the countryside, that same poll found some 65 percent saying Palin "represented the values of rural communities."[87] Charles Webster, the state GOP chairman in Maine, commented, "I see her as being somebody who the average, what I call 'working class guy,' relates to. Somebody who's plain-spoken, somebody who hunts and fishes. And this is Maine—we're in the country up here."[88] Ruben Navarrette Jr. wrote, "Because I grew up in a small town with a population of less than 15,000 people, I was disgusted by the insults and condescension coming from those who think of themselves as the enlightened elite. Meanwhile, in small towns, I detected great affection for Palin."[89]

That did not happen by accident. In Alaska, Palin was careful to hone her nonurban, working-class identity. She grew up in the Matanuska-Susitna Valley, located between Fairbanks and Anchorage, a working-class area boasting homesteaders who had settled half a century earlier—well before the region swelled into an Anchorage exurb.[90] Throughout her political career, she pitched herself as a "valley girl," and she was never shy about tracing her complex path through four different colleges over a six-year span, one of which was a community college. As governor, she would bring her kids into the office and occasionally hold meetings with one on her hip. She was a proud military mom; her son Track was a private in the Army. The family shopped at Walmart and drove around in a family-size, gas-guzzling Chevy Suburban. Palin's husband at the time, Todd, was a commercial fisherman and a champion snowmobile racer. She posted photos of him at races—as well as herself and the rest of the family shooting guns, on hunts, and at fish camp. Unlike other politicians who would sometimes discover some rural connection a few weeks before Election Day, Palin was country through and through. She knew how to shoot a rifle and filet a salmon.

Palin's 2008 GOP convention acceptance speech line drew a stark contrast between rural politics and Obama's stint as a grassroots organizer in Chicago: "I guess a small-town mayor is sort of like a community organizer, except that you have actual responsibilities." During that speech, she also told the audience the nation grows "good people in our small towns, with honesty, sincerity, and dignity," and that they "do some of the hardest work in America." Later, during a campaign stop in rural Ohio, Palin commented, "The smell of the hay, the smell of the cut grass is just beautiful." To rural voters, Palin reflected the core values of freedom, hard work, self-reliance, and family. That she would kick off the vice-presidential debate against Joe Biden with a shout-out to one of her children's elementary schools hit the mark perfectly.

Palin appeared to stumble in an early interview with Katie Couric over policy questions, McCain's record, not having a passport, and not reading national newspapers. That interview, and several others just like it, sent shivers down the spines of political operatives in both parties—and Tina Fey's caricature of Palin on *Saturday Night Live* seemed devastating. But they only reinforced her credentials with rural voters. She was not one of them! In a ten-year retrospective piece on Palin's rise published in the *Atlantic*, Couric and Brian Goldsmith note the following: "At the time,

Palin might not have been able to name a single newspaper or magazine—but she did read where the electorate, at least a significant part of it, was moving. Her candidacy revealed that long-standing political norms were being pushed aside by a new style of divisive, personality-driven populism. A decade later, it's clear that Palin was more than a historical footnote; she was the harbinger of things to come."[91]

Palin stood for a genuine movement, Frank Rich, writes: "The essence of Palinism is emotional, not ideological. . . . The real wave she's riding is a loud, resonant surge of resentment and victimization that's larger than issues like abortion and gay civil rights."[92]

Obama believed he could reenergize a winning left-leaning coalition by focusing on the economic concerns of working-class Americans of all stripes. Even as early as 2004, when he burst on the scene at the Democratic National Convention, Obama understood the traction that the GOP was gaining among blue-collar whites who used to be part of the Democratic coalition. As noted in a recent account of those early years, "When Mr. Obama scolded pundits for slicing America into red states and blue states, it wasn't a dopey celebration of national harmony. It was a strategic attempt to drain the venom out of the culture wars, allowing Democrats to win back working-class voters who had been polarized into the G.O.P."[93]

Later, as president, Obama tried to make good on his ambitions when he set his sights on perhaps the greatest blue-collar economic pressure points: the spiraling cost of health care. As the details of the Affordable Care Act (ACA) unfolded in the spring of 2009, and as federal legislators headed home for the August recess, an explosion of anger roiled across the nation, particularly in rural parts. In Boiling Springs, South Carolina (pop. 4,500), a town hall meeting for Representative Bob Inglis was filled with heckling, shouting, and interrupting. One of the participants, who called himself a "conservative, mainstream American," proclaimed, "I consider myself just an average American but there is not a day or a week that goes by that I don't hear talk about revolution in our country because [of] the government."[94] Inglis, an otherwise stalwart conservative, would go on to lose to an even more strident far-right candidate, Trey Gowdy.

Make no mistake, "Obamacare" was an explosive issue in many communities; conservative outrage, particularly over the individual mandate, was not confined to rural communities. And yet, research during and after the ACA debate suggests that rural residents were especially animated, even when controlling for party affiliation.[95] For instance, a 2017 Kaiser Family Foundation study found that even though rural residents confront a greater number of health care challenges and were less likely to have health insurance, they were overwhelmingly more likely to favor repeal of Obamacare than were nonrural residents. Rural Democrats were twice as likely to favor repeal than were urban or suburban Democrats (23 to 12 percent, respectively).[96]

Not long after Obama and his family moved into the White House, the Tea Party took hold across the county. The movement was likely not as grassroots as first reported, given the considerable funds it received in elite GOP circles,[97] but by 2010, it had become a major national force. Chapters spread across the country. The Great Recession set the backdrop for the Tea Party revolt, and the popular narrative at the time was that the Tea Party rosters were stacked with dislocated blue-collar workers. But was the state of the economy and economic concerns actually the forces that propelled such anger and resentment? Any move that the Obama administration made—including many that would aid working-class citizens—was vehemently opposed by Republicans. Republican Senate leader Mitch McConnell's proclamation that his "number one priority" was to make Obama a one-term president was unprecedented, especially because many of the president's policies were moderate, certainly not hyper-liberal. The highly contentious individual mandate, for instance, was an idea hatched years earlier by a conservative think tank. But that did not matter.

It was later revealed that the motivating force behind the Tea Party was not economic dislocation per se but fears about changes in society and, in particular, concerns about race and immigration. For Tea Party activists, Obama was somehow beyond comprehensible categories. In a survey conducted by CBS in the fall of 2012, some 65 percent of Tea Party identifiers blamed Obama for higher taxes even though a vast majority of Americans had just received a tax cut. Nearly 90 percent disapproved of his job performance (compared with 40 percent of Americans over-all), and when asked to offer a specific as to why they disapproved of the president, the number one reason cited was "I just don't like him."[98]

In an extensive, four-year study, a team of scholars found that attitudes about race were intimately linked to support for the Tea Party. In one simple experiment, pictures of Barack Obama with a different skin tone were shown to subjects. Those seeing the picture with Obama's face darkened were twice as likely to express support for the Tea Party than those who saw the picture of Obama with a lighter skin tone. These scholars write, "The Tea Party emerged during a period when white Americans' political power was threatened by the election of Barack Obama, their majority status was threatened by a rising minority population that received wide media coverage, and the Great Recession increased their economic insecurity, a factor previously shown to catalyze racial threats."[99]

Tea Party insurgents were challenging mainstream Republicans across the country, and yet, polling data found that the movement was particularly potent in rural America. A 2010 CNN/Opinion Research Corp. survey, for instance, suggested that about 11 percent of Americans were active supporters of the Tea Party, and of that group, more than one-half lived in rural areas.[100] There were also regional differences. A 2010 study by the Blair Center for Southern Politics at the University of Arkansas found that although the eleven states of the old Confederacy made up about one-third of the nation's population, it accounted for more than 50 percent of national Tea Party membership.[101] As we will explore more in chapter 9, the Rural Voter Survey offers ample evidence that these values and ideas about race, hard work, and government dependence imbue the rural ethos.

As the 2012 election rolled around, it was pretty clear that the truce between Obama and rural voters had ended. There was some movement in his administration on rural-related issues, including a comprehensive farm bill that included price supports, crop subsidies, insurance provisions, and food stamp assistance, which helped support everything from feed corn to dairy cows to sugar, peanuts, fruits, and vegetables. That bill, incidentally, stalled for two years in the House because Tea Party

Republicans were unwilling to find a compromise that might give Obama a win. But to many rural residents, Obama's heart did not seem to be in it. Policy is not politics, and there were some obvious indicators. In his first year in office, for example, Obama took 43 trips inside the United States, but just one was to a rural county. In his second year in office, he visited 104 places, but only six of those trips were to a rural county, which included vacations in Bar Harbor, Maine, and Martha's Vineyard, Massachusetts.[102]

There seemed a growing sense that rural communities were being ignored in the "change agenda" and that the concerns of rural residents were beside the point. For example, there were new EPA rules on strip-mining of coal, which Obama's opponents quickly dubbed his "war on coal." In an effort to appease his environmental supporters, the argument went, Obama was willing to sacrifice rural communities. Voters in coal-mining communities took it hard. In 2008, Obama netted 43 percent of the vote in West Virginia; by 2012, that figure had dropped to 35 percent. (The figure dropped to below 30 percent for Joe Biden in 2020.) Another example of how Obama may have been tone-deaf to rural voters was a move in 2011 by the Department of Labor to ban people under age eighteen from being near certain farm animals and operating certain kinds of farm machinery.[103]

In the 2010 midterms, Democrats suffered historic losses—and the election hardened the Republican hold on rural America. According to one analysis, Republicans picked up thirty-one seats in "pure rural" areas and another twenty categorized as a mix of rural and suburban.[104] In the Senate, Republicans flipped seats in North Dakota, Arkansas, Wisconsin, Illinois, Pennsylvania, and Indiana. By 2011, the unemployment rate in the smallest 30 percent of counties had skyrocketed up to 10 percent, two points higher than the national average. Charlie Cook of the *Cook Political Report* suggested, "Obama has a problem . . . in states with large small-town, rural populations . . . the president has a really, really hard time."[105] In 2012, not only did Obama fare worse in rural America compared with his 2008 numbers, that election saw the largest rural-urban gap that had ever existed in American history . . . until Hillary Clinton ran in 2016.

WHERE DID ALL THE DEMOCRATS GO?

Hillary Clinton was not going to win rural America, but few expected her to do much worse than Obama did. But Clinton's greatest strength to many—her policy acumen, her years of experience, her hard-nosed pragmatism—was her greatest weakness in rural America. That was not because rural voters knew nothing about policy or disdained pragmatism or hard work; we will put those myths to rest in the second half of this book. Rather, Clinton epitomized the image of the urbane, progressive, out-of-touch transnational elite—the carefully constructed counter to the real American, which had helped channel rural frustrations into an identifiable voting bloc.

Trump was particularly attuned to that caricature of Clinton. Cue Trump at a rally in Ohio: "Ohio has lost one in four manufacturing jobs since NAFTA, a deal signed by Bill Clinton and supported strongly by Hillary Clinton. Remember, every time you see a closed factory or a wiped-out community in Ohio, it was essentially caused by the Clintons."[106]

Consider the fact that at the start of each Republican presidential debate, Trump hit hard his promise to make China pay. Yes, immigration was a major part of Trump's appeal, but what really distinguished him in the Republican primary—especially against other immigration-hard-line conservatives like Ted Cruz—was his no-holds-barred approach toward China.[107] "I have many friends, great manufacturers, they want to go into China. They can't. China won't let them. We talk about free trade. It's not tree free trade, it's stupid trade . . . we're being ripped off."[108]

Compare how Trump and Clinton danced around the delicate politics of renewable energy and economic restructuring in rural Appalachia:

Clinton in a CNN townhall: "We're going to put a lot of coal miners and coal companies out of business."

Trump a month later, standing in front of coal miners: "What I told the folks before over at Peterbilt—the plant—incredible . . . you have to get out and vote, because the miners, to a certain extent, they're so down and they've been treated so badly that they haven't been voting. They haven't been going out and voting like they can. . . . And that includes members of their family that have left the mining business . . . they've left coal. And they've gone into something else. And that's fine. . . . And their parents are still in the coal world where they want to be, and that's where they want to be.

Notice how Trump praised rural ways of living; he praised rural livelihoods, acknowledging that they were not just a sacrifice or another "dirty job" people had to do but, rather, something people wanted to do.

It is not that Trump and Clinton held different positions on policies that mattered to rural voters. Clinton could not, and would not, overcome that difference, although, as we will see, the policy gaps are not as wide as either candidate suggested. And Clinton did come back and say she cared for the coal miners "who did the best they could." She acknowledged that they would be affected by her policies seconds after her tone-deaf, almost gleeful remark about putting them out of work. (Seriously, watch it: https://www.youtube.com/watch?v=ksIXqxpQNto.). But as Anthony Flaccavento, a one-time Democratic candidate for Congress from the same rural community where Trump stood with coal miners, put it, it came down to the fact that Trump's "demeanor during [that] speech [was] a master-class in political empathy."[109] Trump played to rural America's sense that they were forgotten by the political elite and that traditional politicians—none more traditional than Clinton— would continue to disparage their ways of life.

Trump continued to court rural voters four years later in his reelection bid against Joe Biden. He bet on rural areas, knowing that elections are won on the margins and that these gaps often decide the difference. He lost, but in doing so, he reconfirmed a new basic fact of American partisanship: that rural voters are increasingly one of the most important segments of the American electorate—for Republican candidates. Compared with other segments of the electorate, the rural gap is just as important, as demonstrated in figure 3.3.[110]

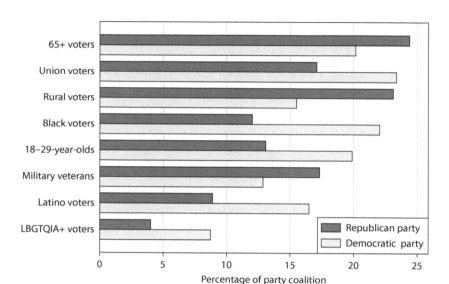

FIGURE 3.3 Demographic groups and their relative importance to the Republican and Democratic vote in 2020

Note: Using data from the *New York Times* National Exit Polls in 2020, we calculate the percentage of each party's total vote share that came from each segment of the electorate, by taking the overall percentage of the electorate represented by the group and multiplying it by the percentage of each group that voted for Joe Biden (Democratic Party) and Donald Trump (Republican Party).

In 2020, everyone talked about the "youth vote," and voters age eighteen to twenty-nine broke decidedly in favor of Joe Biden, with 60 percent voting Democratic and just 36 percent voting Republican. Because young voters constitute 17 percent of the electorate, this meant about 15.6 million more votes for Biden. Young voters, therefore, made up about 19 percent of the Democratic ticket's vote. That's practically the same size as the rural vote. The advantage given to Republicans, as a result of their success in tapping into this rural identity, is more important to their coalition than LGBTQIA+ and Latino voters are to the Democrats and almost as important as Democrats' advantage among Black voters, members of unions, and the elderly.

Trump added fuel to the fire. His winners-and-losers approach played right into rural residents' deep sense that they were falling behind as others were unjustly moving ahead. That said, the transformation of rural partisanship is not just about Trump or the 2016 presidential election. Its roots are deep. In the wake of Biden's dismal showing in rural areas in the 2020 election, former Democratic U.S. Senator Heidi Heitkamp of North Dakota, who herself lost reelection two years earlier, put the matter this way: "If you make it all about Donald Trump then it's transactional, as opposed to an institutional failure that the Democratic Party has had in the last how many years of not paying attention to rural America."[111]

Although we have focused mostly on the tactics and personalities of presidential candidates—primarily because in modern American politics, partisanship is largely dictated by the party's presidential candidates—the consequences can be seen throughout our political system. Even a quick look at down-ballot offices tells a story of huge GOP gains in recent decades.

Throughout the 1980s, Democratic Senate candidates performed equally as well in urban as in rural counties. In figure 3.4, we calculate the county-level vote for each Democratic candidate running for Senate and merge it with our county-level measure of ruralness introduced in chapter 1. For each election cycle, we define "mostly rural" as the one-third most rural counties in the country as a way of accounting for the problem of the shifting baseline (i.e., the country becomes more urban over time). We do the same for "mostly urban" counties by taking the one-third most urban counties in the country for a given year. Historically, Democrats have had the advantage in urban areas throughout this period. But beginning in the late 1980s, support for Democratic candidates drops in rural America; it then plummets during the Obama administration, reaching its low ebb by the 2020 contests for U.S. Senate.

A similar pattern emerges in U.S. House contests. Using relationship files provided by the Census Bureau, we can take each census block that is used to calculate our measure of urbanity and place it within a congressional district. To be sure, some states allow congressional

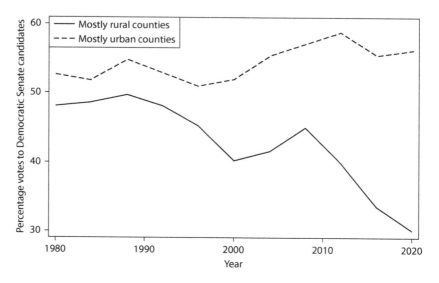

FIGURE 3.4 Percentage of Democratic Senate candidates' vote share from rural and urban counties (1980–2020)

> *Note*: Using our county-level measure of ruralness, we first split counties into mostly rural (0–50 percent of residents live in nonurban blocks) and most urban (more than 80 percent of residents live in urban blocks). Then, using historical elections data from various state archives and David Liep's Atlas of U.S. Presidential Elections (https://uselectionatlas.org/), we sum the total number of votes cast for all Democratic candidates and divide it by the total number of ballots cast in all rural and urban areas.

districts to cross over blocks, but that is very rare, taking place in fewer than five states across the entire time series, and it accounts for less than .01 percent of the total population at stake in the analysis. Figure 3.5 then takes the winners of each congressional race for a given year and considers how each party fared in rural America.

As expected, the average ruralness of each party's congressional district is, well, not very rural. Most Americans do not live in rural districts, so that is not a surprise. Nevertheless, since 2008, the Democratic coalition in the House has basically represented districts that are entirely nonrural. The average level of ruralness for Republican districts has increased as more and more rural residents are represented by Republican members

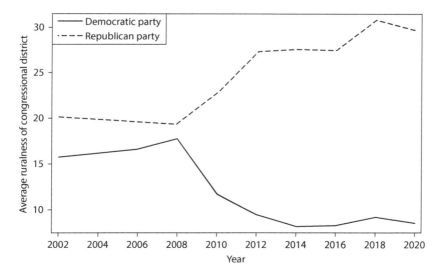

FIGURE 3.5 Average ruralness of congressional district, by party (2002–20)

Note: Using block-level measures of urbanicity, we calculate the percentage of residents living in each congressional district who are rural (living in nonurbanized blocks). Then, using historical elections data from Voteview: Congressional Roll-Call Votes Database (https://voteview.com), we calculate the average proportion of each congressional district that is rural, by the incumbent's partisanship.

of Congress. After the 2020 elections, the average House Democrat represented a district that was 8.4 percent rural; of the 233 Democratic members, 160—almost 70 percent of the party—represented very urban areas where virtually no rural residents lived.

An even more explicit story emerges when we look at state legislatures. As noted earlier, most state legislatures were controlled by Democrats when Ronald Reagan came to office; the New Deal coalition still held sway. But then things started to change, as noted in figure 3.6. Republican gains were remarkable starting around Barack Obama's first term in office.

A savvy reader might surmise that U.S. House and state legislative change were primarily a function of a realignment in the South. There is no doubt that the evaporation of the Democratic Solid South

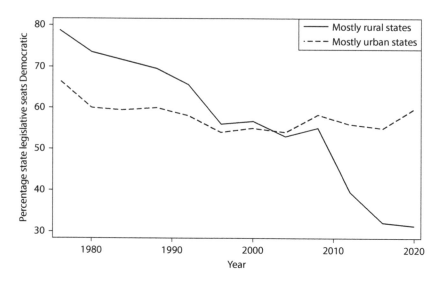

FIGURE 3.6 Percentage of seats in state legislature by state's percentage of rural population (1980–2020)

Note: Using block-level measures of urbanicity, we calculate the percentage of residents living in each state who are rural (living in nonurbanized blocks). "Mostly rural" states include the nineteen most rural states for a given year (the top third most rural), and "mostly urban" states include the seventeen most urbanized states for a given year (the bottom third most rural). Then, using historical elections data provided by the National Conference of State Legislatures (https://www.ncsl.org/), we calculate the average proportion of each state's legislature (both chambers, when applicable) that is controlled by the Democratic Party.

explains some of this trend. Less than one-third of House seats in the South were held by Republicans in 1980; by 2016, that figure had jumped to just under 80 percent. And yet, we find the rural-urban dynamic has even more explanatory power; the change is not merely a southern phenomenon. For example, a vast majority of the remaining House seats in the South that are controlled by Democrats are in the urban areas of the state. A good number of nonsouthern rural states used to regularly send Democratic legislators to Washington, but not anymore. Both North and South Dakota often elected Democrats to the House and Senate in the post–World War II era, which, of course, is not the case today.

We may also consider a few nonsouthern state legislatures. In 1976, some 57 percent of the seats in the Iowa state legislature (House and Senate combined) were controlled by Democrats. By 2020, that figure had dropped to 39 percent. In Montana, for the same years, it went from 55 to 34 percent; in Alaska, it went from 62 to 30 percent; and in Wyoming, the figure dropped from 45 percent to a mere 10 percent. Then, too, even within states that have the largest urban populations, a vast proportion of so-called rural seats in the state legislature are now controlled by GOP legislators. It is also pat, for instance, that legislators from Upstate New York are Republican—that is, except those from seats in urban centers like Albany, Syracuse, and Buffalo.

THE RURAL VOTER EMERGES

In the previous chapter, we told the story of the growing divide between rural and urban voters, but those divisions never materialized to form a national voting bloc. Nativist attitudes found fertile ground throughout rural America in the 1920s, for example, but equally potent localized cross-pressures pulled in different directions. Yankee Republican farmers of post–World War I America would have balked at the idea of forming a voting alliance with southern Democratic planters, and it is hard to imagine midwestern Populists joining ranks, in any sustained way, with plantation farmers back east or with their ranch cousins in the Rocky Mountain West. The data are clear: for nearly two centuries, both major political parties found support in rural America—often at the same time. There was no consistent rural voting bloc in American politics until the past few decades.

What happened? What forces nationalized the rural vote behind one party? This chapter offers evidence pointing to the larger change in conservative politics, which, while lacking a geographic basis, mattered for the cultivation of a rural vote. More important was the emergence of a "real America" narrative that solidified a rural identity behind the Republican Party. By the turn of the twenty-first century, rural

Americans were confronting a similar set of issues—from the decline of small-scale farming, to the disappearance of rural manufacturing, an aging population and population loss. Downtowns and village hubs were drying up, being replaced by the sprawling suburban mall miles away. Infrastructures were withering. Community churches struggled to keep the heat on. Kids moved away.

One need only drive through any of the countless small and midsize towns and villages in every region of the country to witness a decline indistinguishable from one place to another. There were a tragic number of suicides in rural communities throughout the 1980s, and later, the opioid epidemic hit these same places hard, really hard.[112] Declining prospects of future generations, highlighted by the Great Recession, shook all Americans, but rural residents responded to a political message that emphasized how America's future was in the cities and suburbs. To many, rural culture, the more traditional way of doing things, was under assault. This does not mean these communities were giving up or were shriveling away, only that rural communities from across the country faced the same storm clouds, and were willing to try new things and take a bet on an unconventional candidate.

While Trump's candidacy in 2016 was powerful—as was Clinton's unpopularity—the groundswell of changes and fermenting concerns had been percolating for years. Skillful operatives and savvy politicians saw the opening and took it. Kevin Phillips wrote the playbook, but Reagan (and a legion of his operatives), Christian evangelicals, Buchanan, and others crafted a narrative of real America that elevated the image of rural American values—all so they could pound the message that rural America was under assault.

The GOP first tried to capitalize on this deal by placing an unknown and untested Alaska governor on the presidential ticket. As one retrospective account retold, the ascent of Palin was a pivotal moment in American political history, "opening a Pandora's box of divisive, nativist, anti-intellectual, celebrity-driven smash-mouth politics."[113] Former Fox News anchor Megyn Kelly suggested Palin entered the national political scene as "almost a pre-Trump" and "electrified that GOP base like no one I had ever seen."[114] Don Gonyea of NPR remarked, "Meanwhile,

Donald Trump watched Palin's rise as she channeled—and fueled—the anger felt by many voters toward Washington."[115] For our concerns, it is safe to say that Palin's style and rhetoric hastened the rural-urban divide that was set in motion two decades earlier.

For nearly forty years, rural Americans were told that the earth below their feet was giving way due to ignorance and the indifference of coastal elites. Make no mistake, countless sources told them that real America was under assault, and the enemy were the Democrats. It took a few decades to coalesce, but by the time Barack Obama was running for reelection, the scope of success of this top-down strategy was made clear—and it has rocked American politics ever since.

At a 2014 American Farm Bureau Federation convention, Alan Robertson, cast member of the A&E reality show *Duck Dynasty*, told the group, "You realize that we have generations now that don't understand the concept of home, or family, or faith," he complained. "We got people growing up in huge neighborhoods in metropolitan areas that have no idea what you know, what I know."[116] A February 2022 survey published by the Morning Consult found that just 23 percent of rural voters said Democrats cared about their community more than did Republicans. Some 94 percent of Republicans (who made up the vast majority of the pool) had an unfavorable view of Democrats. There are policy differences between the parties, certainly, and those positions might lean rural communities toward the right. But that's not what is driving so many rural voters to GOP ranks. It is the ironclad belief that Democrats are, at best, out of touch and, more likely, hostile to the rural way of life.

Fundamental to this story is not simply the realignment of American party politics. Rather, something unique, something very different has transformed the hearts and minds of rural residents. They have become convinced that Democrats are not only wrong, but toxic. Even moderates or conservatives with long résumés and histories of public service in their state or community are dead in the water if there is "D" next to their name. The solution for many is to simply abandon the party altogether and run as independents—what some have started calling "Plan B."[117]

While we have stressed changes in the Republican Party, we should not overlook how much also falls on the backs of the Democrats themselves. In an op-ed, "How the Left Lost Its Heart," written a few years after the publication of his landmark book, Frank put the matter plainly: "The Republicans . . . were industriously fabricating their own class-based language of the right, and while they made their populist apparel to blue-collar voters, Democrats were giving those same voters . . . the big brush-off, ousting their representatives from positions within the party and consigning their issues, with a laugh and a sneer, to the dustbin of history. A more ruinous strategy for Democrats would be difficult to invent."[118]

The timid, uninspired response of the Democratic Party to these changes will play a leading role in this book's conclusion, as we outline what options might remain. For now, it is enough to say that the third piece—the indifference of Democratic elites—was the icing on the cake. The nationalized rural voter has been mixed, baked, and frosted.

4

LISTENING TO RURAL AMERICANS

I t can be pretty frustrating trying to link contemporary voting trends to historical conditions, especially since hard data about individual attitudes and opinions rarely exist further back in time. We can put our hands on troves of aggregate census and voting data and conduct content analyses of books, media reports, speeches, and campaign ads, but making a leap from this information to attitudes can be tricky. It can even lead us to conclusions that are downright wrong.

Consider what we know—or think we know—about Franklin D. Roosevelt's (FDR) historic victory in the 1932 presidential election. Unemployment rates were sky-high, bankruptcies were endemic, household discretionary incomes were minuscule, and industrial output had stalled. We know that FDR won a clear majority of voters, breaking the Republicans' decade-long hold on power. So it would make sense to infer that the state of the economy was foremost in the minds of voters when they cast their ticket for Roosevelt. This was the Great Depression, after all. Roosevelt was able to oust a sitting president, Herbert Hoover, because he offered better economic policies. As one prominent political scientist would write, "The 1932 election offers a perfect exhibit for the electoral influence of the economy."[1]

But do we really know what was in the minds of voters when they went into the polling booths in 1932? Yes, we know that support for

FDR was highest in communities where job loss was greatest. And yes, we know that after FDR and the Democratic Party oversaw a massive restructuring of the American economy and voters sent them back with even larger majorities in 1936. But is it possible that these economic influences coexisted alongside other issues—forces that were even more weighty to the average voter's decision making? The economy was bad, and FDR made the economy central to his campaign, but it was not the only thing going on in America, even if it is the thing scholars tend to emphasize years later by pointing to troves of aggregate data.

One way to sort out competing explanations and actually gauge voter sentiments is through polling, but modern survey research did not emerge in any systematic way until the 1940s. Students in any college research methods class will hear of the great fail by *Literary Digest* in 1936, when the magazine used telephone books and automobile owner lists to poll voters, only to conclude that Alf Landon would win in a landslide. Of course, most Roosevelt voters did not have phones and cars!

And yet, social scientists were treated to a rare gift in 2018: the uncovering of a large-scale survey from the 1932 election. The poll was conducted for Herbert Hoover's team by the marketing firm of J. David Houser and Associates. It was a confidential survey, with no record of its publication. It was surprisingly sophisticated: "Unlike straw polls as conducted by the notorious *Literary Digest*, the Houser Poll obtained a sample of respondents in a way that matched the demography of the American electorate. A total of 5,235 respondents were interviewed."[2]

What, then, were voters really focused on as they entered the voting booth? The economy, as we commonly think, or something else? "The most striking revelation of the Houser Poll," the political scientist Helmut Norpoth discovered, "is that the Depression was not the dominant issue for American voters in the 1932 election as is commonly assumed. It had a potent rival in the issue of Prohibition. The American people overwhelmingly favored repeal."[3] In fact, the American electorate was not especially "gloom and doom," nor did they think Hoover was doing a particularly bad job managing the economy or that FDR's policies would make the Depression go away. Rather, most Americans were tired of

Prohibition; they wanted to have a legal drink and understood Roosevelt and the Democrats would more likely make that happen. Many things were going on in 1932, and even though the Great Depression is historically paramount in our memory of the time, our projections onto the past do not change what really motivated voters at the polls.

How does this cautionary tale aid our investigation about rural politics? The aim of this book is to detail foundational differences between rural and urban voters and, in doing so, reveal the forces that have led to the novel political landscape we confront. Part of that argument rests on a deep dive into the history of the rural-urban gap. Our historical election data get us to where we are today and tell us that what we are seeing is the culmination of a decades-long process of rural residents coalescing into a distinct voting bloc. Our data are clear: this is an unprecedented pattern. But an even larger issue remains: why does it continue today? What attitudes and behaviors are driving the rural voter?

To answer that question, we turned to survey research to help us better understand the forces that currently roil the country. In chapters 2 and 3, we did what scholars must always do in the absence of individual-level data: we made some inferences about why rural voters were joining together after 1980—Reagan, NAFTA, Palin, and so on—and why they did not emerge as a distinctive segment of the electorate earlier in American history—regional differences, racial divides, and more. We are pretty confident in that story especially since we were able to dig into some survey research after 1980 that, however sporadic, validated many of the patterns we identified in our historical data after the rural voter emerged. And yet, we can be extremely confident in that story only if we are able to tie those patterns to an even greater amount of survey data— objective information we can collect in our own time and consider alongside the most recent developments in rural partisanship.

There is a lot at stake here, even when data such as our county-level measure show an unambiguous pattern. Rural voters supported Donald Trump in 2016 and 2020 more than any other Republican candidate in history; aggregate data show that. But why? Aggregate statistics just do not tell you. It may be easy to look at Trump's campaign rhetoric on immigration, his policies on trade, and his demeanor and disdain for political correctness and assume that this is what drove rural voters to the polls. Lots of journalist and scholars have done just that. But that assumption would be no different than looking around in 1932, noting the long bread lines, and equating support for FDR with attitudes about the economy. Unless you talk to people, you risk getting it wrong.

COMPOSITION EFFECTS AND SURVEY RESEARCH

Let us clarify for a moment that this is not just a historical problem. If we rely only on aggregate, or group-level, data, we risk making the same mistakes about rural voters as we do when talking about any group of people that, while similar on one dimension, are different on many others. All FDR voters had one thing in common; they confronted a national economy in tatters. But their reasons for supporting Roosevelt varied. The same is true of rural voters and why they vote Republican.

Sure, for statistical purposes, it is useful to demarcate specific locales on the map as rural or urban. When all those different people behave the same way, we can spot and measure trends that encompass the entire group. But sometimes our understanding of the group can lead to faulty conclusions about the individuals. Social scientists like to call these bad conclusions "ecological fallacies."[4]

You have already read about one ecological fallacy, which was widely touted in the aftermath of the 2016 election: Hillary Clinton's insistence that she won the places moving ahead while Trump won the places moving behind. Look at a map of those places, and you could muster evidence to support her statement. But that is not to say the conclusion is factually right, either. The places, in general, had some similar characteristics—they generally voted for Clinton and generally made more money. But what about the people living in those places; were they all the same? Of course not.

Now, if you were to take every county that Hillary Clinton won and sum the gross domestic product across all those counties, you would get a distribution like the one in figure 4.1. Pretty nice if you are Clinton, right?

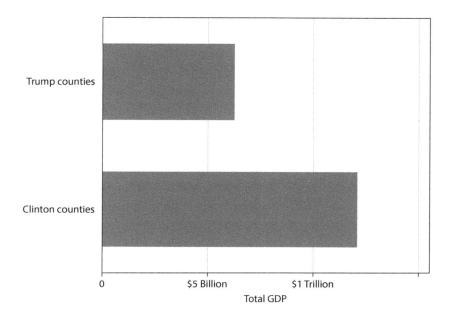

FIGURE 4.1 Total share of U.S. gross domestic product by Trump and Clinton counties in 2016

> *Note*: Figure illustrates the total contribution to national GDP in counties where Hillary Clinton won the most votes in 2016 compared with counties where Donald Trump won the most votes.

The counties she won have a nearly two to one advantage in economic productivity, or, if economic output were votes, we would be looking at a Clinton presidency back in 2016.

However, Clinton was actually committing a mistake similar to Trump's when he celebrated the number of counties he won or the one many analysts make when they take so-called small states and equate that with ruralness. Neither accounts for the fact that these places contain lots of different people; they are composed of complex attitudes and behaviors. What is true, on average, of the group (or place) is not necessarily true of the individuals living and voting there. When we make geographic comparisons, we tend to overlook the fact that geographies—counties, state, countries—contain people . . . lots of them. And in the case of the

2016 election, a lot of those people living in so-called Clinton counties did not vote for Ms. Clinton. They did, however, contribute to that country's GDP.

The basic problem is that the geographies we work with and compare with one another have lots of variation. And sometimes, even though this helps us make comparisons when other types of data are lacking, the analysis can be misleading.

To illustrate, let us change the comparison from one strictly about different places to one about different individuals living in those places. One way to do this is to let only Clinton voters in each Clinton-winning-county contribute to GDP. That will mean Trump voters, who are also a part of those high-performing places, do not get to contribute to Clinton's GDP totals when they happen to live in places she won.

The math is straightforward. We multiply each county's GDP by the vote share Hillary Clinton received in 2016. We then sum the GDP for each county including only Clinton voters' contributions; if Clinton won 60 percent of the vote share in a county, we take 60 percent of the county's GDP and add it to her total. We can then compare Trump and Clinton's share of GDP by taking each of their totals as a percentage of the country's overall GDP.

This significantly cuts down on Clinton's advantage (figure 4.2). In 2016, 48 percent of voters went for Clinton—and Clinton voters were responsible for 53 percent of the country's GDP. Democrats have the advantage, sure, but it is hardly anything to make noise about. Trump won lots of people living in places moving ahead. Nor was Clinton's share of GDP exceptionally large compared with previous Democratic candidates, whose voters have always made up more than their fair share of GDP since 2004. In fact, although 2016 was an exceptional election, which exposed deep rifts in the country, in terms of partisan GDP, it was not as lopsided as it has been in the past, and the divide hardly seems to constitute a tragic rift between voters within the two parties' coalitions.

But wait—we still have not measured the actual behavior of individuals. We also know, for instance, that the wealthiest people in the United States tend, on average, to vote Republican. In 2016, 48 percent of individuals

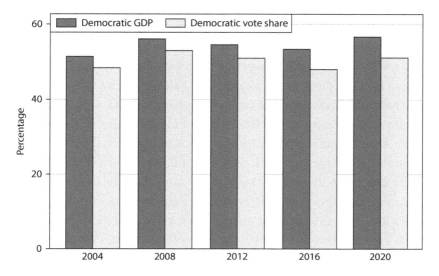

FIGURE 4.2 Democratic contributions to GDP and Democratic presidential vote share (2004–20)

Note: Figure illustrates the total contribution to national GDP in counties where the Democratic candidate for president won, weighted by the proportion of Democrats in that county (darkly shaded bar). The lightly shaded bar indicates the proportion of the national vote that went to the Democratic candidate.

making over $250,000 per year voted for Trump, while just 46 percent of those high earners voted for Clinton. Trump had an advantage among all voters making above $50,000 per year.[5] GDP is not the same as income; it is a socially produced "good." And yet, to the extent those incomes would mean that Republicans, on average, may contribute to GDP at a higher rate, our earlier assumptions do not reflect these differences among individuals. We have allowed Republicans and Democrats to contribute equally to a county's GDP, but this is not true at an individual level. The typical Republican voter's share to a county's GDP is most likely higher than a Democrat's average share. So, even if we make a better comparison, we still do not accurately capture individual-level differences.

And there is one additional piece of the puzzle. Clinton seemed to be suggesting the rationale for her strong support in these areas sprang from voters concerned about growth, opportunity, development. They picked her over Trump because she better represented the future. Some of that was probably true, but we cannot know with certainty. Maybe it was not about economic prosperity, but a hatred for Trump. The lessor of two evils? In short, geography can feed self-serving myths.

There is, of course, evidence in the aggregate data to suggest that rural voters perceive themselves to be unique and different from those who live elsewhere. Often, geographic comparisons give us clues about large changes affecting the many individuals involved. And the rural-urban gap in partisanship is clearly a visible clue of big changes in American politics. But why is that the case? We know rural America is whiter than the national average. We know that if you live in a rural area, you are less likely to have a college degree. We also know non-college-educated whites are more likely to vote Republican—at least in recent elections—regardless of where they live. So, is rural America "redder" because voters out there perceive themselves as different—a distinct group of people who, given the current message of the Republican Party, view this as their best way forward? Or is it the case that rural America is composed of different groups of people who tend to want to vote Republican? Do the people living in rural America actually differ in any meaningful way from those living elsewhere because they are, in fact, rural?

It is critical to sort out the difference between the "composition effect hypothesis" and our own argument about rural identity. There is no "rural voter" or rural-urban divide if geographic differences are driven solely by composition effects—that is, the fact that rural areas are just composed of different groups of people, such as whites or non-college educated voters.[6] Put a bit differently, it is theoretically possible that rural-urban differences boil down to the fact that there are more ideological conservatives living there than the average suburb or the city, or more whites, or more evangelicals. If that is the case, then "ruralness" is not actually an identity; what motivates a person in the countryside to vote Republican is the same as what motivates voters in Queens, New York or Orange County, California (where, collectively, almost one million persons voted for Trump). Overcoming the divide, too, would require different prescriptions—a focus on the group's other characteristics and not their so-called ruralness.

Unsurprisingly, as we will show in the remainder of this book, these divisions are not merely the result of having higher concentrations of Republican-leaning groups in rural America. But we do not take that problem for granted. Proving that the rural-urban divide is more than just composition effects has been a challenge—one we set out to overcome by moving beyond aggregate data, such as census figures or vote returns, and turning to survey research.

The only way to overcome the problem of making assumptions about individuals from the group they belong to is to survey people—a lot of them. That is why we conducted the Rural Voter Survey, the largest survey of rural voters ever undertaken. A wide variety of demographic data tell us what rural America looks like and how it stacks up against other areas in the United States. But until the Rural Voter Survey, those numbers gave us little insight into whether or not rural Americans see themselves differently.

It may seem a bit strange and academic to rest our account on this methodological problem. After all, J. D. Vance lived his tale of rural struggles, right? And Thomas Wuthnow, the author of a widely noted book about the collapse of rural communities, saw what he saw.[7] If economic desperation and communal collapse are present in rural areas, and rural areas support figures like Donald Trump, it seems a bit unnecessary to ask people how they perceive themselves vis-à-vis urban voters. Why spend so much time and effort to dive deeper?

It makes all the difference. If we are to understand the rural-urban divide primarily as a result of composition effects we would vastly oversimplify the American electorate, with dangerous implications. Doing so would fail to consider the intersection of multiple identities and group loyalties. It may have been true twenty years ago, but today, the gaps in partisanship—the intensity of support for the Republican Party in rural America—vastly exceeds what a higher concentration of white, old, and non-college-educated voters would produce. Composition effects may have explained rural-urban differences before, but no longer.

Conflating "rural" with other demographics, particularly whiteness, is especially toxic in American politics, given the centuries-long struggle to secure a modicum of political equality between whites and nonwhites. When rural simply becomes white, the conclusion, according to Brookings scholar Andre M. Perry, is that "Democrats [need] to better understand and empathize with rural voters and the working class—as if there are no Black and brown working-class people living in small towns. What's destructive about these takes is the unstated assumption that the country can't heal if white Americans aren't accommodated first."[8] That is precisely the problem if ruralness becomes nothing more than whiteness, or elderly-ness, or any other demographic pattern imposed on rural Americans without accounting for their different perceptions, values, and ideas.[9]

One danger, which motivated us to write this book, has been muddling of "conservatism" with "ruralness." Again, more Trump voters live in big cities than in all of rural America combined. These analytical errors risk further isolating rural America from mainstream partisan politics, playing into political rhetoric that is beneficial only to those seeking office. It neglects that the rural-urban divide is not just the consequence of some distant sociological or economic forces reigning over small-town life.

WHO AND WHAT TO ASK?

Little survey research exists on rural voters, although scholars have started to take the subject much more seriously since the 2016 presidential election. While the rural-urban divide is a major issue today, it was not always the case in the past. With the rise of globalization—the "flattening" of our world—prominent political scientists dismissed the need for thinking about how attitudes vary over geography.[10] In fact, the leading survey used by political scientists, the American National Election Studies (ANES), a whole host of demographic characteristics, but stopped asking people about where they lived in 2000! As we comb through historical newspaper archives, seldom do we find the major polling firms reporting their findings by geography. We get lots of other "controls," including occupation, race, gender, age, education, and so on, but rarely is geography part of the list.

Sometimes we got lucky, like with our example of the 1932 election noted earlier. Relying on the massive set of commercial and academic surveys collected by the Roper Center at Cornell University, we were able to gain insight into the historical emergence of the rural voter since 1980. We went back to the raw data and parsed out respondents' locations to understand the ways in which voters differed and, almost more importantly, did not differ over the last forty years. And although political scientists dropped community context from their models, fortunately, one other major survey, largely used by sociologists—the General Social Survey (GSS)—includes a measure of residency that enables us to identify rural from urban voters consistently. These data offer rich detail for our historical analysis, largely in chapter 3.

Still, none of these past surveys offers many detailed questions on the dimensions of a rural identity. So in the lead-up to the 2020 presidential election, we launched the Rural Voter Survey as part of a multiyear effort to understand the rural-urban divide.

Two weeks before Election Day, we conducted a 3,000-person national survey of voter attitudes to better understand what was driving voters' decisions in the moment. We saw the rural-urban divide present in the first of these waves. Our findings were near spot-on with national exit polls and county-level returns showing Trump exceeding his share of the rural vote, sometimes by double digits, in the course of four years. Clearly, something was going on in rural America, and it was unlikely to go away, we thought.

And so, a few months later, in June 2021, we launched what is, at this point, the largest survey ever fielded specifically to capture the attitudes of rural Americans. In that wave alone, we surveyed over 10,000 Americans, more than 7,600 of whom lived in rural areas. Then again, in the spring of 2022, we fielded another national survey, once more oversampling rural voters, capturing an additional 1,800 rural responses.

TABLE 4.1 Demographic distribution of the Rural Voter Survey (three waves)

	November 2020	June 2021	June 2022
Number of (unweighted):			
Rural respondents	571	7,683	1,855
Suburban respondents	891	1,855	1,006
Urban respondents	1,660	1,229	985
Average county-level ruralness measure			
Rural respondents	52.79%	56.61%	59.90%
Suburban respondents	16.81%	10.70%	11.34%
Urban respondents	6.15%	7.18%	8.92%
Percentage rural respondents (weighted):			
White	86.3%	87.25%	86.68%
College-educated	28.66%	24.76%	25.76%
Below 35 years old	31.86%	24.82%	25.85%
Over 65 years old	18.47%	20.13%	19.81%
Voted for Trump	60.66%	62.38%	60.80%
Northeast	15.31%	12.80%	13.85%
Midwest	24.09%	29.22%	27.33%
South	47.4%	45.89%	44.11%
West	13.20%	12.10%	14.71%

Note: Table lists the weighted and unweighted demographics for the three primary samples composing the Rural Voter Survey.

But who is rural? In our aggregate study of historical voting patterns, we took great pains to carefully construct a measure of ruralness that is sensitive to the wide-ranging ways in which rural communities exist—both at a single point in time and over time. With survey research, our task is a bit easier. We simply ask, "Which of the following best describes the area you live in? Urban, suburban, or rural?" We know that these terms—rural, suburban, and urban—are not widely used in everyday conversation, so we also gave respondents some clues as to what we were trying to get at: "Urban—Densely populated, city or large town; Suburban—Mainly residential, bordering a city or large town; Rural—Sparsely populated, small town or village." On top of that, we asked them to confirm their characterization early in the survey by inquiring about their specific town—the place listed on their physical mailing address. In other words, if our records indicated that the respondent was from Meadville, Pennsylvania, we asked them to describe that place—Meadville.

But why not use their actual physical location if you have it—which we do? As Zoe Nemerever and Melissa Rogers have argued in an extensive study of this very topic, "Researchers should not assume that people who live in rural areas self-identify as rural or that people living in non-rural areas do not identify as rural. This is an unfounded assumption that could undermine both conceptual understanding and empirical findings."[11] Truth be told, the vast majority of respondents who have an urban mailing address said that they lived in an urban area—and the vast majority of respondents who have a rural mailing address said they were rural residents. But not everyone—not the college student studying far away from their home in the countryside, or the retired pensioner who, while loving all that space out West, still roots for the Mets every chance they are on T.V. People move, but their loyalties, or identities, can stay the same.

Using our county-level measure of ruralness introduced in the first part of this book, we know that the average "urban" person in our survey lived in a county where just around 7 percent of the county population lived in nonurban area. That is a very urban place by our measure, and it is an urban place by our respondents' perceptions. Same with rural. Most rural Americans do not live in the most sparsely populated counties in the country. Counties where every single person lives in a rural area are rare. Fewer than 20 percent of all rural Americans live in a county where 90 percent or more of all residents live in a nonurban census block. A majority of rural residents live in 642 counties—many of them quite large—where a hefty percentage of residents in that same county do not live in rural communities. For example, Worcester County, Massachusetts, is a sprawling county with more than 860,000 residents. Only 21 percent of residents in that county are defined as rural residents, but because the county is so large, that comes out to nearly 200,000 people. There are more rural residents in this county than any other, and it is not a "rural county," on average.

Now, using our measure of county ruralness, we would not call the county as a whole "rural," but we would not be surprised if someone from rural Worcester answered our survey and, indeed, identified as a rural resident; in fact, we surveyed nineteen rural residents from Worcester County, Massachusetts. All that is to say, we are not at all surprised that, on average, our typical rural resident lives in a county that is pretty rural but not overwhelmingly rural. The typical rural resident in the Rural Voter Survey lives in a county where about 55 percent of their fellow county residents live in a nonurban block.[12]

So there it is—thousands of interviews conducted over two years. Honesty compels us to admit, however, that polling has taken a hit lately—especially given the huge miss in 2016 that predicted that Hillary Clinton would sail into the White House. Yes, there have been problems and built-in biases with survey research since the start of scientific polling. Those limitations have become even more problematic in recent years for a host of reasons, not the least of which has been the near disappearance of landline telephones and the invention of caller ID. When is the last time you picked up the phone for some unknown number and told a stranger your deepest thoughts?

The Rural Voter Survey, however, avoids several of these problems. First, our surveys are not meant to predict elections. The largest problem confronting pollsters has to do with the fact that in 2016, and especially 2020, our ability to accurately predict who would and would not show up on Election Day was challenged.[13] Each news organization and academic uses a different "likely voter model," which means there is a bit of guesswork involved in horse-race polling. And sometimes, they guess wrong. Fortunately, we do not have such uncertainty in our work, as we are not trying to predict elections in the future, but instead explain what has already happened. We simply asked whether rural respondents voted. And, if they did, they were a "rural voter." No "maybe/somewhat likely to turnout next November" problem here. We recognize, however, that self-reported voting might inflate actual turnout measures a tiny bit due to what scholars call the social desirability effect. (People tend to say they voted, even when they did not.).

On the other hand, large random sample surveys eliminate over-reliance on certain types of residents. In our research, we uncover a small group of rural residents who are anxious to proclaim their allegiance to Trump and to espouse hard-right policy positions at every turn. We discuss this group, dub the rural rabble rousers, in chapter 9, and suggest too many journalists and even scholars zero in on their opinions and behaviors leading biased, unrealistic accounts. In our surveys each respondent represents a single data point, regardless of their eagerness to be heard.

Of course, there are others problems confronting survey researchers. A big one has to do with low response rates on telephone surveys.[14] Fortunately for us, about ten years ago, large multinational corporations realized there was an untapped source of information they could use to test new slogans, brands, and commercials—men and women sitting in front of computers. Today, most survey research for marketing, general research, and politics is done online, not over the phone. Online surveys encourage broad-based participation in a way the phone calls never could: they pay money. They do not just call you asking you to give up part of your day; you opt in and get something in return. Internet utilities, corporations, and big news media outlets have all found it profitable to recruit ordinary Americans into survey "panels." These are groups of people from all walks of life who, at the click of a button, can get a survey sent straight to their inbox or with a push notification on their mobile phone. People join these panels because they get rewarded. Some get a percentage off their utility bill for completing a number of surveys, while others may get points they can put toward magazine subscriptions or gift cards. Those rewards get paid from the companies' coffers—which is much easier, and likely more reliable, than hiring a phone bank, like in the old days, to call a bunch of random digits.

There is always excess capacity in these panels, and researchers, like us, have been buying into them for the last few years. For businesses, millions of dollars may be invested or sold on the results of these panels. For academics, dozens of high-quality peer-reviewed scholarly articles are published each year based on panel surveys of this sort.[15] These panels also can give us insights into what average Americans think beyond which shade of red the next diet soda label should be.

In politics, one of the most visible panel-based online surveys is You-Gov, and no doubt you have seen results reported from other companies, such as IPSOS. Untold media outlets report their findings from these opt-in panels each month. They have tremendous advantages, allowing us to reach Americans where they are at. Online polls reduce sampling bias, get a more diverse group of individuals to take surveys, and the veil of behind-the-screen anonymity likely generates more honest opinions.

We bought into a set of panels managed by Lucid (now CINT), which specializes in bringing together multiple panels, managed by hundreds of providers, into one. They calibrate these panels to guard against overlap (e.g., same person on two panels taking two different surveys) and prevent individuals known to rush through surveys from participating in subsequent trials. We developed our own set of criteria for who we wanted to take our survey and how well our sample would mirror rural America. Traditionally, it is common to collect a sample using criteria pegged to the national census—or quota sampling. Given the fact that we needed to reach thousands of rural residents, who are often overlooked when relying solely on national, census-based criteria, we employed a different strategy. We used the U.S. Census Department's 2018 American Community Survey to generate new quotas based on regional demographic characteristics of rural areas. We took each of our respondents who identified as a rural resident and then adjusted, or "weighted," some of those responses so our regional estimates for rural respondents matched our census data. We did the same for nonrural respondents. In other words, we made sure that respondents from the rural South reflected what we know about the rural South's racial and ethnic diversity (fewer white respondents than on average, more Black residents than on average).

We made sure the age profiles of our survey data mirrored that of what you might actually find in rural America (i.e., they are older). Funnily enough, that works contrary to how you may think. Old people love taking online surveys; it's the young folk who can be harder to find and who we have to "weigh up" for our sample to match the known population characteristics.

We weighed our data on nearly a dozen characteristics and then excluded anyone who did not vote in the 2020 presidential election.

Ultimately, we care about politics. And if you don't vote, we can't really say your voice matters for what we are trying to explain.

But even if online samples are commonly used in high-profile national polls, you may be wondering, isn't that biased against places with limited internet connectivity? That is, if rural residents have less access to broadband internet, which is true, would certain types of rural Americans be missing in our data? Good question! We were worried about this, too. But in reality, while some rural residents do not have access to high-speed internet, smartphones with data connections are ubiquitous across rural America. We know internet connectivity makes a difference for schooling and growing the economy, which is why expanding broadband access matters for rural communities. But rural America is more connected than you think. Like many parts of the world that lack high-speed internet, phones fill the gap. Our survey enabled respondents to complete these surveys over their phone—and almost half, from all parts of the country, did so. In fact, the Rural Voter Survey was specifically designed to facilitate mobile phone use. Most survey research is not done just online these days; about half of all surveys—in rural, suburban, and urban America—are taken on the phone in someone's pocket.

In sum, the Rural Voter Survey has done what no other scholar of American politics (or journalist) has so far done—survey nearly 14,000 Americans, upward of 10,000 of whom were rural voters across the country, within a small period of time.

Beginning in the next chapter, we report what they told us. We detail the questions we asked, with the specific wording and instrumentation used. We will mainly report the percentages of various responses, but we have also developed models used to see how various answers and attitudes relate to one another. You will note that we often used the exact questions found on other leading surveys—Gallup, YouGov—as a way of validating our own sample.

Our methodologically intricate and unique approach would be something to celebrate if not for the fact that it has unearthed a real danger confronting the United States—a danger we now turn our attention to in each of the remaining chapters.

5

DOWN AND OUT IN RURAL AMERICA?

Route 17 stretches the entire length of North Carolina. Driving south through the Great Dismal Swamp, it feels as if one is entering the "real" South. Tobacco and soybean fields stretch for miles on your right, crisscrossing the state all the way until they brush up against the Appalachian mountains. You know a family has been there for generations when you see the fields brush right up next to the double-wide—hardly a lawn to mow—or when the old farmhouse is just a few yards from the highway. On your left, you are never more than a thirty-minute drive from the Atlantic Ocean and, if you know where to look, a local fisherman who is still selling shrimp out of the back of his pickup truck on the side of the road. It is a beautiful drive, but there is no denying this is a poor part of the country. Near the end of the state road stands a large rectangular warehouse—home to the former Holden Farms Market. Well before farmers' markets were all the rage in the suburbs and chic urban neighborhoods, Holden Farms was simply a place where locals could get fresh greens, some homemade pimento cheese, and, without a doubt, the best tomato sandwich south of the Mason-Dixon line.

Two brothers—David and Kelly—started the market in 1984 when the only thing you could find on Route 17 were Baptist churches and a few small gas stations. The land they built on was so old, they could trace it back through their ancestors to a grant their family received from King George II in 1756. Farmers, fishermen, and some retirees kept the place afloat.[1] But over the last forty years, the local community in Brunswick County exploded, jumping from just 35,000 full-time residents to nearly 150,000: hundreds of new golf course communities were now within an hour's drive, thousands of new beachfront homes, new amenities (all on paved roads!), sit-down restaurants, and shops catering to the seasonal influx of cash that arrived before Memorial Day and stayed put through the Indian summers of September. Route 17 was just two lanes back then; today, parts stretch into six. More people, more business, more money.

Holden Farms closed in 2020, ten years after the Census Bureau declared that Brunswick County was no longer a "rural community." According to family members, business was at an all-time high. Abandoned by David's and Kelly's family members, in the months following David's death, nobody wanted to take on the work. It was hard. Early mornings, unpredictable harvests, and a grueling pace that never stopped. It was simply easier to get one of the new nine-to-five jobs installing cable boxes for the newly moved-in family, or commuting to North Myrtle Beach to manage rental properties.[2] A new family— immigrants from El Salvador—bought the building and rebranded it. Driving south, look right for the sign, "Lucky Day Produce: Faith, Love, Hope."

This little piece of America epitomizes much of what is taking place all over the country. Although it is not the most rural community out there, thousands of rural residents live there, trying to adjust to a new reality of their "former" rural community. It epitomizes the fact that for them, rural America is poor, but it is changing. Rural America is no longer just farms and agriculture; its economy is rapidly diversifying. Rural Americans still value hard work and long hours, but they need immigrant labor to do the jobs that many simply won't. Rural America is a bit more complex than what many may tell you, especially when it comes to its relationship with government and the economy.

It is easy to tell a story of rural decline and rural poverty; that bit has become almost pat. It is what one hears when trying to describe the story of rural America's move toward the Republican Party: rural America is reacting to changes in the broader global economy, shifts that have lifted millions out of poverty but have left rural communities reeling in its wake. Aggrieved, desperate, uneducated, and poor, rural Americans have lashed out against globalization, immigration, and the federal government, which has seemingly made it all possible. Disconnected from the global economy, they failed to see how the rising tide of global trade lifted all boats. Unwilling to adapt—either by moving to cities or getting more education and new skills—they got left behind.

What's worse, according to Thomas Frank's widely read account of Republican partisanship (*What's the Matter with Kansas?*), rural residents never seemed willing or able to connect the dots between their economic misery and the candidates who turned their backs as soon as they were elected: Rural residents, Frank writes, would "vote to stop abortion; receive a rollback in capital gains taxes. Vote to make our country strong again; receive deindustrialization. . . . Vote to strike a blow against elitism; receive a social order in which wealth is more concentrated than ever before in our lifetimes, in which workers have been stripped of power and CEOs are rewarded in a manner beyond imagining."[3]

So the story goes that, caught with their backs against a wall, rural America lashed out, but not in a productive way—a manner that would soothe their economic woes. One can imagine the sons and daughters of David and Kelly looking out at the changing rural landscape, nervous about where their future stood. Immigrants coming into town, driving wages down. Chinese companies buying up old farmland to convert to subdivisions, where New York pensioners—read "LIBERAL!"—would come to retire in droves. Rather than electing politicians who would invest in schools (giving kids a chance to get jobs in new-tech industries), expand infrastructure (making it easier to develop and expand), or shore up flailing welfare programs, they voted out of anger. That's why Republicans do so well, so we have read about time and time again: they tricked them yokels to vote against their economic self-interest!

Yes, and no. Consider the Holden family once again. Stand in the parking lot of the old Holden Farms and stare across the highway. Yes, it is true that in a nearby neighborhood, one in four adults lack a high school education; they simply dropped out of school. Nearby, just 10 percent of adults have a bachelor's degree or better.[4] Of course, that community cannot compete in a digital age. What new Silicon Valley offshoot would open a shop there? Even with massive amounts of money poured into nearby job-training programs, what work would you even be able to find? Most of the population growth has come from retirees on fixed incomes—hardly a model for economic development, save the countless new health clinics and golf courses. Tourists come and go, year in and year out, but it is a volatile business; a single bad weekend in late August can sink a store's entire bottom line. Just like the thousands of rural communities we survey in this book, this little rural hamlet in southern North Carolina would be a risky bet in our global economy.

It wasn't as if Holden Farms was about to go under; business was brisk. And although the owners sold the family store, none of the immediate descendants have willingly left the community their family has called home for almost three hundred years. They all had jobs. Even if it meant a longer commute to one of the shoreline communities, there were means to get by. In fact, there were many signs to suggest that things were improving—just maybe not the way the Holdens and, as it turns out, millions of rural residents may want.

As goes rural North Carolina, so goes the rest of rural America. This chapter will demonstrate that economic deprivation does very little to explain the lock that the Republican Party has in these communities. Likewise, unlike Frank and other mainstream political scientists, we will argue that rural voters—however poor and economically marginalized they may or may not be—are, in fact, connecting their economic situation to policies and politicians that make really good sense to them. They are not voting against their interests, if you understand that their interests are very different from what others may think—especially those who do not live in rural communities. Rather, by and large, rural residents are telling themselves a different story about government, why economic growth seems confined to urban areas (even when it's not), and what they think the future may bring to the places they call home. The trick is to understand those stories.

We should be clear. There are deep pockets of poverty in rural America. In fact, about an hour inland from Holden Farms, you will probably see a level of poverty that many Americans would find unimaginable—more like it was in a developing country on some other continent than a half-day's drive from Washington, D.C. And yet, there is also deep poverty in urban America—just a few blocks down from the nation's Capitol Building! Economic deprivation alone does not account for the changes we documented earlier in this book: the development of a national rural constituency and their overwhelming support of Republican candidates. Something else has happened.

We suggest that while deprivation alone cannot distinguish rural residents from Americans living elsewhere, the way that rural residents experience economic deprivation is fundamentally different from those living in urban and suburban communities. Unlike city dwellers or those living in suburbia, rural residents are especially attuned to inequality and economic progress in their immediate communities simply because those are more integrated places. The fact that rural areas are more economically integrated—poor living next to non-poor—means that an individual's success matters less when thinking about politics. As a result, the narratives of rural deprivation and decline that have brought thousands of rural communities together have morphed into a larger, now national story of a struggling rural America.

That is how economic decline has mattered in rural America and whatever sense of lost hope, alienation, or anger rural residents supposedly feel as a result. First, we show that by a host of objective standards, it would be unfair to say that today, rural America is more economically deprived than other places. There is no doubt that more global trade and the technology revolution gutted manufacturing across America. As we will show, the decline of manufacturing jobs in America has been dramatic—and it was especially devastating for countless small mill towns. This change—the rise of the NAFTA ghost town—helped drive the rural voter into the GOP ranks. And yet, while the jarring consequences of factory closures and free trade can still be felt in the countryside, there is also evidence of leveling off and, in some places, renewal. At the very least, rural places may be a bit less well-off than urban America, but the similarity between these different types of communities begs the question as to why they vote so differently. The initial impetus, sure. But why now?

We find that because rural residents experience economic deprivation as a community, historic economic loss and hardship have helped develop a strong sense of rural identity—a collective sense of belonging that is really independent from one's own economic well-being. Consequently, large majorities of rural residents—even those who are doing fine today—come to see themselves as part of a larger story of economic fragility. Given the dramatic shifts of the last few decades, there is a deep-seated, grinding unease - a dark cloud on the horizon that threatens their community and beloved way of life. Rural residents are much more likely to say that kids growing up in the community will have to move away to live productive lives, and that children living nearby will have a better life than their parents. That type of community-oriented thinking is central to our take on the rural economy, and is a powerful reason why rural voters have developed a sense of shared, place-based destiny.

We do not see the same patterns outside rural America, where poverty is less integrated into the full community. We repeat: a case can be made on both sides as to whether rural America is actually suffering more than urban America. But, as we have said throughout the book, attitudes, beliefs and even gut feelings are what count in politics. And the perception that rural communities are being unfairly held back and sacrificed for the betterment of others—particularly those living outside rural communities—is there.

Those feelings of resentment and anxiety are an extension of rural grievance. This is more than semantics. By "grievance," we mean there is evidence that a sense of rural solidarity around economic issues and government manifests even when there is no "other" to blame or resent. There need not be a bad actor or a scapegoat for rural Americans to develop this sense of place-based solidarity. Indeed, similar to how women, Latino, and Black Americans develop a sense of collective belonging, we find evidence of a similar linked fate in rural America.[5] When scholars use the idea of "linked fate," they stress not just that we all belong and find meaning in the groups we identify with: I am a professor, I am white, I listen to bluegrass . . . Rather, such feelings carry over into a belief that my own personal success in life is tied to the success of the group.

We will show that this mentality exists, particularly around a shared sense that rural ways of life are becoming increasingly difficult to live. Just as linked fate is a notoriously difficult concept to measure, we also rely on multiple indicators of grievance to bolster this finding.[6]

Grievance is therefore central to our understanding of rural politics, and it is hard to discuss rural culture, social capital, or even racial resentment without first making sense of this foundational bond. We will consider it first within the context of rural economies, where it is easiest to explain. Where others look to economic explanations and emphasize the material conditions—the facts on the ground or the money in peoples' wallets—we see complex narratives that rural residents weave for themselves about how they fit into the larger economy and the reasons they give for why they are deprived, even when their deprivation isn't uniformly felt among all rural residents—and even when it is not all that much worse than elsewhere in the United States.

Grievance helps us explain lower levels of formal education alongside minimal desire to spend more on public education. Grievance helps us make sense of the prevailing skepticism toward policy makers and government experts who claim to know how to "fix" the rural economy but who may never have stepped foot in a mine, cut hay, or worked with their hands. Grievance makes us pause and rethink the decision to close up a thriving business like Holden Farms. Was it impossible to keep the lights on? Or did it just make better sense to sell the fields to the next developer moving into town? And yes, even with that nice little windfall, it sure does hurt to have to sell the family farm and see others have to do the same.

Grievance, we will show, ultimately explains why rural voters are so hostile to the Democratic Party and why Republican politicians are so eager to exploit the feelings of mistrust and anxiety that bring rural voters to the polls year after year.

RURAL ECONOMIES THEN AND NOW

Economics looms large in American politics, as it has since the very beginning. In the opening line of Alexis de Tocqueville's *Democracy in America*, published in 1835, he reports that nothing struck him more forcibly than "the general equality of condition among the people," a "fundamental fact from which all others seem to be derived." Setting aside Blacks (both slave and nonslave) and those lacking "sobriety and industry," he found great opportunity for success. "Scratch a rich American," said Tocqueville, and you will find a poor boy."[7] By the end of the nineteenth century, the "by your bootstraps" mythology had become ingrained in the American psyche. "Fortified . . . by the inspirational novels of Horatio Alger and fed by national pride, the American success myth was widely accepted."[8]

Economists Jeffrey Williamson and Peter Lindert offer compelling evidence that on a per capita basis, colonial America (which, of course, was entirely rural) was likely the most income-egalitarian place on the planet.[9] In 1774, among all Americans (including slaves), the richest 1 percent received less than 9 percent of the total income. (Today, the ratio is 1:20.) They argue that colonial America was far more egalitarian than European nations and had a particularly robust middle class. All things are relative, of course, but compared with the rest of the world, America seemed the land of opportunity, made up of hardscrabble farmers.

Due in large part to the toll of the Revolution and the War of 1812, economic inequalities began to build prior to the Civil War. One of the most pronounced gaps in income equality was between rural residents and those in the emerging cities. Rural communities received a bit of a boost just prior to the Civil War, springing from new agricultural and transportation technologies, expanding markets, a flood of immigrants, and low tariffs. "Tariff rates fluctuate . . . but they are generally low enough to discourage customers from retaliating against American agricultural exports."[10]

At about this time, Cincinnati was a modest-sized town on the banks of the Ohio River. Each fall, farmers from the area would bring their swine to one of the town's many slaughterhouses. An English visitor called it the "city of pigs," where "swine, lean, gaunt, and vicious-looking riot through the streets."[11] It seems, as told by David Danbom in *Born in the Country*, during one of the hog-killing events, the British immigrant William Procter, a candlemaker, struck up a conversion with James Gamble, a soap maker. They both needed the lard. By 1837, they had formed a partnership, which would become one of the great consumer products companies in the world, today bringing in nearly $75 billion in annual sales.

The decades following the Civil War were a time of great economic expansion in America's rural heartland. By one account, the number of family farms doubled (from about 2.5 to 6 million) between 1870 and 1900. Likewise, the total amount of acreage devoted to agriculture, as well as the value of that property, also doubled during those thirty years.[12] Three factors came together: expansion of the agricultural frontier in the Great Plains, a burgeoning number of newly arrived immigrants heading west, and the mushrooming populations of urban centers, which drove the demand for commodities.

Historians agree that in many ways, this was the boom time of rural, agricultural America—the golden age of farming. But if that's true, why would we see the rise of farmer-centered political movements during this period, as we chart in chapter 2? It seems that while rural residents may have benefited from changing economic conditions, they also confronted uncertainty. Economic vulnerability—the fear of losing it all—lay at the heart of these movements. Speculation led to investments in land and new machinery, but if the farmer could not ship commodities due to exorbitant rail prices, all would be lost. There were monetary deflationary pressures, too, which helped consumers in the cities but not the farmers who held massive debt. The growing perception was that the robber barons were making fortunes in the burgeoning cities at the expense of the working class and farmers, which echoes modern concerns among many rural residents, as we will discuss. As noted in chapter 2, the Populists, the largest of the farm-centered parties, "blended economic discontent with the social resentments of people who felt the sting of urban contempt."[13] Five years later, they merged with the Democrats and backed William Jennings Bryan for the presidency.

The perception that Democrats stand with the working class and Republicans side with big business was locked in with the election of William McKinley in 1896, and it shaped politics during the Great Depression and its aftermath. Writing in 1964, the political scientist and historian Clinton Rossiter noted, "The fact is that class has now become the most important single force in shaping the political behavior of Americans."[14] But that did not mean farmers and rural residents aligned with Democrats to any great degree. In Roosevelt's second reelection (1940), for example, he clobbered Republican Wendell Willkie nationwide but lost nearly all of the agricultural Midwest.

In the post–World War II years, there were a few dents in the working class/New Deal coalition, such as the robust support that Richard Nixon received from this group in 1968 and 1972 and Ronald Reagan's appeal among blue-collar workers in 1980. And yet, working-class voters seemed to be loyal Democrats for the most part. As we showed in chapter 3, rural residents, as a group, only began moving away from the Democrats in earnest in 1980. The decline of manufacturing and the advent of unfavorable agriculture trade politics certainly played leading roles in this transformation. But the story of class more generally and partisanship is complex. And when race is controlled for, the income/party preference relationship changes dramatically. Put a bit differently, the percentage of white working-class voters casting their lot with Democrats has declined sharply in recent elections. Exit polling from the 2016 election shows that Trump won a staggering 71 percent of votes by white men without a college education. Ron Brownstein of *The Atlantic* offers a telling observation: after the 2016 election, two-thirds of Republican House members represented districts with a below-average level of education. After the 2018 midterms, that figure shot up to three-quarters.[15]

THE CURRENT STATE OF THE RURAL ECONOMY

Unsurprisingly, the seismic changes taking place within the rural economy are often seen as the major reason for why rural residents vote the
way they do. Rural America is suffering; towns are collapsing; families
are splitting apart. In the United States, the only counties where you can
find more than 40 percent of the population living in poverty are rural.[16]
What's a rural resident to do but find scapegoats for their suffering or
blame politicians?

In many ways, rural residents do seem to fit that narrative of economic decline and reactionary voting. There is no denying that, on
average, rural Americans are poorer than Americans living elsewhere.
They are also less willing to trust the government in an age when, every
year, more Americans trust government less. Rural residents are also less
likely to think the government should play a larger role in managing
the country's economic affairs; across the board, rural residents want
to see less government spending on welfare, health care, education, and
infrastructure—all those policies that experts see as the pathway out of
rural deprivation.

Ask any political scientist to predict the winner of the next election,
and they will immediately jump to the set of "fundamentals"—what
does unemployment look like? Is inflation on the rise? Did GDP grow in
excess of expectations, or do most people feel like the country is heading
toward a recession? What does it cost to buy a gallon of gas? People vote
with their wallets.

What do those fundamentals look like in rural and urban America?
On indicator after indicator, we find little evidence to suggest that
things are significantly worse in rural areas. Consider four indicators commonly used by political scientists and economists: income,
unemployment, health insurance rates, and retrospective evaluations
of the economy over the past year (whether it is worse or better today
than a year ago). Our data come from a cumulative time-series file
compiled by the Cooperative Congressional Election Study (CCES).[17]
Using each respondent's county of residence, we classify them using

the measure of ruralness and urbanness that we described in chapter 1 and track average responses among rural and urban respondents since 2006. We begin in 2009 for the health insurance measure, the first year for which we have data.

Consider first the most direct measure of economic well-being: the percentage of rural and urban households making less than $50,000 (top-left panel, figure 5.1). Income means something to voters; it is arguably the most visible way to make sense of how well the economy is doing. Here we look at the percentage of individuals living in rural and urban

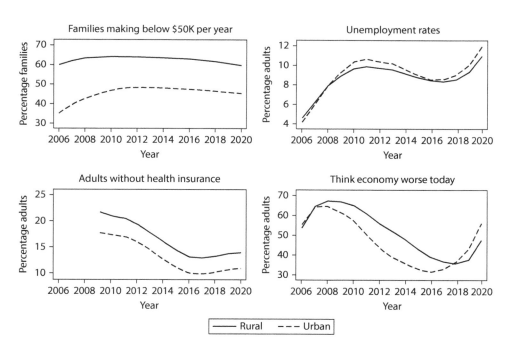

FIGURE 5.1 Perceptions of the economy and economic indicators, by rural and urban (2006–20)

Note: Data for years available from the common content data sets that make up the Cooperative Congressional Election Study (2006–20). Year-specific weights is used to calculate point estimates. Location is identified using respondent county of residence and U.S. Census data for the percentage of county residents living in urban blocks. Urban residents are those living in counties where more than 90 percent of residents live in urban blocks, and rural residents are those living in counties where fewer than 50 percent of residents live in urban blocks.

communities and ask them how much they made the previous year. Not taking inflation into account, incomes in rural America have been pretty stagnant over the past fifteen years, the period when the rural/GOP connection accelerated. Yes, a higher percentage of rural Americans make less than $50,000 a year—roughly the median worker's income for this period. But it is surprising that incomes have been dropping fastest in urban America. Also bear in mind that the cost of living—particularly the cost of housing—is lower in rural areas than in urban settings.[18]

Next, look at unemployment rates during this time (top-right panel). We agree that unemployment may matter more when income is less, but when we ask people whether they have been laid off in the past year—even temporarily—we see that urban and rural workers are just as likely to suffer from fluctuations in the larger economy. The same goes for changes in the percentage of adults who lack health insurance (bottom-left panel). Both urban and rural adults have equally benefited from changes in federal and state law that has increased insurance enrollments—namely, the adoption of the Patient Protection and Affordable Care Act, or Obamacare, enacted in 2010. Even when we just ask people what they think about the economy—whether it is better or worse now than it was a year ago—urban and rural voters largely respond the same way (bottom-right panel). A ten-point gap on economic pessimism simply cannot explain a sixty- or even a seventy-point gap in partisanship.

We are not cherry-picking our data. Elsewhere, we find that equal numbers of both rural and urban residents report that they would be unable to pay for an emergency expense of $400—a common way economists measure economic well-being. On other measures, we find that urban residents are almost twice as likely to report having had a pay cut in the previous year. During the COVID-19 pandemic, rural residents were less likely than urban residents to say their work had been affected by the pandemic; they were 50 percent less likely to have reported losing a job in the year leading up to the presidential election in 2020. And yet, they voted in overwhelming numbers for Donald Trump.

Maybe voting, you say, has less to do with how the rural economy is on any one Election Day and more to do with a long line of economic changes. That is, isn't the rural America we witness today—even if not that much worse off than urban America—at the tail end of a decades-long downfall?

Let us go a bit further back in time, to the 1970s and 1980s, the pivotal years we have highlighted as the inflection point in rural-urban politics. Using decennial census estimates (1970–2000) and the American Community Survey (2010–20), we merge county-level statistics on economic performance with our measure for ruralness/urbanness that we used to track presidential voting returns. We now have data to test the "long decline supposition," and by using objective estimates of economic growth and decline, we can see whether there has been a substantial difference between urban and rural communities.

We'll be brief. We see no major patterns between rural and urban America. Participation in the labor force has stagnated and is just slightly lower in rural America (about ten percentage points; see the top-left panel of figure 5.2). The percentage of families living in poverty has declined since 1970, most significantly in rural America. In fact, as a percentage of families—not counties or towns—urban poverty is on the rise (top-right panel). Poverty has tracked with education rates. Today, whether you are in rural or urban America, it is increasingly difficult to find an adult who dropped out of high school (bottom-left panel). Again, we do not deny the fact that median household incomes are higher in urban America (bottom-right panel). But over the past fifty years, despite massive changes to the economy, the gap between urban and rural areas has not widened.

Wait, we hear you say—this is the age of metropolitan wealth and opportunity. You show me high school diplomas, but I know you need a college degree to get your résumé on the desks at Google and Facebook. The income gap is not widening, but economic productivity and output are increasingly correlated with partisanship.[19] Remember, Hillary won the places moving ahead, right?

Absolutely. Using data from the Bureau of Economic Analysis, we can allocate the entire country's gross domestic product in a given year to specific counties.[20] As we have done throughout the book, we then use our measure of ruralness and urbanness to see how these different places contribute to overall economic growth. It is clear: urban areas

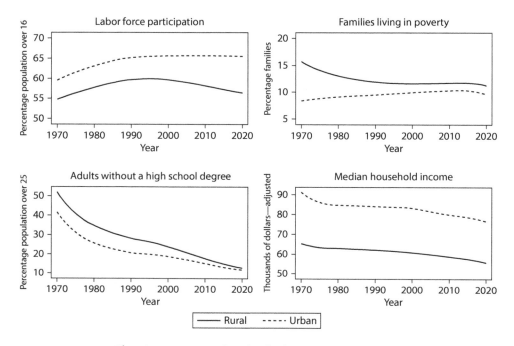

FIGURE 5.2 Changing economies of rural and urban America (1970–2020)

Note: Data come from pooled and interpolated estimates from the decennial U.S. Census (1970–2020). Estimates are at the county level, where urban counties include those in which 90 percent or more of the county population lives in an urban block and rural counties include those in which fewer than 50 percent of residents live in an urban block.

not only contribute substantially more to GDP, but they have done so increasingly year after year (left panel, figure 5.3). And when we take population into account, or consider how much each area contributes to overall GDP, rural populations underperform relative to their actual size. Recall that rural communities account for about 20 percent of the country's population. Our county measure drops some of those residents living in, on average, more urbanized counties, but the conclusion is still clear: productivity is increasingly concentrated in urban areas.

So, how do we square these basic facts? On the one hand, rural America is poorer than people elsewhere in the country, although its relative impoverishment compared with urban areas has not changed all that

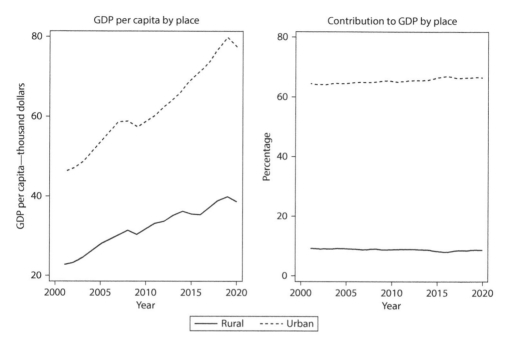

FIGURE 5.3 Gross domestic production in rural and urban America (2001–20)

Note: GDP data come from pooled estimates from the Bureau of Economic Analysis (2000–20). Estimates are at the county level, where rural counties include those in which fewer than 50 percent of residents live in an urban block and urban counties include those in which more than 90 percent of residents live in an urban block.

much in the past fifty years. Both areas have improved; often, rural areas have improved much more. On the other hand, we can clearly see that rural areas' contribution to GDP is just not there. We could round out the figure to add statistics like exports or wealth accrued on capital gains, but all of it would show the same concentration in productivity. Again, we do not challenge anyone who can find data points that make rural America look down on its luck (although, once you are forced to compare it with urban America, we do know the task gets much harder!).

The answer, we argue, has to do with concentrated wealth. For the moment, let's stay with GDP and income. Is it really the case that rural residents are holding the country back? The people and industries driving up GDP year after year are not in the countryside; those data are clear. But who are those people living in the cities, making all that dough, juicing the economy? We saw that incomes were on the decline in rural America. But median household incomes in urban America were also declining. In fact, as we noted in figure 5.1, over the past fifteen years, the percentage of families making less than $50,000 was on the rise. More people are making less money in urban America. And, as we saw in figure 5.2, when we start to take account of inflation—or track the real value of dollars over time—we see that incomes are actually going down in both rural and urban America as GDP goes up nationwide.

What gives? In short, those gains in GDP or income are unevenly distributed throughout society, including within those high-producing urban areas. People at the top of the income distribution are making more than those at the bottom, and they are making increasingly more. In fact, they are making so much more than people at the lower end that they are driving averages up, even as families and individuals at the bottom are making less. It is the familiar story of economic inequality.

There is a geographic component to this, too. When we look at where those affluent people are, we find they are concentrated in urban areas. First, let us compare trends in median household income with the percentage of the population making three times that median amount in that community (we do this to account for differences in the cost of living).[21] These families are not the super rich you may hear about in the tabloids, but they are very well-off. In fact, on average, they represent the top 10 percent of families earning the most in America (left panel, figure 5.4). But in rural areas, only about one in twenty households cross that threshold. They are there, but they are not really all that present in the community. But go into any urban community, and you'll see that these wealthy households are much more common—about one in every ten. They may be tucked into a particular neighborhood, corner of the city, or suburb, but they are there.

Moreover, if we think about where these families are nationwide, we see that as a percentage of wealthy households, they are increasingly gravitating toward urban communities (right panel, figure 5.4).

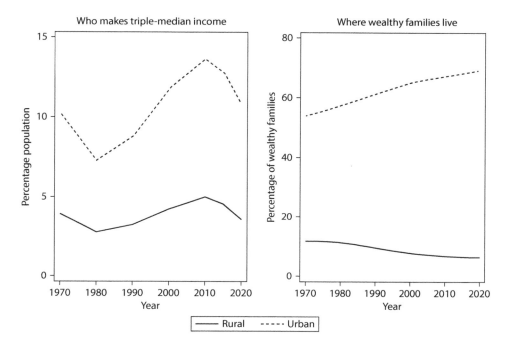

FIGURE 5.4 Economic inequality in rural and urban America (1970–2020)

Note: Data come from pooled and interpolated estimates from the decennial U.S. Census
(1970–2020). Estimates are at the county level, where urban counties include those in which
90 percent or more of the county population lives in an urban block and rural counties include
those in which fewer than 50 percent of residents live in an urban block. Median household
income is first determined at the county level; the left-hand panel indicates the number of
residents making three times that amount, as a percentage of the entire rural or urban population.
The right panel indicates the location of those families making three times their county median
income, as a percentage of all "wealthy families" in the United States.

The really rich, it seems, are increasingly more likely to live in cities.
For example, if we added up all the families in America in 1970 who
made more than three times the median income of their community,
we would note that most of them lived in urban America. Rural America,
though, had as many wealthy households as it should, given its size of
the national population. That is, a relatively equal number of wealthy
families also lived in rural America, and much of that was a function
of family agriculture—where income on a large or even a medium-sized

farm would amplify a family's yearly earnings. As the number of those farms declined, so did rural America's share of the wealth. Where did it go? Urban and, to an even larger extent, suburban America increased their share. The gap between the most-wealthy households in the United States has risen to such an extent that in 2020, of all the families making three times more than their community average, just 7 percent lived in rural America.

Few states capture this phenomenon better than Maine. Residents along the more urbanized southern coastal areas have always had a higher income than those inland and to the north. That's an old story— as it is in many states. But over the past two decades, the number of truly wealthy homeowners (we did not say "residents") has exploded. While the average home sale price statewide is one of the cheapest in New England ($270,000 in 2020),[22] the figure is dramatically skewed by the mushrooming number of multi-million-dollar homes on the market, most of which are being gobbled up by out-of-state buyers in the post–COVID-19 era. We suspect Senator Susan Collins's campaign operatives knew what they were doing when, late in the 2020 campaign, they ran an ad against their Democratic opponent, Sara Gideon, that featured drone aerial footage of Gideon's multi-million-dollar home—and reminding Mainers that she is "from away." And it is also no wonder that inland Mainers increasingly bristle at the state-sponsored moniker, "Vacation-land," plastered on road signs as you enter from the south.

FROM ECONOMIC DEPRIVATION TO SOCIAL SOLIDARITY

Inequality, the concentration of big wealth in the cities, helps us understand why economic deprivation, if not confined to rural areas, has had the effect of solidifying rural residents' collective sense of grievance. We can think of that inequality in two ways. First, we can draw connections between historical and contemporary forces that shape what rural economies as a whole look like. As we just showed, inequality exists in both rural and urban America, but it is growing fastest in urban America.

Next we will show the ways in which inequality also matters for how it relates to the types of economic activity in rural communities. Compared with urban communities, rural economies have become increasingly less diverse. This is not only a reason that inequality has not risen as much in rural areas; it also explains why rural communities, as a whole, experience economic shocks together.

Inequality also matters with regard to how rural residents experience economic hardship in highly visible, day-to-day ways. In short, poverty and economic vulnerability are much more integrated into rural communities than into big cities. We saw this in the 1890s with the rise of the Populist movement in the Upper Midwest, for instance. So, although there is economic deprivation everywhere in the United States, it is felt more keenly among rural residents. Together, these factors amplify narratives of rural decline and relative deprivation, which politicians have exploited into a narrative of "us" versus "them" in recent years.

Historically, rural communities have been less economically diverse than their urban counterparts—more dependent on agriculture, manufacturing, and other smaller, localized services, such as repair work and construction. Clearly, part of the story is that rural America has been upended by the new tech economy, globalization, offshoring, and the premium now placed on jobs that require a college education. Often overlooked is that those changes have taken place everywhere. When we add up the number of jobs in agriculture, forestry, and mining, along with work in construction, transportation, and what the government likes to call "production," we see a dramatic decline in the percentage of adults who work in so-called blue-collar jobs (left panel, figure 5.5). In 1970, nearly one of every two jobs held by a rural worker was in one of those sectors. Today, those industries account for less than one in every three jobs—a 48 percent decline. Although urban communities in the 1970s did not have as many blue-collar jobs, their losses have been almost the same: a 44 percent decline in the same fifty years.

It is worth pausing to reconsider this figure. For both rural and urban areas, the pace of blue-collar job loss has been about the same. But what were the starting points? Fifty years ago, nearly one-half of the rural labor force was blue collar. As these jobs disappeared, the entire fabric—the very character and identity—of many towns was

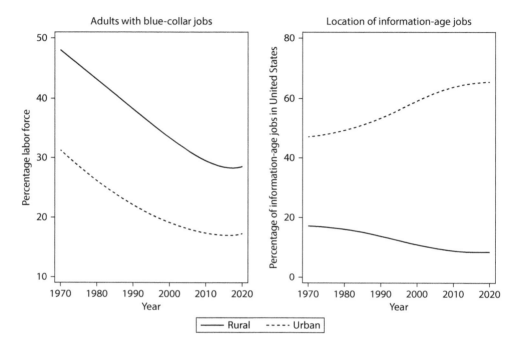

FIGURE 5.5 Blue-collar jobs and Information Age jobs in urban and rural America (1970–2020)

Note: Data come from pooled and interpolated estimates from the decennial U.S. Census (1970–2020). Estimates are at the county level, where urban counties include those in which 90 percent or more of the county population lives in an urban block and rural counties include those in which fewer than 50 percent of residents live in an urban block.

transformed. Those were "the good old day," when the community was buttressed by steady work and pride. We have no doubt that the loss of that pride and prestige among blue-collar workers is a key part of our story.

Moreover, transition to the new information economy has not been even. Urban areas always had a higher share of jobs in financial services, education, science, health care, and entertainment—basically, anything not blue collar or related to public administration (government). But urban America's share of those jobs has increased over the past fifty years (right panel, figure 5.5), while rural America's share decreased, even as it started from a much lower position. The share of the population receiving a college education is growing fast in rural America, but it is growing faster in urban areas.[23] Today, just one in ten jobs in the highly valued information sector is found in rural communities. On average, since 1970, rural communities have lost 60 percent of jobs in the blue-collar sector, as a percentage of all jobs. Consequently, using our measure or ruralness, we calculate that the average rural county in the United States had a median household income of $14,490 compared with $18,394 for urban counties—a 21 percent difference. In 2020, rural households were making considerably more: $53,198 on average. But urban incomes had grown, too, up to $74,071—a difference of 28 percent, seven points higher than in 1980. The gap between rural and urban America has widened.

This does not mean that rural Americans "dropped out"; you may note that they transferred into the information economy at a surprising rate, basically replacing jobs in blue-collar industries with these new jobs. Between 2010 and 2020, the levels of "persistent poverty" as measured by the U.S. government fell in rural areas by almost six percentage points; in metropolitan areas, it actually increased by six points.[24] Most of that decrease in poverty has come alongside more development, which has made the county less rural—a common feature of rural communities nationwide.

Furthermore, as we saw earlier, participation in the labor force has held steady throughout the transformation of the American economy. Likewise, rural residents have become more educated and just as likely to be fully employed as urban workers. In many respects, they have weathered the storm, which was more turbulent in the countryside.

What this uneven development means is that a larger percentage of rural workers experienced this transition. Entire communities had to remake themselves, replacing jobs in agriculture, mining, and natural resource extraction with new industries. More workers felt this transition. More families faced the disruption. More children, growing up in these communities, went off to school but faced an increasingly uncertain future.

Marvin Laucher of Greene County, Pennsylvania, typifies this shift. In 2016, he was a married father of three working in the coal mines of the southwestern part of the state. With mounting job cuts at the mines, and unemployment in the country nearly double the state average, his prospects looked dim. But his sister did computer consulting, and she pushed Laucher to learn how to code. His immediate response was, "Don't you need a college degree for that?" He had a high school degree. But he dove in anyway, and with the help of his sister, within a year, was using HTML, Javascript, CSS, Ruby, and Sinatra to build websites, making $20 per hour. He continued to work driving supply trucks for the mines, but the supplement to his income from the coding has created more stability.[25] He made the change, as did thousands of his rural neighbors. He was not alone, and that is the first big part of the shift.

ECONOMIC INTEGRATION

Inequality is also different in rural America in another way. Let's call it the "everyday sense of inequality"—the type of inequality you can see with your eyes or talk about with your neighbor. As rural residents ourselves, we picked up on this fact before we saw any statistics on the fact. Remember our commute—the one with all the Trump flags? Well, if you looked beyond them and take note of each house you pass by on the way into town, you'd pick up on the fact that each is different—in terms of not just style but size, quality, and pristineness. Right across the street from a massive, newly renovated Victorian farmhouse with a heated garage will rest a double-wide with the screen door hanging off the deck. One lawn is perfectly manicured, the other is littered with junk cars.

But the children of those two families wait at the same bus stop; they go to the same school and play on the same sports teams. The parents help each other out after a snowstorm takes down a big tree on the property line. Even if they run in different social circles on Saturday night, their lived experiences are shared.

Of course, we will not rely on just our intuitions and our own experiences here. Empirically, we know that rural residents are much more likely than their urban counterparts to live next to people with different economic backgrounds. To use another word, we would say that rural communities are more economically "integrated" than elsewhere.

We use that word—integration—deliberately, because we will measure economic integration in rural areas the same way that scholars measure racial integration in cities or public schools. Although multiple measures exist for making sense of integration, we will use one that scholars have used for some time: the index of dissimilarity.[26]

In looking at dissimilarity, we are interested in how far off the residential patterns are from a perfectly integrated community. That is the dissimilarity. How different are the neighborhoods from one another in the same community? Consider three fictional communities illustrated in figure 5.6—A, B, and C. Each of these communities has

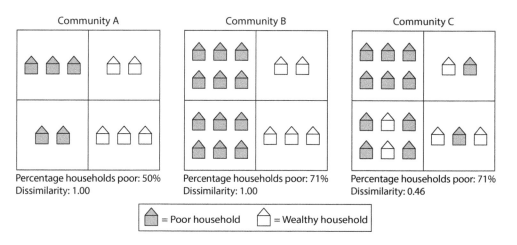

FIGURE 5.6 Three fictional communities and the index of dissimilarity in each

Note: Fictional illustration of population distribution and levels of dissimilarity.

some poor households and some wealthy households. Those house-holds are not only part of one large community (the big square containing all households) but also smaller geographic regions within the community—a neighborhood, for example. Those would be the blocks on each corner in the figure.

Often, we discuss poverty and inequality in reference to the number of poor households as a percentage of the total population. So, in considering community A and community B, we see that community B is poorer than community A because a greater proportion of households are poor. Community B, though, is just as impoverished as community C: the same percentage of households are wealthy or poor in each.

The overall level of poverty or wealth in each community is important. We discussed this earlier in the chapter by taking note of average income levels in rural versus urban communities. We noted that rural commu-nities are, on the whole, less well-off. But that does not explain why rural communities, and not urban ones, think about economic matters using their shared sense of place. What does explain it? Part of the answer is how communities, as a collective, faced economic travails that were much less widespread in urban areas. The other part of the answer comes from how people are distributed in rural communities—who they live next to and are likely to encounter on a daily basis.

In thinking about where poor households are located, and not just how many there may be, we can see that community A is similar to com-munity B in terms of its overall level of dissimilarity, even though community B is poorer than A. We know this because we can take each community and divide it into four neighborhoods. Each neighbor-hood in community A and community B is composed of only poor or only wealthy households. The perfect distribution—a completely inte-grated community—is where every neighborhood (or smaller square) contained the same percentage of households that were poor or wealthy as the entire community (the larger square). In community B, that means 71 percent of households in each of those four smaller squares would be poor (50 percent in community A). That is not what we see. Instead, we see that every neighborhood deviates from that perfect distribution and does so by a significant degree. In fact, it is dissimilar from that perfect distribution to the greatest degree possible, which gives us a numeric dissimilarity index of 1.00.

When communities are more integrated, the dissimilarity index approaches zero. Notice the differences between communities B and C. The percentage of households that are poor does not change; both communities are equally impoverished. However, the distribution of poor households changes a lot. Whereas in community B, there were no wealthy households in the neighborhoods that contained poor households, but three of the four neighborhoods in community C each has some mix of wealthy and lower-income households. Sure, this is not a perfectly integrated community—there are still pockets of segregation. And yet, by and large, poor and wealthy residents are much more evenly distributed throughout the community. Compared with the perfectly segregated community where the dissimilarity index was 1.00, the dissimilarity index in community C is just 0.46. Visually and statistically, if you are wealthy in community C, you are much more likely (nearly twice as likely) to not only live in a neighborhood with at least one poor household but to live in a neighborhood that is as poor as the entire community.

Using the same techniques, we can calculate the dissimilarity index in rural and urban communities drawing on the Census Bureau's American Community Survey. We will define the community, once again, as a county—our unit of analysis for rural voting and partisanship. Counties also have divisions within them, called "tracts" (remember chapter 1?). Urbanized counties have many more tracts than rural counties, and this could potentially matter for making comparisons. Imagine, for instance, if every household in community C were its own neighborhood or tract; it would be completely segregated, since no wealthy tracts would have a poor household. However, although urban counties have more tracts, they also have many more people. The number of tracts per person is actually greater in rural than in urban areas, suggesting that we are actually drawing more detailed neighborhood maps in rural communities, which would bias our results toward finding greater segregation there than in urban ones.[27]

Even with that potential bias working against us, the index also enables us to consider each county separately. That is, even if a county is wealthier or poorer than others (think community A compared with community B), we can still focus on the distribution of wealth within each county. Or, in other words, in calculating the dissimilarity index we do not care about the average wealth of a county compared to another county (rural vs. urban); we care about where the wealth is located within a single community. And we can measure the dissimilarity or integration of multiple factors—not just wealth, but households that receive government assistance, or make below $10,000 per year, or where a child lives in poverty, or where families lack health insurance. That is what figure 5.7 shows for different measures of economic impoverishment in rural, suburban, and urban America.

In each case, rural communities are not only more integrated, they are vastly more integrated. Consider child poverty. There are children in poverty everywhere in rural and urban America. And yet, in urban America, families that do not have a child living in poverty rarely live in the same neighborhoods, or tracts, as those that do. And, again, that is not because there are fewer children living in poverty. In fact, there are more impoverished children per tract in urban America than in rural America. But the reason the dissimilarity index is closer to 1.00 in urban communities is because impoverished children are more concentrated within urbanized counties. The reason the dissimilarity index is closer to zero in rural communities is because you are much more likely to live next to a family that has a child living in poverty and to live in a neighborhood that has a child impoverishment rate consistent with the larger community. Rural America is not perfectly integrated, by any stretch of the statistics. Children in poverty are still invisible to many residents. But rural communities are nearly 66 percent more integrated than urban areas. People living in urban and suburban areas are much less likely to live alongside families that are economically deprived in a very intimate way.

Of course, these statistics do not account for substantial variation in how people experience poverty in different communities. It is impossible to travel to either a big city or a rural community and not see the

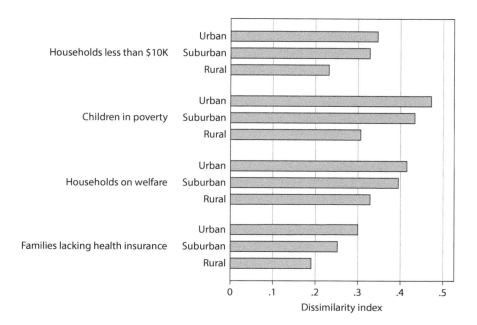

FIGURE 5.7 Exposure to poverty in rural, suburban, and urban America

Note: Data come from census tract-level estimates from the 2020 American Community Survey (five-year estimates). Estimates are at the county level, where urban counties include those in which 90 percent or more of the county population lives in an urban block and rural counties include those in which fewer than 50 percent of residents live in an urban block. Levels of dissimilarity incorporate tract-level and county-level data, which are then averaged into larger rural, suburban, and urban estimates, weighted by the population size of the county.

hallmarks of deprivation and despair—whether in the double-wide that is falling apart or the homeless person on the corner.

Our theory of linked fate, however, rests on the idea that rural grievance has bound together rural residents to think about their community's economic situation, even if they, personally, are doing well. When it comes to culture and social behaviors, we will offer additional evidence for these linking mechanisms. But we are convinced that as it relates to how residents think about economic matters, the degree to which poverty and vulnerable populations are integrated into rural communities is enough to tie residents together.

CHINA SHOCK

We grow more confident in the foregoing conclusion when we look at the evidence that economists and historians have gathered to make sense of changes in rural America since the 1980. These have come together in coherently interwoven narratives about susceptibility to globalization, the decline of manufacturing, and limited opportunities for upward mobility. What is remarkable about these findings is that they implicate all of rural America, whereas, as our pre-1980 story of rural development suggested, previous economic shocks played out differently across the country.

Central to those stories is the rise of an international economy, which has disrupted entire sectors of the American workforce regardless of locale. But rural communities have been especially shaken up, and maybe not for the reasons you think.

The high watermark for this transition, decades in the making, came between 1994, when the United States joined the North American Free Trade Agreement, and 2001, when China's membership in the World Trade Organization (WTO) was approved. The surge of offshoring and outsourcing that accompanied these formal shocks—and what has essentially kept prices on nearly everything we buy in the stores cheap—is referred to by economists as the "China shock." Indeed, the bump in trade raised national standards of living, but it hollowed out communities dependent on manufacturing.[28]

Anyone who has paid close attention to American politics—especially since the Great Recession of 2007–8—knows that declines in manufacturing have been central to changes in American partisanship: the transformation of blue-collar workers as a centerpiece of the Democratic coalition into a fervent part of the Republican Party's base. That transition has played out, in large part, within rural America. Outside the very middle of the country—think the top of Texas straight north—very few rural communities depend on agriculture. Instead, many depend on manufacturing, tourism, and, ironically, government jobs.[29] Prior to and even after the China shock, most manufacturing was concentrated in rural communities; cheap land and labor drew factories out of high-rent urban areas in the mid-twentieth century. In 2014, manufacturing accounted for 15 percent of earnings in rural America and 9 percent in urban America. Comparatively, just 7 percent of earnings in rural America came from the agricultural sector.[30] But China's comparative advantage in manufacturing has created long-run challenges in many of those communities, where earnings were once even higher and more disproportionate. In fact, the industries most susceptible to the China shock were in those rural communities.[31]

Consider Millinocket, Maine. Following World War II, Millinocket and the Great Northern Paper Company had a symbiotic relationship. The town provided a robust labor force, and in return, the paper mill guaranteed a good living for its employees. Millinocket was a vibrant rural town. Schools thrived. In fact, the town had one of the highest high school graduation rates in the state because you needed a diploma to work at the mill. It was a prosperous, proud town—by all accounts a wonderful place to raise a family. By the turn of the twenty-first century, however, demand for domestically-produced paper had withered, and the mill began to cut jobs. The factory closed its doors for good in 2008.

In the wake of the closure, Millinocket (and neighboring East Millinocket) saw a rapid decline in population, plummeting home prices, boarded-up businesses, and shrinking enrollments at local schools. The town's population went from 7,742 in 1970 to 4,466 in 2010.[32] The median age went from twenty-five in 1970 to fifty-one in 2010. Homes were being sold for a pittance, and at Stearns High School, the graduating class went from 235 in 1970 to just 38 students in 2010.[33] A new national monument (environmental preserve) has brought some ecotourism dollars into the area, but the town continues to struggle.

Compared with the entire country, counties whose 1990 employment depended mostly on industries susceptible to international competition and trade were more likely to suffer deep and enduring unemployment through the decade, boosting support for protectionism and, ultimately, the Republican Party.[34] Within those communities, an entire generation of young people experienced a shrinking job market and lost hope as industries that once offered a path to the middle class disappeared.

Concerns about downward mobility—actually being worse off than your parents—was no longer expressed just by young people at the bottom of the social ladder but by the entire community.[35] Not everyone in Millinocket worked at the mill; they all knew someone who did; they all felt anxious, sad, and despondent when it closed.

Given the social and economic structure of these communities—more equal and integrated—these losses created collective anxieties. Moreover, those anxieties were felt across rural America; other nationalizing forces, such as the Republican Party's message about "Real America," reinforced the sense of shared communal decline and pessimism. Well before Trump's candidacy, communities that were more deeply affected by these trade deals became more likely to vote conservatively and for the Republican Party.[36]

Now we turn our attention to the Rural Voter Survey to show the consequences of these developments: how decades of economic anxieties, felt keenly by rural residents across the country, have metastasized into full-fledged grievances against cities, government officials, and the Democratic Party.

FROM ANXIETY TO GRIEVANCE

Anxiety has made it possible for politicians and pundits to exploit rural America's economic vulnerability and transform it into a deeply felt grievance toward government, urban elites, intellectuals, and, in a word, Democrats.

The Rural Voter Survey identifies these links between anxieties about social mobility in different types of communities and the reasons people think their communities are economically precarious. With regard to anxiety, we are interested in how people make sense of their community and how those social orientations—or perceptions about the group's economic fortunes—exist alongside their own personal gains or losses.

First, though, we should point out that, in line with our expectations about economic mobility and economic vulnerability nationwide, we do notice some differences between urban, suburban, and rural areas when individuals are asked to think only about themselves. When we ask individuals about how their own financial situation has changed over the last five years, 62 percent of urban residents indicate that they are better off, while just 45 percent of rural residents do. Among rural respondents, 29 percent say they are worse off, while just 21 percent of urban dwellers do. Suburbanites fall almost perfectly in between.

So, in terms of personal well-being, we see that it is higher in urban areas, but only by a few percentage points. Nearly three in ten rural residents say they are worse off, and that is not too far from the two in ten urban residents who say the same.

In contrast to perceptions about their individual mobility, we also asked respondents a host of questions to gauge their sense of how their community was faring. Recall that central to our understanding of the rural economy is the idea that rural residents, even if they are doing okay themselves, are still making sense of their communities' greater economic decline.

These questions have appeared on numerous surveys since 2018 and versions of them were developed in collaboration with our fellow traveler in rural politics, Kal Munis. We extended and slightly modified questions that Munis has previously validated, and interested readers should be sure to check out his additional findings.[37]

We wanted to be as clear as possible when asking respondents about economic mobility and make sure they knew that we wanted them to think about their communities, not themselves. This can be odd for some, especially people used to taking surveys, which are all about individual circumstances. Other than a few political scientists (ahem!), most people do not care about place, let alone place-based identities. So, we were deliberate in asking people about their towns, but we used their actual towns when posing the question—for example, "Philadelphia is, overall, a better place to live than it was five years ago"; "No matter how hard you work, it is difficult to get by in Ligonier"; "Young kids growing up in and around Fredericksburg will have a better life than their parents"; and "Children growing up in and around Oneonta will be able to live productive lives if they stay nearby."

Few surveys do this, but it is essential to our theory of how geographic inequities are perceived at the community level. If you care about people's actual communities, you need to ask about their actual communities. When we do, we capture a much more vivid picture of economic anxiety in rural and urban America than any other economic statistic will show you. For one, there is simply a lot of economic anxiety out there! Almost half of Americans are concerned that their communities are worse off now than they were five years ago, and nearly one in two Americans are worried that children these days will have a worse life than their parents. As we have said, the economy is tough for all Americans regardless of where they live.

It is also true that the level of economic anxiety is highest in rural communities. On each of the surveyed dimensions, rural residents are more likely to interpret their community's chances for upward mobility and economic prosperity in more pessimistic terms. Only 38 percent of rural residents look at their community and think it is a better place to live today than it once was. A minority—43 percent—of rural residents think children growing up in their community will have a better life than their parents, even if only 30 percent of rural residents think that it is difficult to get ahead in their community with hard work (something we will reconsider in chapter 8). Likewise, 68 percent believe that children growing up in their rural community will have to leave because they will be unable to "live productive lives if they stay nearby" (figure 5.8).

Even when anxiety is high nationwide, it is even higher in rural America. How do rural residents understand what has placed their communities in such a vulnerable position? We asked them to consider four statements:

"The government spends too much money bailing out big cities and not enough helping people who live in communities like mine."
"Over the past few years, rural areas in [Respondent State] have gotten less than what they deserve."
"People who live in cities have too much say in [Respondent State] politics."
"In general, when the government does something, it considers what people living in rural areas know."

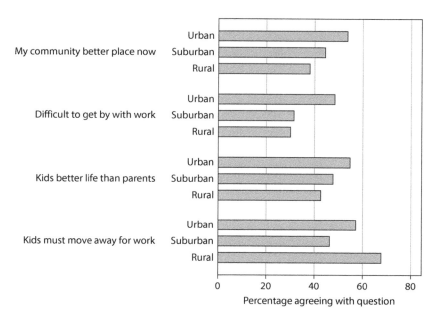

FIGURE 5.8 Place-based anxiety in rural, suburban, and urban America

Note: Data are from the 2021 wave of the Rural Voter Survey. Respondent location is self-described, and geographic averages incorporate poststratification weights described in chapter 4. The figure illustrates the percentage of respondents "strongly agreeing" or "somewhat agreeing" with the following statements: "[Respondent Location] is, overall, a better place to live than it was five years ago"; "No matter how hard you work, it is difficult to get by in [Respondent Location]"; "Young kids growing up in and around [Respondent Location] will have a better life than their parents"; and "In general, young people have to move away from places like [Respondent Location] in order to get good jobs and make money."

These items represent a range of potential reasons why people might have a place-based grievance. First, we are interested in perceptions of who gets what and at whose expense. We used the language of "bailing out" places, since it is common in partisan discourse to speak of bailouts for cities and states, particularly among conservative Republicans.[38] We also asked rural residents whether rural areas in general get less than they deserve.

We consider these perceptions about unjust distribution along-side beliefs about a place's influence. Again, we deeply probe people's *thoughts* about the influence of different types of communities—not people, such as the wealthy or the educated. These are the place-based identities at the heart of our theory. So, we asked about cities and urban areas and whether they had too much say. We also reversed direction and asked whether the government considers the perspectives of rural areas.

For urban residents, we followed the same script but asked about bailing out rural communities and whether rural areas had too much influence. Suburbanites always present a particular challenge. It was easy to ask whether the suburbs got less than they deserved and whether the government considered what people in the suburbs know. But for the "out-group" that we specify in the other two questions—the recipient of an individual's grievance—we randomized whether individuals saw "urban areas/big cities" or "rural areas" in the question.

As with economic anxiety, we see that many Americans express grievances. This should not be surprising. As we saw earlier in chapter 3, trust in government institutions has plummeted since the 1970s; that decline in trust translates, no doubt, into a sense of grievance as measured by our four questions. But also like economic anxiety, we see that rural residents are much more polarized in their views—remarkable all the more, since it is already a polarizing topic. Compared with residents of urban and suburban America, rural residents are more likely to say that big cities have too much influence in politics, and they are also more likely to say that rural areas in their state get less than they deserve. Nearly 80 percent of rural residents agree with the sentiment that too much money has gone to "bail out" urban areas at the expense of rural ones; in contrast, just over 20 percent believe the government takes rural perspectives into account when making decisions (figure 5.9).

Now, an attentive reader of figures 5.8 and 5.9 will notice two findings in addition to the supercharged levels of rural grievance and anxiety that we highlight. First, there is anxiety in urban America as well. Even if it is marginally higher in rural America, why doesn't this sense of anxiety about urban decline and urban prosperity translate into a type of urban shared fate? Likewise, there is resentment in urban America, too. In fact, when we ask urban and rural people about whether their type of community gets what they deserve, almost similar percentages of respondents conclude the same thing: they don't.

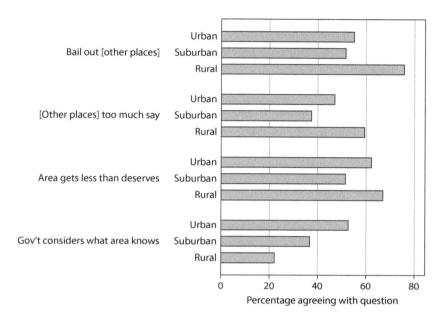

FIGURE 5.9 Place-based grievance in rural, suburban, and urban America

Note: Data are from the 2021 wave of the Rural Voter Survey. Respondent location is self-described, and geographic averages incorporate poststratification weights described in chapter 4. The figure illustrates the percentage of respondents "strongly agreeing" or "somewhat agreeing" with the following statements: "The government spends too much money bailing out [big cities, rural areas] and not enough helping people who live in communities like mine"; "Over the past few years, [rural areas, cities] in [Respondent State] have gotten less than what they deserve"; "People who live in [cities, rural] areas have too much say in [Respondent State] politics"; and "In general, when the government does something, it considers what people living in [urban, suburban, rural] areas know."

So what do we make of these two findings about urban residents? First, there is nothing theoretically implausible about urban grievance. In fact, as we write in the conclusion, there seems to be a fair amount of resentment from urban areas toward rural areas.

More significant to our argument: we are not as concerned with whether or not a given attitude is present in a community (although that clearly matters) as we are with the relationship between these attitudes. Do they coexist in the minds of urban and rural residents? Does knowing whether someone is anxious help us better predict whether they also hold grievances? Our theory of rural America's shared destiny demands that there be a connection between these perspectives. Only then will politicians and media narratives be able to tap into this shared sense of economic precarity and translate it into something as powerful as the "rural voter."

We will offer a more detailed analysis of this relationship in chapter 10, where we develop a mathematical model that maps a connection between answers to these questions about economic anxiety and the answers to questions about community grievance. We will wait until we consider other factors so we can precisely measure how much weight these economic considerations have when we control for other aspects of ruralness, such as civic pride and racial resentment. That fuller model will also enable us to consider how these two variables—personal well-being and anxieties about the community's economic fortunes—might change depending on the type of community a person lives in.

Even so, knowing that this relationship holds true even under more robust model specifications, consider just the relationships among personal well-being, concerns about the future of one's community (i.e., place-based anxiety), and whether someone has a grievance against the government. Figure 5.10 plots those relationships, where normalized measures of personal well-being and economic anxiety are predictors for grievance. The first thing we can distinguish are the positive and negative relationships. When one variable is higher, does the other variable increase or decrease, given all the other variables in the model? Or, more precisely, when a person has a higher sense of individual mobility (they feel they are doing better off), does that increase or decrease their level of grievance toward government and places not like their own?

For urban residents, we can see that when someone's level of individual, or personal well-being increases, so does their level of economic grievance. Our estimate is positive and statistically significant. That is why the black dot is to the right of the 0 line. In fact, compared with someone who feels much worse off than five years ago, a person who feels much better off is nearly 10 percent more likely to express grievance on those four questions we identified earlier.

Notice, however, that individual well-being for rural residents is to the left of the 0 line; in other words, it is negative. This indicates that for rural voters, as their sense of personal well-being increases (as they

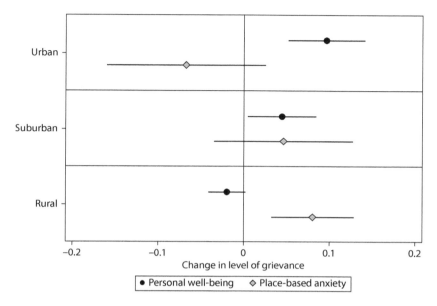

FIGURE 5.10 Relationships among personal well-being, place-based anxiety, and grievance

Note: Figure illustrates the marginal change in economic grievance for a one-unit change in respondent's personal well-being (economic situation gone from much worse to much better) and level of place-based anxiety (no anxiety to maximum amount of anxiety). Data from the 2021 wave of the Rural Voter Survey. Respondent location is self-described, and geographic averages incorporate poststratification weights described in chapter 4.

become better off), their level of grievance actually decreases. To be sure, it is not by that much, and by conventional standards of statistical certitude (or significance), it is about the same as no change at all.

What about economic anxiety? Well, it is exactly as our theory would suggest. For urban residents, any sense of economic anxiety does not have a meaningful relationship to grievance. It is there; we saw it measured earlier. But that does little to explain why someone would also feel aggrieved toward rural communities or government more generally. But rural residents are different story. Here, as we would expect, given how economically and socially integrated rural communities are, the relationship between economic anxiety and grievance is positive and strong. That is linked fate at work.

MEN, WOMEN, AND THE POLITICS
OF SHARED FATE

Without a doubt, the changing American economy has had deeper negative consequences on men as opposed to women. More men have dropped out of the labor force due to automation and the decline in manufacturing, more generally, while the percentage of women working has increased by 20 points.[39] Real wages for women have gone up since the 1980s, while the real wages for men have declined.[40] The transition to an information economy has advantaged those who pursue college degrees. Even though women still lag behind in certain STEM fields (science, technology, engineering, and mathematics), they are closing the gap. Actually, the overall gap in college success between men and women is widening, but to men's disadvantage. Today, six in ten degrees go to women—a discrepancy that is wider than the male advantage over women in 1970.[41] Men are falling behind, and the gender gap in politics is growing.

Rural men are particularly susceptible to the changes just described. Men are overrepresented in the types of jobs that are already overrepresented in rural areas. For example, knowing what we do about the gendered distribution of the workforce, we can look once again at figure 5.5 and conclude that, on the left, most of the decline—roughly 80 percent—in blue-collar jobs affected men, while most of the increase in information sector jobs and services went to women.[42]

Our point here is not to give an exhaustive account of rural men. But the clear gendered patterns of economic change raise an interesting question about the politics of shared fate in rural America. Simply put, to what extent is this really felt only among men in rural America?

Additionally, this question seems appropriate to ask given the fact that men are more likely to vote conservative and were much more likely to vote for Donald Trump in both 2016 and 2020, at least, nationwide;[43] although, to be sure, Trump closed the gender gap by nearly half in his second run, from thirteen to seven points.[44]

We see evidence of the gendered economy in the Rural America Survey, too. Of all Americans, men are more likely than women to say they are better off now than they were five years ago; recall that this is a perception, which may also stem from a sense of wanting to appear as if they are better off. Although we ask about individuals, we are not convinced that respondents do not also think of their families and coearners, for instance. Either way, in urban America, 71 percent of men say they are better off compared with just 52 percent of women (a nineteen-point gap). In rural America, despite the trends we just outlined, men are marginally more likely to say they are better off: 48 percent to 42 percent (a six-point gap).

The takeaway is not that this is definitive evidence that men are doing better. Rather, the astounding thing is that men and women in rural areas personally experience economic deprivation more alike than in urban areas.

Likewise, when we look at our measures of economic anxiety and how it is felt at the community level, gender gaps just do not appear in rural places. Equal percentages of rural men and rural women share a sense that the rural economy is on the decline. Except that when it comes to thinking about whether children will have a better life than their parents, rural women hold noticeably more pessimistic views than men: only 38 percent of rural women think children will be better off compared with 47 percent of men (nine-point gap). There is also a gender gap on that question in urban America: just 44 percent of urban women believe children growing up in their city will have better lives than their parents, but 65 percent of urban men think so (twenty-one-point gap). Again, men in rural America hold perceptions similar to those of rural women.

But even though perceptions of individual and community mobility may not be highly gendered in rural America, it is still an open question as to whether women and men think differently about whom to blame—the alleged source of their anxiety. Well, in what we see as some of the strongest evidence for our theory of shared fate, we find that men and women living in rural America hold resentful attitudes toward both government and urban areas. In fact, summed altogether, women are even slightly more resentful than men (although the real difference is a negligible amount)!

As we have argued throughout this book, there is more to the rural voter than voting for Trump. But we would stress a final point about gender politics in rural America that is pertinent to our discussion of economic anxieties. Fewer developments have been more central to the currents of modern American politics than the growing gender gap in partisanship. Like other nationally representative exit polls and surveys, our study showed a six-point difference between men and women nationwide in 2020.[45] While that is in the single digits, there are a lot of women voters, and that translates into big differences in outcomes. But recall a point we stressed in the previous chapter: those national differences conceal patterns that are substantially marked by geography. In urban areas, there is a gap of just two points: 38 percent of men voted for Trump. But in suburban areas, that gap is much wider than the national average; 56 percent of men and just 42 percent of women voted for Trump. In rural America, there is a gap. It's in the reverse direction. More rural women voted for Trump than rural men by one and a half points. In short, the rural voter is not the aggrieved man.

DOWNTRODDEN AND DEPLORABLE

Many times, as we were writing this book, we were careful to remind ourselves that we are two of the best-paid residents of our own rural communities. (Now, if our college president is reading these words, let's be clear . . . we are not overpaid, just comparatively well-paid.) Most of our neighbors think it's cute—professor in the countryside; boy, is he squirrelly! But there is a lot they don't talk to us about. You hear stories: Edgar ran out of wood in March just when the weather turned bad again, and the program for helping with rising fuel costs was already empty; Linda had to move to the night shift because she couldn't find any affordable daycare for her kids; the only local store that took EBT cards (food stamps) closed, so now there is a move get a vanpool together on the first of the month to take people into town to buy groceries. We do not live those lives. We do see those lives, though, every day.

This is also where survey research really helps. People can be brutally honest, and we would argue that is even more the case when they are responding to our work online than over the phone or in person. Don't get us wrong; plenty of our neighbors are brutally honest about their problems and whom they blame ("Fuck Biden"). With the Rural Voter Survey, we have an even more vivid portrayal of that honesty all across rural America.

And it is all across America. Rural Americans—women, men, young, old, poor, and well-off—are anxious about their future, and that uncertainty has morphed into full-bore grievance.

As we were putting the finishing touches on this chapter, an op-ed appeared in the *New York Times* by Art Cullen, editor of the *Storm Lake Times*, a twice-weekly newspaper published out of Storm Lake, Iowa (pop. 11,256).[46] It was written in the wake of the Democratic National Committee's decision to drop Iowa from the lead position in the 2024 presidential contests—a spot it had held since 1972. The Democrats, Cullen argues, are getting their "derrières handed to them" all over rural America, and in exchange, they decided to ditch Iowa. Democratic candidates never really liked coming to Iowa; it was an awkward arrangement, he suggests, and it is certainly true that Iowa is not as diverse as other states. Given the outcome of the 2020 Caucus, Joe Biden doesn't owe Iowa anything. But Republicans, he writes, are sticking with Iowa. Democrats see it as a lost cause.

And then he turns to grievance. Sure, family farms are fading from the landscape; yes, everyone thinks they pay more than they should in taxes. But the heart of the matter—what Democrats can't seem to understand— are the anxieties and fears that spring from a withering rural economy. "The old brick factory haunts along the mighty Mississippi River are dark, thanks to Ronald Reagan and Bill Clinton and everyone else who sold us out for 'free trade.'. . . Your best hope in rural Jefferson was to land a casino to save the town. . . . John Deere tractor cabs will be made in Mexico, not Waterloo. . . . The resentment builds to the point of insurrection when it is apparent that the government is not here to help you."[47]

A few days before the 2022 midterm election, Donald Trump returned to Sioux City for a rally. "The Iowa way of life is under siege," Mr. Trump bellowed. "They loved him," wrote Cullen, but "Democrats viewed the crowd as deplorable and told Iowa to get lost."

6

A WASTELAND OF ALIENATION?

Many families still run the cattle farms that once fed the former bustling mill towns along the Kennebec River in central Maine. They connect these rural communities to the past but struggle to remain afloat and compete with cheaper goods from larger ranches out of state. As we were writing this chapter, a massive end-of-summer storm came through town. Lightning struck a tree on one farm; in the blink of an eye, the family lost eight heifers, totaling upward of $15,000—enough to sink a small family business on the eve of a long winter. It made front-page news in the local paper. Condolences poured through on the town's Facebook page. A neighbor urged them to start a GoFundMe campaign to help recoup their loss. In two days, they reached their goal, and got $10,000 more than they asked.

What is even more remarkable about this story is that this farm has the same barn we described in the introduction—with TRUMP 2020 emblazoned on its side. The young farmer made waves on that same Facebook page months earlier as creating a nuisance for doing a burnout in his car down Main Street—easily identified because of the large American and MAGA flags flying out of his truck bed. But when the crisis hit, all that went by the wayside. And that was not the first time the community has lifted up this family; he acknowledged so in thanking his neighbors for their generosity and spirit. The farm would not exist in the first place if it was not for years—if not decades—of community support for him and his family. Community still exists in rural America.

If you have read anything about rural America recently, you know that is a bold statement. So the story goes, the rural community is breathing its dying breath, snuffed out by methamphetamine, broken families, limited educational advancement . . . you name it. We are told that the hollowing-out of rural communities has left a vacuum, which has been filled with a "mixture of fear and anger," as Robert Wuthnow writes.[1] He is not alone in this assessment; in his 2018 book, *Them: Why We Hate Each Other and How to Heal*, former Nebraska Senator Ben Sasse suggests that many Americans are suffering a sense of despair. At the core of this hopelessness is a historic isolation; we have "fewer non-virtual friends than at any point in decades."[2] With rural Americans' communities evaporating, we might assume they are alone, huddled in their basements, tied to conspiracy theory websites and Facebook pages that add fuel to the grievance fire. But is this actually the case?

Impressions and anecdotes are not our data. They give us insights, especially when they conflict with the simpler stories told by wayward journalists and scholars of a supposedly "simple folk" trying to eke out a rural life. However, as we show in this chapter, these impressions often conflict with our own evidence that details the richness and complexity of community in rural America.

Simply put, when you talk to rural Americans, they tell you a different story. To be sure, we were skeptical that the type of communal bonds we personally witness in rural Maine would extend to other parts of the country. But we were also skeptical that all of rural America was as alienated and downtrodden as many were saying. In fact, we were skeptical that the decline in rural communities was anything worse than the decline taking place all over America. And so we asked more questions on this topic than any other as a way of trying to understand more fully what the state of community is across the country. It was easy to anticipate stories of despair and isolation, but what we found was story after story of hope and solidarity. We heard some concerns about community decline, school closures, and declining church attendance. Overall, though, rural Americans did not translate that into helplessness or rage.

There remains a pride and social connectedness in rural areas unlike almost anywhere else in the United States.[3]

The aim of this book is to detail foundational differences between rural and urban voters and, in doing so, reveal the forces that have led to the novel political landscape we confront. Building on the last chapter, which documents the economic upheaval in rural areas and the collective sense of economic precarity, here we explore community structures and how rural and urban voters think differently about their place-based communities outside of an economic lens. The core of our analysis comes not from piecemeal accounts from a few towns here and there, but from thousands of individuals living across rural America. Just as we showed that residents of rural communities are more likely to consider the economic well-being of their communities when thinking about the economy, we find that rural residents are especially outwardly oriented when it comes to making the larger social community a part of their personal identities. And just as rural residents are more likely to witness poverty because they live in economically integrated places, so, too, are they more likely to emphasize common characteristics of rural communities and define their place as important to who they are. Where rural residents draw on their shared economic experiences to make sense of the economy, they also have a heightened sense of shared destiny, or social cohesion, when it comes to thinking about the value of civic life.

Much has been written on the withering state of community in rural areas, and we do not shy away from these arguments. We ask the same questions but take a comprehensive approach, touching on the general themes that have emerged from what other scholars and journalists have found in their little slivers of "real America." Nor do we deny that parts of rural America are deeply suffering—the hamlets of Appalachia described by J. D. Vance, or the impoverishment of indigenous communities that have faced centuries of government-sponsored discrimination. Rural America is complex, but the general pattern that exists is different from the common narrative.

First, we largely confirm that there has been rapid decay in social and political trust in rural communities. Both rural and nonrural Americans are becoming more distrustful—we know that. Distrust in institutions is a pervasive social phenomenon. In rural America, distrust is at its lowest levels in decades. Even among members of the same party, distrust of government institutions and political figures bottoms out when you cross over into the countryside.

Theory and existing empirical work suggest that the bottoming out of social trust should go hand in hand with the decline of "social capital"— the term social scientists use to describe many ways in which people engage in their community. There is much to support that idea. The opportunities for rural residents to step beyond their private lives and enter the social realm are, in fact, shrinking. Among several other indicators are the closings of hundreds of community schools across rural America—historically a key community institution—and the boarding up of more and more churches.

However, we find that while rural Americans are feeling these institutional forces, so are most Americans. The decline in social capital is not just a rural phenomenon, it is an American one. Social engagement is on the decline just about everywhere—a result of new technologies, government policies, and the types of lives people now value. It is not just a rural situation, but it does help explain the unique attitudes held by rural Americans in more nuanced ways than often discussed. In fact, on many measures, and in many parts of rural America, social capital is high.

Many argue that this decline in engagement goes hand in hand with another way we can think about community: how the desire to be a member of a place fits into personal identities. Many Americans have stopped engaging in community life because they simply do not want to connect. As a culture, we are becoming even more individualistic. People engage less because, well, they do not want to engage. However, our data show that we should not conflate concerns about the decline of social capital with an analogous decline of community belonging. Rural communities throughout the United States are defined by close interpersonal connections and a sense of small-town connectedness.[4] Such a distinction was once at the heart of modern sociology—a discipline motivated in part by seeking out the differences between urbanizing communities and the more traditional communal structures.

In this vein, one of the most impressive accounts of the decline of contemporary rural communities was penned by Timothy Carney in 2019. In *Alienated America*, Carney argued that in areas where opportunities for community engagement abound, we find safety nets, sources of knowledge and wisdom, and places where people can exercise their social and political muscles.[5] He continues, "Why do some people believe the American Dream is dead? I think the answer is this: because strong communities have crumbled and much of America has been left abandoned, without the web of human connections and institutions that make good life possible. More of America is a wasteland of alienation. Less of America is the 'village.'"[6] He concludes that the "erosion of civil society, leaving individuals adrift and families isolated, is at the core of America's social, economic, and poetical tumult."[7] People in rural America are less happy, he argues, because their community networks have evaporated.[8] America's decay, Carey argues, springs from broken places.

Our evidence suggests that this is not the case. A decline in social engagement does not necessarily go hand in hand with a decline in social cohesion. Elsewhere in America, that might be true. Only in rural America do you see this disjuncture between a lack of community engagement and a robust sense of belonging—a pride in community and sense of place—alongside limited community contacts and hollowed-out civic institutions.

For instance, it is true that rural Americans, like urban and suburban Americans, are less likely to go to the PTA meeting or gardening club and less likely to volunteer than they once were. Rural Americans, however, remain extraordinarily proud and attached to their local community. Rural Americans want to be in touch with others, even as they lack the meaningful institutions to connect in traditional ways. That is not true in other parts of the United States. It distinguishes rural America from the rest of society. Simply put, rural Americans do not see themselves as alienated and isolated.

And that matters for how social bonds in rural Americans matter in politics. Rural voters are growing more distrustful, but not toward one another. They are distrustful of the "other" living "over there." Once again, place is central to how rural residents understand themselves and how they make sense of politics: who is with them, who respects them, who has their interests in mind. The evidence is clear that any attempt to regain a political foothold in rural communities must start with addressing the deep skepticism and distrust that has been brewing for decades and which has been central to the creation of a coherent rural voter. It might mean that outsiders should be careful stepping into rural America and seeing nothing of value left worth saving.

THE IMPORTANCE OF TRUST

On the surface, rugged individualism would seem to be the protagonist of the American story. Founding documents chart the rights and liberties of individuals, while discrete institutions check and balance each other. Our electoral system leans against tickets and platforms and in favor of localism and "candidate-centered" politics, and once in office, rogue legislators become "profiles in courage" rather than outcasts or pariahs—for the most part. Undoubtedly, our economic system also rests on hyperindividualist footing.

Below this surface we find that the story of America has really been the story of community. The late historian Arthur Schlesinger noted, "at first thought it seems paradoxical that a country famed for being individualistic should provide the world's greatest example of joiners."[9] On close inspection, we find that American individualism means freedom from governmental restrictions and constraints, not merely the ability to head off on your own. And that is where civic life comes into play.

In the absence of governing authority, and as a matter of necessity in a new, uncharted land, local voluntary groups flourished in Colonial America. Geographic isolation, autonomous religious associations, and no fixed social classes powered civic engagement and local communities. The "associative spirit," noted Schlesinger, "flowered in a profusion of local capitalistic enterprises, notably for building toll roads and establishing banks."[10] The response to growing fears of

British taxation and land acquisition was the formation of local protest groups. So strong was the tendency to rest faith in local communities that the principal chore of the Constitutional framers was to convince Americans that the prospect of a secure life was better in a large, extended republic—a hard sell, to be sure. "The Antifederalist looked to the classical idealization of the small, pastoral republic where virtuous, self-reliant citizens manage their own affairs and shunned the power and glory of empire."[11] And while George Washington may have later warned his fellow Americans about the "spirit of party," he leveled few disparagements at local clubs and associations. After all, Washington himself was a member of a Masonic fraternity in Virginia from the age of twenty until his death.

The move to join was hastened in the early decades of the nineteenth century. During his travels through the states in the 1830s, Alexis de Tocqueville noticed that "the power of association has reached its uttermost development in America."[12] He observed a society in which the "commitment to voluntary associations was constant and unyielding."[13] The catalysts during this period included increased commerce, new roads and bridges making travel less difficult, growing literacy rates, and, in particular, the expansion of the popular press. The so-called penny press burst onto the scene in the 1830s, and a decade later, the partisan press was thriving. Even the smallest town boasted multiple newspapers; citizens were voracious consumers of any social, economic, and political news—as well as gossip!

The rise of public schools in the 1840s, coupled with the lyceum movement, fueled a growing interest in public affairs, and labor unions emerged as industry blossomed in the growing towns and cities. "People of kindred interests could be quickly assembled, agitation organized, mass meetings held, committees put to work."[14] An array of changes ushered in during the Jacksonian democracy period gave the average citizen a role in public affairs. Empowered by these opportunities, citizens joined local party committees. It is telling that in many communities, turnout for local elections was higher than for congressional or presidential elections.

Life in American cities was difficult around the turn of the twentieth century; the horrors of factory working conditions, overcrowding, filth, and poverty were all too real. But this is also the time when leisure became more common. The dreariness of the factory grind, growing health problems among workers (which threatened production), and the Progressive Movement merged to usher in shorter workdays and a six-day work week. Electric lighting in urban areas allowed for evening entertainment. Vaudeville shows, Wild West reenactments, motion pictures, and professional sports (particularly baseball) were popular.

Along with this change came a growing interest in community affairs. Writing about the implications of increased leisure after the turn of the century, Claude Fischer suggests the development of organization over spontaneity became a central theme. "Beginning in the 1880s, membership in fraternal and civic clubs grew rapidly. . . . In the early 1930s [one study] found that over 40 percent of Newburyport, Massachusetts residents belonged to one or more of 357 associations."[15] Whereas young boys had once flocked to the sandlot to play baseball, by the 1940s, they were playing in Little League, organized by their parents.

At about the same time that associational life was burgeoning in the cities, the agricultural West was expanding—spurred on by bumper crops (for a period) and the Homestead Act, which was created during the Civil War and lasted until the 1930s. Many of the immigrants who arrived on the Eastern Seaboard in the late 1800s quickly headed West with dreams of finding cheap land and beginning a new life. Towns sprang up across the plains, and so did associational life. Granges and Farmers' Alliances became vehicles for farmers to organize and petition the government, and local civic community groups flourished. (The Vassalboro Grange #332 still hosts potlucks, theater productions, and the community seedling sale.) At the center of all this were the local schools and community churches. "The spurt in associationism at the end of the nineteenth century was greatest not in the burgeoning metropolises (though it was visible there), but precisely in the smaller cities and towns of the heartland."[16]

The idea of America as a "nation of joiners" was given an empirical foundation in the 1963 oft-cited comparative work, *Civic Culture: Political Attitudes and Democracy in Five Nations* by Gabriel Almond and Sidney Verba. Following World War II, America had a distinctive "participant civic culture" and a widespread orientation to social life. Pay no mind to low election turnout or the widespread discrimination of a race of people in the South; American democracy, they argued, was buttressed by an unusually positive orientation toward public affairs and civic engagement.[17]

Not only did Americans join together, these community connections, it turns out, were critical to its functioning democracy. Social capital has just that: value. Social capital is the network of personal relationships that enable a community to function. It facilitates cooperation and reciprocity with others—what a team of scholars call the "norms that lead to positive ties among individuals and groups and stimulate more pro-civic actions."[18] Or, simply put, it is what builds trust.

Communities rich in social capital are high-trust communities, which produce procivic attitudes, leading to vibrant community affairs. A meta-analysis of thirty-nine recent studies suggests that communities plush in civic engagement and social capital enhance the well-being of the broader community.[19] On the other hand, communities with lower levels of trust can see destructive outcomes, such as social isolation, low levels of community engagement, and poorer physical and mental health. A senior fellow at the Brookings Institution, Isabel Sawhill, put it this way: "Without a certain degree of social trust, without norms of appropriate vs. inappropriate behavior, without strong institutions that uphold unifying and transcendent values, neither democracy nor the economy will flourish." That is, trust is the glue that makes a democratic society work.[20]

As individuals step beyond their private lives to connect with the community, they develop a sense of reciprocity—a belief that by helping others, you can assume others might help you somewhere down the line. Francis Fukuyama, in *Trust: The Social Virtues and the Creation of Prosperity*, writes that engagement and trust often go hand in hand, and many of the lessons may apply to changing rural communities.[21] Social engagement eases individual anxieties about change and creates a reserve of optimistic attitudes that bolsters cultural cohesiveness and prosperity. Absent engagement, but alongside a strong desire to protect community distinctiveness, such reciprocity fails to materialize in the political realm. Distrust toward institutions and political leaders follows in its wake.

Needless to say, trust is on the decline throughout America—but it is particularly waning in rural America. In figure 6.1, we return to the time series we constructed using the General Social Survey and consider average levels of agreement with the following three questions, asked repeatedly since 1970: "Most people try to be helpful"; "Most people would take advantage of you"; and "You can trust most people." It's clear that the largest changes in the past fifty years have taken place among rural Americans. Rural residents in 1970 were more likely to think

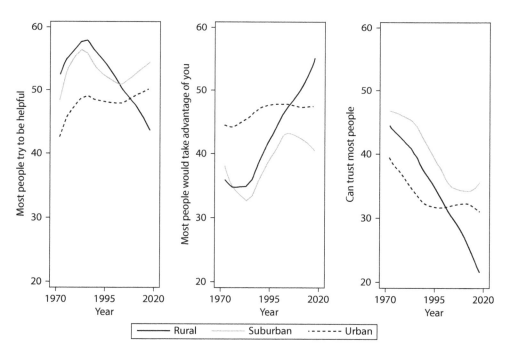

FIGURE 6.1 Declining social trust in rural, suburban, and urban communities (1970–2020)

Note: Using data from the General Social Survey, we identify respondents from rural areas (counties having no towns of 10,000 or more people) and urban areas (central city of 112 largest Metropolitan statistical area). The three panels illustrate the weighted average of respondents for the following questions: "Would you say that most of the time, people try to be helpful, or that they are mostly just looking out for themselves?"; "Do you think most people would try to take advantage of you if they got a chance, or would they try to be fair?"; and "Generally speaking, would you say that most people can be trusted, or that you can't be too careful in dealing with people?"

others try to be helpful and, conversely, less likely to think others would take advantage if they had the chance. They were more likely than urban residents to say people could be trusted.

But all that has changed. The decline of trust has been steep and consistent, beginning roughly in the 1980s. There is a large literature on declining levels of trust in the United States, but few works have zeroed in on rural attitudes. We have to be a bit speculative here, given that we cannot go back in time and ask additional follow-up questions, but our assumption is that forces we detailed in chapter 3 are intricately connected in creating a heightened sense of cynicism in rural areas. As we discussed, the rhetoric of "us versus them"—the creation of a "real America" that is against everyone else—became particularly sharp during this period. Local rural economies were changing rapidly, especially in the wake of NAFTA, and there was a growing sense that the future of America lay in metropolitan areas. Global economic interdependence did not seem to bode well for rural life. There were other destabilizing issues, including huge swings in traditional norms of behavior, increased immigration, the redefining of gender work roles, and an avalanche of new technologies. We also see the growing prominence of nationalized news programs, including Rush Limbaugh's and Fox News. To be clear, many of these changes affected all Americans—urbanites and suburbanites are more distrustful, too. But something took off in rural America in particular. The anger and cynicism in rural America is a world apart.

We know that distrust has become especially pronounced in rural communities, and not only because of our time-series analysis. Distrust matters in how citizens relate to one another but also how they think about government. One follows from the other, and so we expect—and find—that distrust of government is especially pronounced among rural residents.

Here we focus primarily on Republicans, given the set of questions we asked about prominent elected officials, such as Joe Biden and Anthony Fauci. It also lets us consider distrust as it varies over geography and not just partisanship, since distrust in government has been a major political tenet of modern conservatism.[22] That is, are rural Republicans more distrustful than Republicans in other parts of the country? Let us consider general political sentiment, as measured by a few "feeling thermometer" questions we placed on our Rural Voter Survey. For each of the following groups, we asked respondents how "warmly" or "coldly" they felt on a 0–100 thermometer scale.

Regardless of where a Republican voter lives, they are likely to have very cold feelings toward the Democratic Party and President Joe Biden (figure 6.2). Not surprising. What is surprising is that stark differences

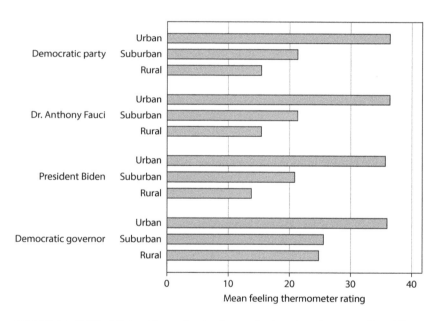

FIGURE 6.2 Political distrust in rural, suburban, and urban America among Republican voters

Note: Data from the 2022 wave of the Rural Voter Survey. Respondent location is self-described, and geographic averages incorporate poststratification weights described in chapter 4. The figure illustrates the mean feeling thermometer rating for self-identified Republicans toward the listed groups and public figures. The prompt read as follows: "We'd now like to get your feelings toward a number of groups in the U.S. on a feeling thermometer. A rating of zero degrees means you feel as cold and negative as possible. A rating of 100 degrees means you feel as warm and positive as possible. You would rate the group at 50 degrees if you don't feel particularly positive or negative toward the group." Responses to "Democratic governor" include only Republicans living in a state with a Democratic governor; for those respondents, the actual governor's name appeared in the prompt.

exist among Republicans depending on where they live. Rural Republicans are downright "icy" toward the Democratic Party: 15 degrees! Compare that with the lukewarm attitudes of urban Republicans, who at least break the freezing mark at 36 degrees. Similar trends exist for specific figures. Joe Biden is abhorred among rural Republicans—13 degrees cold, nearly three times colder than how Republicans living elsewhere feel about the president. And this trend includes governors for those rural Republicans living in states with a Democrat living in the governor's mansion. Ice cold.

Distrust and cynicism, in other words, are simply part of the rural experience. But does that mean rural residents are any less engaged?

SOCIAL CAPITAL IN RURAL AMERICA

As we have said, historically, one of the key ingredients of building public trust has been civic engagement. When we connect with others, cohesion is forged, an intuitive sense of reciprocity and belonging. Why think the worst of your fellow citizens when you're all in it together? But what is the state of civic engagement—what social scientists call "social capital"?

Beginning in the 1970s, levels of social engagement throughout the United States started to plummet. A small cottage industry developed to study the countless ways in which American society was turning inward and away from community, whether from rising divorce rates, adolescent crime, or other factors. One of the most widely discussed studies on the state of associational life in America has been *Bowling Alone: The Collapse and Revival of American Community* by the Harvard sociologist Robert Putnam. Published in 2000, Putnam's book sounded an alarm that is still being heard. As noted in a twenty-year retrospective, "It is difficult to overstate the influence of Putnam's thesis. His argument and evidence understandably caused much concern."[23]

With truckloads of data, Putnam charted a steep decline in American associational life. In every dimension, from modes of political participation to civic engagement, religious involvement, workplace connections, informal social meetings, and philanthropy, the decline of social capital was steady and significant. Most community organizations—like the Rotary club, PTA, League of Women Voters, Lions club, and the Grange—had nearly collapsed. "Many Americans continue to claim that we are 'members' of various organizations, but most Americans no longer spend much time in community organizations."[24] While the number of nonprofit associations grew dramatically from the 1960s to the 1990s, many of these new groups had few actual members. It had been, according to Putnam, a "proliferation of letterheads, not a boom in grassroots participation."[25] As for religious participation, he noted a steady decline, downwards of 50 percent, in church attendance since the 1950s.[26] The trend for informal connections, like going out to dinner with friends, going to the movies, or attending sporting events, had similarly declined. The percentage of Americans occasionally playing cards with a group of friends, for instance, went from about 16 percent in 1975 to just 8 percent in 2000.[27] One of the reasons Putnam's book was so informative is that it placed America's current social behaviors in historical context, tracing their decline over time.

As for the culprits of the decline, Putnam was somewhat equivocal. Changing family life patterns, including dual-wage-earner and single-parent homes, was part of the story. But so was the rise of electronic entertainment—above all, television. Suburban sprawl and pressures of time and money were likely part of the problem as well. Perhaps most significantly, Putnam suggested that a generational change was at work, in which one cohort accustomed to potluck dinners, card clubs, weekly lunch meetings and, yes, bowling leagues was being replaced by an anonymized, suburban, television-watching generation.

The best way to describe the current state of nationwide social capital and civic engagement is that it is muddled. On the one hand, many of the trends discussed by Putnam have continued. According to Gallup polling, for instance, the number of Americans who report no religious affiliation has gone from about 2 percent in the post–World War II period to a whopping 20 percent in 2020.[28] The percentage of Americans who report they "never" attend religious service is now higher than for those who say they "infrequently" attend.[29] Likewise, work associations and unions, which Putnam calls important institutions for sustaining social and professional ties, have continued their downward drift. About one-third of American workers were unionized in the 1950s; today, that figure stands at just 12 percent.[30] A similar decline can be seen in professional associations. Even though the number of registered nurses doubled in the last two decades, the American Nurses Association membership fell by 50 percent.[31] There was a surge in volunteering following the 9/11 terrorist attacks, but since then, the percentage of Americans who say they are involved in at least one voluntary association has been cut in half.[32] The "giving rate" of charitable contributions has also declined.[33] If we add to the picture the rise of the gig economy and the dramatic increase in the number of Americans working from home during the COVID-19 pandemic, we see that workplace connections are likely at an all-time low.

Much of our academic theorizing—including Putnam's—suggests that lower engagement and heightened levels of distrust should put a stranglehold on rural communities; they should lack the social glue to collectively solve problems or even identify as a cohesive bloc. Rural residents should talk to one another less and feel less invested in the future of their community. They should lack the social capital that makes democratic politics possible.

Our Rural Voter Survey replicated much of Putnam's measurement strategy, asking about social capital in broad terms—from formally joining civic organizations, to simply heading out to the neighbors' for dinner. While we lack the extensive time-series data Putnam used to document decline in social capital, we leverage nearly ten thousand responses to better understand how urban, suburban, and rural residents engage with one another. Our survey is a single snapshot in time. We cannot go back and find answers to our questions from a bygone era. What we lack in time, however, we gain from the ability to make accurate and holistic comparisons between rural and urban America.

We asked urban, suburban, and rural respondents a number of questions to gauge their social engagement. Figure 6.3 offers a quick look at four measures of community engagement, and breaks them down by geography. The first thing to note is that regardless of where Americans live, engagement is low. That is, on average, less than one in two American adults "got together with neighbors and others who live in your local community" or "participate in non-religious groups, such as sports teams, book clubs, PTA, or neighborhood associations" less than once a week or more. We even asked people to consider a hypothetical question: "Setting aside the details like the day and time, if there was a community celebration in your area—like a picnic or a craft fair—would you

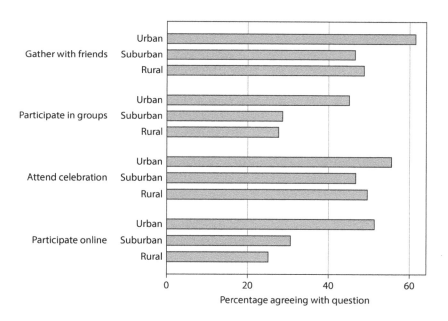

FIGURE 6.3 Social engagement in rural, suburban, and urban America

Note: Data from the 2021 wave of the Rural Voter Survey. Respondent location is self-described, and geographic averages incorporate poststratification weights described in chapter 4. The figure illustrates the percentage of respondents who responded "once a week or more" or "once or twice a month" to the following questions: "How often do you get together with neighbors and others who live in your local community?"; "How often, if at all, do you participate in non-religious groups, such as sports teams, book clubs, PTA, or neighborhood associations?"; and "Some groups are local. But people also connect with larger groups from all over the state or country using the Internet. How often, if at all, do you participate in these online groups?" The figure also displays the percentage of respondents who said "Yes, I would attend the event" to the following question: "Setting aside the details like the day and time, if there was a community celebration in your area— like a picnic or a craft fair—would you attend?"

attend?" Just 50 percent of American adults, on average, said yes. And that is just a survey response; we weren't actually asking them to show up! Even on the least taxing form of engagement—whether they participated in any online groups—just a quarter of Americans indicated that they got together over the internet a few times a week or more. We see low levels of social engagement and assume it is lower now than it has ever been. Putnam's thesis still holds water.

But is it any lower in rural America? Not really. In a strict comparison of urban and rural residents, urban residents are more likely to get together with neighbors, participate in nonreligious groups, attend that fake celebration, and connect online. But urban America does not vastly outperform rural residents. That gap is highest when comparing online engagement (twenty-six points), but on other questions, the gap is hardly the stuff of alienated wastelands. In fact, the 40 percent of Americans who live in urban areas is a bit exceptional. Comparing rural America with the suburbs (where the other 40 percent lives), we see rates of social engagement that are near equivalent to what rural residents tell us.

Some of urban America's exceptional quality has to do with who lives there and not necessarily the fact that it is urban. Again, these other non-geographic confounders are something we will control for all at once in developing the Rural Voter Model in chapter 10. For the time being, it is helpful to consider one such alternative explanation. In figure 6.4, we look at the same four questions but instead think about how responses vary over different generations: millennials (born after 1981), gen X (born after 1965), boomers (born after 1946), and the pre–World War II generation (born before 1946). When we look at the participation of millennials in rural America, we see nearly identical levels of social engagement to that of urban America writ large. We know that urban residents are likely to be younger; and younger urban residents participate more than the urban average. The difference between urban and rural America is partly the result of composition effects, as more young people living in urban areas boost their engagement.

Mostly, though, the evidence of community collapse specific to rural America is simply lacking. It is low, but it is not especially low in a relative sense. And what is surprising is that our data cut against Putnam's

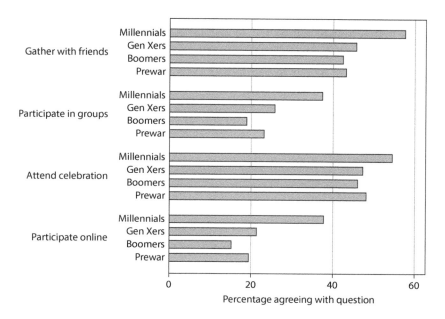

FIGURE 6.4 Social engagement in rural America, by generation

Note: Data are the same as those displayed in figure 6.1, but for only rural residents, disaggregated by year of birth: millennials (born after 1981), gen X (born after 1965), boomers (born after 1946), and the pre–World War II generation (before 1946).

worry of generational change. At least in rural America, younger residents are much more likely to engage with others than older residents—a fact not true just for expected behaviors like getting online but also in formal organizations like the PTA, civic clubs, and other community organizations.

Reported behaviors like getting together with friends tell us a lot. It also matters how residents of these communities describe social capital in their own terms. Of course, we cannot ask them "what's the level of social capital in your community?" For good reason—most Americans don't use the terms we academics concoct. Instead, we pushed respondents into one of two assessments about their community overall: either they believe they live in a community where residents like to come together, or they think they reside in a place where folks tend to prefer staying to themselves. We may call this a blunt, direct measure of perceptions toward the social connectedness of the respondent's community (table 6.1). Overall, 52 percent noted that most people in their community tend to stay to themselves. As for a geographic breakdown, once again, our data suggest that while residents in urban areas report higher levels of engagement, rural respondents note higher levels than do suburban residents. But the difference is minuscule.

Yet another dimension of community connectedness is political engagement. If there is one clear exception to the civic decline thesis, it is political action. The 2000 election witnessed the lowest turnout level in generations, particularly among younger Americans, sounding warning bells about declining faith in elections and government institutions. Generally speaking, Americans were not talking about politics, following public affairs, or giving their money or time to candidates. They were not especially partisan. The number of independents and split-ticket voters had reached record levels.

That's all changed. Americans are more engaged, attentive, and partisan than at any time in generations. Turnout in the 2020 election, at 66 percent nationwide, was the highest in more than a century. According to a study conducted by the Pew Research Center, upward of two-thirds of Americans now regularly engage in overt forms of political engagement, including donating to campaigns, attending protests or meetings, contacting officials, and expressing their views on social media. A case

TABLE 6.1 Description of community engagement in rural, suburban, and urban America

	Urban	Suburban	Rural	Total
Often get together	53.78	44.00	49.34	48.31
Everyone does their own thing	46.22	56.00	50.66	51.69

Note: Data from the 2021 wave of the Rural Voter Survey. Respondent location is self-described, and geographic averages incorporate poststratification weights described in chapter 4. The question read, "Which of the following best describes the area where you currently live?" Response choices were "People are active in the community and often get together" or "People are not that active in the community, and everyone does their own thing."

can be made that Donald Trump single-handedly spurred a higher level of civic engagement. Writing in the *Atlantic*, Eric Liu of the Aspen Institute notes, "Since the early 1970s, the nation's civic health . . . has been in steady, severe decline. . . . But now millions of people, once cynical bystanders, are participating earnestly." He points to marches, packed congressional town hall meetings, and protests at airports, campuses, and street corners. "Membership in the ACLU and the League of Women Voters has swelled, as have subscriptions to leading newspapers." The ranks of the MAGA team is filled with first-time participants in politics. Trump has given voice to communities long disregarded by cosmopolitan political elites.[34]

On the one hand, higher levels of distrust could mean that citizens are mad, ready to kick the bums out of office, and increasingly willing to mobilize. Especially after the 2020 election, when trust in the election itself was called into question, no doubt many images of rural voters painted for you include the cynical protester standing on the street corner with their "big lie" poster held up high (he no doubt has a cowboy hat on).[35] This type of engagement is not constructive of social reciprocity and community bonds; it is destructive and would actually seem to support the alienation hypothesis.[36]

At the same time, though, political scientists know that distrust is likely to have a depressing effect. That is, people with the lowest levels of trust are the least likely to participate in politics.[37] Why join the fuss when it will not make any difference?

We asked Trump and Biden voters in the 2020 election some questions about how they participated during the campaign. These participation measures account for the fact that our respondents voted—a low bar, for sure, but it is important to note that our respondents already have some propensity to engage in politics, and our queries tap higher-cost forms of participation. Most Americans do little more than vote—fewer than 30 percent will even put up a sign, and fewer still will donate money to a campaign (13 percent). Only the most active, engaged, and politically committed voters choose to do much more than show up on Election Day. Nevertheless, even small differences—a couple of percentage points—tell us a lot about how politically engaged segments of the population are.

But our concern here is with geography. Are rural voters any more or less likely to participate in politics as a result of their declining trust? Are they lashing out, participating at higher levels, but in a way that cuts down on community connectedness? In figure 6.5, we distinguish between Biden voters and Trump voters, because it is certainly possible that one candidate was better than the other at energizing voters. (And yes, we are being sarcastic.) But regardless of whichever candidate they supported, our evidence shows that engagement is always lower in rural than in urban communities. Often, it is much lower. Suburban engagement is not great, either, and sometimes it is lower than rural engagement, but the general pattern of diminished trust and lower engagement

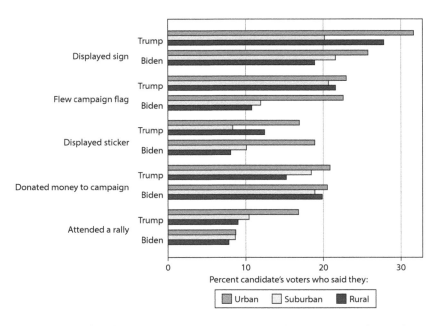

FIGURE 6.5 Political engagement among Trump and Biden voters in rural, suburban, and urban America

Note: Data from the 2021 wave of the Rural Voter Survey. Respondent location is self-described, and geographic averages incorporate poststratification weights described in chapter 4. The figure illustrates the percentage of Trump or Biden voters within rural, suburban, or urban areas who indicated that they did each of the listed activities.

holds. As other research has found, while distrust is simmering in rural areas—in part because of heightened inequality—and produces support for conservative candidates, it does not necessarily raise levels of political participation.[38]

There is one aspect of political participation that is distinctive in rural America, however. Engagement among rural Democrats is abysmal. They are there, and they show up to vote, but especially in the visible ways people show their support for candidates, Biden voters were reticent to slap a bumper sticker on their car or put a sign in their yard. (The percentages for each bar are among Biden or Trump voters, which already takes into account the differences between geography in how many live in rural, suburban, or urban America.)

This difference seems related less to trust (Democrats, in general, reported modestly higher levels of trust than Republicans) and more to the fact that throughout rural areas, Democrats are in the political minority. They want to keep their heads down. Shortly before the 2022 midterms, an AP reporter traveled to central Pennsylvania to get a sense of what it's like to be a Democrat in rural parts. Here's what he found: "The party's brand is so toxic . . . that some liberals have removed bumper stickers and yard signs and refuse to acknowledge publicly their party affiliation." One of the Democrats quoted in the piece suggested, "The hatred for Democrats is just unbelievable. I feel like we're on the run."[39]

MORE DATA ON RURAL ENGAGEMENT

Maybe you're still not buying it. You may be shaking your head, asking us, "But haven't you read J. D. Vance's book about the collapse of community in Appalachia?" A key theme in his memoir, *Hillbilly Elegy*, is connections. Not until he attended Yale Law School did Vance come to appreciate the importance of networks—and how they were missing in his childhood towns in rural Ohio. The social capital that once existed in the small towns and hollers of Appalachia have evaporated, Vance suggests, along with steady employment. Left in its wake are dead communities rife with young white men adrift, addicted to drugs and social media. There are broken homes, indifferent parents, poverty, and economic collapse.

From Vance's vantage point, in the wake of crumbling communities comes a contradiction between what "hillbillies" believe and how they act. Hillbilly families are said to stick together, but divorce rates are high, domestic abuse is rampant, and alcoholism is ubiquitous. His people believe in hard work, but many are lifetime welfare recipients, and able-bodied men cling to disability checks. People help each other out, but struggling kids are adrift, and distressed adults can languish unnoticed. His book is in many ways responsible for getting journalists, pundits, and politicians to think about broken communities and missing networks.[40]

But how accurate is Vance's account? There has been no shortage of critiques of the book. In one of the chapters in an edited volume *Appalachian Reckoning*, Ivy Brashear, the chief blogger with the Institute for Rural Journalism and Community Issues, offers a full-throttled rebuke: "[The book] displays a willingness to sell out his family members by tapping into a long history of distorted, false, and intentionally made stereotypical images of central Appalachia. . . . People will read his book and assume all Appalachian people, if they are smart, are trying to actively run away from their culture."[41]

The *Washington Post* reporter Christopher Ingraham has likewise written a good bit about rural America, including his 2019 book, *If You Lived Here You'd Be Home by Now: Why We Traded the Commuting Life for a Little House on the Prairie*. Instead of what some might call drive-by journalism, Ingraham left his urban life to live in Red Falls, Minnesota, population 1,400. His take on rural social capital is quite different than what Vance, Carney, and others would suggest: "The relative scarcity of people means that those of us who do live here have to forge closer personal bonds to solve the sorts of problems that, in more populated places, are typically handled by anonymous professional bureaucracies."[42]

In no small part because of the media tidal wave surrounding Vance's book, in 2018, the Joint Economic Committee, chaired by Senator Michael Lee of Utah, issued a comprehensive report titled "The Geography of Social Capital in America." The study sprang from the premise that there has been a withering of social capital in the United States, particularly in rural communities. The goal was to create a social capital index that could be used by policy makers, community leaders, and researchers. In creating an index, the committee sought to build a single measure that encapsulates a number of behaviors. They gathered their data at the county level, with statistics on 2,992 of the 3,241 counties across the country (accounting for over 99 percent of America's population). Some of the variables used in the index center on family interactions, social support groups, political engagement statistics, and crime rates. As with most indices, one could quibble with certain parts, but inclusive measures usually capture important trends. In statistical terms, there is a high degree of construct validity, meaning the variables are highly correlated with one another—which you would expect.

These data capture a number of ways in which individuals in urban, suburban, and rural America engage beyond what we asked in the Rural America Survey, and the aforementioned index is a helpful tool for making comparisons, keeping in mind the concerns we raised about geographic or group-based comparisons earlier in the book. Figure 6.6 helps us visualize this comparison.

The first thing we can note are regional and even state distinctions. Many of the states with the highest engagement scores are located in the midcontinental north, including Utah, Wyoming, Colorado, the Dakotas, Minnesota, and Wisconsin. A second bloc of high social capital states are found in New England, especially Vermont, New Hampshire, and Maine. Conversely, the states with the lowest social capital scores tend to be in the South and Southwest, including Florida, Louisiana, Nevada, and New Mexico. The authors of the report write, "A clear 'north-south' divide is apparent, and the clustering of states into similar contiguous blocks suggests that geographic differences may have deep-seated roots in

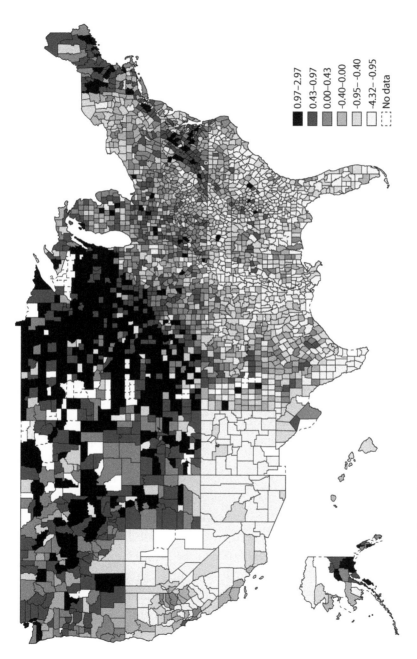

	0.97–2.97
	0.43–0.97
	0.00–0.43
	-0.40–0.00
	-0.95–-0.40
	-4.32–-0.95
	No data

FIGURE 6.6 Social capital across America

Note: Map displays the average "social capital index" for each county in the United States, as described by the U.S. Senate's Joint Economic Committee report, "The Space Between: Renewing the American Tradition of Civil Society." Darkest-shaded counties are those with the highest levels of measurable social capital.

historical immigration and internal migration patterns, regional culture, and perhaps even features of climate and topography."[43] As we discussed in chapter 3, much of American politics has nationalized, and regional distinctions have fallen by the wayside. However, important differences still exist in making sense of how different communities, spread across the United States, engage with one another.

Still, as we argued earlier, you cannot take these regional distinctions and simply infer that by "South" we mean rural, as is too commonly done. Houston, San Antonio, Dallas, Austin, Fort Worth, Jacksonville, Charlotte, El Paso, Nashville, Atlanta, Orlando, and Miami, among others, are southern cities that are also on the list of the fifty largest cities in the United States. South does not mean rural.

As such, we took the Joint Economic Committee's index and merged it with our rural measure, introduced in chapter 1, and created averages between different types of communities all over the country. As with some other analyses already presented, we try to account for the wider variety of ruralness, so we consider very rural (more than 75 percent of residents live in a non-urban area) and somewhat rural places (between 50 percent and 75 percent of residents live in a non-urban area). Table 6.2 also summarizes some of the differences. When we move from regional and state differences to rural differences, we also see a relationship—but it is the opposite of what we might expect. Overall, somewhat rural and very rural counties have higher social capital scores than suburban and urban areas. The index scores range from -4.3 to 2.9. The score is -0.7 for urban areas, -0.09 for somewhat rural areas, and 0.07 for very rural areas. There is a lot of variation in urban and rural America, but, on average, rural areas have higher levels of community engagement on this index.

Looking at some of the particular measures, we see that rural counties do not fare quite as well with some of the more institutional measures, and the percentage of unmarried mothers is a bit higher in rural areas. And yet, more localized civic engagement measures show that rural counties fare better. For instance, in urban areas, there are roughly eight membership organizations per 1,000 residents, but in rural areas, that figure jumps to about thirteen. There are roughly twice the number

TABLE 6.2 Key differences between rural and urban social capital

	Urban	Most rural	Somewhat rural
County-Level Index	−0.70	0.07	−0.09
Membership organizations per 1,000	8.31	12.72	12.57
% Births to unmarried women	34.20	38.35	38.69
Religious congregations per 1,000	0.73	2.65	2.05
Violent crimes per 100,000	450.56	197.94	235.38
Membership organizations per 1,000	8.31	12.72	12.57
Charitable contributions as share of AGI, middle-class itemizers	3.70%	4.58%	4.41%

Note: Table displays the average "social capital index" for each county in the United States, as described by the U.S. Senate's Joint Economic Committee, "The Space Between: Renewing the American Tradition of Civil Society" (December 18, 2019, https://www.jec.senate.gov/public /index.cfm/republicans/2019/12/opportunity-rightly-understood-rebuilding-civil-society -with-the-principle-of-subsidiarity). The most rural counties are where 75–100 percent of the county population lives in nonurban census blocks. Somewhat rural counties are where 50–74.99 percent of the county population lives in nonurban census blocks. Urban counties are where 0–24.99 percent of the county population lives in a nonurban census block (or where 75.01–100 percent of residents live in urban blocks).

of nonprofit organizations per 1,000 residents in rural areas than in urban communities. Rural areas also fare much better in the "informal civic engagement subindex" than do more populated places. The most pronounced difference relates to crime levels: the index notes some 450 violent crimes per 100,000 residents in urban areas but just 235 in somewhat rural and 197 in very rural areas. Elsewhere, 2.7 percent of rural residents report being victims of a crime, while over 5 percent of urban residents do so.[44]

Again, we might take exception to some of the items on the Social Capital Project index, and the way the committee operationalizes some of the measures can seem a bit biased. For example, the "number of organizations" measure does not account for how big they are. And the report recognizes that the "lack of data at the county level on indicators related to social capital reduces the accuracy of local estimates." But the clearest takeaway from the report is that when we introduce a broad range of civic engagement–related measures, rural areas hold up pretty well.[45]

A CLOSER LOOK AT RURAL CHURCHES, SCHOOLS, AND DRUG ABUSE

Although we find the data convincing, maybe you are thinking back to that story you read in the *New York Times* about the rise of Christian nationalism or the *NPR* story on the long bus trips many rural students have to take to get to school.[46] You're right to do that: schools and churches are pillars of any community, but especially in rural America. Has there been a deterioration of particular types of civic and community organizations—institutions that historically held rural communities together—such as churches and schools?

The relationship between social capital and religious life has been well documented. Putnam, in his chapter on this dimension in *Bowling Alone*, suggests that churches have a "unique importance in American civil society."[47] Charles Murray, in *Coming Apart*, writes that religion's role as a source of social capital is "huge."[48] Wuthnow notes, "Religion holds an important place in holding the community together, whether it is preaching and the potlucks, or conducting weddings and funerals."[49] Carney finds that to the true believer, the church is no mere institution; when it comes to people serving as neighbors, "churches do heavy lifting."[50] We know that churchgoers are more likely to engage in secular volunteer activities and give more time and money to community causes. Putnam, with coauthor David Campbell, penned a full-length volume on the interplay of religion and community life, published in 2012, called *American Grace: How Religion Divides and Unites Us.* They suggest, "communities of faith seem more important than faith itself."[51]

Religion is a belief system held by individuals that gives their lives meaning and purpose. But what Putnam, Murray, Wuthnow, and Carney are all pointing to are the ways in which religious community matters outside of one's own personal beliefs. Religious communities—and in rural America, this has generally meant Christian churches—are a particular form of social engagement. That is not just the stuff of squirrelly academics. Echoing Putnam and Campbell, a minister of a small congregation in Collierstown, Virginia, writes, "In rural communities, the church plays a more important role than just offering a meeting place for the local congregation. It brings stability and supports the whole community."[52]

At one level, the story of community collapse in rural America is confirmed by the sharp decline in rural churches, which dates from the end of World War II. Along with the modernization of agriculture came a decline in rural-centered industry—an even larger source of employment. The countless small mills, factories, and workshops that dotted the rural landscape began to close, and along with those closures, the rural populations declined. Congregations withered, and churches closed. As noted by Pamela Riney-Kehrberg, after World War II, "rural schools, rural churches, and small towns lost their constituencies. . . . The United States truly became an urban nation."[53]

The initial response was for churches of the same denomination in nearby towns to share administrative costs and limit the number of full-time employees. Enter the "traveling rural minister," whereby one clergy would drive from town to town on Sunday mornings. As a pastor at Seventh-Day Adventist churches in rural Indiana, Melvin Matthews spent the better part of a long career driving from church to church. "It's a bit frustrating for me to spend more time actually traveling than ministering," Melvin commented after two services and over one hundred miles on the state highways in southern Indiana. Duke University's Mark Chaves, who studies religious trends in American congregations, notes that today, only about half of rural churches have a full-time clergy person [54]

Then, the 2008 Great Recession proved to be a perfect storm for the demise of many rural churches. Combined with population loss, growing secularism, generational change, and the growth of megachurches in suburban and urban areas, rural church foreclosures skyrocketed starting in 2008. According to one account, banks were simply no longer willing to grant struggling religious organizations forbearance. In 2010 alone, some 270 churches were sold after defaulting on their loans, a large number of which were located in struggling rural communities.[55] The Flat Rock Church in Lithonia, Georgia (pop. 1,924), first opened its doors in 1860. It took out an $850,000 balloon loan in 2005 to construct a three-hundred-seat addition. In May 2010, the loan became due, there were few funds to make the payments, and the bank foreclosed.[56]

We asked several questions to try and tap into how personal beliefs and attending church might matter for social capital. On the one hand, our data suggest that rural residents are probably a bit more religious than residents in other geographic areas, given how often they report praying (see chapter 7). This is consistent with an earlier Gallup report finding that rural Americans have slightly higher levels of religiosity.[57] But on the other hand, our data show that they are less likely to attend church services than are urban residents. Roughly 38 percent of urban respondents report they attend church service once a week or more—a figure that drops to 29 percent for rural residents and 26 percent for suburban residents (figure 6.7). Likely the closure of community churches have made attending services more difficult for rural residents. And yet, that less than one-third of rural respondents report regularly attending church services is surprising and certainly noteworthy—especially given the role that faith plays in the lives of so many rural residents.

Like churches, schools have served a similar function in bolstering social engagement in rural communities. Ever since the growth of mass public education in the mid-1800s, the school has been a stand-in for the public square. Schools are structurally independent communities that "foster competence and character in individuals, build social trust, and help children become good people and good citizens."[58] But, of course, they are more than that. Beyond providing our kids' education, schools serve as a cultural center for the moral community. In neighborhoods, towns, and cities across America, schools serve as the focal point for public gatherings. They are the physical places that tie private citizens to the public sphere. We attend sporting events, hold community meetings, watch a play, listen to a concert, see our children grow, and often vote at "the school." They are much more than classrooms, auditoriums, and gyms.

We asked respondents, "Setting aside what happened during the pandemic, which of the following best describes the public schools in your area?" The options ranged from "struggling" to "flourishing." The findings reported in figure 6.7 suggest no statistical difference based on respondent's geography. If anything, rural respondents were a bit *less*

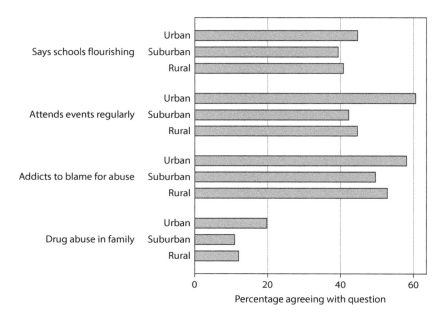

FIGURE 6.7 Engagement in schools and attitudes toward drug abuse in rural, suburban and urban America

Note: Data from the 2021 and 2022 waves of the Rural Voter Survey. Respondent location is self-described, and geographic averages incorporate poststratification weights described in chapter 4. The figure illustrates the percentage of respondents who responded "flourishing" to the question, "Setting aside what happened during the pandemic, which of the following best describes the public schools in [Respondent Location]?"; who indicated the answer option "often" in response to the question, "How often, if ever, do you attend events (football games, plays, concerts, discussions) at schools in your area?"; who said "strongly agree" or somewhat agree" to the question, "Drug abuse is primarily the fault of individuals themselves, drug addicts."; and who indicated "yes" to "Has drug abuse ever been a cause of trouble in your family?"

likely to say schools in their areas are struggling. About the same number (35 percent) of respondents from urban, suburban, and rural areas said their schools were flourishing.

We also took the opportunity in the Rural Voter Survey to ask about resident's attitudes toward drug abuse and violent crime, particularly as they are connected to social capital. The objective facts about the incidence of crime and drug abuse are one way to understand the rural-urban gap. But drug abuse and crime also sever the bonds of social trust in communities. (Recall that Senator Lee's study includes several measures of drug abuse, with the clear conclusion that the drug epidemic is a national crisis, not a rural one.) In rural areas, though, we find that on average, individuals are more likely to view drug abuse differently than urban residents. Just over half of rural residents agree with the idea that drug abuse is mostly the fault of drug addicts themselves (as opposed to, say, Big Pharma). Although the numbers are not overwhelming, more urbanites are likely to place the blame at the feet of individuals. Likewise, when we ask respondents whether violent crime is more prevalent in cities than in rural areas, we see that urbanites—not rural residents—are more likely to agree.

Rural residents are not immune to the grips of America's ongoing drug crisis, particularly as it is centered on opioid abuse. And yet, residents themselves are not thinking about this crisis in any outlandish way. They are not blaming individuals more than expected or overwhelmingly passing the buck. And, contrary to how many urbanites have tried to portray rural residents, they are not fanatics when it comes to seeing urban areas as crime-ridden "hell holes," no matter what Donald Trump says.[59] They see crime in their own communities, and they see drug abuse ravaging rural areas. They see it to the same extent as city dwellers because both Americas are reeling from its dangers.

These questions only scratch the surface. For example, we could think of additional ways in which local schools reinforce social capital in rural communities. Schools are places to gather, but they are also the conduits for the cultivation of civic skills and community ties. By volunteering, going to sports games, attending parent-teacher conferences, working concession stands, and carpooling with neighbors, Americans learn the foundational skills to be productive participants in a democratic society. As their children create friendships in class and the drama club and while prepping for the science fair, families become interwoven. These bonds are the fabric of community cohesion and trust.[60]

Particularly in rural America, schools are often the cornerstone of the local economy. They can be the largest employer in the area, providing secure jobs, retirement plans, and health insurance—increasingly rare commodities. Schools require a large number of employees, including teachers, administrators, custodial staff, coaches, and counselors. There are buildings to construct, food to deliver, parking lots to plow, and grounds to be maintained. Parents and others are drawn to the town center each day, filling the stores, cafes, and auto repair shops.

As with churches, it is no surprise that there has been a decline in the number and viability of rural schools over the past few decades. As with the rise in drug-related arrests (not to mention deaths), these social phenomena affect entire communities.

Federal accountability regulations, rising operating costs, and dwindling enrollment have put the squeeze on small-town school budgets. There is a growing need for child psychological and social services and substance abuse counseling. In rural communities, this usually falls on the school; local schools are usually the only source of help for a range of behavioral health disorders, and the cost of providing these services has become staggering. Due in large measure to skyrocketing special education costs, battles over rural school budgets are as ubiquitous as they are intense. School districts lose funding because of reduced revenue from property taxes—stemming from a shrinking population and economic decay. That is nearly always coupled with declining enrollments. And when schools are in a state of decay, fewer people move to the area, and businesses shy away. It can create a community death spiral. The outcome of higher costs and declining revenues is usually school closure. A town's demise can come in fits and starts over a long period, but when the local school is boarded up, the death bells chime with a deafening resonance.

There are two options for a community with a shrinking population and declining economic base. One is to close schools entirely. According to the Wisconsin Department of Education, since 2002, the state has closed 564 schools.[61] Of that number, 183 were in towns with fewer than ten thousand people. That equates to 32 percent of school closures. In Arkansas, the situation has been even more dire. In the last decade, the state closed 211 schools, 121 of which were in rural towns.[62] That comes out to 57 percent of the school closures. This is happening all over rural America.

Outright closures represent the so-called nuclear option; both faculty and staff are let go, and the remaining students are bused long distances. Several years ago, a report documented the travel times for rural kids in five states: Arkansas, Georgia, New Mexico, Pennsylvania, and Washington. Some 85 percent of the rural districts in each of these states reported that the longest trips for elementary children was in excess of thirty minutes, and 25 percent said the longest rides were over one hour![63] To put this in context, the report notes that the average commuting time for adults during those same years was twenty-two minutes. As noted in another account, rural student bus rides also tended to be more arduous, traversing poorer roads and more hilly or mountainous terrain than those experienced by suburban students. What is more shocking is that many rural elementary children are "double-routed," an efficiency measure whereby they ride the same buses as middle and high school students.[64]

National statistics on current rural bus rides are scarce, but an account in the *New York Times* profiled the long journey for some kids in rural Utah. According to the article, many children in the state sit on bouncing, jarring rides for upward of four hours each school day. "Because school districts are closing down thousands of small country schools across the nation, experts say the bus rides taken by poor rural students . . . are getting longer and rougher."[65] As noted by a scholar who has studied the problem, "Apparently being rural and poor is sufficient justification, in practice, to impose long rides on some young children."[66]

The second option for declining communities is school consolidation. This happens when two or more schools with shrinking enrollments and/or funding consolidate into a new campus at a central location. While this might be a better option for rural communities than complete closure, it is not without drawbacks. West Virginia has been consolidating school districts for decades. The economic ramifications has been massive: according to West Virginia Public Broadcasting, the state has spent over $1 billion on school consolidation in the last two decades. As more and more schools are consolidated, students are forced to travel longer distances. The number of children who ride buses more than two hours a day has doubled. Because of these long travel times, West Virginia spends a larger portion of its education dollars on transportation than any other state.[67]

There are certainly positives to school consolidation, not the least of which is usually a spanking new facility with state-of-the-art infrastructure. Many of these new facilities are impressive and can spark a sense of pride; new buildings rise out of the cornfields and vacant land like Emerald City. But for parents, the growing distance to school leads to fewer volunteer hours in the classroom and for extracurricular activities, and they are less likely to have a relationship with their kids' teachers.

There can be a loss of identity for the community when disparate schools are consolidated. It may seem silly to some, but friction among students and parents can arise when rival schools are merged. And, of course, there can be a big economic hit to the community when local schools are shuttered and students are sent to a consolidated building— often in a remote but centralized location. David Thompson notes that the money spent on consolidated schools is partly returned to the local community only when school employees spend their salaries at local businesses. "By shuttering smaller schools, consolidation takes that money out of the small-town community."[68]

COMMUNITY COHESION IN RURAL AMERICA: DISENGAGED BUT PROUD

As you have seen, our data echo studies that suggest Americans are not especially engaged in traditionally defined community life. Again, we cannot go back in time, but we certainly have the sense that civic connections were more robust "back in the day." On the other hand, there is little evidence to suggest that social capital is significantly worse in rural areas—especially compared with the suburbs. Why, then, do so many journalists and scholars keep saying that rural community life is withering in comparison to other areas?

Some of the misrepresentation has to do with selling a simple, salacious story. As we discuss in chapter 7, stereotypes of rural life abound in pop culture movies, film, and music, so it can be easy—even rote—to pigeonhole these communities in conventional ways. It is certainly true that many rural communities look run-down, with vacant stores and dilapidated buildings all too common. So-called windshield surveys (driving through an area to get a feel for things) likely push some to conclude that rural communities are hollow, worn out.

Another reason—likely the biggest—is that too often, journalists and scholars focus on a narrow dimension of community: the extent to which citizens leave their private lives to engage in community events. Key here is the viability of community institutions like churches, clubs, and nonprofits. Most, but not all, of Putnam's work relies on these sorts of measures. Much of Senator Lee's work was fixed on the breadth of community engagement. This makes perfect sense, given the benefits to individuals, local communities that spring from associational life.

And yet, there are other dimensions of community life that beg our attention: the desire to belong to a particular place. Our findings suggest that community—as an idea and value—is highly desired in rural areas across the country. Rural towns are, by and large, much more cohesive than urban and suburban communities. The fact that rural residents are less engaged in recent decades but place so much importance on community is one reason the "wastelands of alienation" thesis seems more visible in rural communities than elsewhere. We are not arguing that urbanities and suburbanites do not care about community, their place. Rather, we are arguing that when speaking for themselves, rural residents are quicker to define themselves by where they are from and the communities they live in.

When we interviewed Americans about the importance of community, we had a very distinct type of community in mind: communities rooted in place. That is, there are a lot of different communities in the United States, reflecting our rich diversity and pluralistic values. Americans are members of churches, synagogues, mosques, and temples. These are religious communities, which, for many, offer necessary bonds grounded in fellowship, service, and worship. Americans are also members of volunteer organizations, college alumni associations, and small-business groups—even professional sports fans identify as part of a larger community. Geographic communities are like these other communities in some ways. They offer friendship, opportunities for service, and social bonds. They are also unlike these other types of communities in that they are highly exclusive and politically relevant. I can decide tomorrow to root for the Raiders, but it is different from the decision to pack my bags and move thousands of miles away. And even then, nothing guarantees that your community will "adopt" you. One of us recalls, on moving to Maine, a short visit to the local town office. A man at the counter joked with the clerk, "Although I've been here just forty years and am still the new family on the street, I wonder if the town might consider changing the speed limit!"

Since our subject is rural America, and since these are communities that, by definition, are geographically exclusive and, by default, represented in politics, we asked Americans all over the country about whether this type of community—their place—was important to who they are.

One way to make sense of the importance of community is to simply ask residents how long they have lived there. This is a very conservative measure, and it is tied a bit to the average age of residents; we asked respondents to tell us the number of years they have lived in the same town or city. The results may surprise you. Overall, Americans are staying put; our data confirm other sources that show migration rates in the United States are at historic all-time lows.[69] But you are a little more likely to stay where you are if you are in a rural community, especially if you are a millennial (age twenty-six to forty-one) or a member of the prewar generation (age seventy-seven to one hundred or above).

Now, this is surprising not for the small differences in how long rural residents have lived in their hometown, compared with others, but because of the big differences in how rural Americans assess changes in their community. As you can see in table 6.3, when rural residents are asked to describe how their community has been doing, they are more likely to hold pessimistic views about it. Just over half say they are "sure my community is going to be a better place to live in five years." Recall that this animated a sense of economic anxiety we discussed in chapter 5. Perceptions about social mobility and community flourishing are lower in rural America than in other parts of the United States.

TABLE 6.3 Social cohesion in rural, suburban, and urban America

Percentage agreeing with statement:	Urban	Suburban	Rural	Total
"I am sure my community is going to be a better place to live in 5 years"	61.79	57.06	53.61	57.79
"If given the chance, would you move away?"	42.08	23.77	21.36	29.04
Millennials (Post-1981)	47.51	34.48	33.74	39.58
Gen X (1965–80)	42.45	20.70	19.13	27.84
Boomers (1946–64)	22.86	14.96	11.39	15.30
Prewar (Pre-1945)	13.09	6.87	5.37	7.57

Note: Data from the 2021 wave of the Rural Voter Survey. Respondent location is self-described, and geographic averages incorporate poststratification weights described in chapter 4.

It would make perfect sense, then, to assume that respondents who have a dim view of the future of their community would be the most likely to want to leave. In other words, wouldn't those who believe their community's economic future is dire also be interested in leaving? That's not what we found.

When we asked whether rural residents would get up and leave if they had a chance, they flatly rejected our offer, as reported in table 6.3. We appreciate that a resident may wish to stay or move for any number of reasons, but it is also reasonable to assume this query would tap a general feeling of attachment respondents feel to their place. We also couched this question and in a set of several other community-related questions. Given the despair, anger, and resentment we are told rural residents harbor, we would expect them to be interested in moving away. Why not get out of the heck out of that dying community, that desert of civic life? Instead, we find rural residents are much *more* likely to want to remain in their community than urban and suburban residents. Just one in five rural residents said they would move. Conversely, a full 17 percent of rural residents said they would not be anxious to move even if they believed their community was headed for big trouble. That figure is 12 and 10 percent for urban and suburban respondents, respectively.

This finding is not a reflection of age, as one might assume. Although it is a bit higher for millennials—33.7 percent would go—that is nowhere near as high as the 47.5 percent of millennials living in urban areas who would bolt if given the chance. And this is not just a reactionary response to our survey. Rural residents want to stay where they live, and they *do* stay precisely because their communities are central to their identity.

We also used a straightforward, open-ended query: "What are three qualities that come to mind when you think about communities like your own?" Open-ended questions like this enable respondents to express attitudes and opinions in their own words without the constraints of researcher-created response categories. Findings can be rich, complex, and unexpected.[70] Table 6.4 provides the results, averaged over different geographies.

The first item we explored was simply whether the respondent expressed a "positive," "negative," or "neutral" feeling about the community. Given the precise language used by the respondent, is it fair to say that each one expressed good, bad, or indifferent feelings about where they live? Overall, most respondents had positive things to say about their community, which we would hope, but averaging over geography yields some stark differences. Whereas 45 percent of urban respondents offered a positive assessment, that figure jumps to 63 percent for suburban respondents and a whopping 79 percent for rural residents.

The evidence grows when we then look at the general theme of those positive responses. By and large, most rural residents mentioned something positive about the pace of life in rural areas: "Peaceful, community driven, slower paced." There was one word repeated over and over again: "quiet." But alongside those pace-driven descriptions were also remarks about neighborliness and friendliness. And the second-largest category of responses picked up solely on that theme, exactly in line with what our analysis of social capital in rural communities suggests. Rural

TABLE 6.4 Survey results by geography

Open-ended descriptions	Urban	Suburban	Rural	Total
Positive words	44.53	62.77	79.45	62.48
Neutral words	20.09	8.48	5.77	10.92
Negative words	35.38	28.75	14.79	26.66

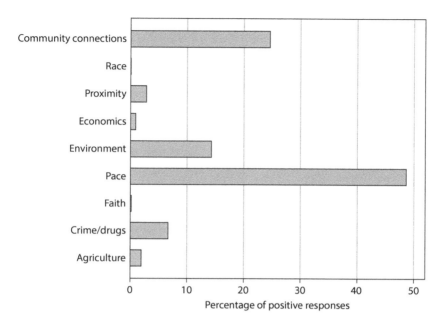

FIGURE 6.8 How rural residents describe their community

> *Note*: Data from the 2022 wave of the Rural Voter Survey. Only rural respondents are included, and averages incorporate poststratification weights described in chapter 4. Categories determined from open-ended responses to the prompt: "What are three qualities that come to mind when you think about rural communities like your own?" Intercoder reliability of each prompt measured 94.3 percent.

America values its community connections (figure 6.8). Here is a sample of some responses:

> "You know the owners of the local businesses. Most of the people are friendly. There is no hustle and bustle, everything moves slower than in the big cities."

> "People participate in things. They appreciate whatever things to do are there. They help each other."

> "Neighbors helping each other, and you can go to a small town and have lunch with someone you know everyday."

"People take care of each other, in other words if someone needs help the neighbors will band together to give assistance."

It is also important to note that whereas we asked about social relationships in specific geographic communities, the GSS data discussed earlier ask respondents to think about people in general. As such, while we can see that rural areas are becoming more skeptical of "most people," rural residents maintain relatively high levels of social trust within their own rural community. That is, whom do they distrust? Those living outside real America.

We also asked rural Americans to come up with five words that describe people living in rural communities within their specific state. We gathered more than twelve thousand descriptors and fed the list to a Latent Dirichlet Allocation (LDA) topic modeler, specifying the Gensim library (Think, ChatGPT, but for the specific purposes of classifying and grouping together lots of text).[71] The distribution returned to us confirmed what we found in other surveys and through manually coding other responses. Overwhelmingly, rural residents described their neighbors living in rural America using positive terms—over 90 percent of the time. Thematically, rural residents were most likely to use words or phrases related to the following.

(1)   Friendliness (59.2 percent of the time): "nice," "outgoing," "caring," "kind," and "generous."

(2)   Simple lifestyle (15.1 percent of words): "down-to-earth," "relaxed," "slower paced," "leisurely."

(3)   Family-oriented (12.6 percent of words): "family-oriented," "dedicated," "community," and "loyal."

(4)   Hardworking (11.4 percent of words): "hardworking," "dedicated," and "diligent," especially in relation to their work as farmers or laborers.

(5)   Conservative (7.5 percent of words): political connotations, including "conservative," "Republican," and "pro-Trump."

Of course, it is possible that people, in general, like to describe people in positive terms. So we also asked urban residents to describe people living in big cities within their state. The list they gave us is very different. Thematically, urbanites were most likely to describe other urban people using terms and phrases related to:

(1) Positive Descriptions of life (35.2 percent of words): "excitement," "entertainment," "fast-paced."
(2) Negative Descriptions of life (27.4 percent of words): "noise," "violence," and "dirt."
(3) Positive Personality Traits (22.1% of the time) "kindness," "caring," and "friendliness."
(4) Negative Personality Traits (18.6 percent of words): "rudeness," "greediness," and "snootiness."
(5) Cultural diversity (15.3 percent of words): references to different races, ethnicities, religions, and cultures.

Nobody loves a wasteland of alienation, but Rural America loves rural America.

RURAL PRIDE AND RURAL POLITICS

In some ways, J. D. Vance has played a leading role in this chapter. His 2016 book is well-written and revealing—and it certainly made sense that it would quickly climb the bestseller lists that year. It is no wonder that his take on rural politics would be in high demand in the wake of the 2016 election. The great geographic divide had been growing for more than three decades, but the rush to explain Donald Trump's upset win put rural voters in the spotlight. Few were surprised when Vance's book was turned into a movie.

One of the key themes of his book, an unfortunate piece of "hillbilly culture," is learned helplessness—a pessimism and despair born from adversity; an ironclad belief that nothing can change. As he leaves to attend Ohio State University, Vance is awash in optimism. Back home, the gloom remains. "There was something almost spiritual about the cynicism of the community at large, something that went much deeper than a short-term recession. . . . As a culture, we had no heroes, certainly not any politician."[72]

At first, Vance was an outspoken critic of Trump. He did not vote for Trump in 2016, calling himself a "never Trumper," and even suggested that much of the former president's support sprang from racism. In a private message to a former college pal, Vance wrote, "I go back and forth between thinking Trump is a cynical asshole like Nixon who wouldn't be that bad (and might even prove useful) or that he's America's Hitler."[73] In fact, in an interview, Vance offered an interesting theory about Trump's support and the decline of social capital. He suggested that white, working-class Americans wouldn't be lured by Trump if they attended church. "I think Trump provides that sense of community that many in the white working class would have, if they actually went to church. I think if folks went to church a little bit more they may not be as excited or as attracted to the sort of social experience that Trump provides."[74]

But all that was before Vance set his sights on the U.S. Senate seat for Ohio. His conversion to Trump's graces is, on one level, easy to understand. In the 2022 midterm elections, few Republicans in red states who failed to get Trump's endorsement made their way through a GOP primary. But it is possible that Vance also came to understand that his assessment about despair, fatalism, and helplessness had only a certain level of appeal. The real energy, the drive and momentum in conservative politics is a sense of distrust and grievance, tied to a deep love of place. Rural America is awash in grievance, and it certainly has a profound love of place. Former U.S. Senator Claire McCaskill of Missouri summarized the turn of rural politics this way: "It's a complicated stew, and it started before Trump, but there is no question that Donald Trump mainlined rural grievance."[75] In the desperate desire to stem the tide of change and to keep their beleaguered communities together, rural voters had found a cause and someone who celebrated, not denigrated, rural life.

On Election Day, Vance beat his opponent—a working-class Democrat, Tim Ryan, 53 to 47 percent. But that was only after Republicans poured millions of dollars into a state where Trump and Republicans won handedly. Ryan, it seemed, was well positioned to challenge Vance. He fits the mold of Ohio's now-senior senator, Sherrod Brown, a Democrat. He spoke openly about his resistance to Nancy Pelosi's leadership and attacked China's trade policies. He was a proud Ohioan, born and bred in the small steel mill towns that are a part of the economic decline in rural America. He was, nevertheless, a Democrat—a long-time partisan unable to distinguish his candidacy from his support of Joe Biden and the House majority. Vance's principal strategy—his only strategy—was to tie Ryan to electric vehicle subsidies, Democratic industrial policies pursued during the Obama administration, and the rising cost of fuel.

There may be a silver lining tied to Ryan's homespun sense of place and pride in Ohioan communities. Trump won rural voters in Ohio by forty-four points in 2020, but Ryan closed that gap to just fifteen points— an incredible shift given the historic voting trends in rural America, and rural Ohio in particular. Surprisingly, Ryan did worse in suburban and urban communities than Biden did in 2020. Our analysis of exit polls suggests that if Ryan had maintained his urban and suburban advantage, his conversion of rural voters would have put him within a single point of victory. Nothing suggests that this trade-off is zero sum. Ryan's doing better in rural America was not necessarily the reason he did worse outside it. There are national forces and local issues in every election. What we know is that even though rural voters marginally approved Vance, the real Republican stronghold in Ohio was suburbia.[76] A Democrat showed up, played up his strong local roots, celebrated the lives lived in rural Ohio, and was rewarded.

What both Ryan and Vance know is that rural America is not down and out; they are also bound to a larger cause—the fight to preserve their communities. They are cynical of politics and distrustful of outsiders but not alienated from each other. They relish where they live, and that a strong sense of place, coupled with a sense of a shared destiny, has redefined electoral politics.

7

CLINGING TO THEIR GUNS
AND RELIGION?

When John Denver sat down with two friends to write "Take Me Home, Country Roads," talk of an abyss between rural and nonrural cultures would have seemed strange. Released in 1971, the song became a huge hit in rural areas, but it was also played endlessly on pop radio stations from New York to San Francisco, eventually climbing to number 2 on the *Billboard* charts. It was released during a turbulent period in American politics, certainly, but the song taps feelings of nostalgia and a simpler time, so its broad appeal made sense. As noted by one commentator, "Through countless adaptations, the enduring success of 'Country Roads' seems to lie in its transcendent ability to evoke feelings of home and belonging."[1] Denver's songs celebrate the beauty and frailty of nature and the traditions of rural life. It made little difference that he was a hippie, a die-in-the-wool Democrat, and frequent critic of Republican officials or that he would rail against American foreign policy.[2] His songs hit a sweet spot in the American psyche by celebrating rural life and the people who lived it.

At the same time Denver was crooning about dirt roads in West Virginia and the mountains of Colorado, *The Waltons* burst into American living rooms. Set in rural Virginia during the Depression, the nine-season television series charted the early life of John-Boy Walton, his parents, grandparents, and five siblings. Times were tough, but life was simple and harmonious on Walton's Mountain. Economic hardships were present—it was the Depression, after all—but there was never a trace of anger or resentment toward elites, politicians, or those in far-off cities. Their poverty seemed, well, quaint—like something out of a 1940s Frank Capra film. At the end of the pilot, the mother, Olivia, asks her husband, who had just quit his job in the city, how they would survive. "But John," she asks, "what are we going to live on?" John responds, "Love, woman. Love." There was no racial animus—the family was quite friendly with the poor Black family down the road—and any hint of alcohol abuse was couched in never-ending jokes and storylines about the beloved "recipe."

And *Little House on the Prairie* rounded out the ideal rural life. First aired on television in 1972, countless Americans tuned in to watch Pa, Ma, Laura, and her sisters struggle to survive frontier life at the end of the nineteenth century. The show was about family, hard work, and community. There is self-reliance, but the Ingalls family gets by with the help of friends and neighbors in Walnut Grove. The virtues of rural community life were made vivid every Wednesday night.

The celebration of rural life in the early 1970s crossed ideological boundaries and demographic groups, but it was particularly attractive to baby boomers. Starting in the late 1960s, as many as a million young Americans left their homes in the suburbs and cities and moved to farmhouses, remote mountaintops, and woodland clearings to grow their own food and live closer to the earth.[3] The back-to-the-land movement created one of the most unusual demographic shifts in American history, briefly reversing two hundred years of steady urbanization.[4]

But things started to change in the 1980s. A decade after Denver's "Country Road" topped the charts, Hank Williams Jr. released "A Country Boy Can Survive." It, too, jumped to the top of the country music charts— but flopped on pop radio stations. The song could not have been more different than Denver's upbeat lyrics and melodies or the tranquil scenes on Walton's Mountain. Williams sang of a culture under assault, a way of life besieged by urbanization and change. Country folks can endure, we are told, by clinging to the skills and values that can be found only in rural America. "I had a good friend in New York City," sang Williams.

"He never called me by my name, just Hillbilly. My grandpa taught me how to live off the land. And his taught him to be a businessman." Above all, the song is about defiance: sure, look down on the rural way of life, but we have skills that matter, when push comes to shove, and we'll stick together. We are a distinct people, bound by community, character, and a novel skill set.

Williams's song was just the start of a long cultural development in American society—the creation of a national, rural identity, built in reaction and opposition to an increasingly urban-centered portrayal of what it means to be a successful, modern, dare we say "cultured" American. The result is that rural culture has now become nationalized—dependent on a few key flashpoints in nearly all parts of the country. What is more, the transformation of rural culture has largely been a response to the stereotypes and caricatures that have increasingly portrayed rural America as an intolerant backwater. That is, the nationalization—and to some extent, the "hardening"—of rural culture has been a defensive move. Although anecdotal, we confess that one of most common words we have seen in the long emails responding to our op-eds and public talks is that these "uncultured" people deserve little attention in our forward-looking society. That matters, not just for urban views, but in how rural residents see themselves. And the strident change has *not* come about by new residents moving in and others moving out. The change has been too rapid. Instead, we find a shift among existing residents. There has not been, as social scientists might say, a change of place but, rather, a change of heart.[5]

This chapter will explore the widening gulf between urban and rural culture. "Culture" can be an amorphous term—anything and nothing at the same time. We explore culture in two ways. First, we look at some of the common values and ways of living that rural residents hold regardless of their religion, age, level of education, and so on. We explore the cultural-political glue that binds rural residents together. The picture is multidimensional, and we take up distinctive elements in different chapters. For instance, rural residents have a strong sense of community, which we discussed in chapter 6, and they have a common understanding of what constitutes "hard work," a key topic we take up in chapter 8. Both of those are a part of rural culture, but here, we zero in on these additional cultural components: gun ownership, religious attitudes, views on abortion, ideological conservatism, and patriotism.

In short, the hackneyed portrayals of a culturally deprived, out-of-touch backwater are misleading. That is because on some of the most fundamental issues—what it means to be patriotic, who you should trust to make decisions, what rights are owed to individuals—rural and urban America are actually not that divided. On major cultural issues, we are deeply divided by partisanship, but seldom by geography.

In earlier chapters, we presented the real forces driving rural distinctiveness as those related to competing ideas about economic anxiety and place-based grievance, as well as how rural residents think about their community, particularly their civic pride. Race and widespread attitudes about the value of hard-work also drove the divide. But when considering some of these other ways in how rural, suburban, and urban Americans see themselves, the gaps are just not nearly as consequential. Our evidence again comes from the Rural America Survey, as well as a few aggregate data sources. In some ways, the divisions we explore next are the least consequential for understanding the rural-urban divide, even as they sit at the heart of a widening partisan gap and the epicenter of perceived geographic differences. Our conclusions largely stem from teasing out the composition effects of partisans in rural and urban areas. We would be convinced of a rural culture gap if rural conservatives and rural progressives behaved or thought differently than their partisan or ideological brethren living elsewhere. That would suggest that geography is doing some work and that on these profound cultural issues, local, rural context matters.

However, with the exception of gun culture, rural residents are not outside mainstream values. They are, on average, more likely to hold conservative or right-leaning positions on many issues, but those ideas are found all over the country. Indeed, as we have repeatedly stressed, although there are fewer Republicans in urban areas, as a percentage of a city's population, there are many more Republicans there than in all of rural America. Even if conservative values are found in a greater degree in rural areas, it is a mistake to call those values "rural" when a majority of Americans who subscribe to them live outside rural communities.

And yet, we do not neglect the fact that almost everyone has a picture in their heads that rural America is very different from urban America—that rural Americans do, in fact, have different values from the Republican family living in suburbia or the big city. This is not a function of proportions. Even if we live in very politically homogeneous communities, we know that not everyone agrees. So why do Americans, both rural and urban, think they belong to different cultures when, in fact, they do not?

Cultural perceptions have built up over generations, and they will continue to define what it means to be a member of "rural America" long into the future. Modern forms of entertainment, or pop culture, have come to reflect and even reinforce the idea that rural residents are, well, just different. How Americans spend their free time has always varied by geography, but today the chasm between rural and urban life-styles and perspectives is enormous—extending to music, movies and television, the sports we play and watch, the stores and restaurants that take our money, the cars we drive, and the beer we drink. Pop culture also provides powerful cues to rural residents about how the broader culture views them and to nonrural residents about what we might make of those who spend their days in the countryside.

Pop culture and attitudes feed into one another. Art imitates life, and life mirrors art. In rural America, however, the portrayal of rural residents as simple-minded, folksy, racist, backwards . . . you name it . . . well, it has not been taken so lightly. In fact, our data show that rural residents' perceptions of how the entertainment media portray them is a major source of rural grievance—a simmering anger that has politicized their distinctive identity and put them in the service of exploitative politicians willing to wage war on behalf of the "real America."

Statistically, most of our readers will not be from rural America, so the image in your head of what rural America is like will have been formed from the artfully crafted stories you have witnessed on television and at the movies. Most will not realize how one-sided and even distorted these pictures have become. The second half of this chapter offers a survey of the rural entertainment media landscape over the past century. There is a reason most people living in urban and suburban parts scratch their heads when they think about rural issues and rural people—who but the uncultured, least-educated, backward-thinking would want to live in flyover country? That is the picture that has been painted for you!

GUN OWNERSHIP AND HUNTING

It is only honest to admit that most of us depend on the media to make sense of one another—including the communities in which we actually live. Not everyone has access to thousands of survey responses. What are some of the actual cultural differences? There must be regional and geographic variation in how Americans live, what they value, and what they fear. What sets rural culture apart? In 2017, a *Washington Post*-Kaiser Family Foundation survey was conducted of nearly seventeen hundred Americans—including more than a thousand living in rural areas.[6] Nearly 70 percent of the rural residents reported that their values differed from those of people who live in big cities, including about 40 percent who said their values are "very different." Surprisingly, less than 20 percent of urbanites suggested rural values are "very different" from their own. But that was a look at the perception of general attitudes and beliefs—not a measure of what those actual values were. How does rural culture differ from culture in other parts of the country? To what extent do rural Americans actually hold different values, and to what extent are these perceived differences simply false?

Perception of "two Americas" is rampant, and these fake constructs become especially problematic when they warp how politicians see and portray the "other America." Speaking at a San Francisco fundraiser in 2008 while running for the Democratic nomination, then candidate Barack Obama regaled his audience with tales of his travels through rural America. "You go into these small towns in Pennsylvania and, like a lot of small towns in the Midwest, the jobs have been gone now for 25 years and nothing's replaced them," Obama said. "And it's not surprising when they get bitter, they cling to guns or religion." Even Hillary Clinton described Obama as an "elitist" in response. Ouch.[7]

Poor wording? Yes. But might there also be a glimmer of truth? Sure, many urbanites—mainly progressives and Democratic voters—who hold these views about rural culture view it as a by-product of some larger force in American society: economic collapse, diversification, liberalization of certain mores. Confronted with this new version of "progress," rural Americans retreat and get bitter. What Obama shared, and what many urbane progressives were willing to confirm, was a story of rural peoples' knee-jerk bitterness in reaction to change throughout the rest of America.

We have already thought about and dismissed the common explanation of how rural politics plays out in terms of economic decline, job losses, and rural poverty. Yes, times are tough, but poverty needs to be politicized for it to cement an idea of a rural people, unfairly treated by the undeserving other, "over there." And when it comes to cultural values like gun ownership and religiosity, we also find that the image of the bitter rural resident clinging to backward beliefs is one-dimensional.

Let's start with guns. No doubt gun ownership is more common in rural America. We hear it every Saturday afternoon—there's always somebody shootin' somewhere; and don't forget to wear your blaze orange on the hiking trail come November. According to our data, just 37 percent of urban residents own a gun. That number is actually smaller in suburban areas: 34 percent. In rural America, though, over half of households surveyed—54 percent—have a gun. Rural residents are more likely to own a weapon by a large margin.

Of course, there are two ways of reading this finding. Yes, more rural residents own guns than urbanites; we did not ask about the number of guns owned, which may be important in a country where there are more guns than people. But large percentages of both urbanites and suburbanites also own guns. Accounting for their respective population sizes, there are many more gun owners outside rural areas than in rural areas! Stated a bit differently, a vast majority of the gun owners in America live in urban and suburban communities.

We may wonder, then, if all those urbanites and suburbanites are also clinging to their guns. In rural America at least, the numbers seem to track well with the percent of the population who hunts. In rural America, for instance, over four in ten respondents said that someone in their household hunts. When we consider both questions together, we find that 60 percent of rural residents who own a gun also hunt.

We get a very different picture elsewhere in America, where just over a quarter of urban residents—26 percent—say someone in their family hunts. It is even lower in suburban America (22 percent). And in those two areas, smaller proportions of gun owners actually report someone in the family hunting. That is, in rural areas, there is a pragmatic element to gun ownership. We do not and cannot equate gun ownership in rural America just with hunting, however. Home defense and simple hobby shooting are undeniably reasons for owning a firearm. Some 40 percent of the rural residents who own a firearm do not hunt. There is, though, a rural-urban divide, but one that might suggest that nonrural residents are the gun "clingers" in this case.

When it comes to gun politics in America, we recognize that hunting is often seen as a side distraction to much larger issues involving various types of weapons and the ease with which they can be bought. Believe it or not, many hunters favor strict gun control laws (including one of the authors of this book). We are not trying to simplify an incredibly complex and deeply emotional issue for many Americans. In addition to asking people whether or not they owned a gun, we asked a set of questions about potential gun regulations and the causes of gun violence in the United States.

As we have stressed throughout this book, there is only so much we can discern from demographic or aggregate data alone. It's easy to overlay population density data with levels of gun ownership, for example. But to understand gun politics, we need to ask about perceptions, attitudes, and beliefs. At the onset, it should be noted that we asked the following questions about two weeks after the mass shooting at Robb Elementary School in Uvalde, Texas, where a single gunman killed nineteen students and two teachers. It was the third-deadliest school shooting at the time of this writing. Undoubtedly, it affected responses even if, as we believe, attitudes toward guns are less contingent than other types of views surveyed throughout this book. We have good reason to believe that it increased favorable attitudes toward gun regulation regardless of where respondents live. As such, while we find some surprising attitudes in favor of gun regulation among urban, suburban, and rural Americans, we do not want to suggest that when push comes to shove, rural residents—and rural gun owners in particular—are going to easily accept more regulation. Besides, plenty of ideas with majority support languish in the American system, especially when they encounter stiff, organized opposition from well-funded interest groups. Still, as we have been throughout this book, we are interested in the differences between groups and not just attitudes overall.

Here, it seems, Obama's line may have hit the mark—maybe. On a range of issues, rural residents are much more likely to express pro-gun absolutist positions. While there are more gun owners outside rural America than inside, attitudes among rural residents—whether or not they own a gun—are intense. There is strong agreement throughout the United States for raising the age to buy a firearm to twenty-one years, but rural gun owners are about eight points less likely to favor that change than are nonrural residents (figure 7.1). Raising the age limit has become a more popular proposal in recent years, especially in the aftermath of school shootings such as Uvalde (where the eighteen-year-old gunman legally bought his weapon). On other issues, the gap between rural and nonrural residents widens. Clear majorities of nonrural residents favor a ban on assault weapons. Not so in rural America, where barely a majority indicates approval and nearly six in ten gun owners reject the proposal. Interestingly enough, at least, on average, equal percentages of rural and urban residents support the idea that some teachers should be able to carry guns in schools: 48 percent of rural residents compared with 47 percent of urban ones.

The teachers with guns debate, however, highlights an important point: geography matters, but so does partisanship. Democrats in urban areas are not like Democrats in the suburbs, and that is why support

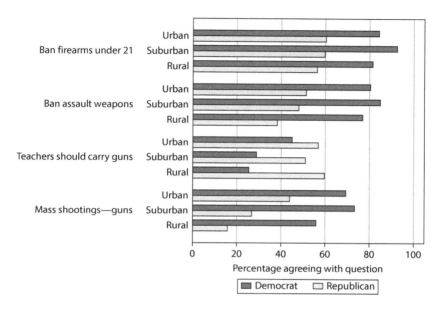

FIGURE 7.1 Gun ownership and values in rural, suburban, and urban America

Note: Data from the 2021 and 2022 waves of the Rural Voter Survey. Respondent location and partisan identity are self-described, and geographic averages incorporate poststratification weights described in chapter 4. The figure illustrates the percentage of respondents "strongly agreeing" or "somewhat agreeing" with the following statements: "Americans under 21 should NOT be able to buy firearms"; "Government should ban the sale of military-style assault weapons in the United States"; "Simply put, mass shootings happen because there are just too many guns in the United States"; and "If we want to protect America's kids, teachers should carry guns."

trends a bit higher in cities. And as we can do with that policy, so we can do with other policies. Once we take into account the partisan differences between these urban and rural areas, we find that rural voters are not all that different. That is, the gaps in rural and urban support for guns largely stems from partisan composition effects. Republicans have a decided opinion on gun control and hold those opinions regardless of where they live (and again, many, many more Republicans live outside rural communities than within them). Compare the lightly shaded bars in figure 7.1 between different geographies, and you will see that rural

Republicans are ever-so-slightly less favorable to gun control measures than urban or suburban Republicans. Rural Democrats, on the other hand, largely adopt the same position as national Democrats.

There is one question we asked for which geographic differences do exist in responses between Republicans. Most dramatically, especially given the fact that we fielded this set of questions weeks after a deadly school shooting, rural residents reacted strongly against the idea that, "Simply put, mass shootings happen because there are just too many guns in the United States." Rural residents as a whole (70 percent) and rural gun owners in particular (80 percent) disagreed with that idea. Rural Republicans disagreed to a large extent (84 percent), especially compared with urban Republicans (56 percent). Throughout the country, strong majorities—even among gun owners in urban America—agreed, but not in rural America. In fact, rural Democrats were less likely to agree with the idea than urban Democrats (even though a bare majority still did).

What are we to make of high rates of agreement with potential gun reforms but strong outlier preferences on the fundamental values of gun ownership as a way of life? We insist that guns are just a part of rural ways of living. It is a cultural "thing" that explains why rural residents have come to see themselves as different. In this case, perceptions match reality. Rural residents and rural gun owners are particularly drawn to the idea that "hunting is a part of our national heritage," for example. Nearly 85 percent of rural Republicans agree with that idea, as do 60 percent of rural Democrats—statistically much higher than the 40 percent of urbanites who believe so. Hunting, in short, is also a part of gun culture in rural America.

As incredible as this may seem, only a short time ago—as late as the 1980s—many high school kids in rural communities would bring their shotguns and rifles on school buses and store them in a broom closet or the principal's office so they could hunt after class. It was also commonplace for high school students in rural communities to store rifles on racks in pickup trucks and leave them in the school parking lots.[8] After-school hunter and gun safety classes remain ubiquitous in most rural communities.

Consider, also, a brief anecdote from our state of Maine. Democrat Janet Mills was elected in 2018, the first woman governor of the state. Like most statewide Democratic candidates, she fared poorly in rural areas but scored huge majorities in the south and along the coast. She was easily reelected in 2022—beating the former governor, Paul LePage, who was making a comeback bid. Not long after her second win, a few progressive state legislators began pushing for tighter gun control regulations. Maine is one of the most lenient states in the nation; for example, anyone can purchase a pistol without a permit, and all types of guns can be sold at shows or through classified ads without controls. But Mills rejected the move offhand. It would go against Maine's rural heritage. In fact, a 1980s amendment to the state constitution stipulates that the right to bear arms "shall never be questioned." Maine is progressive in many ways, including being a leader in the battle for marriage equality (easily passing a statewide promarriage referendum in 2012), but by a wide margin, voters rejected a 2016 measure to mandate background checks on all private gun sales. Gun ownership and hunting in Maine are cultural traditions.

This attitude is also clear when asked about hunting and in an expressive, almost annoyed reaction to the thought that widespread gun ownership is to blame for tragedies like Uvalde. It is not that there are no policy-oriented middle grounds, though. That certainly explains why even progressive politicians from rural areas—what few there are (like Janet Mills)—steer clear of gun control policies. It's widely known that even Bernie Sanders voted against expanding background checks in the 1990s. In a 2015 interview, and in uncharacteristically moderate language, Sanders suggested a middle ground on guns: "We need a sensible debate about gun control which overcomes the cultural divide that exists in this country."[9]

Don't mistake us. The rural-urban divide is a major barrier to having a sensible debate about guns, but not because rural residents are rabid, unreflective, gun-toting fanatics. Rather, the same politics and narratives that drive the partisan gap also play out in a "real America" that values gun ownership and hunting. Consider the recent book, *On Target: Gun Culture, Storytelling, and the NRA*, in which the political scientist Noah Schwartz offers a compelling take on why the National Rifle Association carries such weight in rural communities. He argues that the key tool used by the NRA is carefully honed stories that link gun ownership to legends of America's past and to a simpler time when families and communities were united. "The NRA idealizes rural life, telling stories of fathers and sons bonding in the duck blind, of friends plinking tin cans off of a wooden fence with their dad's old .22, or of America's heroes returning from the fight overseas to tend the farm and raise a family"[10] There are cowboy heroes, renowned hunters, frontier families, trappers, and stalwart outdoorsmen. Other stories paint urban communities as dangerous and crime-ridden, the consequence of liberal policies and culture. These created narratives link gun ownership to the assault on rural communities. It does not matter whether or not you own a gun, "they" are out to end your way of life.

CHRISTIANITY AND EVANGELICALISM

What about religion? When they aren't out shootin' their guns, are rural residents flocking to church to pray (maybe for more guns?). We took a similar approach as described earlier. However, in this case, and like many other reputable surveys—including the Pew Research Center, which for years has explored religious attitudes in the American public— we find that religion does little to explain the widening gulf between urban and rural America, especially once partisan differences are taken into account.[11]

We start with two straightforward behavioral measures: "How often do you pray and attend church?" If we were to zoom in on the make-believe towns found in the TV shows *Hart of Dixie* and *Virgin River*, we might expect to find the streets emptied on Sunday morning until the pews emptied onto the streets and everyone flocked to the local barbecue joint. But on the whole, that is just not what is taking place throughout most of rural America.

In fact, rates of church attendance are lower in rural America than they are elsewhere (see figure 7.2). Some of the reason for that, as we

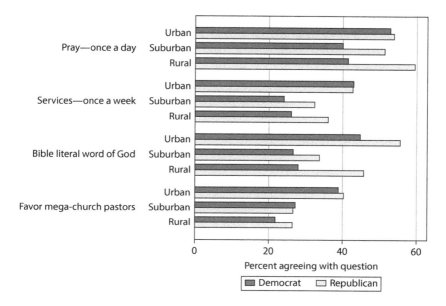

FIGURE 7.2 Religious beliefs and practices in rural, suburban, and urban America

Note: Data from the 2021 and 2022 waves of the Rural Voter Survey. Respondent location and partisan identity are self-described, and geographic averages incorporate poststratification weights described in chapter 4. The figure illustrates the percentage of respondents who indicated "once a day" to the question, "People practice their religion in different ways. Outside of attending religious services, how often do you pray?"; those who indicated at least "once a week" to the question, "Aside from weddings and funerals, how often do you attend religious services in your community?"; who, when asked, "Which of these statements comes closest to describing your feelings about the Bible," answered "The Bible is the actual word of God and is to be taken literally, word for word"; and who gave "Mega-Church Pastors" a score of 50 or higher on a 0–100 feeling thermometer.

explored in chapter 6, is institutional: small churches have been closing their doors during the last few decades throughout the United States, but especially in rural parts. Even so, we are left with a chicken-and-egg problem. Maybe rural residents are not going to church as much as urbanites—where 38 percent still attend at least once a week—because there are few churches. That may make sense given that rural residents report praying just as frequently as urban Americans—and slightly more than suburban Americans. This may explain the partisan differences in church attendance between rural and urban communities. Both rural Democrats and rural Republicans are less likely than urban partisans to attend religious services on a weekly basis.

As with gun ownership, these simple behavioral patterns tell only part of the story. Are rural communities bastions of religious extremism? We asked Americans some questions meant to explore how intense, or even "extreme," individuals' religious beliefs were. Again, we were operating under the idea that many Americans—maybe even you—believed that rural residents not only attended church and prayed more often than "normal" folks, but held religious views that put them outside the mainstream, especially those related to Christian evangelicalism.

As it turns out, you would be better off searching for those views in urban areas as opposed to rural ones. We asked respondents whether they thought the Bible was the "literal word of God." Not even accounting for the fact that there are higher proportions of non-Christians in urban America, rural Americans were less likely to agree with the idea. Likewise, it has been common to think of rural America as the hotbed for Christian evangelicalism, epitomized by the huge megachurches, where attendance often exceeds ten thousand people per week and sermons are broadcast nationwide.[12] As the story goes, 80 percent of white Christian evangelicals voted for Donald Trump in 2016, and we know that rural America loves him. Ergo, it is rural America's "clinging" onto religion—particularly Christian evangelicalism—that is keeping America back.

But readers of this book, we hope, may begin to scratch their heads. Why would that be more common in rural America, where populations of entire towns and counties are often well below ten thousand? Good thinking. As with so many issues we have explored, these quick comparisons fail to take into account multiple factors that explain certain political trends—not the least of which is that most rural Christians are not evangelical and most evangelical congregations are found in suburban and urban America. In fact, when we ask about attitudes toward megachurch pastors, the favorability rate is lowest among rural residents. Rural America is overwhelmingly more Christian than average, and it is becoming more so as the country grows secular and diversifies. But it remains the case that voters in the United States are religious no matter where they live. It is not a defining part of rural politics but politics in general.

Nowhere is the religious divide in American politics more pronounced and consequential than in the heated debates over abortion access and rights for individuals identifying as LGBTQIA+. As we surveyed in chapter 3, abortion politics has been a frontline issue in the ascendancy of modern conservatism. Thomas Frank described abortion, along with guns, as one of the "cultural wedge issues" that had "hallucinatory appeal" among poor whites in rural Kansas who had gravitated to the Republican Party in response to its deft manipulation of voters' concerns.[13] Today, similar arguments are made about the politics of so-called bathroom bills and the use of Child Protective Services to arrest parents supporting gender reassignment surgery for their children.

Given the concentration of practicing Christians in religious areas, it is not surprising that a great deal of commentary has equated rural politics with a steadfast conservatism on these issues. But again, the Rural Voter Survey offers us a different take. As with other prominent surveys that have considered the geographic distribution of abortion attitudes, we find no evidence that rural America is any more conservative than average. We asked respondents whether "abortion should be ILLEGAL under ALL circumstances" as a way of measuring unequivocal positions on an issue full of equivocation. On average, 18 percent of Americans strongly agreed and 17 percent of Americans somewhat agreed. In rural America, just 19 percent strongly agreed and only 12 percent somewhat agreed, meaning that total agreement was somewhat less in rural than in nonrural America. And that is without accounting for heightened Republican partisanship. In fact, if we consider only Republican partisans, rural Republicans are ten points less likely to agree with that very prolife sentiment than are urban and suburban Republicans.

Similar patterns exist when asking about LGBTQIA+ issues. Admittedly, the Rural Voter Survey did not exhaustively cover every single issue affecting millions of rural residents, including over three million rural residents who identify as LGBT, according to the Movement Advancement Project's study of LGBT people in rural America. As that group rightfully points out, "General societal stereotypes and pop culture portrayals of

LGBT people suggest that LGBT people live solely in urban settings, while stereotypes and portrayals of rural communities rarely, if ever, include LGBT people—except as targets of anti-LGBT violence, or as people yearning to leave their rural home to migrate to 'more accepting' urban areas." In reality, not only do LGBT people live in rural America, but many enjoy living in the countryside. "In discussions with LGBT people living in rural communities, researchers find that for many LGBT people in rural areas, living in a rural area may be just as important to who they are as being LGBT."[14]

This is not to diminish the significant barriers that LGBTQIA+ people face; rather, it is a call to recognize that those barriers exist across the entire landscape of American society. When we asked respondents whether they agreed or disagreed with the idea that "you are born a male or female, and cannot switch," nearly 65 percent of Americans agreed. Average agreement in rural areas was just three points higher than in urban America. There is no hard evidence to suggest that rural residents are any less tolerant of LGBTQIA+ people than are Americans in other settings.

NATIONALISM, PATRIOTISM, AND MILITARY SERVICE

While the stereotypes of the gun-clinging, churchgoing extremists may be overrepresented in Hollywood—and in some campaign rhetoric—there are other cultural distinctions embedded in the myth of "real America," and at the top of the list are attitudes about America itself.

It is deeply ironic that so much of the "two Americas" rhetoric centers on the idea of who loves their country the most. Patriotism, and what it means to be patriotic, has become a central fault line in American society, not just between urban and rural parts of the country but also between the two parties and liberals and conservatives. At the same time, it is hard to gauge this patriotic divide; often, patriotic language and symbolism are mere window dressings for differences about policy or self-interest.

Meadville, Pennsylvania (pop. 13,000) is the Crawford County seat. That area of the state, south of Erie and north of Pittsburgh, is conservative through and through, but Meadville boasts a hospital, lots of lawyers, and a two-hundred-year-old liberal arts college (Allegheny). In other words, there is a small island of moderates and progressives in a sea of far-right conservatism. It is places like this where the "battle of true patriotism" is fought time and again.

Not long after the United States invaded Iraq in the spring of 2003, a group of women began holding silent antiwar vigils in the town square, Diamond Park, every Saturday. They called themselves the Women in Black. It drew a good bit of local media attention. Quickly, a response emerged on laws and roadways in the countryside: red-and-white yard signs with the message, "Support the Troops." Soon, the antiwar group began printing near-identical signs, this time saying, "Support the Troops: Bring Them Home." Not to be undone, yet another set of red-and-white signs were printed: "Support the Troops: Period."

Tension between the groups became more and more intense as the war dragged on. In 2007, things reached breaking point when both groups held rallies in the park at the same time. It was an ugly day, with screams and taunts volleying back and forth. "If you don't love America, leave!" According to one observer, "One group thinks that the war is moral and legal, and they say 'support the troops' by supporting the mission, while the other group thinks the war is illegal and immoral, so they say 'support the troops by bringing them home.'"[15]

More recently, as more and more video footage of the January 6th insurrection has been made public, we have learned that many of the rioters expressed deep love for their country. While they were breaking down barricades, shattering windows, and ransacking offices and hallways of the nation's capital, many were also voicing heartfelt patriotic messages—some in tears. We also learned that 10 percent of the rioters were military veterans. Eric Hodges conducted a content analysis of the remarks made by forty of these veterans during the chaos. Most, it seems, believed they were acting out of love for their country and the founding fathers. One was heard commenting, "We need all the patriots of this country to rally the fuck up and fight for our freedom or it's gone forever. Give us liberty or give us death." Another said, "We are very skilled patriots ready for a fight," and still another: "We can't lose our America."[16]

But we all know that "patriotism" is a political cue—and has been so since the Vietnam War. Are rural residents protective of their country; are they patriotic? Indeed, they are. So, too, are most Americans. We asked respondents whether they are "extremely proud to be an American," and a majority of voters strongly agree (figure 7.3). Only 8 percent of respondents tell us they strongly or even somewhat disagree with the thought. Americans are, by and large, patriotic. It is,

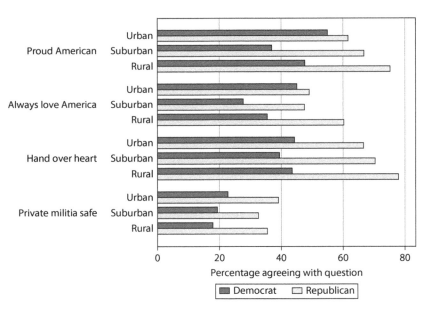

FIGURE 7.3 Patriotic attitudes in rural, suburban, and urban America

Note: Data from the 2021 and 2022 waves of the Rural Voter Survey. Respondent location and partisan identity are self-described, and geographic averages incorporate poststratification weights described in chapter 4. The figure illustrates the percentage of respondents "strongly agreeing" or "somewhat agreeing" with the following statements: "I am extremely proud to be an American"; "Proud Americans love their country no matter what"; "Americans should put their hand over their heart when they hear the national anthem"; and "People who join private militias or other paramilitary groups are dangerous."

however, remarkable that even in a very patriotic country, where it is socially undesirable to criticize the idea of America (as opposed to a specific leader), that rural Americans are even more patriotic than average. And given the overwhelming majority of "proud Americans," we may not be surprised by the large majority of respondents who also agreed with the statement, "proud Americans love their country no matter what." Suburbanites were the least likely to strongly agree, at just 35 percent. Some 47 percent of rural voters and 43 percent of urban voters agreed with that idea.

We had to get creative in how we pose questions to gauge patriotic attitudes, as it is a nuanced topic. In one survey, we asked people to think about a common patriotic act: whether they "should put their hand over their heart when they hear the national anthem." One of us, for instance, has noticed a big difference when attending his kids' sporting events. Everyone rises. That's to be expected. But some place their hands over their heart while others do not. Is this simply a variable custom, or is it an indicator of robust patriotism? Might it be yet another tribal marker—a not-so-subtle wink and nod to others about your politics? It seems that rural residents pick up on this cue. Many Americans support the idea—at least while clicking through on a survey—but statistically higher percentages of rural voters—63 percent of them—strongly agree with the idea compared with just half of urbanites.

This one surprised us. We thought, given the resentment rural residents feel toward progressive-leaning, blue cities, that rural Americans might express—even if only facetiously—a desire to simply break up with urban American. For instance, in February 2023, Rep. Marjorie Taylor Greene, who represents a primarily rural district in the northwest corner of Georgia, made headlines by suggesting a "national divorce" whereby red and blue states go their separate ways. So, we expected that when asked, "Given the gap between Democrats and Republicans these days, splitting up the nation makes good sense," rural residents would, at the very least, respond the same as partisans elsewhere. Not so. In one of the largest gaps we have identified so far, rural residents were much more likely to oppose the idea of breaking up the nation. Whereas almost a majority of urban voters indicated this was a good idea, just under a quarter of rural residents felt the same. Twice as many urban residents as rural residents strongly agreed with this statement. Moreover, there was no apparent partisan gap, either. Rural Democrats and rural Republicans were just as likely to disagree with the thought of tearing America apart. It seems likely that patriotic attitudes are tied to the idea of America itself—that despite all our differences and disagreements, the United States should remain together.

Another way in which patriotic attitudes manifest in the rural-urban cultural divide is through support for the U.S. military. Again, in terms of support, we are more interested in rural residents' values and attitudes toward the U.S. military as an institution and its members. Recall from our discussion in chapter 3 of Sarah Palin's high approval in rural areas due, in no small measure, to her being a proud military mom. There is some evidence to suggest that rural, Black, and poor men were more likely to be drafted to fight in Vietnam, given the college deferment, but since then, there has been little difference between urban and rural Americans when accounting for who serves or served in the military. As for more recent service, our samples show that a slightly higher proportion of rural Americans have an immediate connection with U.S. military institutions:[17] Some 40 percent of rural respondents indicated that a member of their family had previously served in the U.S. military compared with just 25 percent of urban and 34 percent of suburban respondents (figure 7.4). Ironically, the relationship is inverted when looking at current service: a higher percentage of urban residents— 16 percent—say that a member of their family is currently serving compared with just 9 percent of rural residents.[18]

We used a novel question to gauge levels of support for the military: "Imagine you are getting ready to board an airplane. Which one of these people should be allowed to board first: an emergency room doctor, an elementary schoolteacher, or a member of the military?" Overall, some 23 percent said doctor, 13 percent said teacher, and 63 percent said member of the military. For rural residents, the figure for the military shot up to a whopping 76 percent. Perhaps surprisingly, the largest group saying "member of the military" was rural women, at 80 percent.

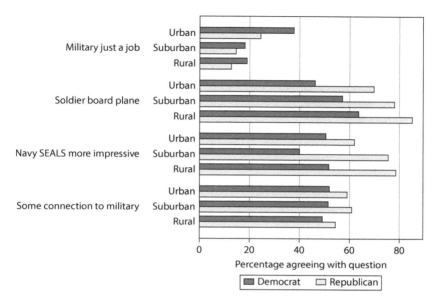

FIGURE 7.4 Attitudes towards the U.S. military in rural, suburban, and urban America

Note: Data from the 2021 and 2022 waves of the Rural Voter Survey. Respondent location and partisan identity are self-described, and geographic averages incorporate poststratification weights described in chapter 4. The figure illustrates the percentage of respondents "strongly agreeing" or "somewhat agreeing" with the statement, "Serving in the military is just a job. They don't deserve special treatment." It also lists the percentage of respondents indicating "soldier" as opposed to "elementary schoolteacher," or "ER doctor" to the question, "Imagine you are boarding an airplane. Which one of these people should be allowed to board first?" Respondents were also asked, "In your view, which one is more impressive . . . being accepted to a special part of the military, like the Navy SEALs, or being accepted to an Ivy League college, like Harvard or Yale?" Finally, some connection to the military means that respondents either currently served, previously served, had immediate family currently serving, or had immediate family previously serving in the U.S. military.

CONSERVATIVE VALUES

While anecdotal evidence about guns, religious beliefs, and patriotic values may dominate the stereotypical discussion of the rural-urban divide, there are at least two other ways we can consider whether rural voters have a distinct "conservative culture." Maybe rural residents are not any more or less religious than nonrural residents—especially once we account for partisanship—but conceivably they express religious beliefs differently when it comes to politics. Likewise, perhaps rural residents are not fanatical when it comes to policies that have been fully nationalized but hold more strident beliefs about government intervention in less salient policy debates—especially those related to rural issues, such as environmental protectionism and free trade. Conservative, sure. But a different brand of conservatism?

Let's start by considering different measures of conservatism and the variety of possible ways in which conservatives think about politics (figure 7.5). Some have argued that modern-day conservatism is

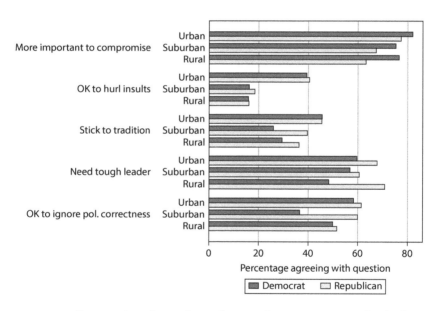

FIGURE 7.5 Conservative values and attitudes toward government in rural, suburban, and urban America

Note: Data from the 2021 and 2022 waves of the Rural Voter Survey. Respondent location and partisan identity are self-described, and geographic averages incorporate poststratification weights described in chapter 4. The figure illustrates the percentage of respondents "strongly agreeing" or "somewhat agreeing" with the following statements: "It is more important for elected officials to find compromise solutions rather than stick to their principles"; "It's fine when politicians name call and hurl insults at the other side"; "It is more important to stick to established traditions than to find new ways of doing things"; "The only way our country can get through the crisis ahead is to put some tough leaders in power and silence the troublemakers"; and "People should say whatever is on their mind, even if it makes some people feel bad."

defined by an entrenched, hostile view toward the values of political compromise.[19] For example, some reputable polling outfits have consistently found—especially during Obama's presidency—that Republicans were less willing to compromise than Democrats, at least in the abstract.[20] The Rural Voter Survey confirms this general trend. On average, 78 percent of Democrats believe it is more important for elected officials to compromise than to stick to their principles, while 68 percent of Republicans think similarly. And those numbers almost perfectly reflect the rural-urban divide: 69 percent of rural residents compared with 79 percent of urban residents prefer compromise.

A similar pattern emerges when asking rural Republicans about whether we should "put some tough leaders in power and silence the troublemakers." Scholars continue to disagree about the relationship between authoritarianism and conservatism and how closely linked these two ideologies are philosophically.[21] Those differences are important, but for our purposes, we are simply interested in whether rural conservatives are more likely than nonrural conservatives (or Republicans) to agree with the idea. Are rural voters more likely to accept authoritarian views? It seems they are—but only by about five percentage points, on average. That is outside the statistical margin of error, but it is hardly a distinguishing feature of a conservative-rural ideology.

In fact, most of the evidence points in the opposite direction. While none of these questions offers us a perfect window into the minds of political conservatives, across a majority of other measures, rural residents are typically less conservative than their urban counterparts. In fact, rural Democrats often have as much in common with rural Republicans on these abstract principles as they do with members of their own party living in urban areas. Consider a straightforward measure: "It is more important to stick to established traditions than to find new ways of doing things." Surprisingly, a roughly equal percentage of urban Democrats and urban Republicans support this idea. To be sure, it is still a minority view; just 34 percent of Americans, on average, support the notion, but that is almost exactly how much rural Republicans support it: 37 percent.

Although this has do to more with the style than the substance of any conservative ideology, many wondered whether modern American conservatism has lost its former "elitist" bent, and if that has been replaced with a cruder form of right-wing populism. Especially after the election of Donald Trump, this populist label has often been associated with a style of campaigning that uses "incendiary political language and insulting rhetoric."[22] To what extent does this variant of American conservatism find favor in rural America? It turns out that, at least in the abstract, rural voters are among the least likely to support candidates who hurl insults and also the least likely to agree with the idea that "people should say whatever is on their mind, even if it makes some people feel bad."

Values and general dispositions toward politics are one thing, but what about specific policies? It is hard to find issues in contemporary American politics that are not fully "owned" by one of the two major political parties.[23] American voters know what Republicans generally believe about taxes and military spending and that Democrats prioritize social welfare programs and environmental protection. Even if they do not know the specific policy implications, they know how to line up the two parties.[24] This is a bit problematic for studying rural culture, because so many political positions are wrapped up with cultural differences. While it is impossible to completely sort out those distinctions, the Rural Voter Survey asked a set of questions about policies that were most likely to tap into rural-specific, and not Republican-specific, considerations. Even then, we found few issues on which Republicans and Democrats living in rural communities diverged from partisans nationwide.

On free trade, for instance, we discovered what other national polls have found: Americans are less divided on the topic now than they once were.[25] Particularly since Trump's election, Republicans are the most likely to support the idea that "it is better to get in a trade war with countries like China, than see more jobs go overseas" (figure 7.6). Support tops out around 80 percent. However, support is nearly as high for Democrats, including Democrats living in urban areas. In fact, rural Democrats were the least likely to support the idea, even though, as we explored in chapter 5, as a percentage of the labor force, rural communities have suffered the most blue-collar job losses in the period after NAFTA. Some of this effect, we contend, may be regional. Rural Democrats living in the Northeast and West were least likely to support a trade war, whereas a majority of those living in the South and Midwest—arguably areas more affected

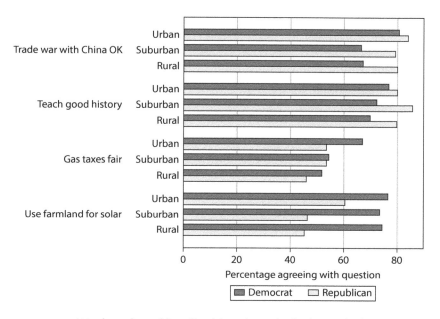

FIGURE 7.6 Attitudes on key public policy debates in rural, suburban, and urban America

Note: Data from the 2021 and 2022 waves of the Rural Voter Survey. Respondent location and partisan identity are self-described, and geographic averages incorporate poststratification weights described in chapter 4. The figure illustrates the percentage of respondents "strongly agreeing" or "somewhat agreeing" with the following statements: It is better to get in a trade war with countries like China, than see more jobs go overseas"; "Schools need to teach more about what is good in American history, and not the bad"; "Gasoline taxes make sure that everyone who uses roads and bridges pays their fair share to maintain them"; and "One way to reduce the cost of electricity is to use open land in rural areas for large solar panel farms and windmills."

lately by recent trade policies—were. We also should recognize that these attitudes are deeply intertwined with the politics of Trump's presidency; we would not be surprised if there were stronger geographic differences in 2015, before Trump announced his candidacy, than in 2021, after four years in which trade wars, tariffs, and rhetorical attacks on Chinese trade practices dominated the president's agenda.[26]

Likewise, Americans are less divided on the issue of school curricula than commonly believed. We asked respondents to react to the statement, "Schools need to teach more about what is good in American history, and not the bad." The partisan gap is pretty narrow within urban and rural areas, and the geographic divide is minimal. Again, heightened support for that idea is largely a function of Republican partisanship in rural areas, and not ruralness per se.

On policies that are more specific to rural land use and livelihood, our survey showed some geographic differences, but the evidence does not suggest that rural areas are hotbeds of conservatism. When it comes to thinking about whether gas taxes are fair (something rural residents, regardless of ideology, might oppose because they simply have to drive more and have limited access to mass transit), rural Republicans are slightly less likely than urban Republicans to oppose gas taxes.

Democrats and Republicans living in rural areas have much less in common with one another when it comes to one major environmental issue: the construction of solar fields on former farmland.[27] Throughout rural America, grassroots movements and well-funded industry-backed organizations have mobilized to prevent the development of solar farms.[28] Opposition, we found, is concentrated among Republicans living in rural areas, but their attitudes do not significantly diverge from those of Republicans living elsewhere—especially in the suburbs.

We know that there are ideological divides between liberals and conservatives in the United States and that people living in rural America are more likely to consider themselves conservative. But when it comes to policies and attitudes toward politics, there is little evidence to suggest that rural America is outside the mainstream of what modern conservative politics entails. We do not find much evidence indicating a dramatic turn to the right in the countryside. If you think the Republican Party and conservative positions are extreme, you're likely to think that many rural residents are extreme. But your concern is with partisanship, not geography.

RURAL CULTURE IN MASS ENTERTAINMENT

If the cultural gap between rural and urban life is more modest than most of us may have imagined, it begs the question of the source of so many misperceptions. Why is our view of the other tribe so wrong?

If we are social animals and learn about our tribes through culture, it would make sense to spend a bit of time discussing the portrayal of rural life in popular entertainment—and the effect it may have in fostering confusion and resentment. "Cultural memory" is a fairly new conceptual framework used by social scientists to bridge social, economic, political, and other aspects of human life. Scholarship in this area has become pronounced in recent years as a way of exploring questions of identity, the politicization of imagery, and the weight of narratives to frame political disputes.[29] In short, cultural memory is the knowledge one calls on to interpret the world, a store built by experiences, beliefs, and values.[30] Fictional media—film, television, music, as well as various forms of advertising—have acute power to shape cultural memory.

The preponderance of nineteenth- and early-twentieth-century literature on rural life reflected the pastoral tradition; the idealization of rural life and landscapes we discuss in chapter 2. In a recent anthology, the editor writes that for nearly half a century, native literature was faithful to the cult of the village, "celebrating its delicate merits with sentimental affection, essential goodness and heroism which, as the doctrine ran, lie beneath unexciting surfaces."[31] In his introduction to a 1937 reprinting of *Main Street*, Sinclair Lewis tells the reader, "Back in 1905, in America, it was almost universally known that, though cities were evil and even in the farmland there were occasional men of wrath, our villages were approximately paradise."[32] In her 1926 review of rustic literature, Dorothy Anne Dondore, in *The Prairie and the Making of Middle America*, suggests, "the portrayals of the rural community reveals a discouraging number of peaceful villages, beautiful girls, unfortunate youths, charming old ladies, and sweetly sentimental love stories."[33]

Not a wisp of discord, bigotry, racism, sexism or ethnic or religious discrimination can be found in Thornton Wilder's play, *Our Town*, written in 1938. The growing scourge of alcoholism in rural America is brushed aside in Grover's Corners, New Hampshire, as it was a generation later on Walton's Mountain: "Right good for snake bite, y'know." A modest revolt against the bucolic narrative arrived in the 1930s,[34] but for the most part, literature during this period echoed the celebration of country life. It is certainly reasonable to assume that this tract reflected concerns about the growing diversity of cities and the upheaval of the Industrial Revolution.

During the Great Depression, Hollywood sought to depict small-town America as a refuge. Nothing captured this view better than the sixteen films in the *Andy Hardy* series, which ran from 1937 to 1946. "In Andy's tidy town, Carvel, there is no poverty, father knows best, and the great question of the day is whether the perky teenagers will be able to put on a song and dance show. Carvel was utopia—neighborly, fair, decent, bursting with generalized good will."[35] So popular was the series that the mayor of Hollywood held a special ceremony in 1941 to present a plaque to the actors playing the Hardy family, whom he dubbed "the first family of Hollywood." That same year at the Academy Awards, the series received a special Oscar for its "achievement in portraying the American way of life."[36] Several other series, stretching from 1939 through 1950, followed a similar route and were equally popular. These films offered an oasis from economic strife and the brutalities of foreign wars. "What was absent in most Depression films about small towns was the Depression, either because the film was set in another era or because the town portrayed was oddly untouched by widespread hardship and unaware of its prevalence elsewhere."[37]

The trend continued for post–World War II movies, for the most part. In Capra's *It's a Wonderful Life* (1946), likely the most small-town-friendly movie ever made, we learn that earnest, hard-working men can be saved from corruption and greed in the small community—the places where a crisis can be averted by the outpouring of gifts (and cash) at a moment's notice. In films like *Oklahoma!* (1955), we marvel at the blissful simplicity and quaintness of rural America.

But cracks in the pastoral facade were beginning to show. A number of films during this period also explored the rigidity of rural life, from the repressed hopes and dreams to stifling sexual mores. *Storm Warning* (1951) confronts the role of the Ku Klux Klan in a small town, *Bad Day at Black Rock* (1955) addresses anti-Japanese bigotry, *The Phenix City Story* (1955) looks at political corruption in Alabama, *Peyton Place* (1957) confronts repression and hypocrisy in a small New Hampshire town, and *Splendor in the Grass* (1961) explores sexual repression in a tiny village in Kansas.

In 1960s television, we find villages and small towns bursting with simple, wholesome characters. No series better depicted the "backward but wholesome" theme better than *The Andy Griffith Show*, which ran from 1960 to 1968. Set in Mayberry, North Carolina (pop. around 5,000), Griffith, as sheriff Andy Taylor, guides his family and friends through a series of zany predicaments. Taylor may have been naive and unsophisticated, but he was stalwart and shrewd. Enter the noble rube. In Mayberry, "kids scurry around at reasonable paces, making low-grade mischief while dirtying their short-sleeve plaid shirts or striped T-shirts. Quirky characters wander about in a landscape of picket fences and healthy storefronts."[38] The show was wildly popular, racking up numerous Emmys and other prestigious awards.

In fact, *The Andy Griffith Show* was so popular that several other rurally based sitcoms were soon produced, including *The Beverly Hillbillies*, *Petticoat Junction*, *Hee Haw*, and *Green Acres*. So many of these shows were aired on CBS that the station soon garnered the nickname of "Country Broadcasting System." The theme here was a bit different and certainly more nefarious. In *The Beverly Hillbillies*, for instance, we find a poor, backward Appalachian family, somehow still dependent on hunting for food—with Civil War–era muskets, no less. But "Pa" misses a shot at a rabbit, and "up from the ground comes bubbling crude." With their new riches, they pack up their truck, *Grapes of Wrath* style, and move to Hollywood. If you have money, of course you would leave the outback. And in each episode, we see zanier and zanier behavior by members of the family, who somehow cannot shake their hillbilly ways. The centerpiece of this genre is to laugh at the backwardness and unsophistication of the hayseed. At the very same time that many were beginning to balk at sitcom tropes and stereotypes of women and minority groups, everything was fair game when it came to rural America.

That was certainly not universally true, but generally speaking, the portrayal of rural and small-town life in pre-1980s film and television reverted to the antiseptic celebration of country life. This was likely in response to the turbulence of the 1960s. We get *The Waltons* and *Little House on the Prairie*, as mentioned at the beginning of this chapter, and a number of other similar films and programs, like *Paper Moon* and *Where the Red Fern Grows*. The narrative was rather simple: rural communities are close-knit, traditional, God-fearing. Racial animus was absent, and drug use and alcohol abuse were rarely mentioned. Drunken characters were recurrent, of course, but they were just wacky characters! Poverty—or at least hardship—was there, too, but noting that cleverness, hard work, and help from friends could not be overcome. And who would want to be the grumpy, rich Mr. Potter, anyway? Better off being poor . . . but well-liked! There is no trace of resentment toward the metropolitans. No one ever wants to leave Walnut Grove. Life in the country may be difficult, sure, but the narrative of small-town rural America was nostalgic—simple lives in simpler times. Again, it was a backlash over the 1960s.

One clear exception was *Deliverance*, released in 1972. The film is about four friends, businessmen from Atlanta, who embark on a river-rafting trip on the Cahulawassee River to explore the Georgia mountains wilderness before it is flooded by the construction of a dam. Looking for their launch site, the group gets lost and comes to a hamlet with a gas station. The locals are barefoot, dirty, backward, and inbred—barely able to utter complete sentences but somehow whizzes at playing the banjo. The men get their gas, find the launch site, and head off—only to be tracked down by two of the locals. When finally confronted, the rustics are seen to be not interested in the men's money or fancy camping gear but, instead, hell-bent on terrorizing the "city boys." Taking their depravity to a new level, even by Hollywood standards, one of the businessmen is sodomized—all the while being forced to squeal like a pig.

Deliverance was hugely popular, the fourth-largest-grossing film that year and nominated for three Academy Awards, including for best picture. It is hard to overstate the significance of the film in the transformation of the rural narrative—particularly with regard to the rural South. According to one account, "The imagery, stereotypes, and symbols produced by the film still inform popular perceptions of the South, even by those who have never actually watched it."[39] The film scholar Pat Arnow suggests that the movie "is still the greatest incentive for many non-Southerners to stay on the Interstate."[40] Anthony Harkins, in his book *Hillbilly: A Cultural History of an American Icon*, writes that the movie was "the most influential film of the modern era in shaping national perceptions of southern mountaineers and rural life in general." Harkins continues: "The film's infamous scenes of sodomy at gunpoint and of a retarded albino boy lustily playing his banjo became such instantly recognizable shorthand for demeaning references to rural poor that comedians needed to say only 'squeal like a pig' . . . or hum the opening notes of the film's guitar-banjo duet to gain an immediate visceral reaction from a studio audience."[41]

Within a few years, the noble bumpkins and laughable hayseeds had been replaced by backwater outlaws. The new horror show villain was the inbred, aggrieved rustic. The redneck nightmare was born. Instead of seeing rural Americans as our quaint but quirky cousins, they become the "other." It became pat for horror films to be set in the countryside. The *Texas Chainsaw Massacre* (1974), *Halloween* (1978), *Something Wicked This Way Comes* (1983), *The Blob* (1988), *The Blair Witch Project* (1999), and untold other dark, creepy films were set in rural villages. Stephen King's books and movies were wildly popular, and nearly all his stories during this period were set on farms and in the woods. What can be more frightening than "children of the corn" or a wild farmhouse dog named Cujo? Taking a page out of a 1977 film, *The Hills Have Eyes*, a recent horror franchise, *Wrong Turn* (2021), takes things up a notch by suggesting urban visitors who stumble into the countryside risk being eaten by the residents.

By the turn of the twentieth century, we see another variation: the redneck reality show. *Ax Men, American Loggers, Life Below Zero, Ice Road Truckers, Duck Dynasty, Hillbillies for Hire, My Big Redneck Family,* and many others saturated the airways. By one estimate, some 127 rurally centered reality shows had hit the airways by 2016.[42] The subgenre is particularly brutal in its portrayal of southern rural life, such as in *Here Comes Honey Boo Boo, Buckwild, Moonshiners, Swamp People, Party Down South,* and *The Legend of Shelby the Swampman.*

While these shows steer clear of overtly vilifying Americans who live in the swamps and woodlands—they are not cast as the demented, inbred murderers and rapists of the horror films—we get a steady diet of bizarre behaviors by dimwitted characters. We learn that some men in the backwaters of Louisiana rarely don shoes, shoot their pistols out the windows of their floating homes, and sometimes drive tractors to the store—all the while waving to neighbors. These "folks" rely on nature for basic necessities to survive, even though they drive new snowmobiles and have barns crowded with expensive construction equipment. They fish with bare hands, make up words not in the English dictionary, eat triple-fried foods at fairs and cookouts, and are always on the edge of lawlessness.[43] "Of course, the producers [of these programs] don't hesitate to add twangy music and edit the shows to emphasize the broad physical humor found in grabbing an armadillo by the tail and then capping his achievement with a rebel yell."[44] As for rural youth, the picture is especially bleak; they are relentlessly depicted as violent, naive, crude, hyperactive, ignorant, and sexually promiscuous.

The theme of rural sitcoms shifted as well. A decade later, the sophisticated urbanite was forced either to endure rustic life or tame the hillbillies. Joel, a New York City doctor trained at an Ivy League school, is forced to practice in a tiny Alaskan community in *Northern Exposure*. Zoe, also a New York doctor, learns the charms of small-town Alabama in *Hart of Dixie*. In *Virgin River*, Melinda, a nurse practitioner, answers an ad for work in a small town in northern California only to find—spoiler alert—that life in rural America is not what she imagined. Rather than the rustics wanting to leave for the big cities, we now find the rustics as too ignorant, unskilled, or addicted to make the move. The highly popular, Emmy Award–winning show *Shitt's Creek* finds a formerly affluent family living in a ramshackle hotel in a rural community—actually, a town the father had somehow purchased when he was still rich. The family comes to appreciate the quirky, wholesome ways of the locals, but, of course, they leave as soon as their fortunes reverse.

In *Ozark*, a series that ran on Netflix from 2017 to 2021, we are given a professional family forced to flee their suburban home to hide from a gangster drug lord. They head to the Ozark Mountains of Missouri, where they find poverty, drug addiction, crime, and crude residents. There are lots of rundown trailers. Again, it's a tough hit for rural southerners. The gap between urban, sophisticated Americans and the "other" is made vivid. In a *New York Times* review, the television editor Jeremy Egner makes a telling observation: "This story about urbanites confronting a heartland culture they don't understand coincidentally captures a dynamic that has received plenty of attention since Donald J. Trump won the presidency. Initial 'Ozark' scripts were written long before the election. But Mr. Bateman [who plays the protagonist] allowed that the parallels between 'a pseudo-intellectual guy who thinks that he can go down to the sticks and big-city these simple folk' and President Trump's critics, flabbergasted by his victory, 'weren't lost on us.'"[45]

Needless to say, the actual residents of the area were none too pleased with the series. One noted to a reporter, "It is a horrible representation of the Ozarks. The show depicts crime and corruption in a region that heavily depends on tourism. Not only that, it is filmed in Georgia, not Lake of the Ozarks like people think!"[46]

It is difficult to chart the course of country music over the last few decades in a few paragraphs, much less a single volume. There are numerous works on this topic, and we are indebted to Ken Burns and his team for the sixteen-hour documentary, *Country Music*, released in 2019. We note that the popularity of country music mushroomed in the 1990s. Urban, suburban, and rural Americans young and old could not get enough of Reba McEntire, Billy Ray Cyrus, Alan Jackson, Faith Hill, and others. Part of its growing popularity was a drift into pop styles. As noted by one music critic, the 1990s "began with artists pushing back against an increasingly pop sound. It ended with some of the most pop-oriented country songs that had ever been released to country radio."[47] Two of the artists who successfully straddled the fence were Shania Twain and Garth Brooks. Conservative themes were less obvious, and one might even suggest some of country music's broad popularity sprang from artists pushing new, previously taboo themes. Certainly the Dixie Chicks (now the Chicks), and their quick fix for the wife-beating Earl, springs to mind.

Likely since 9/11, country music has once again taken an ideological turn—and, in doing so, resurrected deeper geographic connections. "Country music and conservative politics [were once again] both seen as guardians of the hard-working, God-fearing, freedom-loving 'real America.'"[48] Progressive, edgy themes faded. In 2003, country radio basically blacklisted the Dixie Chicks over front singer Natalie Maines's criticism of President George W. Bush's handling of the war in Iraq. By 2004, Gallup had found that nearly 60 percent of country fans identify more strongly with Republicans compared with 11 percent who identify as liberal and around 30 percent who say they're political moderates.[49]

We would not want to go too far by making broad pronouncements, but country music during the last decade seemed to have doubled down on lyrics linked to patriotism, family, community, hard work, loyalty, and Christian values. We can also hear the rejection of elites, outsiders, and the need to go to college. Kenny Chesney's 2016 hit, "Rich and Miserable," underscores this idea: "Go to school to get a job / Don't make enough to pay it off / And on and on it goes."

A key issue is not whether country music echoes conservative themes, because it does; rather, it is whether or not there are geographic differences in the audience. Is country music, with its turn to patriotic and Christian themes, especially popular in rural America? In 2018, a team of scholars conducted an empirical analysis of music preferences, controlling for an array of demographic variables, including population density.[50] Sure enough, rural residents were much more likely than nonrural residents to listen to country and gospel music. "These results broadly track and reflect America's more basic political and economic divide. . . . It appears that these cultural divides are long-standing and deeply ingrained in America's political-economic and geographic divides."[51]

So what does this brief look at popular culture tell us about contemporary rural politics? Country music, ripe with themes of patriotism, family, hard work, resentment, and antielite/anti-intellectualism, is popular across the country, especially in rural parts. We know there are some clear consumer differences, too. For example, in 2016, Donald Trump won 22 percent of the counties that boast at least one Whole Foods Market but a whopping 74 percent of those that had at least one Cracker Barrel restaurant.[52] A number of studies have found auto racing to be more popular in rural than in nonrural communities,[53] and there may be inklings that The Apprentice was especially popular with conservative rural voters.[54] Those sorts of differences reflect divergent attitudes and beliefs—many of which are linked to political messages.

A more significant finding, however, is how rural residents see themselves depicted in movies and films since the 1980s. Is it possible that this portrayal has contributed to their confusion, isolation, and anger toward the broader culture? At the same time that many Americans are pushing against persistent derogatory stereotypes, when more and more are demanding an end to ugly tropes and labels, rural America remains fair game. Some of this springs from the fact that the creators are themselves alien to the types of communities they wish to depict. But another possibility is that pop culture needs a villain, buffoon, or foil. The target has shifted over time—from people of color and immigrants, to space aliens, communists, Arabs, strong women, and other groups. In the last few decades, the foils have been rustics. As noted by James Gimple, "The disrespect is felt most acutely by the fact that dominant cultural institutions, including mass media, are predominantly urban in location and orientation. [Rural voters] see themselves as misunderstood and mischaracterized by these media, as well as dismissed as out-of-touch and retrograde by urban populations."[55]

At best, television and movies depict rural people as simple, behind the times, heavily accented, and peculiar. They are shown working the land or engaging in related rural occupations, certainly blue-collar jobs, suggesting that they are perhaps not smart enough or have enough gumption to make a living in a big city.[56] Equally often, the stereotype is ghastly. Tropes of rural Americans as ignorant, wild, drunken, and lazy are ubiquitous. Tiffany Verbeck put the issue this way: "I remember watching The 'Amanda Show' [on Nickelodeon] in the late 90s and seeing the running segment called 'Hillbilly Moment.' The two actors emerge from a shabby cabin wearing overalls, a straw hat, and sloppy hair. They giggle, mouths wide with missing teeth on full display, and talk like a parody of my dad."[57]

To fully appreciate the depth of this rural stereotype, we recommend you pull up the video "Hillbilly Moment—A Meaty Loaf!" on YouTube.[58] One can only shudder to think of the uproar if another program on Nickelodeon, or any other media outlet, ran any analogous stereotypical depictions of Blacks, women, Asians, members of the LGBTQIA+ community, or any other group. But, of course, the uproar would be so loud and sustained that it could not happen. And yet, ugly typecasts of rural Americans barely raise an eyebrow.

In 1999, Monster.com, the global employment website, ran a series of ads dubbed "When I grow up." In each of these commercials, young kids look into the camera and say things like, "When I grow up I want to be lackadaisical," or "average," "a poor role model," "utterly repulsive," "spend money I don't have," and the like. One kid says, "When I grow up I want to complain about everything." Each ad ends with a line on the screen: "What do you want to be?" The message, one would guess, is that if you do not want to be a loser, or raise kids that are losers, jump on Monster and get a good job. Nearly every one of these kids—the losers—are staged in a rural setting. They are in barns and fields, out in the woods, and of, course, some are wearing flannel coats and goofy hillbilly hats. One of the ads—the one that was aired during the Super Bowl—opens with a kid wearing "the hat," sitting on a decrepit farm-house porch, looking into the camera, saying, "When I grow up I want to file all day." After all, a picture is worth a thousand words.

In the fall of 2022, a new interactive horror video game was released, dubbed *The Quarry*. It was an immediate hit, downloaded by millions of Americans. The game depicts a family that runs a summer camp for kids in the countryside. But they also have a secret curse: they become werewolves at night. When the teenage camp counselors try to leave, they get stuck and have to deal with the werewolves and the crazy family. The goal is to escape the rural hellhole. The main character, the most threatening and ominous of all, is Bobby—an oversized "redneck" draped with overalls and a dirty mechanics cap. A menacing Lenny, right off the page of *Of Mice and Men*.

This review, which is certainly not exhaustive, shows that the cre-ators of popular entertainment—the writers, directors, producers, and artists—have never really gotten things right. Literary authors following the pastoral tradition gave us charming, quaint caricatures of rural life, where the slow, old ways become an oasis from the cold, grinding reali-ties of America at the turn of the century. These themes aligned with the white, elite-centered country movement, touched on in chapter 2. Right about the time that the Cold War villain became less threatening, we got the rural nightmare—an endless stream of horror films that place naive characters in the foreboding bleakness of decrepit farms, dark woods, and mysterious swamps. Anxious to cash in on the reality rage, television producers then flooded the airways with outlandish rural "characters." Certainly, all residents of Appalachia make their own moonshine, and everyone in the mountains out west dine on beaver meat and tan hides. More recently, urban residents are shown to be stuck in strange rural communities filled with charming, good-natured, bizarre residents.

But are rural residents aware of these stereotypes? If so, do they find them off-putting? We asked Americans what they thought, in general, about how movies and television shows represented their type of community: urban, suburban, and rural. That is, what do urban residents think of the portrayal of urban characters, what do rural residents think of how their lifestyle is shown, and so forth. Readers may be thinking: hey, cities aren't portrayed all that nicely either; ever see an episode of *The Wire* or *Law and Order*? And yes, they would be right. We could write a history of urban life and all its egregious misrepresentations, like the one we did earlier (you can check out a few in our footnotes!). But nowhere does the misrepresentation resonate as loudly as it does among rural residents.

Consider the first question we ask in table 7.1: "How often do movies and television portray people who live in [urban/suburban/rural] areas in a fair and accurate way?" Just about half of urban respondents say "always" or "most of the time" when thinking about cities and urban areas. Even if you think the *Law and Order* effect overestimates crime in urban areas (and it does), urban Americans at least think that on the whole, movies and TV get it about right. And yet, compare that with rural respondents; on average, just 23 percent thought that media portrayals of their communities were accurate all or most of the time. Interestingly, suburbanites, too, were not very happy with the way life in the suburbs has been portrayed, but even in that case, their perceptions of an antisuburban bias were not as extreme or pervasive as among rural residents.

Our question shows that when asked about their own communities, rural residents feel misrepresented in popular portrayals of rural life. But how do all Americans think rural life is portrayed? We asked all our respondents, regardless of where they lived, a question about how

TABLE 7.1 Perceptions about media portrayal in rural America

What do you think? How often do movies and television portray people who live in [your area] in a fair and accurate way?	Urban respondents	Suburban respondents	Rural respondents	Total
Never	5.89	6.64	8.71	6.73
Sometimes	18.18	29.57	33.95	25.71
About half the time	26.48	35.55	34.51	31.60
Most of the time	29.07	22.16	16.70	23.95
Always	20.39	6.09	6.14	12.01

Generally speaking, movies and films about country life in rural communities portrays residents as ...	Urban respondents	Suburban respondents	Rural respondents	Total
dumb rednecks	17.49	11.66	17.05	15.11
simple-minded but kind	22.36	30.71	26.72	26.48
hard-working	32.47	27.72	28.12	29.76
clever and sophisticated	3.71	2.25	1.70	2.75
a mix—it depends	23.98	27.66	26.41	25.9

Note: Data from the 2022 wave of the Rural Voter Survey. Respondent location is self-described, and geographic averages incorporate poststratification weights described in chapter 4.

movies and films portray "country life in rural communities." The most common response—made a third of Americans, with slightly fewer rural residents—was to say something to the effect of "hard-working." And another third jotted down the neutral option: "it depends." But many Americans—regardless of where they lived—were quick to pick up on the stereotypes we identified earlier. Rural folk are "simple-minded, but kind," unless they are just portrayed as "dumb rednecks." Only 3 percent said that rural Americans were often portrayed as clever and sophisticated.

The reality of rural life is much different, much more complex. Scary movies may suggest that rural parts are unsafe, but in reality, violent crime is roughly 40 percent higher, on a per capita basis, in urban areas than in rural communities.[59] Are rural folks "simple-minded," when you consider that a surprising (and growing) number of business entrepreneurs come from nonurban communities?[60] And yet, humans are cognitive misers, so when we are offered the pop culture cue, the goofy hayseed or backwater outlaw jumps to mind. As suggested by the rural culture scholar Emily Satterwhite, "Whether over-romanticized or over-vilified, it hides the complexity of what's really going on in terms of the intertwining of the fates of urban and rural [areas], and the mobility of people between the two, and the shared values that occur across both."[61]

What is the outcome, and who cares? Endless bits about backward, hardscrabble, slow, dimwitted rural people define the "other"—a group not like us, holding the rest of America back. Urban progressives are well versed in the "givers versus takers" argument—where conservative, usually rural, states rail against big government while at the same time taking more from the federal government than they contribute. We are all in this together, sure, but those hayseeds are so different— and they are dragging us down. Charming, wholesome, and quirky gets you only so far.

THE DANGERS OF STEREOTYPES

Around the time that Hank Williams Jr. is singing about country boys surviving the cultural onslaught, we find film and television depicting rural characters as something to be tolerated, if not feared. There is a defensiveness in his song, a sense of the rural culture under assault. One take is that rural residents are trying to push the broader culture in their direction—to send it outward. That's likely not the case. The defiance in Williams's song suggests a protective posture—a desperate desire to preserve. As noted by the Brookings Institution's scholar Bill Galston, "The United States in the early 1950s resembled the country as it had been for decades. By the early 1970s, everything had changed, stunning Americans who had grown up in what seemed to them to be a stable, traditional society and setting the stage for a conservative reaction."[62]

In recent decades, there has been a partial rehabilitation of rural characters in entertainment. We still get the rural villains in horror movies and video games, but there is also now a stream of reality television programs and "zany" sitcoms about the rustics who are certainly odd but goodhearted, dimwitted but resourceful, backward but savvy. And no program better encapsulates the myriad stereotypes and tropes—and, in some ways—realities of rural life than *Duck Dynasty*.

Duck Dynasty was a reality show that ran on A&E from 2012 to 2017. It centered on the Robertson family from West Monroe, Louisiana, as they managed their successful duck call and hunting products production plant, Duck Commander. There are several brothers and their wives, the parents, and a wacky uncle. The show was extremely popular, netting upward of $100 million in advertising revenue per season. The widely hyped fourth season preview, for example, drew in an estimated 12 million viewers, the most-watched nonfiction program in history.[63] Early in the show's running, in 2013, the *Wall Street Journal* ran a piece entitled, "The Politics of Who Watches 'Duck Dynasty.'" Market research suggests that the program was particularly popular with Republicans, evangelical Christians, and older Americans.[64]

As with so much modern entertainment, *Duck Dynasty* offered a muted look at rural culture. The men of the family boast long beards, and they nearly always don camouflage outfits in the office and at home. They are self-described "rednecks" but also evangelical Christians. Horseplay and disagreements abound, but feuds are never too serious, and the family always comes together by the end of each episode to say grace and thank the Lord for his blessings. Continuing the tried-and-true tradition of sitcom wives, the women of *Duck Dynasty*, while powerful in their own way, work to keep their men on task—no easy feat given the men's distractibility. They patiently put up with the foolery and misguided schemes, folding their arms and shaking their heads. "[The Robertsons] aren't exactly the Waltons," noted one reviewer, "but they're an affectionate, devout brood that works, plays and prays together."[65] Another noted, "it's a family that many of us would like to have, or hang out with. . . . It makes people happy."[66]

There are many successful business entrepreneurs in rural communities, but it is doubtful that they have so much time on their hands for hijinks—and that they wear camouflage to the office. As a *Washington Monthly* commentator suggested, "A&E appears to have taken a large clan of affluent, college-educated, mildly conservative, country club Republicans, common across the nicer suburbs of the old south, and repackaged them as the Beverly Hillbillies."[67] According to another critic, the men on the show habitually invoke a "redneck identity" and frequently scorn so-called yuppies. "The show discursively configures rednecks as authentically masculine and yuppies as feminine, which therefore implies the superiority of the former over the latter in this patriarchal context."[68] And while there are certainly many close-knit families in rural America, the harmony of the clan seems exceptional. Come to find out, one of the couples later revealed that problems in their marriage spring from issues of infidelity—and another member admitted battling drug addiction.[69] "It's not so much that the Robertsons' show is scripted, so much as the actual family is sort of a creation of network executives."[70]

One of the biggest misperceptions may have to do with the role of religion in rural America. One observer suggested that faith became the show's "elevator pitch," and it has made the Robertsons ideal Christian icons.[71] But as our data reveal, on several measures, rural families are no more devout than those in urban or suburban areas. And it was more than holding hands and praying at the end of each episode. The patriarch of the family, Phil Robertson, gave an interview for *GQ* in which he spoke at length about the Bible and a litany of issues linked to the nation's mounting immorality crisis—including "homosexual behavior" and "bestiality." He went on, "Neither the adulterers, the idolaters, the male prostitutes, the homosexual offenders, the greedy, the drunkards, the slanderers, the swindlers—they won't inherit the kingdom of God."[72] Robertson was especially outspoken about the sin of abortion, a few years later saying it is "just plain evil."[73]

But is it not true that most rural residents favor strict abortion limits and are opposed to marriage equality and LBTQIA+ rights? Maybe not. Many were surprised when, in the immediate wake of the Supreme Court's decision to overturn abortion protections, voters in Kansas—yes, Tom Frank's spellbound Kansans—would overwhelmingly reject a constitutional amendment to ban abortions. And it was not even close;

the measure failed by eighteen percentage points.[74] In fact, a deep dive into the results suggest support for the measure was not particularly pronounced in the smallest communities. The abortion vote was almost even in many of the areas that gave Donald Trump upward of 80 percent of the vote in 2020. As one observer noted, "Urban liberals everywhere may have spilled their Starbucks when reading about these overall Kansas results."[75] There is no evidence to suggest that rural voters hold views that are closer to Phil Robertson than to average folks around the country.

And yet, *Duck Dynasty* probably hits the mark in at least two ways. Throughout the show's five seasons, the Robertsons and their friends make a number of patriotic gestures and clearly celebrate military service. They are "proud to be Americans." They are self-stylized representations of the "real America." Second, and more significantly, there is an unabashed celebration of guns, gun culture, and hunting. This certainly aligns with our data. As the story goes, during the negotiations for creating the show, the family laid out three ironclad stipulations. First, they would not back away from their Christian faith; they were religious, and America would know it. Second, the show would never reveal serious family disputes or any sort of squabbling and backbiting. Finally, they would not back away from their love for guns and hunting—and for taking time off during duck season.

But all told, these differences do not point to some unbreachable cultural chasm separating rural from nonrural America. Guns are tricky, and especially among the young who have grown up in this new age of mass gun violence, there is no gainsaying that it is a polarizing issue. However, it would seem that we are not living in two countries being pulled apart on other important cultural values. Patriotism is popular everywhere, and America remains a steadfastly religious country. Still, the major chasm we identify here is that there is, without a doubt, a belief that there are two different Americas. But it rests on misrepresentations of rural ways of living and rural people. Many of our ideas about the Rural Voter are about as real as *The Beverly Hillbillies*.

8

IRREDEEMABLY RACIST?

Millinocket (pop. 4,000) bills itself as Maine's biggest small town. Even though it is nestled in the far northeast corner of the United States, it represents much about rural America in the ways we've already discussed: manufacturing is on its last legs, and the downtown is rife with vacant storefronts. The average family makes only two-thirds the average American household's income. Area residents constantly fear what its declining population will mean for the schools and if theirs will go the way of so many community churches. Nevertheless, it is a proud town—the gateway to Maine's famous Mt. Katahdin—where residents revel in our state's beloved pristine forests. It's the state's epicenter for snowmobiling, fishing, hunting, and other outdoor recreational activities. Likely because of its deep labor roots, Barack Obama won this town in 2008 with 63 percent of the vote; in 2020, Donald Trump swept it by eleven points.

Millinocket residents woke one late June morning to find their small town in the middle of national headlines. Someone had snapped a photograph of a sign posted on the door of a local insurance agency, which had been in business for more than thirty years:

Juneteenth
~ it's whatever . . .
We're closed.

Enjoy your fried
chicken &
collard greens.

It went viral.

It was the first year that Maine had officially celebrated Juneteenth after President Biden designated it a federal holiday in 2021. The sign is patently offensive and racist, dismissing any need to acknowledge the reason for commemoration, all while playing up a sinister stereotype about Black Americans, whose emancipation from slavery is the very reason for the holiday. Few of us could imagine that in 2022, someone could so callously post such words on their door. And, regrettably, for many Americans, they can imagine it all too vividly, because they experience racism every day, from subtle dismissal to overt harassment.

From the very beginning, race, hierarchy, and exclusion have been central fault lines in American politics. Whether the subject is economic inequality or partisanship more generally, racial and ethnic divides are powerful forces that have traditionally pulled this country apart.

Race and other forms of ascriptivism are important to write about in the context of rural America. Given the fact that Millinocket is nearly an all-white town—98 percent—we know there is deeper curiosity about the episode and what it may represent about life outside more diverse communities. It is reasonable to infer that far from cities and suburbs, where most nonwhite Americans live, such behavior may be tolerated or even encouraged. For some readers, it may not matter that the town manager, the members of the town council, and various civic organizations all denounced the sign in unequivocal terms—or the fact that, to the best of our knowledge, the insurance company no longer seems to be in business after firing the employee who posted the sign. What matters is that it happened in the first place; something must have suggested that it was okay to post that sign in that small rural town.

Others may reasonably wonder, too, what would have happened had someone not snapped the photo. Would residents have just walked on by, condoning such beliefs and complicitly reinforcing white supremacy?

How often do events like this happen in small-town, rural America? And how many of these ideas are never put in writing and posted on doors but, rather, whispered among neighbors, bellowed at taverns, or silently thought?

"Whisper," we hear many say. They voted for Donald Trump! Trump launched his presidential aspirations atop a baseless conspiracy that Barack Obama—the country's first and only president of color—was not born in the United States. In the aftermath of the "Unite the Right" rally in Charlottesville, Virginia, he said there were "very fine people, on both sides" (neo-Nazis and Klansmen were on the *one* side). He elevated the platform and standing of white supremacist groups, such as the Proud Boys, and he responded to the protests in the aftermath of George Floyd's murder by saying, "when the looting starts, the shooting starts." He talked about the "China Virus" and "Kung Flu." He literally launched his campaign by calling migrants from Mexico drug dealers and rapists and then proceeded to ban immigrants coming from most majority-Muslim countries.

So the thinking goes, if Donald Trump epitomizes racism in modern America, then the people who support him do, too. And if rural America supports Trump (which we know they do), then, ipso facto, they must be racist.

In the wake of the 2016 election, *The Nation* published an article by a team of scholars with the declarative headline, "Economic Anxiety Did Not Make People Vote for Trump, Racism Did." Relying on American National Election Study data, the researchers show that attitudes toward race were more highly correlated to a Trump vote than were concerns about the economy or one's personal finances.[1] Put a bit differently, if you had to pick one attitudinal measure to predict a Trump voter, you would be better off knowing attitudes about race than concerns about economic issues. Many other academic works since then have made similar claims; in fact, our model of Trump support in chapter 10 shows just that.

But what about rural voters? In the spring of 2023, two Tennessee state legislators were expelled for breaking rules of decorum in the chamber in a struggle to move gun control legislation forward. It was a bold move by the Republican majority, a feat rarely seen since Reconstruction.

Given that both of the expelled members were black, from Memphis, and that a white woman charged with a similar offense was not kicked out, the move seemed rife with racial undertones. One of the expelled members, Justin J. Pearson, made the point vivid in a speech later that day: "You cannot ignore the racial dynamic of what happened today. Two young Black lawmakers get expelled and the one white woman does not?"[2] Then, in several follow-up assessments by pundits, the rural connection was placed front-and-center. "The confrontation," writes J. D. Tuccille, "represented deep and growing disagreement between rural and urban Americans who hold divergent values, prefer very different laws, and inevitably clash in an excessively centralized country."[3]

Making a rural-racism link is chronic these days. Part of the reason likely springs from the knee-jerk assumption that "rural" implies southern, or that all the Republicans in states like Tennessee came from the rural parts (two-thirds of Tennessee residents live in urban areas). We have worked hard to dispel that myth throughout this book, but there is some evidence to support what we might call the "southernification" of rural culture. For instance, the Public Religion Research Institute (PRRI) conducted a survey in the fall of 2022 on issues related to structural racism and discrimination in the United States.[4] One of the key findings is that support for Confederate symbols and monuments is more likely to follow lines of race, religion, and education—not region. For example, while southern respondents were more likely to suggest these symbols are culturally based, not racist, an equal percentage of rural Southerners and non-Southerners opposed taking down the monuments and removing the flag.

Writing about the implication of the study, one journalist said, "It's the product of a dynamic in which white, rural Americans around the country have adopted the culture of white, rural Southerners."[5] Another commentator noted the decline of regional symbols and regional drawls in rural communities. "Everywhere it's the same cloying pop country, the same aggressively oversized Ford F-150s, the same tumbledown Wal-Marts and Dollar Generals, the same eagle-heavy fashion. . . . Even the accents are more and more the same, trending toward a generalized Larry the Cable Guy twang."[6]

There are other barometers of the rural-racism link. As we charted in chapter 2, the emergence of the Klan in the 1920s was a national phenomenon, but it was especially pronounced in the countryside. During that period, there was growing belief in rural areas regarding the superiority of the Anglo-Saxon race; "better baby" and "fitter families" contests, common in farm communities then, lasted until the 1950s. In chapter 3, we suggested that Lyndon Johnson likely would have fared poorly in rural areas in the 1968 presidential election, had he decided to run, due in large measure to his backing of civil rights legislation.

But, as you would guess, the story of rural racism is more complex. For example, many readers may be surprised to hear that some rural communities held robust demonstrations in support of racial justice in the wake of the murder of George Floyd,[7] or that patterns of race-based housing segregation in rural communities are no worse than in metropolitan areas.[8] Donald Trump was just as popular in Michigan as he was in Mississippi. Kathy Cramer, in her detailed study of rural Wisconsinites noted throughout this book, was reluctant to explain rural consciousness as simply the work of racism—that is, racism being understood as blatant discrimination against people of color: "That's not what's going on here. . . . I observed little overt racism in rural Wisconsin. I searched my field notes for a conversation in a rural community in which at least one person made an [overtly racist] comment. I found exactly zero such exchanges in rural communities, but several in urban and suburban locations."[9]

This chapter explores the rural-racism link in detail and goes beyond overt racism to understand more symbolic or implicit forms of racial animus. Each reader is going to interpret our data through a distinct lens. For some, the link we just connected is enough. There is no need to ask questions or consider demographic change, because, they say, where it counts—at the ballot box—rural America declared itself to be a bastion of white supremacy. Trump made that clear. However, that view may miss some important connections not only for understanding attitudes for some academic reason but also for recognizing areas where the hard work of politics can take place.

The goal of this chapter is to offer a deeper understanding of rural Americans' attitudes on this topic, as it is essential for creating a more just and equitable society. By no means should our data excuse racism, misogyny, xenophobia, or illiberalism—whether confined to rural America or found all over the United States. We hope our data can inform conversations about diversity and inclusion by highlighting misperceptions, identifying areas of common ground, and detailing the ubiquity of racial and ethnic animus in multiple geographic contexts. And although we opened this chapter with a story about an instance of anti-Black racism in rural America, we also consider a wide array of attitudes that reproduce social inequalities in society: attitudes toward immigrants, women, and foreign nationals, to name just a few.

An entire book could be written on the topic, and given the breadth of our data collection efforts, we will present as many of our findings as possible. We are convinced that one reason rural Americans have developed a shared sense of fate is because the racial and ethnic lines that define other political communities are simply not as visible in rural areas. There have been some changes in recent years, but make no mistake: rural America, for the most part, is overwhelmingly white. Undoubtedly, that whiteness makes it easier to unify rural Americans into a coherent voting bloc around issues of economic grievance and anxiety, whereas in other locales, class and color come into greater conflict.

What is more, many politicians use race, ethnicity, and immigration as wedge issues and powerful mobilizing tools. A number of works have documented the role of "covert racism" in policy framing.[10] Nefarious elites use race-centered themes and subtle messages to mobilize support for small government and a host of generally conservative policy options.[11] The "southern strategy" used by Nixon, Reagan, and other GOP presidential candidates captures part of this dynamic, but it extends down to the ballot and across the country.

At the same time, our understanding of racism in rural America is limited by how we can ask people about their attitudes and perceptions. We simply cannot come out and ask, "Hey, do you like black people or not? What about immigrants from Latin America?" Few would offer up an honest opinion, knowing that is socially undesirable to do so. Instead, we rely on well-tested, widely used measures that have been fine-tuned by scholars studying race. But like all survey measures, they are prone to picking up on multiple attitudes at once. Given our findings on economic grievance and rural culture, we are especially concerned that traditional measures of racial animus, or resentment, may also pick up on notions of deservingness and hard work that, at least in the minds of many rural residents, are distinguishable from racialized worldviews.[12] Are hostile attitudes about inner-city residents born from a visceral dislike of nonwhites, or are they linked to the perceived laziness of those living in urban areas? Both are problematic in creating inclusive politics, but getting that story right matters.

Looking at the relationship between hard work and racism, we argue, clarifies some of the complex relationship and offers an explanation for the heightened levels of racial resentment that we document. Values related to hard work are a central tenet of rural identity. That does not excuse prejudice, and in no way does it mean some groups work harder than others. These are perceptions. Additionally, we also consider whether the defining characteristics of the rural voter are limited to whites, regardless of the presence or absence of racial hostility. In this regard, the evidence is much clearer. The sense of shared fate that binds rural residents together economically, culturally, and socially is not an exclusively white phenomenon. Nevertheless, white residents are much more likely to exhibit the characteristics of rural identity we have documented so far throughout this book. For the 15 percent of residents in rural America who largely identify as Black, indigenous American, or Latino, we see similar patterns that bind white rural voters together. Shared fate—whether it stems from economic grievance, cultural values, or civic pride—is about place, not race.

RACE AND RACISM IN RURAL AMERICA

The Rural Voter Survey asked almost as many questions on race, immigration, and prejudicial attitudes as on any other topic. Following the lead of scholars who focus almost exclusively on the measurement of racial animus in contemporary American society, we evaluated racist beliefs in rural America by asking residents about their perceptions of how much racial discrimination exists. We kept the inquiry broad and asked about the United States more generally (rather than respondents' specific rural community), given the limited number of racial minorities in many rural areas and the national implications of the rural vote for racial politics and policies. For most of our rural respondents, few of their neighbors identify as racial or ethnic minorities. Asking about race relations in their community may not make much sense, even if underlying racism is a reason those communities remain predominantly white. Specifically, 41 percent of rural respondents lived in communities where 90 percent of the population identified as white. The average rural community we surveyed was 85 percent white—on par with the percentage of rural residents who identify as white.

But racial identifications are different from racist beliefs. And by racist "beliefs," we mean we are interested in the set of ideas that scholars often refer to under the banner of symbolic racism.[13] At some point in American history, racism was tied to beliefs that stressed the biological differences between races (racialism) or the moral inferiority of certain races given mainstream religious traditions. We touched on this issue in chapter 2. Those are not as common today, although that type of prejudice still animates a great deal of visible hostility toward racial and ethnic minorities, as evidenced by the growing presence of neo-Nazi groups in American politics.

For most Americans, though, racism does not manifest in swastikas or burning crosses. Rather, racial prejudice is underscored by a perception that members of a racial group deviate from the shared values or culture of white America. One way to think about it is through the lens of stereotyping and whether those stereotypes fit the ideal picture of what it means to be "American." Of course, if only racial minorities are stereotyped as cultural deviants, then we have good evidence of how racial prejudice plays out in everyday thoughts and actions. That is what Don Kinder and Lynn Sanders notably described as the source of white America's resentment toward Black and Brown Americans.[14]

How does racial resentment look in rural, suburban, and urban America? In figure 8.1, we limit our analysis just to whites in the sample,

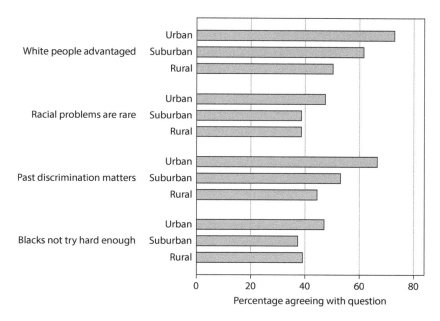

FIGURE 8.1 Racial resentment among non-Latino whites in rural, suburban, and urban America

Note: Data from the 2021 and 2022 waves of the Rural Voter Survey. Respondent location is self-described, and geographic averages incorporate poststratification weights described in chapter 4. The figure illustrates the percentage of respondents "strongly agreeing" or "somewhat agreeing" with the following statements: "White people in the U.S. have certain advantages because of the color of their skin"; "Racial problems in the U.S. are rare, isolated situations"; "Generations of slavery and discrimination have created conditions that make it difficult for blacks to work their way out of the lower class"; "It's really a matter of some people not trying hard enough"; and "If blacks would only try harder, they could be just as well off as whites."

not only for conceptual reasons (some might contend that symbolic racism cannot meaningfully exist in the minds of nonwhite Americans) but also to account for composition effects. As before, if the presence of an attitude in a specific area is solely attributable to the overrepresentation of a certain demographic characteristic, the differences between areas are not a function of geography. In this case, we would be led to believe that racial resentment is lower in urban areas simply because of the fact that more ethnic and racial minorities live there.

Clearly, though, even when we account for composition effects related to race, we see that racial resentment is higher in rural than in urban America. And across the four measures we use, similar percentages of respondents report high levels of agreement. Roughly 40 percent of rural whites agreed with the each of the following statements: "Racial problems in the U.S. are rare, isolated situations," "Generations of slavery and discrimination have created conditions that make it difficult for Blacks to work their way out of the lower class," and "It's really a matter of some people not trying hard enough; if Blacks would only try harder, they could be just as well off as whites." The biggest rural-urban gap exists on this statement in the survey: "White people in the U.S. have certain advantages because of the color of their skin." In that instance, 69 percent of urban whites agree, while just 46 percent of white rural residents agree. All told, this take on racial attitudes in rural America is consistent with the assumptions of most scholars and pundits.

In addition to this standard set of questions, we asked respondents about other events and issues that symbolic racism also likely affects (figure 8.2). The added value of these questions is that the events and issues in question are slightly more varied across geography and even, in one instance, ask about negative stereotypes of "cities." We leveraged the fact that we first went into the field about one year after the murder of George Floyd and the upswell in protest activity against police brutality. Our questions present a mixed picture of how strong symbolic racism remained a year afterward. First, when directly asked, "Agree or Disagree: Police officers deserve our respect," nearly identical majorities of white respondents agreed. But when asked whether "The demonstrators after George Floyd's death were mostly peaceful," we see that rural residents were much less likely to agree. A majority—57 percent—of urban whites agreed with the statement, while just 33 percent of rural whites agreed.

Of course, as we will discuss in our chapter on media effects, all Americans' understanding of those demonstrations stems from how media outlets portrayed certain events and the balance they struck between covering peaceful protests (which engaged millions of people) and select instances of looting (which engaged far fewer but received

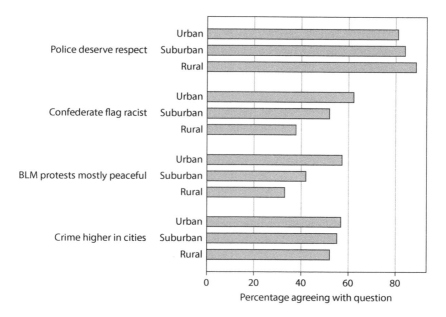

FIGURE 8.2 Racialized attitudes toward current events among non-Latino whites in rural, suburban, and urban America

Note: Data from the 2021 and 2022 waves of the Rural Voter Survey. Respondent location is self-described, and geographic averages incorporate poststratification weights described in chapter 4. The figure illustrates the percentage of respondents "strongly agreeing" or "somewhat agreeing" with the following statements: "Police officers deserve our respect"; "The Confederate flag is racist"; "The demonstrators after George Floyd's death were mostly peaceful"; and "Violent crime is more likely to affect residents of big cities than people living in rural areas."

more coverage). A study conducted by Media Matters, for instance, found that between November 2020 and April 2021, Fox News aired 440 statements on Black Lives Matter protests, the vast majority disparaging the efforts of protesters and organizers, dismissing their concerns, and attacking the individuals behind the movement. The channel was, according to the study, "relentlessly negative in its coverage."[15]

It is also noteworthy that thousands of small towns in rural communities (including Mt. Vernon, Maine!) had their own demonstrations in support of police reform and racial justice; undoubtedly the largest were in urban America.[16] Reporters are increasingly located in urban areas, too. That makes rural Americans more dependent on those media portrayals. We might see the difference in asking about another urban-rural split: "Agree or Disagree: Violent crime is more likely to affect residents of big cities than people living in rural areas." Here, urban residents are more likely than rural residents to agree even though the statement carries potentially-racially loaded language and ideas.

What do these findings suggest so far? First, symbolic racism is present in modern America, and it is present in large swaths of the white population. That much is clear. No matter how we ask the question, majorities of white Americans express ideas that inform much of our academic understanding of how race continues to limit opportunities for social and economic mobility in the United States.

But are rural areas bastions of white supremacy? We see mixed evidence. On the one hand, a majority of whites in these communities excuse their privilege and do not see how past discrimination impinges on the present. On specific issues—whether it is their view about the George Floyd protests or the Confederate flag—there is reluctance to see racism as central to these polarizing issues in American society. And geography matters quite a bit. We also looked at these distributions by age and partisan affiliation, and in both instances, rural residents are more resentful than demographically similar residents of suburban and urban areas.

On the other hand, we see that average responses to these questions give us a slightly more muted image of racial hostility, even on symbolic grounds. On some questions, a majority of rural residents held opinions that were racially tolerant, on average, and did so in parity with whites in different communities. Most disagreed with the idea that "It's really a matter of some people not trying hard enough; if Blacks would only try harder, they could be just as well off as whites," and believed that racial problems were not "rare, isolated situations." On specific issues, rural America is distinctive, but the average difference between their views and those of whites living in the suburbs is often in the single digits.

WHITENESS AND THE POLITICS
OF "HARD WORK" IN RURAL AMERICA

Racism is unavoidable in rural America, just as it is unavoidable in urban and suburban America. Race matters even when the topic is not explicitly racial, as we addressed in the previous section. Consider the scholarly take on racism in the Tea Party movement. As we noted in chapter 3, a good deal of evidence suggests that the driving force behind creation of the Tea Party was attitudes toward race and immigration. The stated rationale for the group's mobilization might have been the Great Recession, shifts in government policy, the growing federal deficit, and the Affordable Care Act; but the strongest correlation was racial animus.

The literature on the topic, which is vast, can generally be separated into four buckets. One approach is what we might call "old-fashioned racism." This theory would suggest, simply, that Tea Party activists were bigots, and the election of a Black president gave them license to mobilize. The more they mobilized, the more racist attitudes were normalized. In fact, one of the foremost architects of the movement, Mark Williams, was kicked out of the National Tea Party Federation for penning an overtly racist letter.[17] As we noted in chapter 3, one experiment found that positive attitudes toward the Tea Party increased when subjects were shown a picture of Barack Obama with artificially darkened skin.[18] That's pretty strong evidence. Moreover, there were a number of news accounts during that period documenting the use of ugly, racist language and racial tropes in Tea Party rhetoric, publications, and posters—especially in the South.[19] A California Republican Party official and Tea Party activist, Marilyn Davenport, portrayed Obama as a chimpanzee, and at rallies, many participants sometimes characterize him as a primate and an African "witch doctor," a modern-day Hitler, a Muslim, and worse.[20]

Closely tied to overt racism is "Obamaphobia." The scholars Christopher Parker and Matt Barreto, in *Change They Can't Believe In*, explore the relationship between Tea Party sentiment and attitudes toward Obama as a person. After controlling for a host of variables, including ideology, partisanship, and policy preferences related to Obama's agenda, they find feelings of antipathy to Obama the most powerful predictor of Tea Party membership. In other words, it is not simply a general attitude toward big government or a close connection to the Republican Party that mattered; instead, it was hatred for the forty-fourth president. Surprisingly, however, in their multivariate model, Parker and Barreto found that measures of racial resentment, while present, are less significant.[21] But how one could truly untangle hostile views of the first Black president from race-related matters is an open question.

Another set of studies suggest that racial attitudes spring from what may be called the "decline of whiteness." Demographic shifts (a rising minority population), coupled with the first Black president, were perceived as threatening the relative standing of whites.[22] Also called "group position theory," the idea is that racial animus is driven by growing threats to the dominant group and efforts to defend their position in society.[23] Diana Mutz described this dynamic in a 2018 paper: "Candidate preferences in 2016 reflected increasing anxiety among high-status groups. . . . Both growing domestic racial diversity and globalization contributed to a sense that white Americans are under siege by these engines of change."[24]

A final bucket, the most common approach, can be called the "symbolic groups status model" or "symbolic racism," touched on earlier. Tea Party activists voiced strong opposition to programs that advance the interest of minority groups—particularly those that help the poor and the "undeserving." At the center of this type of motivation are stereotypes of nonwhites as lazy. Special ire is aimed at leaders (Obama) whom they think enable and aid "those people."[25]

But even here, it is less than clear how much racism drives some attitudes toward government spending. Using data from the Cooperative Congressional Election Study and an embedded experiment, Kevin Arceneaux and Stephen Nicholson find little hard evidence that racial resentment explicitly colors judgments about aid to the poor and the push for small government. They exposed subjects to statements about various government policies while manipulating the picture of the face of the person expressing that view. For example, one subject would be given a statement that the government should "give the unemployed a helping hand" coupled with a picture of a dark-skinned male, while another would get the same statement with the picture of a light-skinned male. Their results suggest that "opposition to government aid is not solely a function of racial resentment. Rather, some degree of racial resentment underlies conservative opposition to support for unemployment aid, and this resentment appears to run deeper among Tea Party conservatives."[26]

That is, separating Tea Party attitudes toward government programs from those perceived to use them is hard. We know that strong conservatives oppose government programs because they violate the principle of limited government; expansion of these initiatives—or even perceived expansion—would cause a stir. We should also not dismiss that fact that a vast majority of Tea Party activists would vehemently reject racist claims. Writing in the *New Republic*, the columnist Jonathan Chait made the following observation in 2011: "The Tea party is organized around traditional right-wing public policy beliefs about government spending, and is almost completely uninterested in what we call 'racial issues.' However, it is also demonstrably true that Tea Party sympathizers hold distinctly reactionary views on racial issues."[27]

In survey research, we also run into the problems of coded language. We know, for instance, that white Americans' attitudes about welfare and crime in the "inner city" are deeply linked to prejudicial ideas and racialized rhetoric that has built up over time.[28] These types of implicit dog whistles are often more successful at animating underlying racial prejudice than overt calls to discriminate against racial minorities.[29] Likewise, Robert Wuthnow makes a similar observation. Racist attitudes, he argues, are linked to perceptions of hard work and the social position of undeserving groups. "The implicit prejudice surfaces most often under the rubric of 'riff-raff,' which meant people on the margins of small towns who did not pull their weight, did not work hard, or use their money responsibly, and expected something for nothing."[30] They received special privileges because of who they were, not because of their work and ingenuity. Wuthnow goes on to say that riff-faff could be anyone—white Anglo, Hispanic, Black, but in communities where there were Black residents, they were the implied referent.

But how do these ideas translate to groups of people outside rural communities, and how much these divides continue to depend on old-fashioned racism as opposed to these implicit prejudices?[31] Some scholars argue that much of white America's tolerance for these racial inequities stems not so much from racism as from other core values that emphasize color-blindness, equal opportunity, and limited government interventionism.[32] To the extent that Black and Brown Americans have had to compete in a vastly unequal society that stresses equal opportunity, they may remain disadvantaged. But do they remain disadvantaged because of racist beliefs or because of ardent beliefs in the ideal of equal opportunity in an unequal society?[33]

We recognize that for many, this may be a matter of semantics and that unequal outcomes between racial groups is racist no matter what the underlying principle. Racism does not require racists, in other words.[34]

We will not wade into that debate, except to raise a set of empirical findings that show the extent to which beliefs about race in rural communities are, in fact, coupled to other attitudes related to the value placed on hard work. It is up to the reader to decide whether or not such an attitude is racist or whether such justifications are important to understand for making sense of racial divisions in American society, especially white rural America. Cindy Kam and Camille Burge offer a helpful analysis of patterns and alternative measures, writing that people highest on the classic racial resentment scale think about racial inequality as a consequence of Black American's "disposition, motivation, or individual choice . . . and deny or diminish the existence of discrimination." Others, however, "interpret differences across Blacks and whites less by pointing to the character of Black Americans and more by identifying structural features of discrimination that undercut the promise of individualism."[35] Some blame the individual; others blame the system.

Still, we should be as clear as possible about what this debate and our data entail. This is not about whether one group is racist and another not. Rather, there are competing notions of what "racism" means and how race is embedded in larger perspectives about politics: whether it is a dichotomy or a continuum; whether one must actively work to dismantle racist systems; or whether color-blindness perpetuates racial inequality more just because it treats individuals as equals. Most white Americans, for instance, believe themselves to be both politically progressive and racially tolerant, primarily because they do not judge individuals by their race.[36] Given the extensive debate among scholars on those ideas, it is unsurprising that we find evidence of that debate in the minds of the American public. And, to a large extent, that debate is reflected in something we might simply recognize as measurement error. Writing in the *Annals of the American Academy of Political and Social Science*, David Wilson and Darren Davis summarize the problem elegantly: "While it is clear that the behavioral nature of racism has changed—based on peoples' expressed willingness to reject racial stereotypes and biological explanations for racial differences in survey interviews—exactly what racism has morphed into is open to debate. Thus, a core problem with contemporary racial attitudes research has been measuring and defining perceptions of African Americans and other minorities in ways that are uncontaminated by other simultaneously evolving attitudes of individuals, conservatives, perceptions of government, and social desirability."[37]

Again, we cannot measure racist beliefs by asking people whether they are racist; there is no "reveal" question. So we ask something we believe taps into a racist sentiments. In doing so, we take a position on what constitutes a racist belief, and many times, those measures are unobjectionable. For example, we asked participants in the Rural Voter Survey, "Do you agree or disagree: The Confederate flag is racist." We did not ask if they flew the Confederate flag or if they knew about its history; just, "is that symbol racist?" Most academics would identify that object as a clear symbol of hate and racial divisiveness or of symbolic racism.[38] We would agree and a vast majority of nonwhite Americans (71 percent) do, too. The fact that only 45 percent of white Americans agree can be seen as further indication that racist beliefs imbue the American consciousness and reinforce the racial divide in public policies and society writ large.

Our point, though, is that we have to think about how multiple measures of racist beliefs stack up. Consider how attitudes about the Confederate flag sit alongside attitudes about white privilege, which we explored earlier. Just among white respondents, 34 percent disagreed both with the idea that "white people in the U.S. have certain advantages because of the color of their skin" and the statement that the Confederate flag is racist. An almost equal percentage agreed with both statements, that the Confederate flag is racist and whites had advantages. Who are the other 30 percent who disagreed with one, but not the other? Are they "sort of racist?" Just over one in five white Americans said they did not think the Confederate flag is racist while also saying they agreed that white people have advantages in society: 10 percent said that, yes, the Confederate flag is a racist symbol, but they were not convinced that white people had advantages. Clearly, there is some tension in what people are thinking and why. Or we may not be measuring what we think we are measuring.

RACIAL ATTITUDES AND HARD WORK

As it relates to our study of rural voters, we notice a deep tension between racial attitudes and other beliefs about how individuals should be rewarded in society and how the government might intervene to reduce wealth disparities between different racial groups. Other scholars have bundled these beliefs into different packages, such as how "individualist" a person is or how much stock they place in "meritocracy." Still others equate Americans' core beliefs of equal opportunity with a demand that the government adopt a race-neutral approach to solving economic and social issues.

Decades of research on American attitudes more generally have shown how white Americans are particularly sensitive to arguments that violate principles of equal treatment and universalism.[39] Beliefs about inequality and what the government should do to address it are highly dependent on individuals' perceptions of social mobility and the causes of economic success.[40] And yet, "individualism" is invoked more readily when the beneficiaries of a government policy are nonwhite; the concept is applied unevenly and in a racialized way.[41]

What we see when we look at our own data is a complicated set of patterns that link rural residents' understanding of hard work with symbolic racist beliefs.[42] The traditional measures of racial resentment are motivated by a resentment toward traditional American values—none perhaps more important than the principle of hard work and individualism, which other scholars have identified as almost uniquely American.[43] It is not surprising that these are connected. Rural Americans' beliefs about cultural and economic uncertainty are not considerations separate from racial inequality. They are bound together in a comprehensive, broader worldview that sees rural communities as unfairly disadvantaged.

These narratives of deservingness, hard work, and whiteness, are similar to what Arlie Hochschild found in her widely acclaimed book, *Strangers in Their Own Land*. A retired sociology professor at UC Berkeley, Hochschild lived in the Deep South for five years, talking to hundreds of residents and conducting an impressive amount of participant observation. She was fascinated by the rise of the Tea Party and what she saw as contradictory interests: given the importance of safe, clean water for the livelihood of so many Bayou residents, why did they so strongly oppose environmental regulations? Wouldn't government protect their interests? She discovered a subculture rich in the ideas of fair competition, hard work, family, and social ascent. But with the decline of manufacturing and rising economic inequality, bayou residents had become angry, resentful, and lost. They had done the hard work and waited in line, but the rewards were gone.[44] Undeserving Americans had "cut in line," and liberal politicians, like Barack Obama, had waved them up front.

But did the Bayou residents lash out at Black Americans and immigrants? Not exactly. Rural residents she talked to scorned welfare recipients and groups favored by the government; and racism, she offers, is ever present in rural Louisiana. But it is intimately tied to notions of fairness, economic mobility, and hard work.

Like Hochschild, when we probed these interconnections, we saw a pattern between our questions about the value of hard work and our questions about race. As with race, we did not simply come out and say, "hey, do you value hard work?" Rather, we wanted our respondents to really identify a position in the places where the values of hard work conflict with other core values. As such, we used forced-choice questions to tease out how much someone believes in the inherent goodness or value of hard work. We asked them to choose one or the other statement: "People are successful in America because . . . somebody along the way gave them some help," or ". . . they worked hard to overcome obstacles." We also asked them to say whether, "Thinking about people who were most successful," do they "work hard and keep at it when times get tough," or do they "maintain a good work-life balance?"

We built several tests to assess how responses to these "hard work" questions varied over our measures or racial resentment. We found similar patterns regardless of the measurement. But to help visualize and interpret how this interconnectedness plays out in the minds of rural voters, let us consider just one measure of racial resentment: individuals' responses to the statement, "Generations of slavery and discrimination have created conditions that make it difficult for Blacks to work their way out of the lower class." This question is about both race and hard work. It is also the question about which urban and rural whites are most different in what they believe. For purposes of the present discussion, we will simplify things. If individuals agreed with the statement, we will think of them as having low levels of racial resentment; if they disagreed with that statement, they have high levels of resentment.

When we divide white rural Americans into these two categories, we can see how attitudes toward hard work vary over different levels of racial resentment. The conclusion is undeniable: racially resentful rural Americans are much more likely to value hard work compared with rural whites who expressed higher levels of racial tolerance.

For instance, as we note in table 8.1, regardless of their underlying racial attitudes (whether they are resentful or have lower levels of racial resentment), most rural whites believe people are successful when they work hard to overcome obstacles. However, whereas 64 percent of non-racially resentful rural whites agreed with that statement, the level of agreement jumps to 86 percent for racially resentful rural whites. Very

TABLE 8.1 Hard work and racial animus among rural non-Latino white Americans

	Low racial resentment (55.89% of rural non-Latino whites)	High racial resentment (44.11% of rural non-Latino whites)
People are successful in America because they . . .		
work hard and keep at it when times get tough.	46.9%	57.1%
maintain a good work-life balance.	53.1	42.9
If you were giving a young man advice, would you tell them to take . . .		
a physically demanding job that pays really well.	67.3%	84.6%
a comfortable office job that just pays okay.	32.7%	15.4%
In your view, which one is more impressive, being . . .		
accepted to a special part of the military, like the Navy Seals.	59.6%	82.6%
accepted to an Ivy League college, like Harvard or Yale.	40.3	17.5
People are successful in America because . . .		
somebody along the way gave them some help.	33.2%	13.9%
they worked hard to overcome obstacles.	66.8	86.1

Note: Data from the 2021 and 2022 waves of the Rural Voter Survey. Respondent location is self-described, and averages incorporate poststratification weights described in chapter 4. The figure illustrates the percentage of white respondents who finished each statement with the listed phrases. Those with high racial resentment agreed with the statement, "It's really a matter of some people not trying hard enough; if Blacks would only try harder, they could be just as well off as whites"; and respondents who disagreed with the statement, "Generations of slavery and discrimination have created conditions that make it difficult for Blacks to work their way out of the lower class." Those with low racial resentment answered in the reverse.

few respondents—14 percent—believed the past discrimination against Black Americans does not matter and believed people are successful because they get help. Attitudes toward hard work are nearly uniform among racially resentful whites. Across each indicator, the percentage of respondents expressing preference for the hard work category bumps up for the racially resentful—and always by double digits!

To be absolutely clear, this correlation between hard work and racial resentment does not mean there is no racism in rural America. It may explain *why* there is racism. Those who believe that past discrimination does not matter, for instance, are much more likely to value hard work. That finding only alerts us to a potential underlying cause of racism and how principled beliefs in a certain view of success reinforce the racial divide in our politics.

The likely connection between hard work and color-blindness extends beyond this one question: it implicates whether white rural residents think Black Americans work hard enough or whether they are systematically disadvantaged in the labor market, as well as what sorts of government policies should redress those inequities. This belief in the value of hard work, generally, seems to extend to a belief that hard work can overcome discrimination faced by racial and ethnic minorities. Given the deep and lasting disparities in economic opportunity between different racial groups, we personally think this belief is wrong. But rural Americans are overwhelmingly convinced that, at least in their own communities, it is possible to get by if you work hard enough (see chapter 5). And they believe that even as they express anxieties about their community's economic future. We conclude, then, that for many rural residents, the reason for their misplaced beliefs does not emerge from pure, unbridled racial animus; rather, it comes from damaging stereotypes, misinformation, and an unchallenged faith in meritocracy, both as an ideal and as it might exist within their own rural community.

What's more, we find that those connections are more tightly braided in rural America than in suburban and urban America. Hard work takes on a peculiar meaning among rural whites. Consider, for instance, the answer to a set of questions we posed about the "hardest" and "easiest" jobs from a list: doctor, teacher, accountant, carpenter, farmer, and waitress. Three of those jobs are classic examples of blue-collar work— occupations that require employees to work with their hands and be on their feet. (Although, as spouses of public school educators, we know that they are also constantly on the move!) Important for our analysis, none of them requires a college degree.

When we consider who chose the last three—classically defined as blue collar—and who did not, we see enormous differences between locales. Among just white respondents, 75 percent of rural residents listed one of those blue-collar jobs as the hardest. In fact, a full 60 percent selected "farmer." Barely a majority of urban residents—52 percent—felt similarly toward blue-collar workers; just over 40 percent thought the same of farmers, specifically. Rural and urban residents view work differently, and their frames of reference are decidedly shaped by the places in which they live.

BEYOND RACE: ATTITUDES TOWARD IMMIGRANTS, WOMEN, AND OUTSIDE CULTURES

Race is one of many divisions in American society. Although it is a profound one, it by no means captures the extent to which rural America's beliefs in hard work, individualism, community, and equal economic opportunity translate into views toward other disadvantaged groups, including immigration, which is intricately bound to the story of economic restructuring.

Immigration and the rapid rise in the number of Latino Americans is one of the most contentious aspects of American politics. Well before Donald Trump's candidacy, immigration reform vexed both political parties, and voters have been remarkably fickle on this issue. As it has played out in rural America, Latinos make up a small proportion of the population—and an even smaller proportion of the voting population, which is the subject of our book. But that is changing. Although rural America has lost population in the last two decades, parts of rural America are becoming more populated largely as a result of Latino immigration. In areas that have lost population, those losses, too, were offset by an increase in Latino residents.[45] Since the last census, 95 percent of rural counties have become more diverse, in large part because of Latino immigration.[46]

These changes are not confined to the areas of the country you might expect (i.e., the Southwest); they have affected rural communities far from the U.S.-Mexico border. Moreover, the Latino population is younger; the demographic change represented by the growing number of children and young adults portends even more demographic diversity in the decades ahead.[47]

To better understand how these demographic shifts have played out politically, the Rural Voter Survey went beyond attitudes toward Black Americans and racial equality, even though we know those attitudes are highly correlated, and increasingly predictive of other racial views and partisanship.[48] As Michael Hout and Christopher Maggio summarize, "While Republicans' views of immigration and their racial resentment have changed very little since 2010, Democrats' views of immigration have become far more positive and their racial resentment has declined substantially. The consequences of these trends were borne out dramatically in the 2016 presidential election. In combination, the two attitudes predict well who voted for Trump and who voted for Clinton."[49]

But as we have seen, correlation between two measures is never perfect, and often, the more interesting story is between the lines, masked by averages, and that vary on different measures.

Let's start with attitudes toward immigration (figure 8.3). As we did earlier, we will consider only how these beliefs manifest among white voters, although including other racial and ethnic groups in the estimates does not substantially expand the differences between rural and urban America. Part of that reason is that, overall, there are no substantial differences between different geographies when it comes to attitudes toward Latinos and immigration.

In rural America, it is true that statistically higher percentages of residents believe that automatic birthright citizenship ("No matter where the parents are from, children born on American soil should automatically be a citizen") is a bad policy. Moreover, in every geographic area, voters who disagree with that idea make up a small percentage of the voting population (i.e., most people favor it). And it is true that in rural America, a smaller percentage of voters agree with the direct statement, "Immigrants to the United States make this country a better place to live"—59 percent compared with urban America's 73 percent and suburban America's 69 percent. But on other measures, rural America seems to have more open attitudes toward Latinos. Using a measure meant to gauge more implicit prejudice toward Latinos, we also asked whether "Latinos have a tendency to get involved in gangs and organized crime."[50] A majority of white urban residents agree with that idea (54 percent), but a minority—albeit large (42 percent)—of rural residents agree (see figure 8.3).

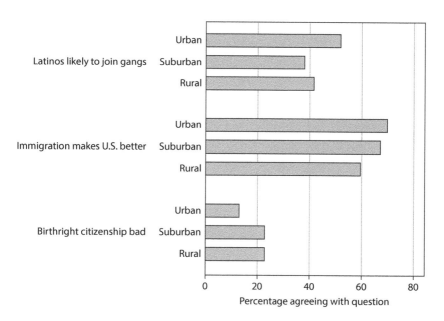

FIGURE 8.3 Attitudes toward Latinos and immigration among rural, suburban, and urban non-Latino whites

Note: Data from the 2021 and 2022 waves of the Rural Voter Survey. Respondent location is self-described, and geographic averages incorporate poststratification weights described in chapter 4. The figure illustrates the percentage of respondents "strongly agreeing" or "somewhat agreeing" with the following statements: "Latinos have a tendency to get involved in gangs and organized crime"; "Immigrants to the United States make this country a better place to live"; No matter where the parents are from, children born on American soil should automatically be a citizen" (reverse coded); and "There is a secretive effort in the United States to increase the immigration of certain types of people in order to replace white Americans."

Just as with race, attitudes towards immigration are interwoven with concerns about rural economy and society. In his book on the decline of civic life in rural communities, the journalist Timothy Carney talked to scores of rural residents. He was, at first, taken aback by the comments of Bob Barrett of Rock Hill, South Carolina, during one of those chats. Although it is debatable whether Rock Hill is "rural" (it would be the largest city in Maine if it moved up here!), Barrett expressed a concern we know is present in rural communities—while in line to attend a Trump rally no less. Barrett commented, "I liked it better then . . . it was better to be an American." He was clearly nostalgic for the good ol' days, which we may assume was tinged with a zeal for white patriarchy, especially when coming from a southern Trump supporter. And sure enough, it wasn't long before he espoused what most would see as anti-immigration sentiments. After a bit of discussion, however, Carney better understood where Barrett was coming from. He was deeply concerned about the effect of immigration on available jobs and how it might drive down wages. He also expressed concerns about the erosion of his community. Carney writes, "We can't deny that racism, in more acute or more diffuse ways, plays a role in American views on immigration. . . . But we should also see wariness about immigration, especially in Trump Country, as bound up with alienation and the erosion of community bonds."[51]

Animosity toward immigrant populations, especially Latino immigrants, is part of a broader set of attitudes that we will call "anticosmopolitan." That is, we mean a willingness to engage with people and cultures outside one's immediate country. We can think about this attitudinally: "Agree or Disagree: It is important that people travel to other countries to gain new perspectives." And we can think about it as a real, lived experience: whether someone has lived most of their life in their current community.

We are not making a normative claim. One of us lives across the street from a lovely elderly couple who have lived in their home ever since they married—more than sixty years ago! They are pillars of the local community and see nothing wrong with staying put. Neither do we. Our point, simply, is that these attitudes are reflective of different

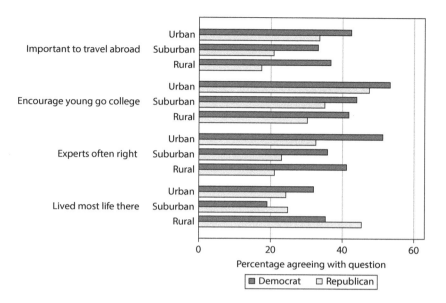

FIGURE 8.4 Anticosmopolitan attitudes in rural, suburban, and urban America

Note: Data from the 2021 and 2022 waves of the Rural Voter Survey. Respondent location and partisan identity are self-described, and geographic averages incorporate poststratification weights described in chapter 4. The figure illustrates the percentage of respondents "strongly agreeing" with the following statements: "It is important that people travel to other countries to gain new perspectives" and "We should encourage most young Americans to go to college." The figure also includes the percentage of respondents who finished the phrase "When it comes to making decisions, government experts . . ." with the option, "get it right most of the time" instead of "almost never know what the right answer is." Finally, respondents were considered to have lived most of their lives in a community if the number of years they lived in the specific location exceeded 50 percent of their self-reported age.

values and worldviews. The data in figure 8.4 suggest that these are meaningful delimiters, too. While most rural people think it is important to travel abroad, just a quarter strongly agree with the idea compared with over a third of urban residents. And while 40 percent of rural residents have lived in their community "all my life," fewer than 30 percent of urbanites have as deep, local roots.

We also could include a more expansive set of considerations, such as whether one believes it is "important to encourage young people to go to college." Again, we look at the gap in the most enthusiastic response. Most Americans, including rural Americans, think we should encourage young people should go to college. But where nearly one in two urban Americans strongly agrees with that idea, rural residents are much less enthusiastic. Likewise, across the United States, we see weak support for the idea that, "when it comes to making decisions, government experts get it right most of the time." On average, 70 percent of Americans think those experts "almost never know what the right answer is." That average is driven primarily by residents outside urban areas. In big cities, residents are much more evenly split in their views about expert authority. Not so in rural communities, where three in every four residents are skeptical about expert or "Cidiot" (read city + idiot) claims.

Differences exist, especially in the lived experience of rural residents, but these attitudes are not completely confined to rural areas. Suburban residents also hold skeptical views about outside authority and are less enthusiastic about basic cosmopolitan ideas than urban residents. Nevertheless, these views are not the result of partisan composition effects either. Even when we confine the analysis to Republicans, rural residents think and behave differently from voters who are already more predisposed to answer conservatively.

We find similarly complex attitudes when it comes to questions about gender and support for traditional family structure. Recall that we considered some other gendered attitudes when we explored whether economic anxiety was more likely to be felt among rural men as opposed to women. In that instance, we saw that the shared feelings of anxiety and grievance were just as likely to be felt by women, even though rural men have been more likely to suffer the consequences of globalization.

Here, we can look at averages across locality, as we have largely done with each analysis of different attitudes. It also makes sense to look at how these beliefs vary by the gender of the respondent as well: how men and women living in urban, suburban, and rural locations view the topic (figure 8.5).

Unsurprisingly, women hold more egalitarian views than men, regardless of where they live. Women are less likely to say "Women are too

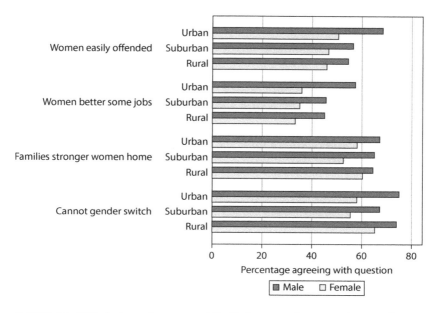

FIGURE 8.5 Attitudes toward women and family, by respondent sex and geography

Note: Data from the 2021 wave of the Rural Voter Survey. Respondent location and gender are self-described, and geographic averages incorporate poststratification weights described in chapter 4. The figure illustrates the percentage of respondents "strongly agreeing" or "somewhat agreeing" with the following statements: "Women are too easily offended"; "When women lose to men in a fair competition, they typically complain"; "In the past, families were stronger when more moms didn't go to work"; and "You are born a male or female, and cannot switch."

easily offended," or "You are born a male or female, and cannot switch." And while a majority of women believe that "Families were stronger when more moms didn't go to work," even though just over a third are willing to agree that "Women are just better at some jobs like teaching and nursing." On these questions related to gender equality and gender fluidity, women everywhere hold similar beliefs.

Location does seem to matter for men, but perhaps not in the direction you may expect. The gap between urban men and women is highest on each of these questions. Nearly 20 percent more men than women living in urban areas think women are too easily offended, compared with a difference of just nine percentage points in rural areas. Likewise, urban men are much more likely to think that women are better suited to certain types of jobs and that you cannot change your gender assignment after birth. Perhaps most significantly, in urban America, men are more likely to see the traditional male-as-breadwinner model of family life as stronger, while in rural areas, men and women hold nearly identical views; to be sure, the average American still views such a family model as "stronger."

As with our analysis of racial divides, the most important takeaway is that regardless of where they live, Americans are deeply divided on these issues. There is a reason they are among the most contentious in American politics and society today. Immigration reform is too often dead on arrival when a new Congress begins its work. The pay gap between men and women may be closing, but men—especially Black men—continue to be left behind; few public policies even attempt to address these gendered inequities. But these are problems that exist despite—not because of—the growing divide between rural and urban America.

HOW GRIEVANCE, CULTURE, AND SOCIAL CAPITAL MANIFEST AMONG NONWHITE RURAL RESIDENTS

We imagine that some of these findings will be especially difficult for rural residents to hear. As our discussion of symbolic racism noted, most Americans recognize that it is morally and socially wrong to be a "racist," even as they harbor prejudicial beliefs. When we travel throughout rural America and speak about our research, rural residents are particularly frustrated over constantly being labeled "bigots" and "racists" when most deeply believe there is nothing wrong with their belief set. Politics has changed, they tell us, not us.

The evidence for our claim, as difficult as it may be for rural Americans to swallow, is undeniable—especially once we look at the various dimensions of racism in rural America. However, even while rural Americans are more racially resentful than urban or suburban Americans, we do not find overwhelming evidence that the logic of rural identity is limited to whites. Racism does not define the rural voter.

For readers who have perhaps jumped to this chapter, or those in need of a reminder, recall that we have identified four unique attributes of rural politics. First and foremost is a shared sense of economic anxiety, which translates into a collective grievance toward government, experts, and outsiders. Second is the heightened sense of civic pride that rural Americans have, which, as it plays out in communities reeling from social decay, has manifested in heightened forms of political participation and engagement. Third is a cultural connection, which is largely evidenced by rural America's overwhelming sense that their ways of life are discounted, mis-portrayed, and dismissed by others living "over there." Finally, we have noted in this chapter the racialized politics of hard work and individualism that distinguish rural Americans' views and help shape a comprehensive worldview through which they filter issues, such as racial inequality and government intervention to address such inequalities.

Those views are rural views. They are, generally speaking, shared by millions of rural Americans who are not white. In the South, this largely means Black Americans, who represent 13 percent of the rural electorate. Out west, the racial diversity is much wider, including 4 percent Native or Indigenous Americans and a large percentage of residents identifying as racially mixed. Once we incorporate our standard measures of Hispanic heritage, we also see higher levels of ethnic diversity between regions. On average, just 7 percent of rural voters are Latino, but that number jumps to almost 17 percent in the West, with the South following at around 8 percent. Here, too, we will point out that in isolating our analysis to rural voters, we likely underestimate—or, at least, omit—a large proportion of ethnic minorities living in rural communities who do not vote because they are not citizens.

Because we sampled thousands of rural voters, we have been able to draw many distinctions among rural voters themselves; for example: men and women, racially resentful and not-so-racially resentful. Given the overwhelming lopsidedness of whiteness in rural communities (although we recognize it varies depending on where you are in the United States), drawing racial distinctions is harder to do. We surveyed just over 10,000 rural Americans, and yet, we recognize that this means just about 1,100 of our respondents identify as nonwhite. Within that group, we are left with about 550 Black Americans, 150 Indigenous/ Native Americans, and a mix of different identifications, sometimes in the single digits. It may not always be fair—and it certainly does not always make good statistical sense—to extrapolate from these data "what Black rural residents think" or "How do Native Americans in rural communities differ from other racial/ethnic minorities?" We care, but we just don't have reliable data.

For this reason, although we have tried to avoid creating underexplored and oversimplified dichotomies throughout the book, we have to rely on one here: white and nonwhite. And in terms of nonwhite, we include respondents who identify as Hispanic or Latino even though they are usually classified simply as "white." This includes about 7 percent of our rural sample, although it is important to note that our survey was conducted exclusively in English. In this regard, it may misrepresent some important attributes of non-English-speaking rural voters.

We will offer further evidence of these patterns in chapter 9, where we pull together a more statistically robust "rural voter model" and combine dozens of questions into composite indices, averaging over each one. But even by looking at just a few of the questions we have already explored, we can begin to see that rural identity is not a phenomenon exclusive to whites, even if it is most pronounced among white residents of rural areas.

Consider, for example, how rural residents—white and nonwhite— think about the economy, or any other marker of rural identity measured in figure 8.6. It is true that racial and ethnic minorities, wherever they live, are statistically more likely to think that children being raised in their community need to move away to have successful careers. That is true in cities and the countryside. It is highest, however, in rural areas, and rural nonwhites are even more likely than rural whites to share that sense of economic anxiety. That anxiety, as we explained in chapter 5, translates to a shared sense of grievance. And that grievance is felt in rural communities regardless of the color of one's skin. In fact, nonwhite rural residents are a tad more enthusiastic in saying that the government spends too

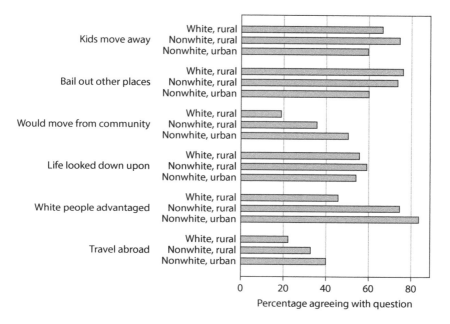

FIGURE 8.6 Key measures of rural identity among whites and nonwhites

Note: Data from the 2021 and 2022 waves of the Rural Voter Survey. Respondent location and race/ethnicity are self-described, and geographic averages incorporate poststratification weights described in chapter 4. The figure illustrates the percentage of respondents "strongly agreeing" or "somewhat agreeing" with the statements described in figures 5.8, 5.9, 7.1, and 7.4 and table 6.3.

much money bailing out cities.. True, there is some resentment among nonwhite urban residents when they are asked whether the government bails out rural communities, but this attitude is pretty unique to them; white residents of urban areas (not pictured in figure 8.6) do not join their neighbors in expressing that type of geographic resentment.

What about culture and civic pride? Again, we see that rural residents—regardless of race—have more in common with one another than do rural residents and urban residents. Rural minorities are much less likely to want to leave their communities—a large majority want to stay—whereas a majority of urban minorities want to leave. They are also more likely to say that their rural way of life is looked down on by people living in big cities and urban areas—even more than white rural residents. As with economic grievances, we also see that urban nonwhites feel they are looked down on by people living in rural communities. As before, this finding is confined to urban minority groups; it is not shared by urban whites.

Our focus is on attitudes in rural America; we offer no theory as to why racial minorities living in cities feel this way. We conjecture that we would find similar evidence if we asked whether "whites" looked down on urban residents' way of life, since it is easy and often reasonable to equate ruralness with whiteness.

Of course, on one dimension, the effects of geography are nonexistent: racial attitudes. Here, the linked fate that binds racial minorities—particularly Black Americans—operates across the geographic lines we have constructed. On each question intended to gauge racial resentment or hard work or views about racial events in the news, racial and ethnic minorities—regardless of where they live—have more in common with one another than they do with whites, including whites living in rural communities. On other ideas wrapped up with race—anticosmopolitanism, gender hierarchies, and traditional values—there is much greater diversity among racial and ethnic minorities than we often discuss. For example, while white rural residents are the least enthusiastic about the need to travel abroad to gain new perspectives, nonwhite rural residents are also comparatively less enthusiastic than urban residents. In short, when it comes to racial politics, racial identity trumps other attitudes and behaviors.

"YOU DIDN'T BUILD THAT"

A lot of American politics is racial politics. Consider how quickly the politics of hard work and race were wrapped together when Barack Obama—the country's first Black president—was campaigning for reelection in 2012.

In making the case for expanded government spending, Obama rallied a campaign crowd by telling them, "If you were successful, somebody along the line gave you some help. There was a great teacher somewhere in your life. Somebody helped to create this unbelievable American system that we have that allowed you to thrive. Somebody invested in roads and bridges. If you've got a business—you didn't build that. Somebody else made that happen."[52]

The president's "you didn't build that" line was the rhetorical shot heard 'round the countryside. It was deeply unpopular in conservative circles, and small business owners—over half of whom reported feeling dismissed by the comment. Mitt Romney pounced. Given that there are somewhere over thirty million small businesses in the United States, and assuming that several voters are linked to each, Obama's suggestion that others made it happen seemed an electoral gift from the gods. A columnist for the *Washington Post* dubbed it Obama's " 'you didn't build that problem,' " and he went on to note several other lines by the president that might cause some grief: "In the decades after World War II, there was a general consensus that the market couldn't solve all of our problems on its own" "Only government can break the vicious cycles that are crippling our economy;" and "A lack of [government] spending leads to lost jobs which leads to even less spending."[53] The *Atlantic* writer Andrew Cline observed, "Even by the most favorable interpretation, the president uttered something worthy of enormous controversy—a philosophical rewriting of the American story."[54] Day after day, Romney pushed the message that Obama and the Democrats could not care less about the toil, sacrifice, and risks of business owners. "Come here and talk to Brian [Maloney, owner of a trucking company] and you'll learn that in fact he did build this business," Romney said at a campaign event.[55] One month after Obama said the line, a Google search for "you didn't build that" had 70,000 hits per day.[56]

But it was also no wonder that in first reporting on the story, Fox News played up how rural people reacted to Obama's message.[57] Republican candidates toured the backwoods playing that message on repeat; Romney's ad against the president featured a folksy-sounding metal fabricator located in rural New Hampshire, whose praise of work ethic was overlaid by images of barns, pickup trucks, and open country. David Brooks, writing in the urbane *New York Times*, nevertheless used the comment as a way of framing Romney's limited appeal outside small towns: "These economic values played well in places with a lot of Protestant dissenters and their cultural heirs. They struck chords with people whose imaginations are inspired by the frontier experience."[58]

Before the dreaded comment, the story of Obama's win in those types of communities, including the Iowa Democratic Caucus in 2008, was legendary. How did a novice senator from Illinois beat the hands-down favorite, Hillary Clinton . . . in the Hawkeye State? Believe it or not, in the final weeks of the general election, several polls had Obama and John McCain essentially neck and neck in the rural areas of thirteen swing states.[59] Essentially tied in rural areas? When it was all said and done, Obama won some of those states and lost others, but he did better with rural voters throughout the country than the previous Democratic candidate, John Kerry. He was no darling of the rustic, not by a long shot. But Obama's solid showing offered reasons for optimism, if perhaps limited. By the 2012 election, all that was gone—and by the end of this administration, the eradication of the rural Democrats was near complete. "It was over the course of the Obama presidency that Democrats ceded an unprecedented amount of power in rural America."[60] The carnage lay everywhere—Senate seats, House districts, state legislatures, and governors' mansions. Progressive rural politicians were nearly wiped out.

How did this happen? Numerous forces were at work, some policy centered and others beyond Obama's control. We tackled this topic in greater detail in chapter 3. But an unflattering explanation gained momentum as Obama handed over the keys to the White House to Donald Trump. Rural voters, many surmised, could not stand to see a Black man in the White House. And the racism, rage, and rebellion of the anti-Obama Tea Party era morph into Donald Trump and his racist backers. Why else would Trump get huge numbers in rural parts?

Some of the evidence presented in this chapter buttresses that claim of racism. On a range of race-related questions, responses from rural residents veer from those of other Americans—and even from other Republicans—in significant ways. And yet, this chapter also revealed that for many rural residents, attitudes about races are intimately linked to perceptions of hard work, self-reliance, a disdain for government handouts, and the dangers of elites. Is the turn away from Democrats partially driven by the party's greater representation of racial and ethnic minorities (as evidenced by candidates they have run and by their support in the electorate)? Yes. Is the turn away from the Democrats partially driven by the party's economic platform, which many see as a violation of equal opportunity and color-blind deservingness? Yes. Many of our rural friends and neighbors would take great umbrage at these characterizations of rural racial attitudes and still insist that America is the land of opportunity.

9

RADICALIZED BY FOX?

The certification of county-level primary election results is rarely a contentious issue. Sometimes a few charges of impropriety occur in a precinct or two, and there may be some grumbling about the results from a particular city or town. Those events have always been minor. But that was before 2020, when election fraud was big news, whether or not you believed it to be true.

Consider what occurred in Otero County, New Mexico, in the summer of 2022. Located on the U.S.–Mexico border, the county boasts roughly 66,000 residents. It's primarily rural, centered on the small city of Alamogordo, whose population approaches 30,000 people.

The state's primary election was on June 7, and about 25 percent of its registered voters came to the polls to pick candidates for each party, including for the three U.S. House races and statewide offices, like governor and secretary of state. It was a sizable turnout for a primary election. In Otero County, about 7,500 residents turned out; they also picked nominees for sheriff and the state House.

The tabulation and certification process was running smoothly when, unexpectedly, the three members of the county election commission decided they would not certify the totals. They could not point to any irregularities or problems, but they would not verify the results. Many in the county and across the state were confused and worried by this pronouncement, given that if the commissioners did not approve the results, the voters of the county would be disenfranchised; their votes would not be counted.

The issue soon drew both state and national attention. First, the state Supreme Court ruled that without evidence of irregularities, the commissioners would have to okay the results. Then, after refusing to relent, the New Mexico attorney general's office issued a statement that each of the commissioners could be fined and removed from office if they did not certify the election.[1] In the end, two of the three commissioners agreed, enough to end the standoff.

The lone holdout was Couy Griffin, founder of a group called "Cowboys for Trump." An outspoken supporter of the former president, Griffin was known for his incendiary comments, including having said in 2020, "The only good Democrat is a dead Democrat."[2] As to why he would never certify the results, Griffin was clear: "My vote to remain a no isn't based on any evidence, it's not based on any facts, it's only based on my gut feeling and my own intuition, and that's all I need."[3]

At the time, Griffin was also being tried for entering a restricted area during the attack on the Capitol on January 6, 2021. He would later be found guilty and sentenced to fourteen days in federal prison, and he was stripped of his post on the county commission. In addition, a U.S. district judge ruled that he was disqualified from holding public office because he violated the insurrection provision in section 3 of the Fourteenth Amendment. The same judge said Griffin was barred from serving in any civilian, military, or federal office—in any state.

Otero was not the only county in New Mexico where election commissioners challenged the integrity of the primary results. In rural counties throughout the state, commissioners were met with screams and angry protests. As noted in one account, when Torrance County commissioners indicated at a widely attended public hearing that they were going to approve the results, they confronted a chorus of shouts and jeers: "Shame on you!" "Cowards and traitors," and "Who elected you?" The commissioners pleaded for patience and said concerns about election security would be addressed at a future time. "The time and place to fight this battle is not by canvassing this election," Chairman Ryan Schwebach told the crowd.[4]

After all the certification battles had ended, New Mexico secretary of state Maggie Toulouse Oliver released a statement saying she was relieved. "We note that the Commission admitted that they did not have any facts to support not certifying the election results," she said. "It's unfortunate that we had to take action to make sure Otero County voters were not disenfranchised . . . and it is a shame that the Commission pushed our state to the brink of a crisis by their actions."[5]

So why would the certification of a state primary election—a set of contents for which there were no claims of irregularities or problems—cause such a stir? Why would all these rural counties come to the edge of disenfranchising their own voters and draw national attention from newsrooms in distant cities?

Part of the answer is obvious. Following the 2020 election, President Donald Trump and several of his allies claimed that Dominion voting systems, the same system used in New Mexico, had been manipulated. It was part of an elaborate scheme to steal the election for Biden.[6] Even though there was no evidence to back up any of these claims, and Dominion had entered into a set of libel suits against the networks that had aired those false accusations, the conspiracy claims ran wild through the summer and fall of 2022. Officials at Dominion would comment that the action by the Otero County commissioners was "yet another example of how lies about Dominion have damaged our company and diminished the public's faith in elections."[7] That explains why commissioners picked up on the story.

But as to why the media's story is focused on rural areas demands another, more nuanced answer. Many may think this is just another example of how the concerns of rural residents have shifted from local matters to far-off national battles, driven by manipulative conservative television commentators. With the decline of local news, a topic discussed in detail in the pages to follow, it is reasonable to surmise that rural residents are left with little else but Fox News commentators and other right-wing channels, conservative satellite radio, and, of course, the dark web. The conservative echo chamber, we might assume, rings loudest in the dimly lit basements of angry rural residents, particularly pissed-off men. So the story goes, it is just natural that internet-spawned conspiracy theories have found fertile soil in the American heartland. This is just the latest chapter: Edgar Welch, the guy who stormed Comet Ping Pong Pizza in Washington, D.C., with an assault rifle to free children held in a Democratic sex ring, was from a small town in North Carolina. All those militia compounds, well, they are located in the countryside!

Our data tell a different story. Pieces of this narrative fit, but not all. For example, while it is true that rural voters are now getting most of their news from national sources, so, too, are all Americans. Fox News is more prevalent in rural than urban areas, but not overwhelmingly so, and not after controlling for partisan composition. More Fox News viewers live outside rural America than within; millions more people ready to challenge the integrity of elections reside in the suburbs and cities. Likewise, while conspiracy theories have become surprisingly pronounced among Republicans, there is scant evidence to suggest that rural voters are more likely to believe these wild claims than are nonrural Americans. The American media landscape is changing, but the story of how it plays out in rural parts is not as clear as even the media want to tell.

This chapter explores those two distinct aspects of media politics in rural America. On the one hand, we rely on aggregate and individual-level data to chart how media habits have changed in rural America. But what explains the knee-jerk assumption that rural residents—like Edgar Welch of "Pizzagate" and Couy Griffin of the Otero County/Dominion voting machines debacle—are especially animated by national politics? We offer evidence that the narrative of radical rural voters ignited by wild conspiracy theories and a conservative media bubble is driven in part by national media outlets. In chapter 7, we explored how rural residents are more apt to feel they are misrepresented by popular media portrayals; here, we have evidence that the number of news media accounts highlighting polarizing, ideological radicalism in rural areas far outweighs their prevalence in American politics.

Media misrepresentation is not deliberate. Our analysis pinpoints a subgroup of rural voters who are indeed animated by ideological talking points and conspiracy theories. These radically engaged rural residents—mostly men—make up just under 10 percent of the rural voting population. They are vocal and active; they are the ones who turn out at local events making outrageous claims about everything from COVID-19 vaccines and the teaching of critical race theory in schools to cancer-causing wind turbines and schools putting litter boxes in the bathrooms for "furry" students. In other words, there is a reason the media paint such a distorted image of rural politics. They are routinely covering the most engaged residents, who differ in fundamental ways from the average rural voter. In this way, the media reinforce the rural-urban divide, fomenting distrust among all rural residents and painting a wild picture in the heads of nonrural residents about what those backwoods people truly value.

THE DECLINE IN LOCAL NEWS

The story of local news in the twenty-first century in the United States is one of decline. Several recent studies have documented the disturbing trend toward fewer and fewer media outlets. Penelope Muse Abernathy of the Hussman School of Journalism and Media at the University of North Carolina–Chapel Hill has spearheaded a research project to document what her team is calling emerging "news deserts." These are communities, either urban or rural, with limited access to credible and comprehensive news and information that feeds democracy at the grass roots.[8]

Drawing on an extensive data set of media operations, Abernathy charts the steep drop in local news outlets since the high point of 2004. The analysis looks not only at newspapers but also digital sites, ethnic news organizations, and public broadcasting outlets. An array of forces—from declining ad revenue to the mushrooming number of online competitors and the financial pressures of the Great

Recession—have led to shrinking number of local outlets and a growing number of communities without any local news sources. Between 2018 and 2021, more than three hundred newspapers closed, an additional six thousand journalists were fired, and there were more than five million fewer print newspaper subscribers.[9] Moreover, since 2018, the number of communities with no local news whatsoever went from thirteen hundred to eighteen hundred. Unsurprisingly, they were concentrated in rural areas.

The increasing presence of news deserts goes hand in hand with coverage deserts, even in places where a newspaper may still operate. In *Ghosting the News: Local Journalism and the Crisis of American Democracy*, the *Washington Post* media critic Margaret Sullivan describes how "ghost newspapers" have taken over—essentially chain-owned operations that rely almost exclusively on national wire reports and little local coverage. Local reporting, other than the most rudimentary (weather, sports, obituaries, "happenings around town"), has evaporated. Local and regional news outlets are, she argues, "under siege in a very, very extreme way because [they've] been hit very hard by the economic and social and technological issues that went to the heart of their business model. [T]hen something happened and that something was called the Internet, [and it] kicked the legs out from under the business model of newspapers."[10] Others have called these "zombie news outlets," but the idea is the same: news organizations in name only.

Summarizing these developments, political scientists Danny Hayes and Jennifer Lawless emphasize three related indicators of decline. First, total circulation of newspapers has simply dropped: in the early 1990s, it was about 65 million, which came to about 68 percent of American households, but by 2018, that figure had fallen to 29 million—even though the population had increased during the same period. Second, at the heart of that decline was advertisement revenue, which went from about $50 billion in 2000 to roughly $20 billion today—a 71 percent decline. Something had to give, of course, and that was the third factor: the number of employees at newspapers. In 2004, there was an average of 8.1 newsroom staffers for every newspaper operating in the United States. Today, that figure is 5.5.[11] Hayes and Lawless note a comment by a reporter at the *Billings Gazette*, who could not say how many reporters had been fired from the paper of the year because he "quit counting after 30 rounds of cuts." "With advertising moving online and to other sources, local newspapers were shrinking to a degree that shocked almost anyone who had worked in the newspaper business."[12]

The upshot is that of the remaining local news outlets, there has been a change in the types of news stories covered. The biggest casualty has been local politics. After conducting an analysis of the largest newspaper in each of the 435 congressional districts, Hayes and Lawless write of a "catastrophic loss of local news reporting." Local news withered in urban, suburban, and rural outlets. They reference, for example, the *New Hampshire Union Leader*, which a few decades ago used to publish on average seven local news stories a day; it's now down to about four.

The evidence is overwhelming: local news outlets (particularly newspapers) and local news information have been in decline for two decades. The powerful economic forces of shrinking advertising revenue, the rise of social media, and instant access to countless online sites have shaken the already precarious local news business model. On top of all that, the changing demographic of local news readers and viewers paints a foreboding picture: they are much older. As noted by one observer, "There is no hope for the old model of local news to bounce back, and anyone who tells you otherwise is arranging deck chairs on the *Titanic*."[13]

As one might guess, the hardest hit have been outlets in rural communities. Forces just described have put additional pressure on outlets in communities of all sizes; major news outlets have downsized as well. But in rural areas, there has been a double whammy: the shrinking population leading to declining advertising revenue. Surviving news outlets in urban and suburban areas have been forced to close their rural bureaus to save money. According Abernathy, "More than 500 newspapers have been closed or merged in rural communities since 2004. Most of these counties where newspapers closed have poverty rates significantly above the national average. Because of the isolated nature of these communities, there is little to fill the void when the paper closes."[14] Coupled with the declining readership of more regional newspapers, Kathy Cramer, in her study of rural Wisconsin, found much the same: "Many of the papers are published by the same company, Gannett, and use the same pool of reporters, not reporters located in a specific community."[15] In 2002, the Northwestern University/Medill Local News Initiative issued a stark report, with this summary: "This is a nation increasingly divided journalistically, between those who live and work in communities where there is an abundance of local news and those who don't. Invariably, the economically struggling, traditionally underserved communities that need local journalism the most are the very places where it is most difficult to sustain either print or digital news organizations."[16]

Local television has fared somewhat better in terms of profit margins, but they have done so mostly by shifting from local political news to entertainment—sports and weather in particular. Americans still watch their local weathercaster's reports. And as with many small newspapers, the independence and "local" nature of these stations has shifted, springing from ownership trends. One of the most prominent owners of local television stations is the Sinclair Broadcast Group, which boasts nearly two hundred stations. A controversy arose in 2018 when anchors at each of the Sinclair outlets were directed to read the same script on the potential "fake news" coming from other stations. The owners of Sinclair are conservative, and many observers saw the "must-run" segment as a not-so-subtle attempt to protect Donald Trump when his relationship with Vladimir Putin was drawing scrutiny.

Our data confirm this story. We asked a series of questions in the Rural Voter Study related to respondents' news consumption habits, including the preferred means of getting news. Some 21 percent of urban residents said it was from newspapers, a figure that dropped to just 10 percent for rural residents. Conversely, whereas 44 of urban residents said they preferred to get their news via television, that figure jumped to 52 percent for rural Americans. In short, both the aggregate data trends and our individual-level data analysis suggest that local news outlets and local news stories are fading from the political landscape, especially in rural areas.

THE NATIONALIZATION OF NEWS

In place of local news, an ever-greater share of media coverage focuses on national themes and personalities. The explanation is simple: it costs a lot less to run national wire service articles than to send a reporter to cover a city council meeting or state legislative hearing. And neither local television stations nor local news internet startups have yet to fill the void created by the loss of local newspapers. Consequently, Hayes and Lawless suggest, "When newspapers stop telling citizens what was happening in city hall or on their county commissions, there was no other place where citizens could find it."[17]

In 2022, former Obama communication consultant Dan Pfeiffer penned a book on the growing power of Fox News and internet sources in the increasingly nationalized battleground of electoral politics. In charting the shift from local reporting to national news stories, he tells a tale of Obama's remarkable run in Iowa in 2008. Local media, he argues, was critical to the win. After every campaign event in small towns and hamlets, Obama would sit down for a one-on-one with a reporter from a local paper. "The weeklies were the lifeblood of their community, and it was a big deal when Obama sat down with them, . . . a gesture of respect." But that would never work now, writes Pfeiffer. "The people in those towns have no access to local news. If they pay attention to politics, they probably get their political news from national outlets, more likely right-wing sites shared on Facebook."[18]

The decline of local outlets does not mean Americans are paying less attention to politics; quite the opposite. Filling the local vacuum is national news. According to Gallup, about 23 percent of Americans were paying close attention to the national news in 2000. By 2020, that figure had nearly doubled to 44 percent.[19] This trend has been especially acute for strong partisans and older Americans. Recent scholarship suggests that when citizens rely on national sources, they are more likely to highlight areas of conflict between the two parties.[20] Conversely, local newspapers serve as a moderating force by sharing agreed-upon information and setting a common agenda. Local news media also cover stories that feature members of the community who are known and respected. Those figures may be wrong-headed on a particular policy dispute, or be one of "those Democrats," but they certainly are not the evil villain.

At first glance, it would seem that rural America would be particularly susceptible to these nationalizing tendencies, given the significant decline in local media coverage. With fewer local outlets and less coverage by regional media, the vacuum would be filled by national television programs, internet sites, and satellite radio stations. Pfeiffer's story makes perfect sense in that world.

But that's not what the data illustrated in figure 9.1 suggest. We asked all respondents, "How much time do you spend paying attention to national news?" and a similar question on "local news." As for urban respondents, some 43 percent reported they pay "a great deal" of attention to the national news, which is in line with the previously noted Gallup estimates. And yet, this figure drops to 34 percent for suburban respondents and to just 27 percent for our rural respondents. A similar pattern emerges for our query on local news: 41 percent of urban respondents pay a "great deal" of attention to local news, which drops to 29 percent of suburban respondents and a meager 25 percent for rural respondents. Conversely, rural residents were twice as likely to say they pay "very little" attention to the national news as urban residents (22 percent to 11 percent, respectively). As with the Gallup data, when we control for age and strength of partisanship, these figures climb a bit, but the overall pattern remains the same.

Faced with fewer and fewer local media outlets, it is simply not the case that rural residents (on the whole) have shifted their attention to national news stories and outlets, as many Americans have. Rather, with the decline in local news, rural Americans have become more susceptible to simply dropping out of political media altogether. They still vote come Election Day, but they do little to follow the news in between. One reason: when asked whether or not media covered stories that were relevant to their geographic community, rural residents were the least likely to agree. Nearly a majority of rural voters—45 percent—said the news is irrelevant to their local communities—a number twice as large as that of the average urban respondent!

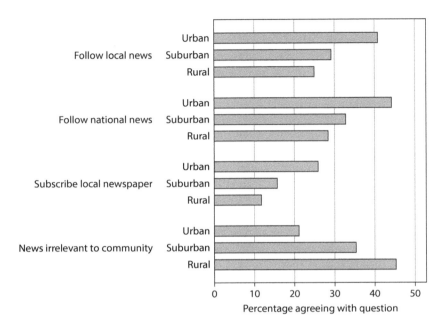

FIGURE 9.1 Engagement with news media in rural, suburban, and urban America

Note: Data from the 2022 wave of the Rural Voter Survey. Respondent location is self-described, and geographic averages incorporate poststratification weights described in chapter 4. The figure illustrates the percentage of respondents who said "a great deal" or "a modest amount" when asked, "People are busy and they can't always pay close attention to everything, but generally speaking, how much time do you spend" with the response selections "paying attention to national news?" and "paying attention to local news?" The figure plots the percentage of respondents who said "yes, online" or "yes, hardcopy" when asked, "Do you subscribe to a local newspaper?" And when asked, "How often do national news outlets cover stories that are important to communities like your own?" respondents who said "A bit less than they should" or "Way less than they should" were classified as saying news was "irrelevant."

WHAT ABOUT THE INTERNET?

While it is certainly true that rural communities are losing local outlets and local news at a staggering pace, hasn't the internet filled the gaps for those still trying to stay engaged? Sure, the daily rag may be gone, but rural residents can access the World Wide Web, right? Yes and no.

There are, generally speaking, two ways to consider internet access in different parts of the country: whether or not there is fast internet (broadband, for example), and whether or not residents have access to smartphone service. From there, you can also discuss how many residents have tablets, home computers, and so forth.

Rural access to the web has been an issue since the dawn of the internet age. In 2000, about 40 percent of U.S. households had access, a figure that dropped considerably in the countryside. In the early years, internet was delivered through the traditional landlines that were also used for telephones and cable television. Early providers included CompuServe, The Source, and America Online (AOL). By today's standards, these dial-up services were incredibly slow, but, of course, there was nothing to compare them to.[21] Waiting thirty seconds to download a news article, or five minutes for a short video, seemed normal.

Digital subscriber lines (DSL), also known as broadband, carried the internet signal through existing phone lines at a much faster speed. But, again, there were geographic barriers; the closer the subscriber was to a city center, the faster their internet service.[22] A 2014 report by the Federal Communications Commission stated the issue bluntly: "Americans living in urban areas are three times more likely to have access to Next Generation broadband than Americans in rural areas. An estimated 15 million Americans, primarily in rural communities, don't even have access to entry-level broadband in their homes. 41 percent of America's rural schools (not students) couldn't get a high-speed connection if they tried."[23]

The push for faster internet transmission in rural areas has been relentless—and the rollout of 5G, the newest technology standard for wireless networks, has reignited the debate over rural access. This has meant the installation of new fiber-optic lines called "cable residential broadband," which has exacerbated the geographic digital divide even more. As one analyst noted, "DSL, cable, and fiber optic lines all required expensive infrastructure buildout; services were typically limited to urban and suburban areas." Moreover, "it doesn't make much sense . . . to run a cable all the way outside towns to provide internet to just a few homes, which means that people in rural areas are being left behind in this technological revolution, with slow dial-up or—in some places—no Internet at all."[24]

Connectivity in rural areas has gotten better (in both breadth and speed) in recent years, but the digital divide remains. A 2021 Pew study found that while 79 percent of urban residents reported having broadband service, only 72 percent rural residents had it. When it comes to desktops, tablets. and other hardware, the figures are nearly identical: about 80 percent of urban and suburban residents report having a desktop computer, and the same is true for just 72 percent of rural residents. Another research team found that upward of 42 million Americans were without broadband internet access.[25] As you might imagine, there is significant variation by population density. Simply put, the access gap is a function of the rural-urban divide.

The contours of the internet access issue have remained more or less unchanged for two decades. In order to provide rural residents with fast internet access, the speed necessary for much of today's online commerce, culture, and education—not to mention home entertainment and video games—massive investment in the construction of rural broadband is needed. The Biden administration earmarked some $65 billion for the construction of high-speed internet access in the United States as part of the 2022 Bipartisan Infrastructure Law. A disproportionate share of those funds will be spent in rural communities.[26]

As for mobile service—the ability to get online through a smartphone or another device—matters have improved in rural areas, but here, too, there can be limitations in the countryside; dead spots are all too common. Rural residents have fewer provider choices, often pay higher fees, and get lower-quality service.

So what do our survey findings suggest about rural internet usage? For starters, it's important to bear in mind that all the respondents in our study had access to the internet—either through home computers, a tablet, or a smartphone. The figure is 100 percent because, as you will recall, the survey was conducted online. This is a built-in structural bias in our sample but, we think, not a significant one—particularly given that we are less interested in overall results than in subgroup variation.

For instance, there are some clear geographic differences when it comes to accessing news. We asked a general question on the respondent's "preferred way to get the news." The categories included newspaper, radio, television, social media, and websites. Overall, some 23 percent of respondents noted either social media or a website. For urban residents, where newspapers scored the highest (21 percent), either social media or websites was noted by 19 percent, and in suburban areas, the number was 27 percent. Some 26 percent of rural residents noted either social media (11 percent) or websites (15 percent).

We asked an open-ended question about respondents' primary source of news, and the results fit this pattern; urban respondents are a bit more likely to say newspaper, with a modest uptick in internet sources for suburban or rural respondents. There is some evidence that rural residents are more likely than nonrural residents to use the internet for news, but the difference is not overwhelming.

We also asked, "Outside of work, how much time do you usually spend online (computer or phone) each day?" Overall, 35 percent of urban respondents said they were "connected" at least six hours per day. This figure drops to 26 percent for suburban respondents and to 27 percent for rural Americans. As for the other response categories, there was no significant difference between the three groups of respondents. For example, nearly identical percentages of each said they were online between one and three hours per day (roughly 38 percent).

It is worth mentioning that a growing pool of social science research suggests that heavy internet usage, particularly time with social media, likely contributes to sharp partisan polarization and highly negative attitudes toward those on the other side (dubbed "affective partisanship"). For example, a 2021 meta study conducted by a team of researchers at New York University found that frequent time online greatly intensifies ill feelings about the opposition. Numerous studies suggest that Facebook, Twitter, and YouTube are especially powerful in this regard. Not surprisingly, belief in conspiracy theories tends to increase with heavy social media use.[27]

Not long after the Biden administration set aside $45 billion of the infrastructure law to improve broadband access in rural areas, Michael

Rea, a resident of Winchester, Virginia (pop. 28,332), ripped off an angry letter to the editor of the *Winchester Star*. He had a beef with the appropriation, but not exactly the way you may think: "[It's] designed to ensure that every resident of the USA will have access to the Internet. The primary impact of this initiative will be in rural areas. This initiative will be a boon to right wing conspiracy nutjobs who will no longer be restricted to right wing news outlets to spread their lies. Soon those rural residents who crave the latest nonsense about how the Left is trying to destroy the American way of life will be able to log onto the Internet 24/7 to get the latest fevered rankings."[28]

Rea is certainly not alone in thinking the internet may lay at the heart of the rural voter transformation. He and others do not think it is merely a coincidence that the rise of the rabid conservative rustic happened at the same time the internet took off. But the survey evidence clearly suggests that most rural residents do not spend a disproportionate amount of time on the web, nor do they get most of their news from online sources or posting wildly on social media. As with so many topics in this book, our survey results push back on the traditional picture that we have about rural residents. Why is that?

THE NEWS MEDIA'S PORTRAYAL OF RURAL AMERICANS

As it turns out, the story of media and rural politics is one of rampant misconceptions. Just as the news media are quick to pounce on stories of election commissioners gone berserk, average citizens are worried about what investments in broadband would mean for all the "conspiracy nutjobs" living out in the countryside. There is a reason, though, for why most jump to the conclusion that wild internet conspiracy theories and rampant social media use explain the changes we are seeing in rural America. It is the same reason the national news paints a picture of rural America that is so wildly different from the one we offer in this book, be it about economics, community collapse, race, or culture.

Consider a National Public Radio (NPR) story aired the day before the 2022 midterm elections. The correspondent, H. J. Mai, traveled to Sheboygan, a small town in eastern Wisconsin, to chat with rural voters about the upcoming election. After some frustration in finding anyone willing to talk (the Green Bay Packers were playing, after all), Mai found a home littered with yard signs for various GOP candidates, including Senator Ron Johnson and the gubernatorial candidate, Tim Michels. He knocked on the door, was invited in, and talked for a while with the husband and wife. A few days later, we all heard the story while driving from work or picking up the kids from soccer practice.[29] Mai is an experienced, thoughtful reporter. He really wanted to talk to rural voters and tell their story. He was not malevolent or out to get anyone. He just did what all journalists do. And that's the problem.

Media means just that—mediation, a *mediated*, or in-between. Most of our readers—statistically speaking—do not live in rural areas. Even if they did, they do not live in *all* rural areas at the same time. Just like anything newsworthy, we require mediation to make sense of broad themes, national patterns, and invisible abstracts, including the rural voter. Those mediations depend on who is willing to talk to you. And maybe those people are just different when it comes to mainstream media.

Even when they venture into flyover country to get that juicy interview or shot, journalists will almost invariably paint an unrepresentative picture of what is going on. Our problem is not that they do not spend much time in rural settings, or that they do not fact-check or try their darnedest to get it right. It is simply that when reporters do show up, they talk only to people they can see and who want (badly) to talk back to strangers. That's exactly what happened in Sheboygan. And these folks—the ones anxious to talk to a reporter and who have a dozen campaign signs in their yard—are just different from the average rural voter. That interview, though, shapes our perceptions. Again, humans are cognitive misers; we take the cues and make generalizations. We all do it—day in and day out. The snag, of course, is that these stereotypes become entrenched.

And this type of reporting happens at NPR. Setting aside public broadcasting and non-profit reporting, we also need to acknowledge that most media are profit-driven. They need to sell papers and ad space, get more listeners, and push for clicks and higher ratings. Sensational stories do the trick. A recent book by the journalist Matt Taibbi, *Hate Inc.*, charts the growing incentives for the media to boost ratings by portraying the other side as different, even crazy. "The primary product the news media sells is division."[30] Even if one were reading the local paper as an indicator of what was going on nationwide, a quarter of all homes would be on fire, half of all drivers would be arrested for drunk driving, and every tree would have a cat in it. (Seriously, as we wrote this sentence, all these stories were in the morning's paper!)

Visual media are even worse. Newspaper or television stories of rural politics nearly always profile the outspoken, the guy with the really big Trump billboard or the gal who refuses to sit down during the town hall meeting. In the fall of 2020, CNN sent a reporter to rural Pennsylvania to touch base with voters in a "pivotal county" that Donald Trump needed to win. The opening shot of the story, plastered all over the start of the article, was of the "Trump House." Clad in work jeans and a ball cap, the owner of the house, Leslie Rossi, stands in front of his massive two-story dwelling, which is painted red, white, and blue and draped with American flags across the roof, windows, and doors. The lawn is littered with signs for Republican candidates, particularly for the top of the ticket. The Trump House, it seems, is a big attraction in southwest Pennsylvania. Rossi, who apparently spent "countless hours in 2016 pushing disaffected Democrats and never-before voters to choose Trump," is a key figure in the story. He's an interesting guy—and his willingness to dedicate his entire home to the cause is, well, exceptional. The average rural voter, right?

Consider an op-ed penned by one of the authors of this book (Jacobs), along with Kal Munis, published in the *Washington Post* a few days before the 2022 congressional midterm elections. The piece centers on the myriad misperceptions of rural voters. They write, "Anyone who has spent time studying rural communities knows that rural residents hold deep and pervasive grievances about how they're viewed." And yet, the editors chose to open the article with a picture of a neon-blue billboard from Worthington, Pennsylvania, that reads

"God Knows Trump Won."[31] Read chapter 7 of this book! Talk about a misperception . . .

We ultimately tell a different story about rural voters because we do not have to knock on doors. We use survey evidence, which capture a larger array of voices. Journalists and editors sometimes use polling data to cover stories; although, as we've noted, rarely do they do a cross-check by geography. One reason for that is suggested by Nikki Usher in her book, *News for the Rich, White, and Blue: How Place and Power Distort American Journalism*. She argues that news outlets confront a "market failure," where only nongeographically based outlets are able to survive. Citing several data sources, including several noted earlier, Usher found that more than eighteen hundred communities no longer have regular access to local news. The larger, digital-oriented outlets, often located in urban areas, pull back on their coverage of rural areas. The coverage that exists comes from reporters sent to cover the story rather than someone embedded in those communities. Compounding the issue, these drop-in reporters are often demographically distinct, much less likely to have a blue-collar background. The "delocalization" of news contributed, she suggests, to the media missing the rise of Trump in 2016, among other things.[32] From our vantage, the phenomenon that Usher documents leads reporters to find easy, flamboyant stories that are digestible anywhere in the United States. They get the juicy story (and the picture, of course!) and head back to the home office in the city.

Adding fuel to the fire, we all know that to cover stories, reporters need to incorporate quotes from local officials, experts, or residents. That makes sense; it is good reporting. But to do that in rural America would entail traveling to those communities to find "the local" in person, which can take a lot of time and resources. Not to worry: "person on the street" and "local expert" interviews can now be garnered from Twitter and other social media outlets. It's a lot easier—and cheaper—to scroll through websites than to drive out into the countryside. "Journalists use Twitter to track the shape and scope of public opinion on issues, but they may also use the website to find exemplars and VOD pop quotes," Yanna Krupnikov and John Barry Ryan write.[33] Here again, there is built-in bias toward the loud, the deeply engaged. A heck of a lot of average rural, urban, and suburban Americans do not post about politics on social media. In fact, according to a 2021 Pew study, upward of 70 percent of Americans never or rarely post about political or social issues—and, of course, the ones who do are much more likely to be partisan extremists.[34]

To better understand the distorted picture of rural Americans, we conducted two content analyses of national coverage of rural politics. First, we did searches on Media Cloud, an open-source platform that allows users to track the frequency of words and phrases used in outlets over a defined period. We took a comprehensive look at the top 50 newspapers in the country, according to a 2019 PEW media study, from January 2011 to September 2022. These are traditional papers of national record, such as the *New York Times* and the *Washington Post*, in addition to regional city papers. The *San Francisco Chronicle* had the most stories on "rural America" since 2011, clocking in at 282. As we discussed, many Americans no longer get their news from papers, even those published online, so we crossed this list with the top digital news outlets, adding 37 possible sources for news about rural America on websites, such as Buzzfeed, MarketWatch, Politico, and NPR. We searched for "'rural' AND 'America,'" or "'rural' AND 'United States.'"

Discerning trends over time and dramatic swings is key to understanding the data. In figure 9.2, we look at articles that include "rural" and "America" anywhere in the content. One finding is the growing number of articles since November 2016, which makes sense, given what we know about the scramble to explain Donald Trump's win. For example, about a week after the election, Politico ran a piece titled "The Revenge of the Rural Voter," and NPR ran a segment, "Rural Voters Helped Donald Trump Defeat Hillary Clinton." Notice, though, that they confirm a data point rural residents are already attuned to: rural America was largely neglected by major news outlets before Trump.

Aside from trying to explain Trump's win, there are two other big jumps. The first begins in 2019 and continues for about two years. The initial part of this surge were articles linked to the presidential election, but it was sustained (unlike the 2016 spike) due to the coverage surrounding the COVID-19 pandemic. There was a great deal of reporting

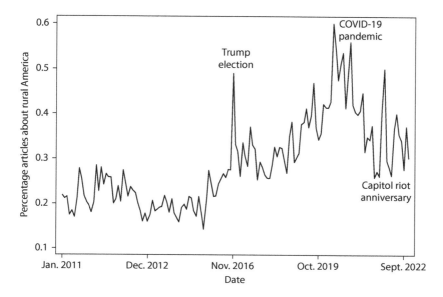

FIGURE 9.2 Percentage of news articles about "rural America" (2011–22)

> *Note*: Daily time-series count of all news stories and all stories containing the words "rural" and "America" sourced from Media Cloud, the fifty top U.S. newspapers of 2018, and the top thirty-seven digital native sources of 2018, based on research from the Pew Research Center (2019).

on why some Americans were pushing back against social-distancing measures, school closings, and vaccines—and we learned that a disproportionate number were rural Americans. For instance, a 2021 Kaiser Family Foundation survey found some differences in vaccine hesitancy rates based on geography.[35] This theme was highlighted in countless news outlets—which helps explain the spike in rural news coverage. For example, in 2021, the *New York Times* ran a piece titled, "Faith, Freedom, Fear: Rural America's Covid Vaccine Skeptics,"[36] the *Atlantic* ran a story with the headline, "The Rural Pandemic Isn't Ending,"[37] and *FiveThirtyEight.com* published "Why Being Anti-Science Is Now Part of Many Rural Residents' Identity."[38]

But does spike in "rural America" stories make sense in this case? The Kaiser survey found that 15 percent of urban and suburban residents said they would not get a COVID shot. For rural residents, it was 20 percent. Conversely, some 72 percent of suburban and urban residents said they would definitely or probably get a shot; for rural residents, it was 64 percent—an eight-point difference. So the geographic divide is real but, in our view, not dramatic. (These figures also mirror the findings in the Rural Voter Survey.)

What is dramatic is the news coverage. Again, excuse the anecdote, but it is revealing that when we asked students in our classes—a majority of whom come from suburban and urban centers across the United States, "raise your hand if you think a *majority* of rural residents refuse to get vaccinated." Every hand but one went up; that student was from rural Maine. Our guess is that most Americans would probably be surprised to hear just 20 percent of rural residents were unwilling to get a COVID shot and that this figure was only five percentage points higher than for nonrural residents.

The media, we argue, told a story about rural vaccine hesitancy that is incompatible with the survey-driven facts that two-thirds of rural folks—a large majority—were ready to roll up their sleeves, and at a rate just slightly lower than the rest of the country. That is not even touching on the media framing of the issue. Consider, for instance, that vaccine hesitancy among Black Americans was the same as for rural residents, according to the Kaiser study. This example is not an excuse for rural vaccine hesitancy or an apology for the troves of disinformation that circulated in rural communities (we heard it all with our own ears). Rather, it is an illustrative case of how the mediated portrayal of rural behaviors diverges from actual rural behaviors.

Similarly, the next jump in figure 9.2 happened in January 2022, immediately following the insurrection of the Capitol, followed by another spike a year later on the anniversary of the riot. It may have made sense for reporters, in their frantic efforts to disentangle the type of Americans who stormed the Capitol, to once again zero in on rural politics. And yet, the men and women who stormed the Capitol were not disproportionately rural.[39] We confirmed from a list of stories associated with the date stamp that the articles were, indeed, about January 6th. But given the empirical reality that rural Americans were no more likely to be at the Capitol riot than suburban or urban Americans, it does little to explain why there would be a spike on the one-year anniversary.

These trends are useful for making sense of broad swaths of time. Clearly, these patterns are a major part of the story of how rural America does or does not get covered. Searching by key words also has its disadvantages, so we did a deeper content analysis of stories meeting those search criteria in *The New York Times*. Yes, the paper is housed in urban New York; most people in America also reside in urban areas. That's key and we are not saying that a story about rural life needs to be on the front page every day. But in wanting to know more about how rural areas are covered from the outside, the *Times*, as the preeminent newspaper of record, has a newsroom with comparatively loaded resources to cover these issues. It matters how they cover rural America.

All in all, we identified 407 articles about "rural" "America" or "United States" published in one of the news sections of the *Times* between September 1, 2019, and November 1, 2022. We exclude op-eds and opinion pieces. Each of those news articles boasted a substantive sentence or more about "rural America," validating our search terms. Even then, only 63 of those articles made rural people or rural communities the focus of the article.

Even if it is just quickly mentioned, any mention of rural America matters. For example, in a massive cover story for the *Times*'s magazine edition, there are two paragraphs (out of twenty-six) dedicated to how COVID-19 relief spending is transforming rural economies. It may not be much, but even if most of the story is not focused on rural areas, it still is coverage, helping paint a picture in one's head about rural America's needs and wants. (One would walk away from that particular story thinking that all they talk about is broadband access . . .)[40] That is different from a story exclusively focused on trying to understand rural voters, but it still helps. What do these data points tell us? They confirm our earlier analysis: yes, rural places got more coverage after Trump; also, it's largely superficial, brief, and secondary to the larger story. In two years, just sixty-three articles were about "rural America" and the 46 million Americans living there.

Unsurprisingly, the three years we focused on were dominated by news coverage dealing with COVID-19. Lengthy or brief, 28 percent of stories that contained some analysis of rural America were about the pandemic. Even so, that was not the largest issue covered. As our longer time series hinted at, rural America was largely written about in the context of elections and partisan polarization. Fully one-third of all articles dealing with rural America were mostly about politics—and not political decisions related to COVID-19, which we decided to categorize as a pandemic story. Even so, we are sure we are undercounting the impression that readers were left with about rural politics and partisanship. Donald Trump made an appearance in half of all stories addressing rural America, whether or not it was about politics.

Don't get us wrong. As political scientists, we think politics is important. But we do not think politics—particularly presidential politics—is the only way to understand rural life. To be sure, there is coverage of rural economies and the people living there. Another magazine cover story does a deep dive into the "tragedy of America's rural schools."[41] The article recognizes that "Nationwide, more than 9.3 million children—nearly a fifth of the country's public-school students—attend a rural school. That's more than attend the nation's 85 largest school districts combined. And yet their plight has largely remained off the radars of policymakers." Reporter Nicholas Casey did his homework, traveling to New Mexico to tell the story of how lockdowns exacerbated economic hardships in a small rural hamlet largely unaffected by disease, explaining, in part, one reason residents were so hesitant to embrace public health orders.[42] Do not confuse our findings here: there is coverage, and some of it is very good.

Most of it is not, though, and most of it reinforces our findings about both news nationalization and a bias toward sensationalist coverage. Of just the news articles dealing mostly with rural people or rural communities, only two have what we might call an optimistic or positive perspective on what is happening in rural America. One is about a rural community in our home state and how Chinese investors were funding the redevelopment of an old paper mill, promising hundreds of new jobs. The other reminded us that, well, broadband—it's coming!

We know bad things happen in rural America; clearly, with their economic anxiety and grievance, rural Americans are attuned to social and economic decline in their communities. But recall, rural residents are also immensely proud of where they live and don't want to leave. They see a community spirit in their neighbors, and they feel it themselves. All we can point out from our analysis is a massive disjuncture between what is covered—really, what is not covered—and how rural Americans may want to be depicted if they had such a choice. Maybe it is not the place where roads will "Resemble Cuba in 20 Years," or the town in a "Death Spiral," where "Everything Is Going the Wrong Way" (to pick just a few headlines). This is not to deny that problems exist in rural America; rather, it is to raise the question about whether anyone reading the *New York Times* may feel like these places are worth saving.

Misrepresentation, then, is part of the story. In the drive to chart the contours of the rural voter, the media too often highlight extreme characters. Kicking off your piece from the "Trump House" may be novel and generate more clicks, but there are a lot of rural residents who are not game for splashing patriotic colors on the siding or stapling flags on their rooftops. That person does exist in rural America, however, so in some ways, reporters have a small part of rural politics right. But it is a small part—a small group of rural Americans, roughly 8 percent—who have come to define their political and social identity around being very informed and deeply engaged. They are hyperattentive to the news and are primed to push an aggressive, in-your-face brand of activism. We call them "Rural Rabble-Rousers."

ENTER THE RURAL RABBLE-ROUSER

In our surveys, we took a look at the levels of respondents' media engagement. Who pays a lot of attention to the news in cities, suburbs, and tiny villages? These are the "deeply engaged," to use a concept pioneered by Yanna Krupnikov and John Barry Ryan. For these Americans, politics is not just something they read about here and there; it is part of their day-to-day lives. These people do not just read books about politics (like books about rural voters); rather, these types of people make the consumption of political news and information part of their identity (if we sold T-shirts with our book, they would wear them).

To search for these deeply engaged voters, we combined two measures that appeared on the Rural Voter Survey: first, if the respondent reported following the news very closely—the top response category—and second, if they posted something about politics on social media in the last twenty-four hours. As we would expect, most Americans are not part of this group; overall, about 14 percent of respondents meet both criteria. And, unsurprisingly, given the larger patterns detailed earlier, rural Americans (8 percent) are much less likely to be deeply engaged than urban Americans (23 percent). Suburbanites are marginally more likely to be deeply engaged than rural voters (9 percent). We believe these geographic differences are a function not of news access but of interest and engagement—particularly when controlling for age differences by geography.

The overall gap between urban and rural engagement is less important for our purposes—although it is worth noting that one implication is that coverage of urban issues will draw on a larger and potentially more representative proportion of urban residents. Rather, our focus is on how deeply engaged rural residents differ from those not deeply engaged. Given that our overall sample is so large, narrowing our rural voter pool to just 8 percent for the deeply engaged group leaves us with more than five hundred respondents—certainly plenty to allow us to make some generalized assessments.

As table 9.1 reveals, the deeply engaged rural resident is quite distinct from other rural Americans. Demographically, this person is much more likely to be a younger male with a college degree. When we turn to attitudinal measures, differences really pop. For example, on several of the measures dealing with attitudes toward the respondent's community, the deeply engaged are more optimistic. Whereas 36 percent of the less engaged group said their community is a better place today than in previous years, that figure jumps to 61 percent for the deeply engaged. Why more optimistic? It could be motivated reasoning—they had their

TABLE 9.1 Unrepresentative characteristics of the deeply engaged rural voter

Rural voter characteristics	Not deeply engaged (92.43% of rural residents)	Deeply engaged (7.57% of rural residents)
Average age	49 years	38 years
Male	47.9%	66.4%
Self-described: very conservative	20.5%	27.0%
College degree	24.3%	31.1%
Below $50k per year	60.1%	65.2%
Anxiety and grievance (chapter 5)		
Personally much better off today	20.0%	47.4%
Community is a better place today	36.4%	61.2%
Kids better life than parents	41.0%	62.8%
Government considers rural perspective	19.5%	54.3%
Measures of engagement (chapter 6)		
Attends church once/week or more	28.8%	53.5%
Gets together with neighbors weekly	22.1%	46.7%
Wore a Trump hat	10.6%	28.4%
Flew a Trump flag	12.7%	23.3%
Attended Trump rally	5.3%	10.5%
Cultural conservatism (chapter 7)		
Fine when politicians hurl insults	12.7%	54.6%
Fine to ignore political correctness	20.1%	47.6%
Americans always love country	45.6%	59.3%
Gun ownership	54.0%	48.8%
Abortion always illegal	13.3%	45.2%
Rural always/mostly portrayed accurate	19.6%	59.3%
Racial/sexist attitudes (chapter 8)		
Racial problems rare	36.9%	63.8%
Latinos join gangs	41.1%	60.6%
Cannot switch genders	48.2%	58.1%
Women easily offended	49.1%	64.4%

Note: Data from the 2021 and 2022 waves of the Rural Voter Survey. "Engaged" voters are those who "posted anything about politics on social media" in the last twenty-four hours and said they followed the news "very closely." Averages among rural residents incorporate poststratification weights described in chapter 4.

guy in office.[43] Defensiveness of their communities? Fuck you—they might be telling us—we're fine out here!

Clearly, the deeply engaged are resentful that outsiders and the federal government do not consider the perspectives of rural residents. They are sure that cities have too much say in government and rural communities are getting a bad shake. We asked respondents if they thought it was okay for citizens to hurl insults at politicians, a measure of support for more civil political action. About 13 percent of the less engaged rural respondents said yes, a figure that skyrocketed to 55 percent for the deeply engaged. The latter are much more likely to express racist and misogynistic attitudes, and they do not care much for political correctness.

The extraordinary differences between deeply engaged and less engaged rural residents is consequential for how rural residents and the media interact. The contrast between your average rural resident and the one who is simply louder and more likely to be covered by the media is huge. On many items, the figures are different by a factor of two or three. In fact, we cannot find two other variables—like age, gender, income, attitudes toward race, or feelings about the federal government—that divide rural voters in a more dramatic fashion than these two measures of media attentiveness. It is rare to find one or two measures that so neatly and dramatically divide the population on such a range of topics.

In calling this group "Rural Rabble-Rousers," we imply a person, often a male, who is more likely to be noticed because of their significant interest and involvement in media. As Krupnikov and Ryan explain, the deeply engaged are not always animated by a particular issue or candidate; rather, they are animated by a "dispositional interest." The importance they place on following political affairs means that they have a sustained attentiveness to a host of topics, developments, and personalities—a "cognitive appreciation" for knowing. "In other words, [he/she] not only feels the emotion of interest but also holds a belief that something *should* be interesting."[44] Even the most mundane political events will draw the scrutiny of the Rural Rabble-Rouser. There is an "investment of self in politics."[45]

While we use a different measure than Krupnikov and Ryan, we argue that Rural Rabble-Rousers make politics a central part of their identity. Consider a few findings that reinforce this contention. They are three times more likely to say they wore a Trump hat, twice as likely to say they displayed a Trump flag, and twice as likely to have attended a Trump rally—even though they are no more likely to have voted for the former president. They eschew political correctness and are nearly three times more likely to endorse uncivil discourse (the hurling of insults at political opponents) than are other rural residents. Their views on compromise and political correctness suggest a Manichean sense of right and wrong. They are not afraid to be loud, aggressive, and uncompromising. Significantly, the deeply engaged—the ones paying close attention to the news and posting online—are also the most politically active. In every one of our engagement measures, this group was two or three times more likely to answer in the affirmative.

This is not the same as the traditional story of Fox News taking over rural areas. We asked all respondents an open-ended question about where they get most of their news. Rural Rabble-Rousers were about 10 percent more likely than other rural residents to say they got their news from Fox, but they were one-half as likely to say it comes from local news outlets. They really do not care about local politics. On the other hand, they were a whopping three times more likely to say they get news from multiple sources—meaning they are in front of televisions, or listening to talk radio, or online with social media a lot, gathering information from national sources and posting or sharing wherever possible. They "eat" whatever news they can find. Foundational for the Rural Rabble-Rousers is a detailed, extensive understanding of policies, events, and personalities garnered through close attention to numerous media sources. That is, they arrive fully "informed," ready to air their extensive knowledge to anyone who will listen, but especially to the other side. They are not shut-ins; Rural Rabble-Rousers report being twice as likely to gather with friends and neighbors as less engaged rural residents.

We believe the media's portrayal of the rural voter often springs from coverage of the Rural Rabble-Rouser. That's the person screaming at the school board meeting about critical race theory or holding the sign at the intersection against allowing trans athletes to participate. It's easy for reporters to get the "action picture" and the colorful interview. It's the Rural Rabble-Rouser who's screaming, red in the face, at the town hall meeting about COVID-19 policies, or ready to tell anyone who will listen that Dr. Fauci is a scoundrel and a pawn of the Chinese, and why they would never give up their freedom by taking a COVID vaccine shot. And when nonrural Americans head into the countryside, sometimes while simply driving down the interstate, they are overwhelmed by the overt displays of the "faithful": massive signs for Trump, ugly disparagements of "liberals," and crude messages for Joe Biden and Kamala Harris. It's hard to miss; recall, it opened our book!

Mount Vernon, Maine (pop. 1,700), is nestled around several small lakes in the central part of the state. Years ago, it was a hippie, back-to-nature community, but in recent years, many of the residents work in Augusta, the state capital. The hippie vibe has faded, mostly. In the summer of 2022, the town held its annual town meeting, where residents would vote on a range of policy questions. These gatherings are historically sleepy affairs, with a few dozen participants. Not so this time. On the agenda was a move to enhance broadband internet service and a measure to regulate solar farms. Homemade signs littered the roads leading to the school, and the gymnasium was packed. Almost immediately, and at nearly every turn, a handful of men held the floor, referencing newly discovered information about so-called climate change, the trickery of solar power, and the reasons that expanding broadband is a Democratic plot. In the end, the group did not carry the day, but these men set an unfamiliar—and, for many—uncomfortable tone.

Nationwide, over 55 percent of rural residents agree with the idea that "one way to reduce the cost of electricity is to use open land in rural areas for solar panels." We asked. Only 20 percent disagreed with the idea. But if you were to stand in that room—particularly if you were a journalist trying to weave together a story (assuming some newspaper could afford to send you to Mount Vernon, Maine), you would walk away with a very different impression of where average public opinion stands. That is why the Rural Rabble-Rouser matters.

The aim of this book is to better explain the rural voter, and since the Rural Rabble-Rouser is unlike the rural voter in so many ways, we lack the space to dive into what really motivates them. We have reason to believe, though, that their exaggerated involvement stems from these larger structural changes in the nationalization of media outlets and the decline of local news. One additional pattern emerges, which is the Rural Rabble-Rouser's propensity to believe in things that are simply not true.

Rural Rabble-Rousers possess an acute conspiratorial worldview. Conspiracy theories and disinformation are a profound threat to the stability of America's democratic institutions. It is a problem everywhere, and many assume it's especially pronounced in the small towns and villages of rural America. As figure 9.3 shows, however, a vast majority of rural residents—upward of 85 percent—do not cling to conspiracy theories like Democrats running child sex rings. They are no different than the less engaged who live in urban and suburban America; the rates are about the same as for Americans overall. Conversely, the Rural Rabble-Rouser is about twice as likely to hold these distorted views. There are rabble-rousers in urban America, too, but we are limited in analyzing their beliefs given sample size constraints; our concern remains with rural voters.

Over 60 percent of Rural Rabble-Rousers are likely to say the January 6th protests were peaceful. The same goes when asking whether Democratic Party officials run a child sex trafficking ring. One of our surveys asked a "replacement theory" question: "Do you agree/disagree that there is a secretive effort in the United States to increase the immigration of certain types of people in order to replace White Americans?" Some 30 percent of less engaged rural residents (the nine-out-of-ten group) agreed; only 14 percent were strongly in agreement. This figure tripled to 63 percent for the Rural Rabble-Rousers. Most rural residents do not think our political disagreements are so great that the United States should split into different countries (see chapter 7), but among the deeply engaged, such a fantastical idea has majority support! That is how an idea held by a minority of a minority can make headlines, and why politicians, such as Marjorie Taylor Greene, find it advantageous to exploit these issues.

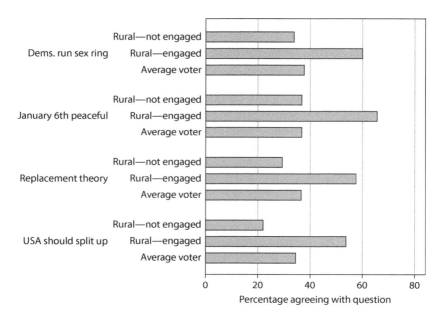

FIGURE 9.3 Political conspiracism and deep engagement in rural America

Note: Data from the 2021 and 2022 waves of the Rural Voter Survey. Respondent location is self-described, and geographic averages incorporate poststratification weights described in chapter 4. "Engaged" voters are those who "posted anything about politics on social media" in the last twenty-four hours and said they followed the news "very closely." The "average voter" is the typical American, weighted according to the national distribution of rural, suburban, and urban individuals. The figure illustrates the percentage of respondents "strongly agreeing" or "somewhat agreeing" with these statements: "It is likely that top Democrats run a child-sex ring"; "The events at the U.S. Capitol on January 6th were mostly peaceful"; "There is a secretive effort in the United States to increase the immigration of certain types of people in order to replace White Americans"; and "Given the gap between Democrats and Republicans these days, splitting up the nation makes good sense."

This group is convinced that governance is rigged and that by immersing themselves in piles of information and listening to the most strident, explicit commentators, they can uncover the truth. The knowledge garnered through their hours with the media becomes a source of power and prestige. In a changing world, where the white, patriarchal order is in decline, good blue-collar jobs are hard to find, and the stature historically linked to manual labor is in retreat, being the most informed can juice self-worth. In other words, it can be empowering for those on the "out" to be "in the know." By doubling down on internet homework, the Rural Rabble-Rouser gets to the bottom of things. And yet, he cannot feel the pride of "knowing" unless others become aware of his expertise. Coupled with this deep knowledge is the urgency to spread the truth—at meetings and rallies and with yard signs, letters to the editor, social media posts, and any other medium available. The markings of the Rural Rabble-Rouser are ubiquitous in rural communities. If you live in a rural community, you know who they are.

Consider how different our story of the rural voter would be if we had to rely just on the attitudes, perceptions, and behaviors of the Rural Rabble-Rouser. Well, in simplest terms, it would be the story you probably already know—or once knew.

CREATING BETTER IMAGES IN OUR HEADS

The rapid expansion of radio, television, and internet news sources held the promise of a more enlightened public. Instant access to mountains of data, countless new sources, and novel perspectives would enliven public debate and drive out corruption, bigotry, and lies. An invisible hand would help weed out false information, leading to more refined understandings and heightened discourse. By allowing individuals to join with the like-minded, social media would give traditionally disenfranchised individuals a greater voice. Many attributed Barack Obama's win in 2008 to the rise of social networking sites, and since then, untold numbers of candidates have solicited and coordinated financial contributions and provided opportunities for volunteers via social media. Much of the energy behind the Tea Party movement stemmed from the widespread and sophisticated use of online coordination. When it first burst on the scene, social media was hailed as a "liberation technology."[46]

But there is more to the story, of course. In the American setting, "new media" has had a direct and sustained consequence on the withering local news outlets and decline of local news coverage. There is no question that we know more about politics, and an endless array of other topics, than at any point in history. We are, if nothing else, well informed. But the declining interest in and knowledge of local happenings has been stark. Most of governance in the United States happens at the state and local levels, but our interests have turned to Washington. The University of Pennsylvania scholar Daniel Hopkins, in his book, *The Increasingly United States*, put the matter this way: "A few decades ago, on local TV news or in newspapers arriving at readers' doorsteps, the media consumer was likely to see a lot of content that was targeted to her based on where she lived. Both advertisers and editors thought about their audiences geographically, and tailored their coverage accordingly. In recent years, though, our reliance on spatially bound media sources has eroded. Cable television and the Internet have introduced a host of new competitors that attract audiences based on a shared interest in politics rather than a shared geography."[47]

As it relates to our investigation of the rural voter, the ramifications are numerous. With the shrinking number of viable local news outlets, the remaining coverage of rural areas is usually done by reporters who often do not know the community or the sensibilities of the men and women who live there. Too often, the easy, click-attracting story is the outrageous—the crazy COVID-19 denier, the gun-toting fanatic, the religious zealot, the culture war warrior, the animated school board protester, and, of course, the rabid Trump supporter. Are these characters found in rural America? Absolutely. But they are also replete in suburban and urban communities. If a community of people continually shake their heads at how they are portrayed, if they feel they are constantly reduced to a caricature, it would make sense that resentment would build—and that a shared fate ethos would gain steam. And it would also make sense that outsiders would scorn all rustics.

Adding to the vicious cycle is the transformation of the news-consumption process, which enables Americans to search channels and sites to match their interests. At the dawn of the internet age, the MIT scholar Nicholas Negroponte prophesied the emergence of the "daily me."[48] Whereas in the not-so-distant past, citizens would open their local newspaper or turn on their televisions to get the daily news, with the internet comes the ability to narrow their choice of stories and perspectives to match their interests and comforts. Each day, we open the daily me. There is an unlimited filtering process whereby certain stories and topics rise to the top while others are pushed aside.

The "echo chamber" phenomenon has been well studied, and we need not recount that literature here. But there is an added dimension as it relates to the rural voter. Humans show a strong tendency to connect and bond with others like them (what sociologists call "homophily"). Birds of a feather flock together, as they say. With the opportunity to customize "news," and with the nationalization of sources, partisan Americans have become strident in short order. In rural America, the homogenization of news has intensified and calcified the sense of shared fate. There are few crosscutting, divergent messages. "The impulse to belong to a clan is deeply human . . . and new tribes continue to form, organized not around ancestry but along fuzzier lines of ideology or demography," writes novelist Laila Lalami. Foundational to tribal connections are idiosyncratic language and shared sources of information. "One faction might speak of 'illegal aliens,' 'traditional families' and 'the life of the unborn,' while the other talks of 'undocumented workers,' 'marriage equality' and 'my body, my choice.' "[49] That language—and the lens through which to interpret new developments—comes via the new media. The rural voter finds legitimacy in certain outlets and deftly rejects contradictory information as fake or liberal pap from the "lamestream media." That is, with the sprawling news deserts and easily customized news we find rural voters "in it together," their fate bound by information solidarity.

There is also evidence to suggest that like-minded groups not only reinforce conformity but also foster extremism. Which brings us to the Rural Rabble-Rouser—the politically active rural Americans who find legitimacy and value in a deep connection to news media and aggressive political action. When Robert Putnam gave us his groundbreaking volume on the decline of social capital in the United States, discussed in greater detail in chapter 6, he paid only modest attention to networks and associations on the internet and the rise of cable news. He acknowledged the growing use of self-help support groups and concluded that the growth of "telecommunications, particularly the Internet," is a clear exception to the trend toward civic disengagement. And yet, "these developments hardly outweigh the many other ways in which most Americans are less connected to our communities than we were three decades ago."[50] He may be forgiven for moving briskly over these topics, given that much of his research occurred before the rise of social media. Facebook was founded in 2004, and MySpace burst on the scene in 2005.

But in some ways, Putnam was prophetic; he warned about the power of the internet to create and foster ideological echo chambers and ferment extremism. He recognized the power of the "net" to transmit information among physically distant people; even in those early days, he found thousands of "far flung, functionally defined networks."

Most important for our concerns, Putnam touches on what he dubs "cyberbalkanization," the ability to restrict communications to people who share precisely our interests. He considered this one of the medium's greatest attractions—but also a threat to building diverse, functioning communities. "Place-based communities may be supplanted by interest-based communities," he argued. Virtual communities offer the allure of utopian collectives. He cites a line from the communications specialist Stephen Doheny-Farina: "In cyberspace we can remake the world out of an unsettled landscape."[51] For a group of deeply engaged rural voters, communities of shared knowledge and grievance become the barricade against the forces of change. But for the average rural voter, the old type of place-based communities is still central to how they make sense of politics. Whether journalists are equipped to recognize that from far away, though, is another story.

10

PULLING IT ALL TOGETHER

Finding the Rural Voter

L et's pull it all together and take a stab at creating a comprehensive picture of the average rural voter. Who is this person; what makes 'em tick? What are the attitudes and beliefs at the core of this unprecedented change? Is this actually just about whiteness or age or conservatism? Are rural voters really all that different from other Americans?

By now we suspect (hope!) that at the very least, you have some appreciation for the fact that the rural voter is complex. The lens through which rural residents interpret politics is filtered by their collective sense of place, shaped through countless shared experiences. Those experiences have given rise to a deep grievance that is oriented toward urban areas, elites, and government experts—in a word, Democrats. How their lives are portrayed in the media only adds fuel to the fire. At the same time, that grievance does not fundamentally alter the extent to which rural residents take immense pride in their community and their desire to stay there. And, to be sure, the shared fate that binds rural voters together is deeply tied to strong notions of hard work and a belief that equal opportunity exists in the United States, or at least their specific rural community. Racial animosity is higher in rural America than anywhere else, and so is the belief that you can get ahead if you just keep your nose to the grindstone.

But how should we interpret all these factors as a whole? How do they relate to one another? In what ways does something like antiurban grievance represent anti-Black attitudes? To what extent does pride in one's community reflect an underlying appreciation for its whiteness or religiosity? Are rural voters more patriotic than other conservative Americans in nonrural areas? Are rural voters just Republican?

Ever since political scientists set their sights on quantifying political behaviors, there has been an understanding that of all the dynamics we may wish to measure, the most confounding are the hearts and minds of individuals. Humans are exceedingly complex. That is, our statistics cannot fully sort out the answers to these questions, but it can help. Similar to the logic we employed in chapter 5 when we were sorting through the relationship between individual economic mobility and more communal orientations, we can develop mathematical models that enable us to simultaneously weigh various factors in predicting an outcome

The key here is prediction. What factors help us better understand whether something is more or less likely and by how much? We surveyed thousands of rural and nonrural voters. Given all that information, we can determine which factors (opinions, attitudes, behaviors) best help us make predictions about the differences between rural Americans and nonrural Americans. For example, if we know that someone has a lot of racial resentment, we can calculate how much that piece of information would help us predict whether someone is a rural voter. If it does, we can say that knowing someone's racial resentment allows us to more accurately place them in a rural setting as opposed to a suburban or urban community. We would then argue that racial resentment is a distinctive aspect of ruralness. If it does not, we are not saying it does not matter in American politics, just that it matters in nongeographic ways; it matters everywhere—or, at least, somewhere other than the rural-urban divide.

To get even more granular, we can think about how our predictions might change when considering other factors, like concerns about economic decline or beliefs in conspiracies. That is where multivariate modeling helps. In short, this technique allows us to consider multiple variables at the same time, while controlling for others. For example, if we knew that someone weighed two hundred pounds, would this person be overweight? Well, that depends on their height. If the person is 6′2″, maybe not. But at just 5′ they would be overweight. You need both variables—controls—and that is what multivariate modeling does.

With our data we can measure the size of relationships for one set of variables (racial resentment and ruralness, for example) while accounting for lots of other relationships: for instance, higher levels of racial resentment among those who are economically prospering versus those who are economically suffering. Every new bit of data may help, but some factors will ultimately be much more important than others once we average everything together. Taking all these beliefs together, which are most helpful in finding that rural voter—and which do little to help us pick out rural voters from nonrural voters? When we set aside our predispositions, stereotypes, and hunches and simultaneously control for all these factors, what are the beliefs that unlock our understanding of the rural voter?

When social scientists model, we rely on averages. For any of the thousands of individuals in our models, the mix of attitudinal ingredients, as it were, is different. Someone may have a lot of civic pride, but they also may be really upset by their belief that Black Americans do not work hard enough. One may be a stalwart evangelical but not particularly patriotic. For any individual, we cannot say what drives their decision to vote for a particular candidate or which attitude is most important to them when they think about their own political identities. But when we take all those individuals together and see how all the attitudes mix, we can get a sense of what goes with what. As has been the case since the first page of this book, or focus is on figuring out what distinguishes the rural voter.

Think of it this way. Imagine we were trying to predict whether some random person lives in Maine. If you knew nothing about that person, you would have a 0.4 percent chance of getting it right (there are 331 million Americans, and very few live in Maine, only 1.3 million). You would have to be really lucky to get that right; the probability of placing them in Maine is low. Knowing that they have a collection of blaze orange Carhartt beanies might increase the probability by, say, 10 percent, and knowing that they think hot dogs should be bright red increases the chance that they are from Maine by 80 percent. (It's weird, we know, but it really would help you identify the Mainers in the crowd!). Both bits of information help, but knowing one of those things really helps.

Our discussion culminates in this large statistical analysis that we call, quite creatively, the "rural voter model." This model relies on groups of questions that measure key concepts introduced throughout this book. We take the questions we have introduced you to in earlier chapters and combine them into new conceptual packages, or indices. For example, we use five questions to create a "patriotism" measure. Nothing new is being introduced here. We defined patriotism in chapter 7 as someone's feelings toward the U.S. military in general, whether they believed in some form of American exceptionalism, their attitudes toward the national anthem, their opinion on splitting up the country, and their personal or family connection to military service. We explored each of those questions individually and explained how it measured a different aspect of "patriotism." Here, we combine those to get an average score of each individual's patriotism, knowing that patriotism is multifaceted and a combination of many considerations.

Our understanding and measures of personal well-being, place-based anxiety, and place-based grievance are discussed in chapter 5. The relationship between civic pride and social capital and how we identify these beliefs inform much of chapter 6. Key hypotheses and questions related to rural culture—including heightened patriotism, religious evangelicalism, and cultural misrepresentation or precarity—are discussed in chapter 7. We discuss measurement approaches for racial resentment and anticosmopolitanism in chapter 8. And finally, our measures for political extremism and the presence of conspiratorial beliefs is at the tail end of our discussion of the media in chapter 9.

The specific questions we use are at the end of this chapter, and each has the same amount of weight in creating an average measure; each of the five factors for patriotism, for example, counts the same in determining someone's overall patriotism. We then normalize each of those larger measures so the lowest value someone can have on our new patriotism scale is 0 and the highest value is 1. On their own, each new package of questions represents a new variable capturing a whole bunch of beliefs that could be statistically related to someone's residence in a rural area. And because they are normalized, we measure the fullest possible level of change. That is, how does our prediction change from knowing that someone has absolutely no patriotic beliefs to knowing that someone else has the most patriotism possible from our questions?

We can also compare, to some extent, how different attitudes matter. That is, knowing that someone is an evangelical may increase the likelihood that they live in a rural area, just as knowing that someone feels culturally precarious helps us predict that that person also lives in a rural area. But when all those items are included in the same model, we can tease out the ones that matter most—and which ones do not matter for helping us identify rural voters.

Surprise. The results tell you what we hope to have already convinced you—there is a distinct rural identity in rural America; the rural voter is not reducible to just whiteness, or racial animosity, or age; the most definitive parts of that identity relate to rural voter's shared sense of place. Figure 10.1 plots the marginal change in the probability of being rural, where points to the right of the vertical line are positive changes (increases in probability) and points to the left of that line are negative changes (decreases the probability). Going back to our "predict the Mainer model" illustration, a blaze orange hat variable would be on the right side of the figure, but not very far to the right. The red hotdog variable would be way out on the right because it matters much more.

Surrounding those points, the line, are the so-called confidence intervals. They measure the amount of variation in people's responses as well as the number of people, or data points, in the model. In brief, the smaller the line that runs through the point, the less variance. We feel a bit more confident in the exact placement of the dot when the line is short. If that line crosses over the vertical, or zero, line, we are not really confident that the measure has any statistical relationship with being rural. It could increase or decrease the probability of our guess

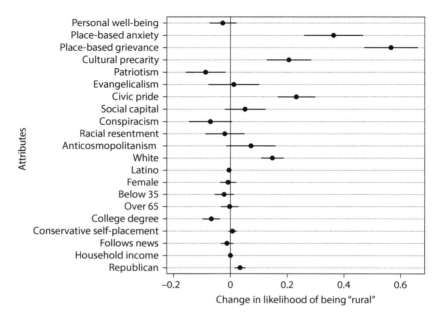

FIGURE 10.1 The rural voter model

Note: Figure plots the marginal change in the probability of being rural for a one-unit change in the attributes listed along the axis, as derived from a binary-probit regression model. Confidence intervals calculated at the 95 percent level surround the point estimate.

that someone is rural; it's not a statistically significant factor for our purposes of identifying rural voters.

To be sure, although we present the results of this model last, we constructed the rural voter model before we even wrote anything in this book. We had to know what mattered and what didn't. Statistical estimates do not tell a great story, and the patterns we explored in earlier chapters contain much more nuance than a dot with a line running through it. But rest assured, this model is not so much a "new" finding, because it is our first, and really, main finding. It supports everything we have written so far, and is especially helpful in supporting claims made throughout each chapter that ruralness matters. The rural-urban divide, in other words, stems from a group-based, shared understanding of what it means to be a "rural voter" in modern America. The divide does not exist because there are more whites in rural America or because there is more racial animosity out in the countryside. Rural identity – that's what we see here.

Recall that our understanding of rural identity is largely informed by notions of linked fate, group consciousness, and a sense that the community's well-being is important to a person's own personal success. Our model gets this. Individuals who said they are better off than they were five years ago are no more or less likely to be found in rural America than in urban and suburban America. Sure, average income and GDP are higher in urban areas, but these places are diverse. Some people are doing well and some are not doing well. Economic well-being or improvement is not confined to urban or suburban areas in any meaningful way. That matters. Take someone off the street and ask them how they are doing. Statistically, if they say they are doing worse today than they were five years ago, you just cannot say that they are more likely to be rural, all things considered. You don't know where they live because people are doing worse (and better) throughout America, in relatively equal proportions.

What really distinguishes rural voters—what would really help us ferret them out in a group—is asking how they think their community is doing. If they told you that things in their town were going south, that children needed to move away, or that their community was getting less than it deserved, our ability to correctly place them as rural increases by a whopping 25 to 50 percent. That's huge.

There is another way of thinking about it, just like we wrote in chapter 5. Yes, there are urbanites who feel like other areas of the country get more than they should, or that children growing up in cities may have to leave. But it is not something that defines one's urbanness. Those people do not represent enough of urban America to allow us to predict whether someone lives there (or anywhere), partially because those questions do not all hang together. That is, an urbanite might say that children growing up in their city might need to leave, but not that their city gets less than it should. But in rural communities, enough voters believe each of those things to be true, which allows us to better predict whether someone lives in a rural community.

The same goes for one's sense of cultural precarity—the belief that the media misrepresent them or that their ways of life are looked down on. As we discussed, this is uniquely a rural attitude, unlike, say, evangelicalism or patriotism. Yes, many rural individuals belong to evangelical religions, and many are patriotic. But knowing that one is evangelical does not help us understand whether or not they live in a rural area because, statistically, those beliefs are just as present in urban and suburban areas. And when considered alongside all the other variables in our model, including demographics, such as race, income, and education, knowing that someone is patriotic actually diminishes, ever so slightly, the chances that they live in a rural community.

When it comes to communal values aside from economic concerns, we have further confirmation that traditional understandings of social capital—how often someone goes to community events or gets together with friends—is not predictive of ruralness. As we described, social capital is on the decline everywhere. Residents may be alienated from one another, but that describes rural residents' views toward their communities as much as it does suburbanites' and city-dwellers' participation in their own places. What is unique, however, is the amount of civic pride rural residents have for their community. Knowing that someone is proud of where they live, that they don't want to leave, and that their community represents a distinctive way of life—well, that means they are much more likely to be a rural American than not. Remember, none of these questions ask about rural areas, specifically. We did not include measures that ask "do you live in rural America" or "are you a rural voter." That would be cheating. Rather, we ask about each respondent's own sense of place. Urban and suburban residents had equal opportunity to indicate to us that they had a common identity informed by shared economic anxieties, grievance, cultural precarity, and civic pride. They did not. Rural voters did.

It is worth pausing to restate an important point. On the one hand, we see that concerns about the respondent's community—the shared economic prospects of the area—matter a lot. The place-based grievance and anxiety measures are to the far right. At the same time, a desire to remain in the community and a sense of civic pride are also powerfully predictive. The rural voter, it seems, is deeply concerned about their community's future but remains proud of where they live. They don't want to leave. Those may not fit easily together in your mind as you look at rural America from afar, but remember, regardless of where people live, they are complex. We all have different attitudes and opinions that do not always fit so nicely together. That's what makes us interesting!

Jumping to the bottom of the graph, we also confirm that responses to the anticosmopolitanism questions—regarding the set of beliefs dealing with expertise, immigration, and the value of holding more encompassing worldviews—are not statistically associated with residing in a rural area. These are conceptually distinct from issues related to cultural precarity and economic grievance, and the model confirms that even after accounting for someone's beliefs about those ideas, knowing that their attitudes about cosmopolitanism broadly construed does not help us predict whether they live in a rural area. Negative attitudes toward immigrants, a skepticism about college attendance, and a lower desire to travel abroad—you can find these beliefs outside rural America to such an extent that they are not distinctively associated with a rural identity.

As with other variables, our multiquestion measure of political extremism or conspiracism fails to predict rural voting. We recognize that it is incredibly difficult to measure the many manifestations of political extremism, especially when it verges on or results in violence. As we discussed, we inquired about many news stories that are clearly conspiratorial and are believed to be on the fringes of the political mainstream (although Trump's "Big Lie" challenges the "fringe" aspect of most conspiracies). Some responses may have been expressive—meaning a way of signaling other beliefs.[1] And, again, a negative finding does not mean you cannot find conspiratorial views in rural America. The rural voter model, based on thousands of survey interviews with American voters, suggests that you are just as likely to find those beliefs outside rural America as within.

A related point: as you may recall in the previous chapter, we uncovered an especially vocal, active group of rural residents, whom we dubbed the Rural Rabble-Rousers. This group is significantly more likely to believe in conspiracy theories than average Americans and other rural residents. They are the loud, aggressive, animated group that often captures headlines. And yet, they make up less than 10 percent of the rural population, which probably helps explain why the conspiracism measure does not help us fine-tune our prediction of the rural voter. They are there, and they can influence rural politics. But they are not the rural voter.

Finally, our predictive model does not uncover a statistically significant relationship with racial resentment. Again, we are not suggesting that racial resentment is absent in rural areas or even that, on its own, racial resentment is not higher in rural America than elsewhere. Just as we saw with measuring levels of patriotism and evangelicalism, clearly, those beliefs are present and a larger share of the population may subscribe to them. The model suggests that those questions are just not good predictors of the rural voter. Put a bit differently, if you were to rely on measures of racial animus or civic pride to predict if a person lives in a rural community, you would be better off picking civic pride. Both are there, but civic pride would better enable you to pick a rural from a nonrural voter with a higher degree of accuracy.

To be absolutely clear, this finding does not diminish the importance of racial attitudes and their influence on politics in rural areas. As we will discuss in the concluding chapter, one implication of our work is that rural areas must confront how these values and beliefs hamstring our ability to build an inclusive and representative multiracial democracy. Other work that we have been involved in describes the interactive value between racial attitudes and other markers of rural identity.[2] The rural voter model is built to predict, after controlling for a host of other variables, whether someone lives and votes in a rural area. All we are saying is that knowing that someone harbors high levels of racial resentment does not tell us whether they live in a rural area because high levels of racial resentment exist across the United States, in suburbs and big cities as well. Racism is present in rural America, to be sure, but it is not a rural phenomenon.

Overcoming racial prejudice is one of the most important challenges confronting American society today; it will require hard work in rural communities. In chalking up racial divisions to the rural-urban divide, we make two mistakes. First, we neglect the fact that there are many parts of rural America where place-based anxieties, civic pride, and rural policies are not white-only. Second, we neglect the fact that racial stereotyping and prejudice are deeply embedded in urban and suburban communities—even if those places are more racially and ethnically diverse than most of rural America.

RURAL VOTERS AND THE DEMOCRATIC PARTY

We started this book with a visual depiction of our drive into the city of Waterville. Now, as we head toward the finish line, in the aftermath of the 2022 midterm elections, we can assure you that the imagery of Trump—the flags, the signs, the hats—are still there. In fact, as the 2024 election approaches, we are likely to see even more rallying around the Trump flag, so to speak.

Trump looms large over rural America. But, as we have been clear to say throughout, the rural voter is not the Trump voter. There is a difference. Millions of rural voters did not cast their ballots for Trump. How do Trump voters and Biden voters differ on the key aspects of rural identity described earlier? We use those same measures of ruralness but now develop two different models. One is the rural, Trump voter model and the other is the rural, Biden voter model.

With the rural voting population split (63 percent for Trump, 36 percent for Biden), we can now determine if the predictive factors for ruralness change depending on whether someone voted for Trump or for Biden. That is, even though both Biden voters and Trump voters live within rural America, maybe our ability to predict their ruralness is different depending on whether they voted for Trump or Biden. Maybe there are two different rural voters?

Sounds tempting, given the images we see even in rural America, but by and large, Biden voters and Trump voters living in rural America hold a shared affinity on many of the domains we have explored throughout the book: economic anxiety, civic pride, and a sense of cultural precarity.

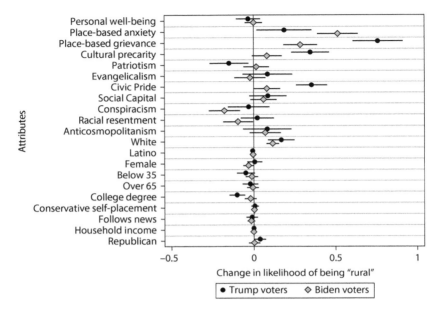

FIGURE 10.2 The rural voter model applied for Trump and Biden voters in 2020

Note: Figure plots the marginal change in the probability of being rural for a one-unit change in the attributes listed along the *y* axis, as derived from a binary-probit regression model. Confidence intervals calculated at the 95 percent level surround the point estimate.

The mix is a bit different, however. The trick in looking at figure 10.2 is to compare the black circles with the gray diamonds for each of the measures (personal well-being, place-based anxiety, etc.). The first question to ask yourself still whether it is statistically significant. Does knowing whether someone is white help you place them in rural America if they are a Biden voter? Does knowing whether someone is white help you do the same if they are a Trump voter? Yes and yes. Whiteness, in other words, still helps you predict ruralness, but it does not help any more or less for Trump or Biden voters. Trump voters and Biden voters in rural America are still, on average, white.

Where are there differences? Three factors help us place voters in rural America if we know they voted for Trump; or, in other words, Trump voters living in rural America seem to have three aspects of rural identity in common: heightened grievance toward government and urban areas, higher levels of cultural precarity, and greater levels of civic pride. To be sure, Biden voters living in rural America also feel this way, and knowing that still helps us place them in rural communities—just not as much. One interpretation is that Trump was especially attractive to rural residents who had heightened levels of these beliefs in rural communities where those attitudes were already more pronounced than in urban or suburban areas.

With Biden voters, some factors that were insignificant in the general rural voter model are meaningful. So, among Biden voters nationwide, how does our prediction for whether or not they live in a rural community change? Three aspects stand out as distinctive. First, place-based anxiety is particularly pronounced in rural America, but rural Biden voters are especially likely to feel the sting of communal economic decline. Trump voters are, too, but the predictive value among Biden voters is higher. In lay terms, we could interpret this to suggest that Biden did especially well among rural voters who were feeling anxious about their community's economic prospects but did not necessarily translate that into a grievance toward government.

Two other factors are negatively associated with predicting rural-ness among Biden voters: for Biden voters, nationwide, as those attitudes become more pronounced, we are more likely to find those voters living outside rural America than within. Specifically, among Biden voters, higher levels of conspiracism and of racial resentment decrease the likelihood of living in rural America. Or, in other words, Biden voters living in rural America are among the least likely voters living anywhere in America to hold conspiratorial views or harbor racial stereotypes.

The Trump and Biden comparison is important; it speaks directly to the election and personality that galvanized all this interest in rural partisanship. But the rural voter has been decades in the making, and as important as Trump's candidacy was for galvanizing a rural voting bloc, just as important has been the long decline in Democratic Party support in rural communities (see chapter 3).

Now, many people dislike Democrats all over the country. Our argument at various points in this book has been that there is something particularly toxic with the Democratic Party brand in rural America—that hostility towards the party it is more than just the partisan divide taking place nationwide. What makes dislike of the Democratic Party so pronounced in rural areas? Something distinctively rural.

Let us demonstrate that point with one additional model, which draws on the logic of the rural voter model (we care about the same factors and their predictive value) and the comparison between Trump and Biden voters. Instead of predicting ruralness, though, now we will predict attitudes toward the Democratic Party. Recall that in chapter 6 we used a set of feeling thermometers to evaluate someone's warmness or coldness toward a number of groups and figures in American politics. Everyone, regardless of where they lived, evaluated the Democratic Party. Unsurprisingly, the average warmth toward Democrats was higher in urban than in rural areas. But why? Is it because there are more Democrats living in urban areas? That is certainly possible and would mean that knowing whether someone is a Democrat (or Republican) would help us predict their warmth or coldness toward the Democratic Party in general. But, importantly, it is unlikely that the prediction would change depending on whether someone was a rural Democrat or an urban Democrat. Partisanship, in other words, would matter in our prediction, but it would matter the same amount for people living everywhere in the United States. That is what we did with Trump and Biden voters (did the rural voter model look different for these two partisans?), and that is what we will do to figure out whether there is just something about the Democratic Party that irks rural voters in particular (figure 10.3).

Many factors leading to dislike of the Democratic Party are not geographic. These would be compositional reasons that average dislike in rural communities is higher than elsewhere—more of that one factor just exists there—but the relationship between that attitude or personal characteristic is the same in rural America as it is in nonrural America. Racial resentment is the perfect example. Higher levels of racial resentment are strongly associated with a dislike of the Democratic Party; the

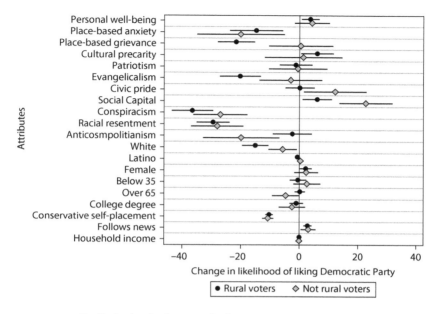

FIGURE 10.3 Predicting levels of support for the Democratic Party in rural and nonrural areas using the rural voter model

Note: Figure plots the marginal change in favoring the Democratic Party on a 0–100 feeling thermometer for a one-unit change in the attributes listed along the *y* axis, as derived from an OLS regression model. Confidence intervals calculated at the 95 percent level surround the point estimate.

point estimate is to the left of the vertical (zero) line, indicating a negative association with the Democratic Party's rating; as racial resentment increases, warmth towards the Democratic Party decreases. But racial resentment is just as negatively associated with Democratic Party warmth in rural America as it is in nonrural America. The Democratic Party, in other words, is disliked by racially resentful Americans, rural, urban, and suburban.

Where is there a difference? In a word, grievance. Again, there are Americans living in big cities and the suburbs who think about politics with an "us versus them" mentality, and they use their geographic communities for making sense of who belongs and who is on the outside. But only in rural America does that translate into a dislike of the Democratic Party. This is the image of real America versus everyone else—a rural America on the ropes, distrusting of government officials, resentful of urban residents' decision-making power, and aggrieved by a sense that they are not getting what they deserve, especially in the aftermath of economic disruptions that have affected their communities in very concentrated and particular ways.

Thinking about these three models together, we have a lot to unpack. But one thing is undeniably clear: the rural voter is not the Trump voter, and although the rural voter dislikes the Democratic Party, they dislike it for a specific reason. And although the rural voter is politically problematic only because of their increasing political homogeneity, the fact that "ruralness" is distinct from "Trumpiness" means there is a political alternative—an alternative made possible only if Democrats show up and compete in rural areas: our concluding thought.

APPENDIX: QUESTIONS USED IN THE RURAL VOTER MODEL

The Rural Voter Survey, which draws on responses and questions from multiple instruments and samples, began in the fall of 2020. The rural voter model relies on questions from just one of those samples from June 2021. We did not impute missing values, nor did we attempt to predict responses to some questions based on demographic data collected across each sample. As such, the rural voter model does not contain every question or concept we introduce in this book. Readers may notice, for instance, that we do not include gun ownership or attitudes toward hunting. (We have data on those attitudes and discuss them in chapter 9.) Those data come from a different sample, not the one that informs the primary construction of the rural voter model. Likewise, we did a much deeper analysis of cultural precarity in our second launch of the Rural Voter Survey. Some of those explicit questions are clearly related to our measure of cultural precarity, but they cannot inform our modeling approach.

The rural voter model relies on estimates from 5,572 individual respondents; 4,009 of those respondents live in a rural area.

Each item is first normalized before the construction of the index. In the subheading, we report the bivariate marginal change in the predicted probability of being "rural" with p values following the point estimate. Unless otherwise noted, answer choices are on a five-point Likert scale of agreement.

Individual mobility: $\frac{dy}{dx} = -0.165$, $p < 0.000$

(1)   I am better off financially now than I was 5 years ago.

Economic anxiety: $\frac{dy}{dx} = 0.699$, $p < 0.000$

(1)   [Respondent-Locale] is, overall, a better place to live than it was five years ago.
(2)   In general, young people have to move away from places like [Respondent-Locale] in order to get good jobs and make money.
(3)   No matter how hard you work, it is difficult to get by in [Respondent-Locale].
(4)   Young kids growing up in and around [Respondent-Locale] will have a better life than their parents.

Place-based grievance: $\frac{dy}{dx} = 0.795$, $p < 0.000$

These questions are for rural residents only:

(1)   In general, when the government does something, it considers what people living in rural areas know.
(2)   The government spends too much money bailing out big cities and not enough helping people who live in communities like mine.
(3)   People who live in cities have too much say in [Respondent-State] politics.
(4)   Over the past few years, rural areas in [Respondent-State] have gotten less than what they deserve.

These questions are for urban residents only:

(1) In general, when the government does something, it considers what people living in urban areas know.

(2) The government spends too much money bailing out rural areas and not enough helping people who live in communities like mine.

(3) People who live in rural areas have too much say in [Respondent-State] politics.

(4) Over the past few years, cities in [Respondent-State] have gotten less than what they deserve.

Suburban residents were randomly assigned to see questions in which the outgroup was defined as "rural" or "urban." Previous work validates this approach and confirms that it does not drive the difference between urban and rural areas.[3]

Cultural precarity: $\frac{dy}{dx} = 0.119$, $p < 0.000$

(1) Children growing up in and around [Respondent-Locale] will be able to live productive lives if they stay nearby.

(2) People in [big cities, rural areas] look down on my way of life.

Patriotism: $\frac{dy}{dx} = 0.130$, $p < 0.000$

(1) Recoded Thermometer Values toward "U.S. Military" on a 1–100 scale. The scale was broken into five categories, representing twenty-percentile increments. As such, a person who felt 0–20 degrees toward the military was a 1, a person who felt 21–40 degrees was a 2, and so on.

(2) An indicator taking on the value of 1 if the respondent serves or has served in the U.S. military or if someone in the respondent's immediate household serves or has served in the U.S. military.

(3) Do you agree or disagree with the following statement? America was chosen by God to be a special place.

(4) Americans should put their hand over their heart when they hear the national anthem.

(5) Given the gap between Democrats and Republicans these days, splitting up the nation makes good sense.

Evangelicalism: $\frac{dy}{dx} = 0.176$, $p < 0.000$

(1) Aside from weddings and funerals, how often do you attend religious services in your community? More than once a week; Once a week; Once or twice a month; A few times a year; Rarely; Never.

(2) Which of these statements comes closest to describing your feelings about the Bible? The Bible is the actual word of God and is to be taken literally, word for word; The Bible is the word of God, but not everything in it should be taken literally, word for word; The Bible is a book written by men and is not the word of God.

(3) You are born a male or female, and cannot switch.

Civic pride: $\frac{dy}{dx} = 0.183$, $p < 0.000$

(1) Which of the following best describes the area where you currently live? People are active in the community and often get together; People are not that active in the community, and everyone does their own thing.

(2) Setting aside the details like the day and time, if there was a community celebration in your area—like a picnic or a craft fair—would you attend? Yes, I would attend the event; Maybe; No, I would not attend the event.

(3) If given the chance, would you move away from your community? Yes, I would definitely move; Maybe; No, I would definitely stay.

Social capital: $\frac{dy}{dx} = -0.139$, $p < 0.000$

(1) Setting aside what happened during the pandemic, which of the following best describes the public schools in [Respondent-Locale]?

The public schools in the area are flourishing; The public schools in the area are doing okay, but not great; The public schools in the area are struggling; The public schools in [Respondent-Locale] have closed.

(2) How often, if ever, do you attend events (football games, plays, concerts, discussions) at schools in your area? Quite often; Sometimes; Hardly ever; Never.

(3) How often do you get together with neighbors and others who live in your local community? Once a week or more; Once or twice a month; A few times a year; Practically never.

(4) How often, if at all, do you participate in nonreligious groups, such as sports teams, book clubs, PTA, or neighborhood associations? Once a week or more; Once or twice a month; A few times a year; Practically never.

Conspiracism: $\frac{dy}{dx} = 0.007$, $p < 0.703$

(1) The events at the U.S. Capitol on January 6th were mostly peaceful.

(2) It is likely that top Democrats run a child sex ring.

(3) Donald Trump got more legal votes than Joe Biden in 2020.

(4) People who join private militias or other paramilitary groups are dangerous.

Racial resentment: $\frac{dy}{dx} = 0.211$, $p < 0.000$

(1) White people in the U.S. have certain advantages because of the color of their skin.

(2) Racial problems in the U.S. are rare, isolated situations.

(3) Generations of slavery and discrimination have created conditions that make it difficult for Blacks to work their way out of the lower class.

Anticosmopolitanism: $\frac{dy}{dx} = 0.298$, $p < 0.000$

(1) Immigrants to the United States make this country a better place to live.

(2) Latinos have a tendency to get involved in gangs and organized crime.

(3) It is important that people travel to other countries to gain new perspectives.

(4) We should encourage most young Americans to go to college.

(5) An indicator taking on the value of 1 if the proportion of someone's life that they have lived in their community is greater than 0.5. We asked respondents, "How many years have you lived in [Respondent-Locale]?" and divided this by their age.

11

BRIDGES ACROSS THE RURAL-URBAN DIVIDE

I t does not go unnoticed that as we cross between our seemingly two different worlds each day, we travel over bridges. Waterville, as its name suggests, is surrounded by water. Those bridges between the rural hamlets that we call home, and the urban hamlet where we work, represent what we are trying to achieve with this book. Why? We have saved that question for last because it is the one that took us the longest to figure out.

Charting the rural-urban divide has been pretty straightforward—or, as straightforward as thousands of survey interviews and millions of historical data points can be. Throughout, we have been motivated to paint as rich and accurate a picture of that divide as possible because we are troubled by it. We are not just curious academics looking for patterned variation but rural residents ourselves; we see the resentment, the grievance, the racism, the longing for community, the pride of place . . . and, yes, the Trump signs.

Of course, at one level, though, it is beyond the scope of our dogmatic social science approach to be troubled by Trump. Sure, we did not vote for him, but most of our neighbors did. We can explain that action by applying our model and thinking about how we, personally, relate to the key set of variables we have constructed. It makes sense. It fits a pattern.

But as we have stressed throughout the book, the rural-urban divide is not just a creature of Donald Trump or any one candidate. And the problems that the rural-urban divide pose go well beyond the partisan disagreements we may have or the policies we may support. As students of American politics, we appreciate the significance of the historic shift in partisan homogeneity in rural communities. We have watched it unfold, increasingly worried about yet another seemingly insurmountable visceral division in our politics. The history of the United States has been, for the most part, the healing of divisions, so witnessing a new divide has been unsettling. But why? People are allowed to disagree. Free societies encourage disagreement. Why is this divide so darn troubling?

Ultimately, we think the rural-urban divide strikes at the very core of our collective political identities as Americans regardless of where we may live. It challenges our ability to work together in the way that other divides do not. You may think one thing about how best to fund public schools and I may think another. What to do about immigration is a contentious matter, as are any number of hot-button issues. Tough choices have to be made. But there is agreement on the set of rules that will determine which policy we select and possibly force us to compromise with one another.

That is not the dynamic of the rural-urban division, though. We believe the Republican Party's dominance over rural areas is bad, but not because we think progressive solutions are necessarily going to work; between the two of us, we disagree over a lot of those issues. Rather, rural areas simply cannot flourish in the absence of competitive elections and viable alternatives. It leads to bad representation and recalcitrant extremism. And given rural America's disproportionate power in many of our governing institutions, the waning of two-party democracy in rural areas threatens how citizens living outside those areas understand and trust their government, too.

The divide between rural and urban, reinforced and strengthened by one-party dominance, is therefore a threat to our American democracy because it creates a sense that the people in the other place are not just different but dangerous. They are not simply wrongheaded about policy questions; they are really bad people. And that type of viewpoint increasingly means that people feel it is fine to challenge the foundational rules of the game that enable Americans to solve problems and bring people living in different areas together.

But we still think it is worthwhile to bring rural and urban people together. The truth is that rural Americans need urban America. In an economic sense, rural residents would forsake many of the basic public amenities they take for granted if urban economies did not subsidize their communities. Culturally and socially, urban America is a vibrant place—a bastion of diversity, new ideas, and opportunity. As Jane Jacobs famously wrote in *The Death and Life of Great American Cities*, "By its nature, the metropolis provides what otherwise could be given only by traveling; namely, the strange."[1] But the rural-urban divide is making urban places and city people seem too strange for rural folks, with big consequences. Rural America is becoming less trustworthy of "the other," which includes academics, experts, and medical doctors, all of whom are disproportionately concentrated in urban areas. Rural areas have some of the highest concentrations of poverty, unemployment, illness, and deaths of despair. There is expertise in rural communities, but tens of thousands of lives were needlessly lost because so many rural residents, steeped in distrust and scorn for outside experts, balked at social distancing and COVID-19 vaccines. Yes, the rural difference in vaccine rates is not as great as media suggest, but it was there. One study found that the more conservative the voting records of members of Congress and state legislators, the higher the age-adjusted COVID-19 mortality rates—even after controlling for racial, educational, and income characteristics along with vaccination rates. The effect was particularly sharp in states not just controlled by Republicans but lacking any meaningful Democratic opposition.[2]

At the same time, urban Americans also need rural America. Again, you can think of it in strictly economic terms. Yes, GDP is higher in cities, but, simply put, cities cannot function without the natural resources, energy, and food that people living in rural areas extract. More importantly, we would argue, urban America benefits, culturally and socially from vibrant rural communities. Rural America is a beautiful, diverse place that enriches the lives of people living in cities. We should not be surprised to hear that if given the opportunity, nearly half of all Americans—including a third of all Democrats—would move to a rural area, according to a recent Gallup poll.[3] We both love traveling to great cities but find fulfillment and calm in our rural homesteads, surrounded by nature. There, as Wendell Berry once posited, we carry out "The care of the Earth [which] is our most ancient and most worthy, and after all our most pleasing responsibility. To cherish what remains of it and to foster its renewal is our only hope."[4]

Both places are better together. We would much rather continue living in a country where both types of communities can thrive and where people and politicians living "over there" can come together to solve the very real problems confronting us all.

It is why we need bridges.

PUTTING RURAL AMERICA IN ITS PLACE

Fortunately for us, many of those bridges are already built. We just need to cross them.

It is only slightly ironic that we close this book by stressing how much rural Americans have in common with the rest of America; we only used that term, "divide" 166 times in the pages of this book! But as it turns out, page after page, we have found that there is more that unifies rural and urban America than divides it. Culturally, by and large, there is no monopoly on certain values in "real America." Proud Americans are found everywhere, as are the religious. If rural America is the home of irredeemable racists, it is because America is the home of irredeemable racists. Socially, Americans of all stripes pine for strong community connections and struggle to build what Putnam called "social capital." And, as Bill Bishop has written, "The creation of a rural energy economy is essential for urban growth. A fight by Great Plains ranchers for open cattle markets is essential for city consumers. People flow from rural counties to urban ones to work and live. There is simply no way to decouple rural from urban."[5]

The real divide comes down to divergent perspectives: how rural America views urban America, and vice versa. That is the source of the rural-urban divide— different perceptions about the other. Rural America sees itself as the economic victim of urban America's unjustly accrued wealth and status; rural America feels that its way of living is devalued by urbanites; rural America thinks its perspectives are discounted by policy makers and government experts who systematically favor the types of growth and policies that benefit urban areas at the expense of rural ones.

We do not deny that there are real, substantive issues underlying these subjective identities and impressions. Countless stories and moments presented in this book support rural America's collective grievance. Do urbanites look down on rural ways of living, profiting off nasty stereotypes? Yes. Have government officials pursued policies that have irreparably damaged the land and encouraged inequality in rural economies? Yes. Do most people living in cities sympathize with these facts and consider how that may fuel resentment? Perhaps, but many in positions of power do not. We hope that as a result of reading this book, more people will come to recognize that few areas have undergone such dramatic and convulsive change in the past sixty years as rural communities, and few places in this country are as economically fragile and misunderstood as those we surveyed.

But as we have documented throughout this book, one of the main reasons these perceptions exist is that politicians are quick to create and exploit misleading images of a divided America to pull voters into their camp. Republican elites did it in creating the myth of real America, and the idea of a collective rural identity is further solidified when Democratic politicians exploit the divide, too, and seem to celebrate that they are the party of urbane-America, the places moving ahead. We really like Hillary Clinton's quote, can't you tell? But she is not alone; consider, also, a few lines penned by the *New York Times* columnist Michelle Goldberg a year after Trump's election: "America is now two countries, eyeing each other across a chasm of distrust and contempt. One is urban, diverse and outward-looking. This is the America that's growing. The other is white, provincial and culturally revanchist. This is the America that's in charge."[6] Progressives exploit the divide, too.

Lest we be accused of drawing a false equivalency, as we detailed in chapter 3, the largest antagonizers of the rural-urban divide have been Republicans. The construction of a real America mythology has served them particularly well come Election Day, even as they have advanced policies and positions outside the mainstream of rural thinking, and have often abandoned rural interests once they arrive in D.C or their state capital. These false and misleading constructions go beyond academic concerns about measurement validity. These are myths made about people, their neighbors, the places they call home. And with these myths, divisive politicians have been able to mask real problems and stoke resentment toward the others living "over there."

At the same time, there are countless stories we tell that should give rural America pause—that compared with poor, unemployed, chronically struggling areas in urban America, life in the countryside ain't all that bad, no matter what Hillary Clinton says. Grievance and resentment cloud rural voters' judgment, making it easy to overlook their interconnectedness with urban areas. Their perceptions may have some merit, but sometimes these perceptions seem to lack grounding in reality—especially among the Rural Rabble-Rousers. What we need to do is rethink how these perceptions and attitudes make their way into our politics and why they largely circulate throughout political discourse unchallenged—why there is no one competing for the hearts and minds of rural voters because we have become convinced that their minds are made up.

THE VALUE OF COMPETITION

The myth of real America and rural America's collective sense of shared destiny reverberates throughout our political system because partisan competition in most rural areas is basically non-existent. Although the single greatest misapprehension by the constitutional framers centered on the role of political parties, our system, and maybe even all democracies, works only because of party competition.[7]

The original criticism of party competition is overwhelming. "The friend of popular governments never finds himself so much alarmed for their character and fate, as when he contemplates their propensity for this dangerous vice," warned James Madison in Federalist No. 10. The problem with parties, he reasoned, was that they would rally self-interest and greed rather than promote the long-term public interest. In a letter to Jonathan Jackson in October 1780, John Adams bemoaned the drift of the country's elites toward party politics in the 1790s: "There is nothing I dread So much, as a Division of the Republick into two great Parties, each arranged under its Leader, and concerting Measures in opposition to each other."[8] And, of course, we all know that George Washington devoted much of his farewell address to the "spirit of parties."

Despite these warnings, the two-party system burst on the scene and, in due time, was hailed as a fundamental element of popular governance. Precisely because our Constitution is so undemocratic, parties filled the void between representatives and the people. According to a famous political scientist in the 1940s, parties "created" American democracy, and that modern democracy is "unthinkable save in terms of political parties."[9] The key mechanism rendered by parties is competition, or what political scientists call "legitimate opposition." In any true democracy, the theory goes, out-of-power groups, vying for public support, check the ruling elite. Competition is foundational.

Two-party competition has been the norm at the national level for more than two hundred years. Many communities and some states were dominated by a single party for various periods, but on a broad scale, the two-party model persisted. There was one great exception, however: the Solid South, stretching from Reconstruction to the 1980s. In sixteen states, eleven of which were members of the former Confederacy, it was a foregone conclusion that nearly all elected posts, from county sheriff to governor and U.S. Senate, would be held by a Democrat. Many of the voters and politicians were conservative, and there was often competition for party nominations, but the winner in the general election was nearly always a Democrat. Until 1976, for example, Alabama had 105 state house seats, 103 of which were held by a Democrat. Louisiana also had 105 state house seats, and 101 were held by Democrats. From the Civil War until 1994,

Democrats maintained a majority of U.S. House seats from the South year after year.

In a number of important ways, the Democratic monopoly in the South shaped national politics and governance for generations. Its legacy is still part of our politics, which gives us insights into how diminished electoral competition affects us all.

The scholar who best charted the dangers of one-party dominance was the Harvard political scientist V. O. Key Jr. in a seminal work, *Southern Politics in State and Nation*, first published in 1949.[10] Key's book, wrote historian Richard Hofstadter, "is significant not merely for what it tells about the South but also for the light it sheds on the mechanics of one-partyism."[11] Key argued that liberal democracies rest on the premise of competition. Issues of substance to voters, matters of deep concern, are raised and fairly debated in the public square. The outcome of that exchange—the policies that are produced—may not please all sides, but action of some sort is likely. The out-of-power group in a two-party system organizes the citizens who have been offended, harmed, or neglected by the policies of the in-power group. They mobilize to address their grievance—and themselves become the "ins."[12] Even if the "outs" are not able to win the election, the fear of losing pushes the controlling elites to moderate and respond. That is also one of the major contributions of minor parties in our system, even if, in the short period, they routinely lose. They raise otherwise neglected issues and demonstrate support around those causes—which pushes the dominant party candidates to respond.

In a one-party system, such as in the Solid South, there are no coherent outs. There is no real political opposition, and few meaningful debates occur about the issues that bear on the public. Big matters are never addressed, and "political leaders frequently have no clear association with ideas and policies, and in some cases even with each other."[13] In the absence of meaningful issues, elections are a battle of personalities; demagoguery reigns. Power springs from personality and style rather than taking the popular side of policy questions. While voters may struggle with an array of problems, elections offer no viable pathway for change. Not fully realizing the limits of the hegemonic party, voters' grievance and anger are directed at "others," and in the case of the South, that meant the federal government—and, more generally, outsiders.

The foremost goal of the Southern Democrat was the "the maintenance of an illiberal society—the withholding of the rights of citizenship from a sufficiently large number to assure minority elections in a putatively majority system," noted the political scientist John Aldrich.[14] But we also know that other issues confronting white residents were neglected, including the deep levels of poverty, inadequate schools, and shameful transportation infrastructure. When Huey Long rose to power in Louisiana in the early 1930s by breaking the mold and addressing the state's abject poverty, there were only three hundred miles of paved roads; all the rest were rutted, temperamental dirt roads that were often impassable during the rainy seasons.[15]

Key's findings about the South parallel the "spatial modeling" framework of party competition introduced by Anthony Downs in his oft-cited volume, *An Economic Theory of Democracy* (1957). Assuming that candidates are rational actors (they weigh the costs/benefits of different electoral strategies), and assuming voter preferences are normally distributed (meaning there are some at both extremes, but most are near the middle), in a viable two-party system, both candidates will move toward the center. That is, there is a high dose of policy moderation on both sides because each candidate will want to attract the most votes—and those can be found in the middle of the ideological spectrum. Conversely, candidates who appeal only to those at the extremes make a small group of voters happy, but they do not win elections. There is a natural, rational force that makes democracy stable.

But again, Downs's model assumes a viable two-party system. The model fails when there is no real competition from the outs, when only one party shows up to compete. Instead, the candidate simply appeases the greatest number of fellow partisans. The trick, also, is to always bear in mind that not all partisans are equally likely to vote in primary elections—the only area of real competition. In one-party states, candidates court the deeply engaged electorate—which is nearly always more ideologically extreme than the overall electorate, even in one-party systems. Given trends in partisan sorting (both rural and urban), combined with gerrymandering and the reliance on party primaries, the Downsian model helps explain how the American electorate could be moderate on the whole but, at the same time, send to Washington one of the most ideologically extreme legislatures in history.[16] Given the data we present throughout this book, we also show that the success of Republicans in rural areas is not simply because voter preferences in those communities are so lop-sided (most voters sit at the far-extremes of the distribution), but rather because no viable competition exists to pull candidates closer to the rural median.

Let us be clear: rural communities have become more ideologically homogenized, but so, too—maybe to an even greater extent—have metropolitan areas. The two changes go "hand and foot"; party competition in rural areas is stunted because party competition in metropolitan areas has also diminished. The pool of voters is, after all, zero-sum. As Jonathan Rodden notes, cities may actually suffer the most electorally given the exceptionally high concentration of Democratic voters in these areas.[17]

A second caveat. We are not suggesting recent trends in rural areas are on par with what America witnessed in the Solid South for more than a century. It is certainly true that many rural areas have become solidly Republican. But Democratic dominance in the South was protected by legal devices long since declared unconstitutional (like the all-white primary) and through mass violence unlike anything we see today. More importantly, Democratic voices *can* be heard, if perhaps faintly, in rural parts of the country; although recall our discussion in chapter 6 showing that political participation was lowest among rural Democrats than anywhere else.

That said, the data are clear: in most areas of the country, U.S. House and state legislative races show only a glimmer of competitiveness. In some places, it is so unfashionable to be a Democrat that you keep it to yourself. Local town councils, school boards, and county commissions are often completely controlled by Republicans. In many (but not all) states with larger rural populations, the legislature is utterly dominated by the GOP. For example, there are 105 seats in the South Dakota legislature. In 2020, Republicans held 94 of them. In Oklahoma, there are 149 seats, with 121 held by the GOP, and in Wyoming there are 90 spots, 79 of which are held by Republicans. But, of course, as we have said throughout the book, sparsely populated states are not necessarily rural. A hefty chunk of Wyoming residents are urban! But where do the Democrats control seats in these otherwise red states? Urban areas, of course.

In these areas, where there is little competition in the general election, the goal becomes appeasing primary voters. If Key and Downs are right, mainstream issues—matters of concern to the full electorate—take a back seat to personality, style, symbolic issues, and allegiance to causes well outside mainstream political discourse. And have they been proven right! As a result of these electoral dynamics, symbolic issues become more important than bread-and-butter concerns. Again, this could happen in Democratically sorted areas as well, but in rural communities, we routinely see candidates emphasize their fidelity to the "stolen election," or the ridding of schools of the teaching of critical race theory, when it's not even being taught, and when most rural voters do not even care. According to one account, Fox News mentioned "critical race theory" nearly two thousand times in less than four months.[18] How many times was suicide rate, childhood obesity, or fentanyl overdoses mentioned? The outcome has been tremendous time and effort in state legislatures aimed at banning CRT teaching. As noted in chapter 7, in February 2023, Marjorie Taylor Greene made headlines for suggesting it's time to consider "a national divorce" between red and blue states.[19] Surely rural residents are with her on this, right? According to our data, only a fraction of Americans would consider such a move—and of that small amount, urban residents were more likely to back it than rural residents. Also, Democrats were more likely to say "yes" than were Republicans!

To be clear, our concern is not with far-right positions, per se. Rather, we are suggesting that in areas dominated by one party, an excessive amount of effort is directed at shoring up the base of the dominant party. There is no incentive to broaden the base or speak to median issues. Fidelity and allegiance are valued over real policy change, and the more narrow the agenda, the better. And although it is easy to do and often done, those issues are not the same ones that, as we have shown over and over again, motivate the rural voter.

Let us again consider the Kansas constitutional amendment referendum in the months following the *Dobbs* decision—the first state, as we touched on in chapter 7, to weigh voter preferences after the ruling. Over the years, GOP officials, in conjunction with organized interest groups such as Kansans for Life, have worked hard to recruit uncompromising antiabortion candidates. With the aid of the state's closed primary system, where only registered partisans can participate, lawmakers with moderate abortion positions were sent packing. And it was easy pickings in rural districts. During GOP governor Sam Brownback's first term in office (which ended in 2014), nearly twenty antiabortion measures were passed by the state legislature.[20] Ever-restrictive moves have been recurrent since then. Yet, polls continued to show that a majority of Kansans opposed complete bans on abortion.[21] As one observer noted, "This imbalance between public opinion and anti-abortion policy made Kansas fertile ground for mobilizing an electorate that had largely been complicit in letting the state move to the far right."[22] And when the voters had their say, they rejected a constitutional amendment to ban abortion by a whopping 59 to 41 percent. Rural voters in Kansas opposed that amendment. And yet, at the same, we also note that as of 2023, of the 165 seats in the Kansas legislature, 114 were controlled by Republicans, including the most rural districts in the state. Sure, there are many issues voters consider at the ballot box. But clearly, there is a big representation gap between what rural voters want and who they can elect at the polls. Can any Democrat candidate pull back the Republicans opponent to the middle? Not if the image of the Democratic Party is continually wrapped up with economic elitism, urban development, and the denigration of rural life.

Kansas is not alone. In an effort to rally the base in one-party states, policy questions are transformed into notions of values and fundamental rights. Compromise becomes impossible because the rhetoric becomes simplistic and overheated. Opponents are not simply wrong-headed but oppressors. Mary Ann Glendon charted the rise of "rights talk" in the 1970s, when liberals framed nearly every social controversy into a clash of rights, which crippled compromise, mutual understanding, and the discovery of any common ground.[23] Both sides do this now (for example, it's a woman's right to reproductive autonomy versus the rights of the unborn). Tea Party activists were keen to pitch every Obama dispute as an abridgement of the Constitution—which explains why nearly all GOP federal office candidates in 2010 proclaimed their devotion to "uphold the Constitution."[24]

The best example in contemporary rural politics would be framing gun control in terms of fundamental rights. As our data suggest, rural voters definitely have distinct opinions about guns; gun ownership is part of rural culture. But majorities of rural voters also favor certain limits. Rights, in contrast, are absolute; there are no limits when it comes to a rights claim. As a result, can any rural candidate talk to voters about commonsense gun control when it is framed as an absolute Second Amendment "right?"

The myth of real America—a community on the ropes and under siege—has fed the rights rhetoric beast, and making it worse is the lack of party competition. Divisive issues are further exacerbated when politicians try to win favor with the base—and when there is no moderating force in the general election.

Evidence also suggests that ideological group homogeneity not only reinforces conformity but fosters a higher level of extremism. Social psychologists have written about the so-called risky shift phenomenon.[25] Simply stated, individual opinions become more intense, more rigid when they are reinforced by like-minded citizens. This process becomes even more intense when positions are symbolic, continually reinforced by the media, and rarely challenged. The vilification of the opposition can become intense when no one feels compelled to say, "Now wait a second, do we really mean to say . . ." If contrary views are never heard at the diner or the VFW hall, and if no one feels obligated to offer a different take at the school board meeting, existing positions become more extreme and calcified. Defections become rare, and defectors are shunned. We can all get trapped in the media-driven ideological echo chamber, but the grip can be eased in competitive two-party communities, where contrary opinions crop up every once in a while. That's not the case in many rural areas—just as it is not the case in many urban areas.

In sum, the homogenization of voting patterns in rural America is not problematic because it hurts the Democratic Party's chances at winning the next election. In writing this book, we could not care less who wins or loses. We care that both parties could be winners or losers. One-party dominance threatens core tenets of democratic governance. We are convinced that democracy is served through the battle of ideas and the struggle to mobilize. When one party, be it in urban settings or the American countryside, thoroughly dominates the political landscape and powerfully stifles dissent, there are consequences. There is less focus on substance and more on style. Effective, consensus-building legislators are replaced by the loudest voices, the ones with the most Twitter followers. And in an age when voters are pulled to national news stories, social media demagogues take a vaulted place. Hofstadter, in that review of Key's *Southern Politics*, put the matter forthrightly: "The essence of 'good' liberal politics is that it manages first to raise issues in a fairly coherent form for debate and then to compromise them in the process of policy-formation without resort to violence and without causing excessive instability in political institutions."[26]

DEMOCRATS NEED TO SHOW UP

Unlike a number of recent works on the woes of Democrats in rural communities, we are not about to detail a prescription for the ailments. We never intended to create a to-do list for presidential or statewide candidates or draft a strategy memo for local-level Democratic challengers. Sure, we thought about how the Democratic National Committee neglects rural parts and why it may make sense for candidates to think about rural policy in nonagricultural terms. And we certainly have some thoughts about how academics and reporters should cover the "heartland." Buy us a cup of coffee, and we'll bend your ear on these and a host of other topics.

Even so, this book does point to one unmistakable conclusion: Democrats need to show up in rural areas.

This verdict comes not from our partisan leanings but, instead, our democratic inclinations (Notice we used a lowercase "d.") American democracy can be greatly enhanced if Democrats in rural areas show up at the polls. By now you likely realize, as we do, that the forces leading to Republican dominance in rural areas are complex and did not happen overnight. But our data also tell us that while there may not be a quick fix, one thing is certain: the cycle of Republican dominance has been driven in large measure by a narrative that Democrats do not care, that they focus their time and attention on helping other areas and the people who are likely to live in those areas. The grievance rhetoric has been a powerful driver in creating a pervasive belief that Democrats do not care about rural Americans, and because Republicans do so well on election night, Democrats do not even show up. That's a mistake.

Democratic candidates should enter the fray fully intending to win, completely devoted to understanding the motivations, concerns, and fears of rural residents. When they do, they may find that the chasm between rural and urban is more a myth than a reality. Democratic candidates may be surprised to find rural attitudes are considerably more diverse than voting results suggest and that they can capture rural voters' hearts and minds without shifting policy positions in any dramatic way. One of the key findings of this book is that while a particular set of concerns and grievances motivates rural voters, there is little evidence to suggest that their take on many policy issues is way beyond that of the mainstream. For example, Democratic candidates do not have to become pro-life absolutists to do well, nor do they have to agree to close the border (let alone ban Muslims from entering the country).

We admit that Democratic success is far from guaranteed. But showing up matters, competition matters, and success builds. It will build a bridge between rural and urban areas and start to dismantle the myth of real America. Still, we know what you are thinking . . .

WHY IS IT THE DEMOCRATS' FAULT?

We are not saying it is. But Democrats should look in the mirror as much as they point fingers. In the aftermath of the 2016 presidential election, liberals were not just distraught, they were downright mad at rural voters. They just could not get why Trump, a billionaire (maybe) Manhattanite could hold such appeal among the white working class—especially in rural areas. Frank Rich, writing in *New York* magazine under the headline, "No Sympathy for the Hillbilly" (replete with a picture of a tractor, no less), dismisses this idea that Democrats hold any responsibility for changing course. "There's no way liberals can counter these voters' blind faith in a huckster who's sold them this snake oil," Rich writes. "The notion that they can be won over by some sort of new New Deal . . . is wishful thinking. These voters are so adamantly opposed to government programs that in some cases they refuse to accept the fact that aid they already receive comes from Washington. . . . Perhaps it's a smarter idea to just let the GOP own these intractable voters."[27]

That would not be the last time a liberal Democrat—from New York City, no less!—trashed the idea that Democrats should show up. While Rich's thinking is misplaced in several respects—which we will respond to in turn—most problematic is the fact that, ginned up with rural imagery and derogatory images, Rich represents a problematic, reactionary line of thinking, which encourages us to see places as black and white or red and blue. Unfortunately, that not only is it wrong, but it widens the division that exists between rural and urban America.

The myth of real America is not the Democrats' fault, and it is understandable that so many Democrats may feel like rural voters are a lost cause. It's taken us a few hundred pages to discount that idea, and nobody can be blamed for thinking it at first.

But just as we find fault in hucksters on the right lampooning latte-drinking liberals, some aspects of left-leaning politics are to blame for the emergence of rural grievance. This goes beyond a thoughtless comment from Obama or Clinton; there is nothing extraordinary about a single gaffe, but they do seem to happen a lot. It is about a much broader disposition held by mainstream liberals and party officials toward their fellow Americans. Nobody is saying that insults, stereotypes, and misrepresentations do not flow the other way. But Democrats should recognize that in at least two instances, they are overrepresented in institutions that are central to the construction—and potential deconstruction—of the real America mythology.

The first is in the institution we call home—higher education. Surprise: the academy leans left. But probably because it is overrepresented by liberals, the academy also leans urban. There are important communities for scholars of rural life; the Rural Sociological Society and the Program in Agrarian Studies at Yale will give you plenty to read once you put our book down. But, by and large, you can walk onto the campus of any major university or large college in the United States—even if in a rural area—and you will find courses on urban politics, urban sociology, and the economies of big cities. Rural politics, not so much.[28] Rural development is a preindustrial phenomenon, not something to think about in the context of Western democracies. That reinforces the idea that rural communities in the United States (and elsewhere) are backwards and in need of reform, when they really have value.

At the same time, we speak endlessly about the diversity of our student bodies, as we should. We seldom think about geographic diversity. Matt Newlin has made it his career's mission to change that, first as director of Rural Initiatives at College Advising Corps and now as the cohost of the podcast, *The Rural College Student Experience*. His work in advising and admissions led him to this unmistakable conclusion: "Only since the 2016 election of Donald Trump have most colleges and universities begun recognizing rural students as valuable members of the campus community, but outreach and recruitment efforts are still designed with urban/suburban students in mind. Colleges don't understand the unique rural populations they are attempting to serve, nor do they make efforts to adjust their services or campus resources."[29]

Discounting geographic diversity has broad social implications; perhaps there is a reason only 29 percent of rural high schoolers immediately enroll in higher education, compared with 37 percent for both urban and suburban kids.[30] We might even argue that in the drive to broaden diversity in college classrooms—which is, of course, a laudable goal—funding initiatives, scholarships, and special recruitment schemes have largely ignored rural students.[31]

It also matters in our classrooms, where we are teaching the next generation of citizens and representatives. Elevating the voices of rural students and rural experiences can be transformative for all involved.

One of us remembers the first time we taught from Kathy Cramer's book on rural resentment. Two students, one from urban northern Virginia and one from rural southern Virginia, stayed after class to discuss it further. The rural student began: "Wow, I cannot believe what all my classmates were saying about how bad schools are in rural areas. Haven't they heard about inner-city schools? We live where we do because of the schools!" The urban student responded: "Yeah, maybe the issue is not that one place is better than another. Both probably need better schools." True story.

The second institution in which Democrats are overrepresented is the media. As with higher education, the media bias is not necessarily driven by some partisan plot. Maybe on some stations, but most journalists are simply trying to eke out a living while working sixty-hour weeks tracking down some public official.

But as we discussed in chapter 9, the media landscape nourishes the myth of real America and feeds the rural-urban divide. Profits dictate strategy, and there is simply no profit to be made in going against giant media conglomerates that nationalize news stories and give the ax to local news desks. But reporters, analysts, scholars, and pundits need to resist the urge to spotlight the flamboyant, the loud, the overstated. There is scholarly evidence to suggest that the way the media cover different groups shapes how others view those groups' level of partisan intensity. For instance, one study found that "when citizens are exposed to media coverage depicting mass polarization, they dislike members of the opposition more, and rate them more negatively on a number of dimensions."[32] The trick is to knock on the door of the resident who does not have a sign in front of their house; according to our data, that would mean about 85 percent of rural residents.

So, it is not solely the Democrats' fault. And, to be honest, the myth of real America is working incredibly well for Republicans, so why would they want to change anything? Democrats, on the other hand, should take note of rural America's institutional advantages, so you may as well start playing the game! As Nick Bowlin in *The Guardian* put it, "As for Democrats who think that this work isn't worth it, or that rural America is somehow unworthy of their efforts, well, the joke is still on them."[33]

BUT DEMOCRATS HAVE ALREADY TRIED TO CARE ABOUT RURAL VOTERS AND HAVE FAILED

Have they? We hear that a lot. This line of thinking was best summarized by Paul Waldman of the *Washington Post*: "That story pervades our discussion of the rural-urban divide in U.S. politics. But it's fundamentally false. The reality is complex, but one thing you absolutely cannot say is that Democrats don't try to help rural America. In fact, they probably work harder at it than Republicans do."[34] For his example, Waldman uses the classic example of government's concern for rural areas: broadband Internet . . . it's coming!

But rural America's unwillingness to translate government policy—benevolently bestowed by Democrats—into votes does not mean they are the "village idiots" some in the media have been willing to label them.[35] Nor do we argue that rural voters fail to vote the "right way," as other low-income Americans supposedly do, in supporting redistributive tax policies and more government spending on programs like job reeducation. Rather, while poverty is not unique to rural communities, we show that the way in which rural Americans think about their economic situation is. When discussing policy, we need to be attuned to those dimensions, largely outlined in chapter 5. Ask a rural resident what they think about broadband internet access. "Fine," they'll tell you, "but will it help me pay my mortgage?"

Consider another classic example: rural areas get more than urban areas in federal spending. Writing in the *New York Times*, Paul Krugman implied that Democrats should just abandon rural America altogether: rural America's beliefs about what it receives and how they are valued is so far off the mark that they are a lost cause. This, apparently, represents the "radicalization of small towns and the countryside."[36]

To start, Krugman's own analysis of "the facts" is just another classic example of poor geographic thinking. Much of his analysis depends on state-level measures for balances of payment (see chapter 1): how much each state sends to the federal government every year minus what it gets back in federal spending. But, as we hope you know by now, those data are problematic for making geographic comparisons between urban and rural areas, because balances of payments are calculated only at the state level. And that is likely to remain the case since it is nearly impossible to allocate some federal receipts to counties or towns (e.g., the corporate income tax); trust us, if we could do that, you would see another chart! But we know that millions of rural residents live in so-called urban states, and many urban residents live in rural states. So why do we keep relying on these false dichotomies? Much federal investment in, say, highways or mass transit cannot be allocated across different types of geographies. And residential patterns and federal spending are also complicated within states. What is a "rural state," anyway, when only four states— Maine, Vermont, West Virginia, and Mississippi —are majority rural?

Krugman's analysis is problematic beyond the general ecological fallacy. He is a policy expert; the title of his newsletter is "Wonking Out." But even this Nobel Prize–winning expert discounted how rural America is more complex than we often think, both politically and economically. And its relationship with urban America is more than the simple dichotomy that the so-called facts often demand.

At the most basic level, policy makers standing outside looking in must rely on averages and raw dollar amounts to make sense of geographic divisions. But, as we discussed in chapter 4, geography is usually a terrible proxy for making sense of how government dollars flow. Progressives like to point to farm subsidies as another policy they have tried to use to win rural voters over: "Ever since the New Deal," Krugman wrote elsewhere, pointing to farm subsidies, "rural America has received special treatment from policymakers . . . which ballooned under Donald Trump."[37]

And yet, while progressive economists are quick to disparage widening inequality in American society (Krugman teaches a master class on the topic), seldom do we discuss the fact that these inequities exist within the rural America. Again, dichotomies—or the "gap instinct"—are particularly prone to fallacious reasoning. But looking beyond the simple divide, some, like Claire Carlson at the *Daily Yonder*, have shown that "while Krugman is correct in saying farm subsidies increased under the Trump Administration, those subsidies didn't predominantly benefit the smaller-scale, rural farmer who made, on average, $9,109 per-farm from two Trump-era subsidy programs . . . [and that] the majority of those subsidy payments went to the largest corporate farms in the country. . . . Some of these farms are run by billionaires who don't live in or represent rural America, but are benefitting from a broken tax system."[38]

Measurement challenges and inequality within rural communities underscore a more difficult challenge for policy makers and politicians who have thrown up their hands and said "we tried!" Both Krugman and Carlson are right; both agree more than they disagree. But national policy makers do not see rural policy the same way as rural residents do. This quest to prove just how wrong rural residents are to think what they think underscores the idea that the value of their lives and the contributions they make to society are determined by someone far removed from their day-to-day experiences.

This means that, overwhelmingly, when we talk about rural policy and rural spending, we often overlook the interconnectedness between rural and urban America and simplify rural economies. We point to massive farm subsidies as proof that rural America is getting more than they realize. Enough with the farms, rural residents may say! Only 6 percent of rural Americans actually have jobs in agriculture, according to U.S. census estimates; that money is padding the pockets of some absentee landlord or giant agribusiness. Even if we broaden the search, data like these miss how federal dollars that go to support mining, farming, and other natural resource extraction makes goods cheaper for all Americans, regardless of where they live. The policy maker's own sense that they "know" what is going on in rural America from a set of misguided data points is just the latest example of overlooking rural America's value and contribution to a larger, interconnected society.

When we fail to acknowledge that interconnectedness, we make it all too easy to split ourselves into warring tribes. That is why rural residents increasingly make sense of their collective situation by emphasizing their declining political, economic, and cultural relevance. Of course, many urbanities—particularly ethnic and linguistic minorities—feel similarly aggrieved, and for similar reasons. But in rural America, problems are felt as a community. Even wealthier rural residents, such as ourselves, see problems down the street. Rural communities are more socially and economically integrated, giving residents collective ownership of their fate.

Objective facts do little to account for this shared sense of destiny and belonging. Millions of Americans are reeling from disruptions in the global economy regardless of where they live. In urban America, they may lash out at the one percent or big tech or gentrification. There are facts to support and oppose that scapegoating, too. We find that in rural America, residents lash out against cities because that is the natural "out group" once one has defined oneself as a member of a geographic community. It is not as much about feelings taking over facts as it is the way in which we all depend on stories to make sense of the world.

Why do rural voters not jump up for joy when Democrats pass big spending bills that will supposedly lift rural communities out of poverty and give them a leg up to compete in the global economy? Won't Joe Biden's massive infrastructure bill help fix roads and bridges in rural parts? Maybe it is that they have heard it all before and just don't believe it. Maybe it is that they simply don't trust that Washington lawmakers have it in their interest to do anything to help rural America because they want to change rural America (make it more like the suburbs and cities that rural residents choose to live away from). And in that regard, the cultural disdain that many urbanites feel toward rural residents, and the lack of progovernment Democrats in rural areas, matters for how these so-called objective economic and political facts are interpreted. That does not mean that policy does not matter or that it is all about candidates' roots. Rural residents can see through some campaigns' attempts to portray their candidate as "one of them."[39] Looks are not what matters—authenticity does, because authenticity is what actually brings a rural perspective to the table.

Sure, point to the fact that urban areas are wealthier than rural ones and that because rural areas are older, sicker, and less economically efficient, they will need urban wealth. Overlook the high degree of inequality in cities that makes it just as devastating to live in inner Miami as in the outskirts of Albuquerque. Divide us into winners and losers so that the winners can keep winning. Your dogmatic insistence on facts is bound to make things worse, not better. Get on the ground and see for yourself what those facts look like in the minds of actual people. They will tell you a different story . . . if Democrats dare to show up.

BUT PROGRESSIVES CANNOT WIN IN RURAL AMERICA

The only way Democrats can win in rural America is to soften their progressive agenda, right? They need to back off on health care reform, tighten immigration, modify stands on reproductive rights, and strip away all the culture war baggage like tolerance toward LBTQIA+ communities and abortion. That's the ticket to success, right? Wrong. While it is fair to say on a host of issues, rural voters are a bit more moderate than the median urban voter, it is also true that the gap is small. More importantly—and this is key to our understanding of contemporary American political behavior—voters need to be convinced that a candidate understands their concerns, that they appreciate their daily struggles and will work to shatter the elite-created obstacles and bring about meaningful change. Candidates need to stand ready to fight.

In the wake of the 2016 election bombshell, many academics and pundits struggled to understand how a candidate with such muddled policy ideas could beat an ultra-prepared candidate with an encyclopedic memory of policy nuances. How could Trump, the dolt, beat Hillary, the wonk? And how did this ethically challenged, values-depraved city slicker win favor in the countryside? Better policies? It was because he promised to tear down the system—a system from which he himself had benefited—to make real changes. To use Maine vernacular, while Trump may have been "from away," he was willing to hear rural concerns.

Democrats do well in rural areas when they show up, too. When the former Democratic Ohio member of Congress Tim Ryan threw his hat into the ring in 2022 to become a U.S. senator, most knew it would be an uphill slog. Not long ago, the Buckeye State was purple, if not blue, but in recent years, it has moved rather hard in the Republican direction; Trump beat Biden in the state by eight points. He would be going up against *Hillbilly Elegy* author J. D. Vance; and Trump, still popular in the state, had stuck his neck out for Vance. It is not a particularly rural state on the whole, but GOP numbers in the Ohio countryside in recent years have been astonishingly large. Ryan would win the major cities, certainly, and he might do okay in many of the suburbs. But he'll get clobbered in rural parts, and that, as they say, would be that.

Ryan threw his heart into it and ran an energetic campaign in every part of the state. But, he refused to shift his stand on abortion, immigration, health care, and issues of racial justice. He was an old-school, card-carrying Democrat, and told naysayers to get over it. At the same time, he was not about to back away from his patriotism, defense of the military, and community values. He talked at length about the corruption in the system and the decline of good manufacturing jobs. At a rally in Dayton, he told the crowd, "You've seen a broken economic system where both parties have sold out to the corporate interests that shift our jobs down to the southern part of this country, then to Mexico, then to China. There is no economic freedom if there's no jobs here in the United States."[40]

And he did something else. He worked hard to convince Ohioans that he was on their side, that he was ready to take on the elites in Washington and corporate America. Almost as if he was responding directly to Hillary Clinton's "producers" line in 2016, Ryan told a crowd, "When I hear people at the national level say things like we have to invest in races where states have an increasing rate of college graduates, that's where we need to campaign, whoa." He said, "We're going to teach the Democratic party that the working-class folks, whether they're white or black or brown men or women or gay or straight, we are the backbone of this party."[41] He was ready to ruffle feathers, to fight, to break some shit. He was proud to be from rural Ohio, warts and all.

Did it work in the countryside? Yes. He lost the election by a few points, but in rural areas, Ryan closed the gap created by Biden by more than thirty points—in two years—with Biden as president. He talked about jobs, health care, dignity, and getting Ohioans a fair shake. He took on both parties where it mattered. Did he magically transform into a mealy-mouthed moderate? Not at all.

Or consider the case of Marie Gluesenkamp Perez's 2022 bid to represent Washington's third congressional district. This is not a majority-rural district, but rural voters living in rural parts made the difference in sending a Democrat to Washington. The daughter of a Mexican immigrant, Gluesenkamp Perez was a thirty-four-year-old mother of a toddler and the co-owner (with her husband) of an auto repair shop.

She was a political neophyte, her only other stab at elected office being a failed bid for county commissioner. The district is of that type that Democrats usually write off: overwhelmingly white (78 percent) and blue collar (73 percent do not hold a bachelor's degree or higher).[42] Trump had won the district with ease in the previous two presidential elections, and her opponent, Joe Kent, had broad name recognition, being a regular guest on Tucker Carlson's show. With Trump's full-throttled endorsement, Kent, most assumed, was a lock; expert election handicappers put Gluesenkamp Perez's chances at one in fifty.[43]

But Gluesenkamp Perez showed up in every community throughout the district. She had a compelling story that seemed to resonate with working-class voters, and she campaigned throughout rural areas, assuming—correctly—that every precinct was in play. She told voters that her party—the Democrats—was out of step with the middle class and too often gave the cold shoulder to rural areas. Gluesenkamp Perez talked about what mattered to voters in the district: health care, child care, good jobs, and schools. She pounded home, again and again, themes that would resonate with all Americans. "We are people that pay our taxes and want good schools and want a functioning society. We are tired of politicking and we are tired of extremists, and we just want to know that our kids are going to have the same or better shot at a good life as we did."[44] She talked about stringent environmental regulations and how they often came at the cost of blue-collar jobs. "My mom grew up in Forks, Washington, which is sort of the epicenter of the spotted owl, and that decimated jobs."[45]

Gluesenkamp Perez criss-crossed the distinct, at each gathering acknowledging voters' "economic fears, their sense of being left out of the political conversation, their disdain for ideological posturing from both sides of the spectrum." She pledged to not support Nancy Pelosi for speaker and to help cut small-business regulations.[46] She argued there were not enough folks in Congress with grease under their nails—and she could speak with authenticity, because she did.

So was she able to convince D.C. Democrats to aid her efforts? Not a chance; the district was a goner.

Or was it? Gluesenkamp Perez won that contest by less than a percentage point—likely the biggest upset in the 2022 midterms. Make no mistake, her story of working-class roots and moderate policy stands did not persuade every single rural voter to her side. Rural counties still went to the Republican. But she made inroads in the rural communities, faring better in those parts than Biden had two years earlier, and that was enough to put her over the top.

And, of course, we could not fail to mention how a Democrat has been able to win in a deeply red part of Maine—Jared Golden, in Maine's Second Congressional District, the second most rural district in America. First, in 2018, Golden did something rare in modern politics: he knocked off an incumbent Republican in a mostly rural district. Second, he has been able to keep his seat even when the voting trends in the district have increasingly shifted to the right.

The story is a bit different; Maine's second district is one of the few jurisdictions that is majority rural. But that makes it tough to disprove that Democrats cannot win. Is he not a progressive? Far from it. Golden is a fierce advocate for government support to spur rural job creation, expand the region's economy, build and maintain better schools, and expand health care. He is a strong backer of reproductive rights, and he talks endlessly about the surge of the opioid crisis in rural Maine. Sure, he sometimes votes against his party on large government spending bills (he was the lone House Democrat to vote against Biden's "Build Back Better" plan in 2022), but he supports an active role for government when he knows it will benefit his constituents.

But we think Golden's policy stands are mostly beside the point. That is, he fits the district. He, too, gets it. He's a former Marine, having served active duty-tours in both Iraq and Afghanistan—and he's not shy about talking about needing help for post-traumatic stress disorder after these tours. He's a good politician, but in keeping with the stoic Maine culture, Golden is far from gregarious. He seems to shun attention. He drives to Washington in his pickup truck (not a stunt), and he defends Maine's gun culture. It certainly did not hurt that Golden's two-time opponent, the pol he frist knocked off in 2018, is a millionaire business entrepreneur who owns an expensive home along the coast. In short, Golden wins because he is genuinely rural.

To drive home the point that Democrats—even progressive Democrats—can win in rural areas if they show up, consider the last figure in the book, 11.1. Along the vertical dimension is the ideology of each member of the U.S. House of Representatives in 2022, as determined by the votes they cast in Congress. The closer you get to -1, the more "liberal" you are and the closer to 1, the more "conservative" you are; conservatives are at the top. It is instructive, and certainly indicative of our political climate, that the ideological distance between party members is so great. There are very few moderates in either party, and all the Republicans are grouped far from the Democrats. Along the horizontal axis is the

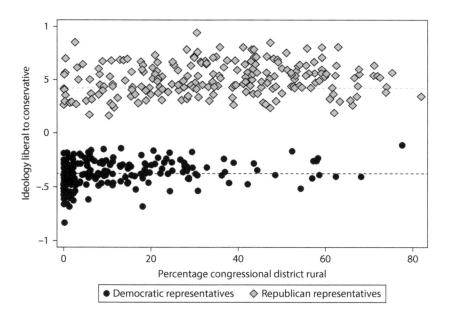

FIGURE 11.1 Partisan control of U.S. House seats by percentage rural district (2022)

Note: Using block-level measures of urbanicity, we calculate the percentage of residents living in each congressional district that are rural (living in nonurbanized blocks). Then, using ideological scores (DW-Nominate) from Voteview: Congressional Roll-Call Votes Database, we plot the average ideology of Republican and Democratic members of Congress by their districts' ruralness. The mean ideology for each party is marked by a dashed line.

"ruralness" of the district. See the black dot farthest to the right? That's Jared Golden.

Given what we have been writing about for hundreds of pages, it certainly makes sense that more of the gray dots would be to the right and that a vast majority of the black dots are on the left (the big cities); most people do not live in rural areas, so most districts are not really all that rural. But note two other patterns, unbeknownst even to us before we did the math. First, there is no relationship between conservatism and ruralness. Even in a more robust statistical model, ruralness does not predict how conservative a Republican member of Congress is. Republicans, in other words, are not necessarily winning in rural districts because they are more conservative. The other point is that there are more black dots on the right side closer together than we might expect, and they are quite like the average Democrat; the dashed lines represent each party's means for ideology. Believe it or not, some rural Democrats are even more liberal than the average Democrat, and it is not because they are representing districts with larger-than-average minority populations. Democrats can win in rural America.

Some rural progressives are starting to take note of that fact. Robert Leonard, who has made a career living and broadcasting in the rural Midwest, is also adamant that Democrats can win without sacrificing their progressive values. He wrote in the *New York Times*, "Democrats should be proud of what the party has been and is and what it stands for, and its values: for smart government being part of the solution, not the problem; for health care as a right, not a privilege; for clean water and air and effective climate solutions; for taxation that doesn't favor the rich; for equal opportunity for all. . . . These are Democratic values. They can play everywhere, including in rural America. Run on those."[47]

To a point, our evidence confirms Leonard's thinking. Again, that is not to say we agree or disagree with his policy positions—just that rural voters are not reflexively hostile to the policies Democratic candidates often support. What really matters is how those policies are framed. It matters if "smart government" is discussed as "smart government for rural America," since rural voters currently think bureaucrats and decision makers do not care or listen to rural perspectives. It matters if "equal opportunity for all" includes an acknowledgment that inequality in rural areas is driven by a different set of policies (e.g., agricultural consolidation, limited vocational training, free trade) than elsewhere. As Tony Pipa, director of the Brookings Institution's Reimagining Rural Policy Initiative, has argued, progressives need place-specific solutions that "put local assets to creative use, unleash entrepreneurial activity, share the benefits widely and retain the value locally."[48] That makes sense to rural voters who see the economy through very local, or place-based, lenses. It means that rural Americans are ready to debate progressive policies and that Democrats need to know that ruralness matters in that progressive argument.

For them to know that, though, Democrats need to show up.

BUT RURAL VOTERS ARE IRREDEEMABLY RACIST

Throughout this book, and especially in this closing chapter, we have tried to make our motivations clear—and what you have to believe to buy our story about rural voters. Foundational to that story is a belief in liberal democracy. That is why party competition matters. It enhances liberal democracy. That is why chronic Democratic absenteeism and weak electoral performance in rural areas matters for us all. It creates unrepresentative outcomes, fuels extremism, and weakens our collective resolve.

Make no mistake, we are deeply committed to the foundational idea that liberal democracies are unequivocally egalitarian places. The goals of building a thriving, multiracial, and multiethnic democracy cannot be sacrificed on the altar of competitive partisanship. The good news is that we do not have to do that.

We understand the argument that if the only way for Democrats to succeed in rural places is to imbue their campaigns with dog whistles and vote against racially equitable policies, then that is not a candidate worth having. We understand that many readers would rather live in a world where there are just a few representatives, all of whom are committed to racial equality, than a world where there are many politicians, but who quickly abandon the goals of diversity and inclusion when the going gets tough.

But we are rapidly moving toward a world in which we do not have to choose either of those options—one in which there are not just a few representatives committed to racial equality but many. Rural voters can be part of that world. But how?

First, when we hear concerns that to win over rural voters, representatives have to be racially conservative, we invariably get historical examples. Support for Jim Crow laws was fueled by southerners, and the South is overwhelmingly rural. Okay. Or how about when Reagan began to convert rural voters into the Republican Party through coded racial appeals?[49] And, of course, there is the fact that rural voters overwhelmingly supported Donald Trump. How can you win them over if he is so popular? A better question might be, do we even want to win them over?

We spent much of chapter 8 working through the politics of race in rural areas precisely because these criticisms are so important. But notice that each of these concerns conflates the past with the future. Often, in doing so, it misrepresents rural Americans. Senators with large rural constituencies supported the 1964 Civil Rights Act; it was not a case of urban versus rural. Coded language moves whites in cities and the suburbs; recall that Nixon's southern strategy focused on driving the wedge on racial politics in the suburbs. With Trump, too, racism lacks a geographic element. You are talking not about rural voters but racist voters.

Historic comparisons tend to overlook the possibilities for a different future—a future, we believe, that clearly involves racially just politics in rural areas. And, as we discussed, most of our understanding of racial politics is distorted by the media's focus on a subset of rural voters who are likely to dominate the headlines—the small group of deeply engaged rural residents whom we call the Rural Rabble-Rousers in chapter 9. For example, this group was twice as likely to believe in white replacement theory garbage than the other 92 percent of rural residents. They are the loud, the overt, the in-your-face characters who drive news stories, but they are not the rural voter.

Racism, as we measure it, is there. Absolutely. It is there and in your own community. But it is not a neat, tight narrative; it has many components. We measure racism by looking at stereotypes and how those stereotypes feed into white Americans' sense that people of color are not working hard enough or are getting an unfair advantage. But recall that the vast majority of rural residents, even if they hold racially resentful beliefs, hardly seem like the irredeemable racists the media make them out to be. To be clear, the data clearly suggest that those people do live in rural America. But do they make up a majority of rural America? Hardly. And while they do make up a majority of Trump's rural coalition, there are millions of votes at stake. A third of rural voters who voted for Trump were in full agreement that whites had advantages just because of the color of their skin; half of rural Trump voters disagreed with the idea that Blacks just needed to try harder to get ahead; and a quarter of his rural supporters agreed that generations of slavery continue to make it difficult for Black Americans. Maybe they were all just lying to us. Maybe not.

How do you change minds? First, you show up. Second, you put your cards on the table. That, at least, is what Dan Bayer, a volunteer with the organization Down Home North Carolina, has seen firsthand. Down Home NC exists to help progressive Democrats win in rural communities. As Bayer puts it, the trick is to address the issue up front: "The main message is, whether we're White, Brown, or Black, we all want safe communities and a shot at a decent life. But those in power use racism to distract us while they pass huge tax cuts for themselves or large subsidies for their businesses. Don't you think we should work together?"[50] A little Pollyannaish? Only if you are thinking it is going to work for everyone. But if you set your sights on the 30–40 percent of rural voters we identify as more mutable on racial issues—those who hold prejudicial stereotypes but do not seem distracted by the race-baiting issues of "inner city crime," "welfare queens," and "urban riots"—then you begin to dramatically change the game.

Changing racial attitudes in rural America—much less all of America—will not be like hitting a light switch. Rather, it is more akin to a dial that is turned click by click. The task is hard. It is also debated.

There are many reasons we continue to struggle with America's "original sin." We note that, as Bayer and others who talk about race in rural communities recognize, our questions about racial stereotypes avoided a lot of the political language surrounding those ideas: "critical race theory," "defund the police," "urban riots." It is not that we think we should avoid those issues. Not at all. But what do those issues actually mean, especially in the context of a quick survey question? Those are terms designed to produce disagreement. Even polling Black Americans produces contradictory messages on racial issues. A reputable poll taken in the aftermath of George Floyd's murder showed that while half of Black Americans feel "less secure" when they are in the presence of a police office, half also agreed that "we need more cops on the street." Anyone following the politically charged debate over defunding the police could pick their fact to support their side, and they did.[51]

But underneath those facts and data points lies a problem that actually sorts out the contradiction nicely. Can it not be the case that a Black person wants to feel safe in America in front of a cop while also wanting more police and a safer community? Why does it have to be only one of those options? Most people, we think, would want to have a conversation about how to make that happen. It is hard to have that conversation when you are not there.

Our evidence shows that with their passionate belief in the values of hard work and insistence that America rewards those who work hard, rural residents would be especially sensitive to tearing down the systemic barriers that keep hard-working people of all colors and backgrounds from succeeding. That would have to be done while acknowledging that racial remedies that cut across color do not have to cut across class. Hard work has broad popular appeal in the United States. There is a reason Barack Obama never uttered "you didn't build that" again, and it was not because he was concerned about losing the rural vote.

So maybe it is not the racial politics of rural areas that liberal naysayers find concerning but, rather, rural residents' fervent belief in meritocracy and competitive enterprise. Maybe it is true that, on average, the system is rigged against us all. But in rural areas, voters see that hard work is enough to get by. Democrats can recognize that both can be true—and maybe even that rural areas are places where hard work does mean something. At the same time, they could also start to show how structural disadvantages in the economy matter just as much in rural areas as they do in urban areas. But to do that, they need to show up.

SYMPATHY FOR THE HILLBILLY . . .
AND THE BUBBAS, BUMPKINS, HAYSEEDS,
HICKS, RUBES, AND REDNECKS

We started this book in the middle of the COVID-19 pandemic. As we all know, because we lived it in very personal, sometimes tragic, ways, it was a calamitous, historic event. The number keeps going up, but as of now, well over 1.1 million Americans have died from COVID-19. It is impossible to calculate the destruction, anguish, and human costs from this period.

One of the great tragedies of the pandemic is that we failed to come together as a nation. Even those of us who study partisan politics, who analyze the ebb and flow of candidates and causes, imagined that the crisis might snap us out of our steady descent into partisan rancor. America came together after 9/11, at least temporarily, so it seemed reasonable to imagine that we would rally as one during this trying time. Americans may disagree about a lot of things, but during times of crisis, we come together.

But that did not happen this time.

A growing body of evidence shows that few factors better predict the severity of illness or mortality than partisan politics, which are deeply embedded in the rural-urban divide.[52] There are varying interpretations as to how this came about, how the bitterness and divisiveness endured and maybe even flourished during a crisis, and from our vantage, there is no escaping the culpability of Donald Trump. Some may disagree. But there is no denying that the geographic divisions were as wide as they were heartbreaking. The pandemic brought to light the very real consequences of the rural-urban divide. It was no longer a matter of abstract social science data, pithy journalistic accounts, or vivid numbers on a spreadsheet. The reality was deadly.

While the gap was likely less than most Americans think, and while some of the partisan divide was due to composition effects, COVID-19 vaccine hesitancy in rural America was a reality—a little higher than in other areas of the country. There was also much greater resistance to social distancing and other mitigation efforts. We will never know the exact number, given the numerous comorbidity factors, but it is likely that thousands of additional lives were lost in rural communities due to a reluctance to follow guidelines issued by the government and to take vaccines created by pharmaceutical companies. But why would people living in rural areas be less likely to take these steps?

This book has shown that rural voters have developed a powerful sense of shared fate, using a narrow lens that guides how they view economic, cultural, and political issues, ultimately generating a shared sense of collective grievance toward urban areas, government experts, and, yes, the Democratic Party. That connectedness—forged by all the elements discussed in the previous pages, as well as by the concerted acts of Republican and Democratic leaders alike, has changed our politics. The rural voter's faith in real America threatens the stability of our democracy. And when the pandemic took hold, their shared fate was strong enough to rally opposition to basic health precautions. It became a badge of honor in some rural circles to flout even the most basic guidelines about interpersonal contact and the seriousness of the illness. Many died because of their fidelity to the tribe.

Urban residents, for their part, were much more likely to heed government and health care professionals' guidelines, often to the point that strict adherence was also a partisan badge. Smart urban progressives also turned their back to science, refusing to drop their masks even while walking alone on hiking trails. But more significantly, they also turned their back to the pleas of rural residents to consider how mitigation rules would cripple family incomes and drastically alter the lives of their kids. When parents and some experts complained about learning loss and the long-term effects of school closures, they belittled legitimate concerns as nothing but unreflective Trumpism. But schooling at home was not a simple matter for many rural kids, and working from home wasn't an option for their parents. Urban progressives dismissed the arguments that rural communities are different and that one-size-fits-all guidelines were wrong. And why shed a tear, the urbane pondered, as the hillbillies, bubbas, bumpkins, hayseeds, hicks, rubes, and rednecks brought it on themselves? Good riddance?

No. We need each other. We need each other to know ourselves. Our interests, well-being, success, and future are wrapped up in the interest, success, and future of the other. We are connected, one to the other, street by street, field by field, block by block. We cannot be immune or indifferent to the well-being of others. Recognizing the complexity of American life—from the thriving metropolis to the new suburbs, to the old villages and quiet, lowly fields and forests—is essential for America's future. It is not an easy task. We will have to do more than just listen to one another to find common ground. Campaigns are hard-fought and there is significant money on the line in changing rural policies so that they benefit everyone in the community, instead of just a few. There are real differences and memories can be long. Democrats in urban areas will not only have to tolerate rural candidates that stray from national talking points, but actively support them; they cannot stand out there alone. When Democrats do show up, rural voters should be ready to jump ship from Republicans who sell local concerns up river, even if just for one election. With time, we might see real competition for rural voters, instead of forsaking a broad swath of the electorate. It is what we should demand of our political leaders and ourselves—to close the rural-urban divide, one bridge at a time.

NOTES

INTRODUCTION: TWO AMERICAS

1. R. Berman, "Trump's Risky Bet on Rural America," *The Atlantic*, November 6, 2020; M. D. Nelsen and C. D. Petsko, "Race and White Rural Consciousness," *Perspectives on Politics* 19, no. 4 (2021): 1205–18; Christina Wolbrecht, Jeffrey R. Dudas, Darren Davis, Edward G. Carmines, Eric R. Schmidt, Deborah J. Schildkraut, and Roger Petersen, "Review: The Politics of Resentment: A Discussion of Katherine J. Cramer's 'The Politics of Resentment: Rural Consciousness in Wisconsin and the Rise of Scott Walker," *Perspectives on Politics* 15, no. 2 (2017): 521–32; and S. Mettler and T. Brown, "The Growing Rural-Urban Political Divide and Democratic Vulnerability," *Annals of the American Academy of Political and Social Science* 699, no. 1 (2022): 130–42.
2. P. Heideman, "What Liberals Miss About Trump Country," *Jacobin*, October 15, 2019; K. Orejel, "Why Trump Won Rural America," *Dissent*, October 16, 2017; A. V. Dam and H. Long, "Biden Won Places That Are Thriving. Trump Won Ones That Are Hurting," *Washington Post*, November 16, 2020.
3. B. C. Thiede, J. L. Butler, D. L. Brown, and L. Jensen, "Income Inequality Across the Rural-Urban Continuum in the United States, 1970–2016," *Rural Sociology* 85, no. 4 (2020): 899–937.
4. Julia Foutz, Samantha Artiga, and Rachel Garfield, "The Role of Medicaid in Rural America" (issue brief, KFF, San Francisco, CA, April 25, 2018).
5. Paul Krugman, "Can Anything Be Done to Assuage Rural Rage?," *New York Times*, January 26, 2023.
6. Bill Bishop, *The Big Sort: Why the Clustering of Like-Minded American Is Tearing Us Apart* (Boston: Mariner, 2008).
7. D. Kurtzleben, "Rural Voters Played a Big Part in Helping Trump Defeat Clinton," *NPR*, November 14, 2016.

8. N. Riccardi, "Trump's Election Day Surge Powered by Small-Town America," *AP News*, November 5, 2020.

9. D. Kopf, "The Rural-Urban Divide Is Still the Big Story of American Politics," *Quartz*, November 6, 2020.

10. Sarah Melotte and Tim Marema, "Gap Between Urban and Rural Congressional Voters Widened in Last 16 Years," *Daily Yonder*, December 6, 2022.

11. D. Byler, "Republicans Now Enjoy Unmatched Power in the States. It Was a 40-Year Effort," Opinion, *Washington Post*, February 18, 2021.

12. Alan Greenblatt, "How Rural America Learned to Love the Republican Party," Governing.com, July 20, 2022.

13. L. Habeeb, J. Nichols, and B. Weingarten, "Being J. D. Vance: Few Understand Better How the Left Lost Rural America," *Newsweek*, June 6, 2022.

14. H. Evich, "Revenge of the Rural Voter," *Politico*, November 16, 2016.

15. J. A. Bill Bishop, "Exit Polls: Romney Improves in Rural," *Daily Yonder*, July 17, 2019.

16. Ron Johnston et al., "The Geographies of Trump's Electoral Success," in *Political Landscapes of Donald Trump*, ed. Barney Warf (London: Routledge, 2020).

17. A. Zitner and P. Overberg, "Rural Vote Fuels Trump; Clinton Loses Urban Grip," *Wall Street Journal*, November 9, 2016.

18. Ruth Igielnik, Scott Keeter, and Hannah Hartig, *Behind Biden's 2020 Victory* (report, Pew Research Center, Washington, D.C., June 30, 2021), https://www.pewresearch.org/politics/2021/06/30/behind-bidens-2020-victory/.

19. Quoted in John Bowden, "Clinton: I Won Places Moving Forward, Trump Won Places Moving Backward," *The Hill*, March 13, 2018, https://thehill.com/homenews/campaign/378070-clinton-i-won-places-moving-forward-trump-won-places-moving-backward.

20. D. Chinni, *Fox News Covid Coverage and Its Penetration in American Communities* (American Communities Project, East Lansing, MI, April 23, 2020).

21. Thomas Frank, *What's the Matter with Kansas? How Conservatives Won the Heart of America* (New York: Metropolitan, 2005), 4.

22. Kim Parker, Juliana Menasce Horowitz, Anna Brown, Richard Fry, D'vera Cohn and Ruth Igielnik, *Urban, Suburban and Rural Residents' Views on Key Social and Political Issues* (report), Social & Demographic Trends Project, Pew Research Center, Washington, D. C., May 30, 2020.

23. Pamela Johnston Conover, "The Influence of Group Identifications on Political Perception and Evaluation," *Journal of Politics* 46, no. 3 (1984): 760–85; Henri Tajfel and J. C. Turner, "The Social Identity Theory of Intergroup Behavior," in *Psychology of Intergroup Relations*, ed. S. Worchel and W. G. Austin (Chicago: Nelson, 1986), 7–24.

24. Michael C. Dawson, *Behind the Mule: Race and Class in African-American Politics* (Princeton, NJ: Princeton University Press, 1995); Katherine Tate, *From Protest to Politics: The New Black Voters in American Elections* (Cambridge, MA: Harvard University Press, 1994).

25. Evelyn M. Simien, "Race, Gender, and Linked Fate," *Journal of Black Studies* 35, no. 5 (2005): 529–50; Gabriel R. Sanchez and Natalie Masuoka, "Brown-Utility Heuristic? The Presence and Contributing Factors of Latino Linked Fate," *Hispanic Journal of Behavioral Sciences* 32, no. 4 (2010): 519–31.

26. John Agnew, *Place and Politics: The Geographical Mediation of State and Society* (London: Allen & Unwin, 1987).

27. Katherine J. Cramer, "*The Politics of Resentment: Rural Consciousness in Wisconsin and the Rise of Scott Walker* (Chicago: University of Chicago Press, 2016), 6.

28. Katherine Cramer, "Analysis: How Rural Resentment Helps Explain the Surprising Victory of Donald Trump," *Washington Post*, December 7, 2021.

29. Amy Fried and Douglas B. Harris, *At War with Government: How Conservatives Weaponized Distrust from Goldwater to Trump* (New York: Columbia University Press, 2021).

30. Nicholas Jacobs and B. Kal Munis, "Place-Based Resentment in Contemporary U.S. Elections: The Individual Sources of America's Urban-Rural Divide," *Political Research Quarterly* (September 7, 2022), https://doi.org/10.1177/10659129221124864.

31. V. O. Key Jr., *American State Politics: An Introduction* (Westport, CT: Greenwood, 1983).

32. Daniel Hopkins, *The Increasingly United States: How and Why American Political Behavior Nationalized* (Chicago: University of Chicago Press, 2018).

33. Walter Lippman, *Public Opinion* (New York: Harcourt, Brace, 1922); Yanna Krupnikov and John Barry Ryan, *The Other Divide: Polarization and Disengagement in American Politics* (Cambridge: Cambridge University Press, 2022).

34. Thomas Ogorzalek, "New Directions in Race, Place, and Space," *Journal of Politics* 81, no. 3 (June 10, 2019): 5.

35. To be sure, place and context have featured prominently in studies of voting behavior dating from Key's (1949) claim that residency and proximity were primary determinants of candidate support. See, for instance: Michael S. Lewis-Beck and Tom W. Rice, "Localism in Presidential Elections: The Home State Advantage," *American Journal of Political Science* (1983): 548–56; James G. Gimpel, Kimberly A. Karnes, John McTague, and Shanna Pearson-Merkowitz, "Distance-decay in the Political Geography of Friends-and-Neighbors Voting," *Political Geography* 27, no. 2 (2008): 231–52; Shaun Bowler, Todd Donovan, and Joseph Snipp, "Local Sources of Information and Voter Choice in State Elections: Microlevel Foundations of the 'Friends and Neighbors' Effect," *American Politics Quarterly* 21, no. 4 (1993): 473–89; Gregory G. Brunk, Subha Ramesh, and John Adams, "Contagion-based Voting in Birmingham, Alabama," *Political Geography Quarterly* 7, no. 1 (1988): 39–47; C. Panagopoulos and K. Bailey, "'Friends-and-Neighbors' Mobilization: A Field Experimental Replication and Extension," *Journal of Experimental Political Science* 7, no. 1 (2020), 13–26.

36. Donald P. Green, Bradley Palmquist, and Eric Schickler, *Partisan Hearts and Minds: Political Parties and the Social Identities of Voters* (New Haven, CT: Yale University Press, 2002); Robert S. Erikson, Michael MacKuen, and James A. Stimson, *The Macro Polity* (Cambridge: Cambridge University Press, 2002).

1. WHO AND WHAT IS RURAL AMERICA?

1.   Anne N. Junod, Clare Salerno, and Corianne Payton Scally, "Debunking Three Myths About Rural America," Urban Institute, October 30, 2020, https://www.urban.org /urban-wire/debunking-three-myths-about-rural-america.

2.   Sarah Low, "Manufacturing Is Relatively More Important to the Rural Economy Than the Urban Economy," U.S. Department of Agriculture. https://www.usda.gov /media/blog/2017/09/12/manufacturing-relatively-more-important-rural-economy -urban-economy.

3.   Kelly Young, "Drug Overdose Death Rates in Cities Surpass Those in Rural Areas," ed. Susan Sadoughi and André Sofair, *NEJM Journal Watch*, August 5, 2019, https://www .jwatch.org/fw115675/2019/08/05/drug-overdose-death-rates-cities-surpass-those -rural.

4.   Carolyn Miller et al., *Main Report* (report, Pew Research Center, Washington, D.C., September 26, 2012), https://www.pewresearch.org/internet/2012/09/26/main -report-13/.

5.   "Sports Fans' Geographical Areas: Shape Their Opinions," Design Sensory Intelligence, accessed April 18, 2023, https://designsensoryintelligence.com/sports-fans-geographical -areas-shape-their-opinions/.

6.   O. E. Okobi, O. O. Ajayi, T. J. Okobi, et al., "The Burden of Obesity in the Rural Adult Population of America," *Cureus* 13, no. 6 (June 20, 2021): e15770, https://www .cureus.com/articles/61370-the-burden-of-obesity-in-the-rural-adult-population -of-america#!/.

7.   Jennifer Bradley and Bruce Katz, "A Small-Town or Metro Nation?," Brookings Institution, Washington, D.C., October 8, 2008, https://www.brookings.edu/articles/a -small-town-or-metro-nation/.

8.   David Uberti, "Drive-By Journalism in Trumplandia," *Columbia Journalism Review*, June 19, 2017.

9.   Thomas Jefferson to John Jay, August 23, 1785, in *The Letters of Thomas Jefferson*, Yale Law School Lillian Goldman Law Library, accessed April 18, 2023, https://avalon.law .yale.edu/18th_century/let32.asp.

10. Sinclair Lewis, *Main Street* (New York: Signet Classics, 1920).

11. Bruce Katz and Jennifer Bradley, *The Metropolitan Revolution: How Cities and Metros Are Fixing Our Broken Politics and Fragile Economy* (Washington, D.C.: Brookings Institution Press, 2013).

12. Quoted in John Bowden, "Clinton: I Won Places Moving Forward, Trump Won Places Moving Backward," *The Hill*, March 13, 2018, https://thehill.com/homenews /campaign/378070-clinton-i-won-places-moving-forward-trump-won-places-moving -backward.

13. Ken Voytek, "Where Manufacturing Is Growing (and Where It Is Not)," *Manufacturing Innovation Blog*, National Institute of Standards and Technology, U.S. Commerce Department, November 19, 2020, https://www.nist.gov/blogs/manufacturing-innovation -blog/where-manufacturing-growing-and-where-it-not.

14. Google Books NGram Viewer, November 14, 2022. https://books.google.com/ngrams/graph?content=rural&year_start=1800&year_end=2019&corpus=26&smoothing=3&direct_url=t1%3B%2Crural%3B%2Cco.

15. Hans Rosling, *Factfulness: Ten Reasons We're Wrong About the World—and Why Things Are Better Than You Think* (New York: Flatiron, 2018).

16. Nicholas F. Jacobs and B. Kal Munis, "Staying in Place: Federalism and the Political Economy of Place Attachment," *Publius: The Journal of Federalism* 50, no. 4 (2020): 544–65.

17. For a review, see Zoe Nemerever and Melissa Rogers, "Measuring the Rural Continuum in Political Science," *Political Analysis* 29, no. 3 (2021): 267–86. See also Kenneth M. Johnson and Dante J. Scala, "The Rural-Urban Continuum and the 2020 U.S. Presidential Election," *The Forum* 20, no. 2 (2022), https://www.degruyter.com/document/doi/10.1515/for-2022-2057/html.

18. Economic Research Service, U.S. Department of Agriculture, "What Is Rural?," last updated October 23, 2019, https://www.ers.usda.gov/topics/rural-economy-population/rural-classifications/what-is-rural.aspx.

19. Economic Research Service, U.S. Department of Agriculture, "Documentation: 2010 Rural-Urban Commuting Area (RUCA) Codes," last updated March 22, 2023, https://www.ers.usda.gov/data-products/rural-urban-commuting-area-codes/documentation/.

20. This is a logarithmic measure—a compressed measure of density—since there is a large degree of variation in population size and density across urban areas.

21. Jacob R. Brown and Ryan D. Enos, "The Measurement of Partisan Sorting for 180 Million Voters," *Nature Human Behavior* 8 (2021): 998–1008, https://www.nature.com/articles/s41562-021-01066-z.

22. A small note on 2020: beginning with the 2020 Census, which had already been plagued by concerns of data irregularities, the Census Bureau changed how it would measure "urban" and "rural" counties, which are traditionally reported about two years after the initial census results. We recognize that this change is an advantage in many respects. Since 1910, the Census has relied on individuals to measure population density for urban areas. The move to measure housing units is more reflective of the concept of "urban residence." The bureau adjusted population thresholds to make households comparable to previous measures that relied on individuals. Of course, at the neighborhood level, the difference between these measures is magnified and did make some previously rural places urban, and vice versa. But at the county level, we are less concerned that this measurement change alters how we distinguish between rural from nonrural counties, since the vast majority of blocks were classified the same in 2010 as they were in 2020.

23. Seldom was a county missing from the U.S. Census's official estimate of ruralness. When a county was missing, we calculated the annual change in the rural population between the two known decennial census estimates to estimate changes in the county population; the largest range between discrete points was 20 years. Throughout the time series, only two states were completely missing from a census report; the archived 1960 census estimates for rurality do not include Colorado or Maryland. For each county in those two states we compute the annual change in rural population between 1950 and 1970.

24. Alexander Keyssar, *The Right to Vote: The Contested History of Democracy in the United States* (New York: Basic Books, 2009).

25. Michael Dubin, *United States Presidential Elections, 1788–1860: The Official Results by County and State* (Jefferson, NC: McFarland, 2002).

26. Bill Bishop, *The Big Sort: Why the Clustering of America Is Tearing Us Apart* (Boston: Mariner/Houghton Mifflin Harcourt, 2009).

27. David A. Hopkins, *Red Fighting Blue: How Geography and Electoral Rules Polarize American Politics* (Cambridge: Cambridge University Press, 2017).

28. Jowei Chen and Jonathan Rodden, "Unintentional Gerrymandering: Political Geography and Electoral Bias in Legislatures," *Quarterly Journal of Political Science* 8, no. 2 (2013): 239–69.

29. Nate Silver, "The Senate's Rural Skew Makes It Very Hard for Democrats to Win the Supreme Court," *FiveThirtyEight*, September 20, 2020, https://fivethirtyeight.com /features/the-senates-rural-skew-makes-it-very-hard-for-democrats-to-win-the -supreme-court/.

30. Osita Nwanevu, "Trump Isn't the Only One to Blame for the Capitol Riot," Opinion, *New York Times*, January 4, 2022, https://www.nytimes.com/2022/01/04/opinion/capitol -riot.html?referringSource=articleShare.

31. Frances E. Lee and Bruce I. Oppenheimer, *Sizing Up the Senate: The Unequal Consequences of Equal Representation* (Chicago: University of Chicago Press, 1999).

32. Philip Bump, "By 2040, Two-Thirds of Americans Will Be Represented by 30 Percent of the Senate," *Washington Post*, November 28, 2017, https://www.washingtonpost.com /news/politics/wp/2017/11/28/by-2040-two-thirds-of-americans-will-be-represented -by-30-percent-of-the-senate/.

33. Emily Badger, "As American as Apple Pie? The Rural Vote's Disproportionate Slice of Power," *New York Times*, November 20, 2016, https://www.nytimes.com/2016/11/21 /upshot/as-american-as-apple-pie-the-rural-votes-disproportionate-slice-of-power .html.

34. Paul Krugman, "Working Out: Facts, Feelings and Rural Politics," Opinion, *New York Times*, October 21, 2022, https://www.nytimes.com/2022/10/21/opinion/rural-america -politics.html.

35. Laura Schultz and Lynn Holland, *Giving or Getting? New York's Balance of Payments with the Federal Government (2023)* (report, Rockefeller Institute of Government, Albany, NY, March 23, 2023), https://rockinst.org/issue-area/balance-of-payments-2023/.

36. Badger, "As American as Apple Pie?"

37. Alex Tausanovitch, *Voter-Determined Districts* (report, Center for American Progress, Washington, D.C., May 9, 2019), https://www.americanprogress.org/article/voter -determined-districts/.

38. Jennifer Cohen Kabaker, "A Closer Look at Small State Minimums in Federal Education Formulas" (blog), New America, February 1, 2012, https://www.newamerica.org /education-policy/federal-education-budget-project/ed-money-watch/a-closer-look -at-small-state-minimums-in-federal-education-formulas/.

39. Aaron M. Renn, "Reforming Anti-Urban Bias in Transportation Spending," New Geography, February 4, 2010, https://www.newgeography.com/content/001391-reforming -anti-urban-bias-transportation-spending.

2. THE DEEP ROOTS OF THE RURAL-URBAN DIVIDE (1776-1980)

1. Andrew Burt, "'These United States': How Obama's Vocal Tic Reveals a Polarized America," *The Atlantic*, May 9, 2013.

2. John Willard Hahn, "*The Background of Shays's Rebellion: A Study of Massachusetts History 1780–1787* (Madison: University of Wisconsin Press, 1946), 33.

3. Michael J. Klarman, *The Framer's Coup: The Making of the United States Constitution* (New York: Oxford University Press, 2016), 90.

4. Alan Taylor, *Liberty Men and Great Proprietors: The Revolutionary Settlement on the Maine Frontier, 1760-1820* (Chapel Hill: University of North Carolina Press, 1990).

5. Thomas Jefferson, Jefferson Quotes & Family Letters, "Extract from Thomas Jefferson to James Madison, 20 Dec. 1787 [Quote] |," Jefferson Quotes & Family Letters, accessed April 24, 2023, https://tjrs.monticello.org/letter/1300.

6. Thomas P. Slaughter, *The Whiskey Rebellion: Frontier Epilogue to the American Revolution* (New York: Oxford University Press, 1986).

7. "From Thomas Jefferson to James Madison, 21 September 1795," Founders Online, National Archives, https://founders.archives.gov/documents/Jefferson/01-28-02-0375. Original source: *The Papers of Thomas Jefferson*, vol. 28, 1 January 1794 – 29 February 1796, ed. John Catanzariti (Princeton, NJ: Princeton University Press, 2000), 475–77.

8. William Nesbet Chambers, *Political Parties in a New Nation: The American Experience, 1776–1809* (New York: Oxford University, 1963), 80.

9. James Trenchard, "The Plan of a Farm Yard—Venerate the Plow." Library of Congress, January 1, 1786, accessed April 24, 2023, https://www.loc.gov/item/2004671570/.

10. Donald Ratcliffe, "The Right to Vote and the Rise of Democracy, 1787–1828," accessed April 24, 2023, https://studylib.net/doc/8347162/the-right-to-vote-and-the-rise-of -democracy--1787%E2%80%931828.

11. David B. Danbom, *Born in the Country: A History of Rural America* (Baltimore, MD: Johns Hopkins University Press, 2017), 121.

12. Danbom, *Born in the Country*.

13. "The Colored Farmers National Alliance and Cooperative Union Is Founded." African American Registry, August 29, 2022.

14. Clayton S. Ellsworth, "Theodore Roosevelt's Country Life Commission," *Agricultural History* 34, no. 4 (1960): 155–72.

15. Charles Postel, *The Populist Vision* (New York: Oxford University Press, 2009).

16. Elizabeth Sanders, *Roots of Reform: Farmers, Workers, and the American State, 1877–1917* (Chicago: University of Chicago Press, 2009).

17. Frederick Jackson Turner, "The Significance of the Frontier in American History, 1893," National Humanities Center, accessed April 24, 2023, http://nationalhumanitiescenter .org/pds/gilded/empire/text1/turner.pdf.

18. Sanders, *Roots of Reform*, 147.

19. Nicholas F. Jacobs and Sidney M. Milkis, "2. The American Party System and Populist Upheaval: Mediating Anger and Discontent, 1800-1945," in *What Happened to the Vital Center? Presidentialism, Populist Revolt, and the Fracturing of America* (New York: Oxford University Press, 2022).

20. Jeffery A. Jenkins and Boris Heersink, *Republican Party Politics and the American South, 1865–1968* (Cambridge: Cambridge University Press, 2020).

21. Walter Dean Burnham, "The System of 1896: An Analysis," in *The Evolution of American Electoral Systems*, ed. Paul Keppner (Westport, CT: Greenwood, 1981).

22. Clayton Ellsworth, "Theodore Roosevelt's Country Life Commission." *Agricultural History* 34, no. 4 (October 1960): 155-72, https://www.jstor.org/stable/3741109.

23. E. A. Ross, *Changing America: Studies in Contemporary Society* (Chautauqua, NY: Chautauqua, 1915).

24. Tom Arnold-Forster, "Rethinking the Scopes Trial: Cultural Conflict, Media Spectacle, and Circus Politics," *Journal of American Studies* 56, no. 1 (February 2022), 142–66, https://doi.org/10.1017/S0021875821000529.

25. Edwin Grant Conklin, "Bryan and Evolution," *New York Times*, March 5, 1922, as cited in T. Arnold-Foster, "Rethinking the Scopes Trian: Culture Conflict, Media Spectacle, and Circus Politics, *Journal of American Studies* 56, no. 1 (2022): 142–66.

26. James M. Gregory. *The Southern Diaspora: How the Great Migrations of Black and White Southerners Transformed America* (Chapel Hill: University of North Carolina Press, 2005).

27. Danbom, *Born in the Country*, 131.

28. Michael Swinford, "Urban-Rural Tensions, 1880–1930," in *The Routledge History of Rural America*, ed. Pamela Riney-Kehrberg (New York: Routledge, 2018), 249.

29. Rayford Whittingham Logan, *The Negro in American Life and Thought: The Nadir: 1877–1901* (New York: Dial, 1954).

30. Thomas C. Leonard, *Illiberal Reformers: Race, Eugenics, and American Economics in the Progressive Era* (Princeton, NJ: Princeton University Press, 2017).

31. Florence Sherbon, "Fitter Families for Future Firesides," *Public Historian* 29, no. 3 (2007): 69–85, https://doi.org/10.1525/tph.2007.29.3.69.

32. Linda Gordon, *The Second Coming of the KKK: The Ku Klux Klan of the 1920s and the American Political Tradition* (New York: Liveright, 2018), 60.

33. "Klansville U.S.A.," American Experience, PBS, https://www.pbs.org/wgbh/american experience/films/klansville/.

34. Gordon, *The Second Coming of the KKK*, 170.

35. Gordon, *The Second Coming of the KKK*, 139.

36. Cindy Alexander, "Statistics: Immigration in America, Ku Klux Klan Membership: 1915–1940s," Gilder Lehrman Institute of American History, accessed April 24, 2023, https://www.gilderlehrman.org/history-resources/teacher-resources/statistics -immigration-america-ku-klux-klan-membership-1915.

37. See "Mapping the Second Ku Klux Klan, 1915–1940," Virginia Commonwealth University, VCU Libraries, accessed April 24, 2023, https://labs.library.vcu.edu/klan/.

38. Charles Eagles, *Democracy Delayed: Congressional Reapportionment and the Urban-Rural Conflict of the 1920s*. (Athens: University of Georgia Press, 1990), 3.

39. Hiram Wesley Evans, *North American Review* 223, no. 830 (March–May 1926), 33–66, https://www.jstor.org/stable/25113510.

40. H. L. Mencken, "The Scopes Trial: Bryan," *Baltimore Evening Sun*, July 27, 1925.

41. Charles Eagles, "Urban-Rural Conflict in the 1920s: A Historiographical Assessment," *Historian* 49, no. 1 (1986): 26–48, http://www.jstor.org/stable/24446743.

42. John Dewy, "The American Intellectual Frontier," *New Republic*, May 10, 1922, https://cryptome.org/0001/us-thought.htm.

43. Nicholas F. Jacobs and Sidney M. Milkis, "Extraordinary Isolation? Woodrow Wilson and the Civil Rights Movement," *Studies in American Political Development* 31, no. 2 (2017): 193–217.

44. Eagles, "Urban-Rural Conflict in the 1920s," 28.

45. Ira Katznelson, *When Affirmative Action Was White: An Untold History of Racial Inequality in Twentieth-Century America* (New York: Norton, 2005).

46. David M. Kennedy, *Freedom from Fear: The American People in Depression and War, 1929–1945* (New York: Oxford University Press, 2005), 193.

47. Todd Arrington, "James A. Garfield and 'Rain Follows the Plow,'" National Park Service, U.S. Department of the Interior, April 2013, https://www.nps.gov/articles/000/james-a-garfield-and-rain-follows-the-plow.htm.

48. Ryan Stockwell, *The Family Farm in the Post-World War II Era: Industrialization, the Cold War and Political Symbol* (PhD diss., University of Missouri-Columbia, 2008), https://mospace.umsystem.edu/xmlui/bitstream/handle/10355/7196/research.pdf.

49. Paul M. Sparrow, "FDR and the Dust Bowl," National Archives, Franklin D. Roosevelt Presidential Library & Museum, accessed April 24, 2021, https://fdr.blogs.archives.gov/2018/06/20/fdr-and-the-dust-bowl/.

50. Brandon McBride, "Celebrating the 80th Anniversary of the Rural Electrification Administration" (blog), U.S. Department of Agriculture, February 21, 2017.

51. Franklin D. Roosevelt, "Fireside Chat, September 6, 1936," The American Presidency Project, accessed April 24, 2023, https://www.presidency.ucsb.edu/node/209049.

52. Ira Katznelson, *When Affirmative Action Was White* (New York: Norton, 2005).

53. Wilson J. Warren "Beyond the Rust Belt: The Neglected History of the Rural Midwest's Industrialization After World War II," in *The Rural Midwest Since World War II*, ed. J. L. Anderson (DeKalb: Northern Illinois University Press, 2014), 72–102.

54. Patrick J. Carr and Maria Kefalas, *Hollowing Out the Middle the Rural Brain Drain and What It Means for America* (Boston: Beacon, 2011).

55. Linda Lobao and Katherine Meyer, "The Great Agricultural Transition: Crisis, Change, and Social Consequences of Twentieth-Century U.S. Farming," *Annual Review of Sociology* 27 (2011): 103–24.

56. Kendra Smith Howard, "Ecology, Economy, Labor: The Midwestern Farm Landscape Since 1945," in *The Rural Midwest Since World War II*, ed. J. L. Anderson (DeKalb: Northern Illinois University Press, 2014).

57. Michael Pollan, *The Omnivore's Dilemma: A Natural History of Four Meals* (New York: Penguin, 2006); Tom Philpott, "A Reflection on the Lasting Legacy of 1970s USDA Secretary Earl Butz." Grist, February 8, 2008, https://grist.org/article/the-butz-stops-here/.

58. Nathan A. Rosenberg and Bryce Wilson Stucki, "The Butz Stops Here: Why the Food Movement Needs to Rethink Agricultural History," *Journal of Food Law and Policy* 13, no. 1 (2017): 12–25.

59. Dennis Roth, "The Johnson Administration and the Great Society," Federal Rural Development Policy in the Twentieth Century, United States Department of Agriculture.

60. Ronald Reagan, "A Time for Choosing Speech," October 27, 1964, https://www.reagan library.gov/reagans/ronald-reagan/time-choosing-speech-october-27-1964.

3. MANUFACTURING THE MYTH OF "REAL AMERICA" (1980–PRESENT)

1. Christopher Cadelago, "Barbershop Confrontations, Profane Signs, and Despair: Pro-Biden and Alone in Rural America," *Politico*, March 4, 2022.

2. Michael Sokolove,"Will Trump Win Pennsylvania Again?," *New York Times*, September 10, 2020.

3. Sokolove, "Will Trump Win Pennsylvania Again?"

4. "Joe Biden Won in Pennsylvania, Flipping a State Donald Trump Won in 2016," *Politico*, January 6, 2021.

5. David Byler, "Trump Lost, But He Won Millions of New Voters. Where Did They Come From?," *Washington Post*, January 5, 2021.

6. David A. Hopkins, *Red Fighting Blue: How Geography and Electoral Rules Polarize American Politics* (Cambridge: Cambridge University Press, 2017).

7. Hopkins, *Red Fighting Blue.*

8. Nicholas F. Jacobs and B. Kal Munis, "Place-Based Imagery and Voter Evaluations: Experimental Evidence on the Politics of Place," *Political Research Quarterly* 72, no. 2 (2019): 263–77.

9. See Nicholas F. Jacobs and Sidney M. Milkis, *What Happened to the Vital Center? Presidentialism, Populist Revolt, and the Fracturing of America* (Oxford: Oxford University Press, 2022).

10. Hugh Heclo, "Sixties Civics," in *The Great Society and the High Tide of Liberalism*, ed. Sidney M. Milkis and Jerome M. Mileur (Amherst: University of Massachusetts Press, 2005).

11. Ezra Klein, *Why We're Polarized* (New York: Simon & Schuster, 2020).

12. Patrick J. Buchanan, "America First—and Second, and Third," *National Interest* 19 (Spring 1990): 77–82.

13. Robert D. Novak, *The Prince of Darkness: 50 Years Reporting in Washington* (New York: Three Rivers, 2008), 225.

14. Kevin Phillips, *The Emerging Republican Majority* (Princeton, NJ: Princeton University Press, 2015).

15. Dov Grohsgal and Kevin M. Kruse, "How the Republican Majority Emerged," *The Atlantic*, August 6, 2019.

16. Grohsgal and Kruse, "How the Republican Majority Emerged."

17. David Corn, *American Psychosis: A Historical Investigation of How the Republican Party Went Crazy* (New York: Twelve, 2022), 104.

18. Corn, *American Psychosis*.

19. Grohsgal and Kruse, "How the Republican Majority Emerged."

20. Daniel Bush, "Have Republicans Lost the Suburbs?," *PBS News Hour*, November 1, 2016.

21. Richard Cohen, Charlie Cook, and Michael Barone, *The Almanac of American Politics* (Bethesda, MD: Columbia Books & Information Services, National Journal, 2021).

22. R. Shep Melnick, "From Tax and Spend to Mandate and Sue: Liberalism After the Great Society," in *The Great Society and the High Tide of Liberalism*, ed. Sidney M. Milkis and Jerome M. Mileur (Amherst: University of Massachusetts Press, 2005), 387–410.

23. Sidney M. Milkis and Daniel J. Tichenor, *Rivalry and Reform: Presidents, Social Movements, and the Transformation of American Politics* (Chicago: University of Chicago Press, 2018).

24. Linda Greenhouse and Reva B. Siegel, *Before* Roe v. Wade: *Voices That Shaped the Abortion Debate Before the Supreme Court's Ruling* (New Haven, CT: Yale Law School, 2012).

25. Dave Davies, "'Reaganland' Author Revisits the Roots of American Conservatism," NPR, August 26, 2020.

26. John C. Green, *Religion and the Culture Wars: Dispatches from the Front* (Lanham, MD: Rowman & Littlefield, 1996).

27. Green, *Religion and the Cultural Wars*, 13.

28. Green, *Religion and the Cultural Wars*, 15.

29. Corn, *American Psychosis*, 104.

30. Corn, *American Psychosis*, 134.

31. Barry Sussman, "Grenada Move Earns Reagan Broad Political Gains, Poll Shows," *Washington Post*, November 9, 1983.

32. "CBS News/New York Times Poll: National Survey, January 1989" (Ithaca, NY: Roper Center for Public Opinion Research, Cornell University, 1989), data set, https://ropercenter.cornell.edu/ipoll/study/31091338.

33. "CBS News Poll # 1985-JUNEHIJK1: Flight 847 Hijacking Survey #1," CBS News (Ithaca, NY: Roper Center for Public Opinion Research, Cornell University, 1985), data set, https://ropercenter.cornell.edu/ipoll/study/31090686.

34. Chicago Council on Foreign Relations, "American Public Opinion and U.S. Foreign Policy, 1987: General Public," Gallup Organization (Ithaca, NY: Roper Center for Public Opinion Research, Cornell University, 1986), data set, https://ropercenter.cornell.edu/ipoll/study/31089291.

35. CBS News/New York Times, "National Survey, January 1987" (Ithaca, NY: Roper Center for Public Opinion Research, Cornell University, 1987), data set, https://ropercenter.cornell.edu/ipoll/study/31091260.

36. Steven M. Teles, *The Rise of the Conservative Legal Movement* (Princeton, NJ: Princeton University Press, 2008).

37. Danny Hayes, "Candidate Qualities through a Partisan Lens: A Theory of Trait Ownership," *American Journal of Political Science* 49, no. 4 (2005): 908–23.

38. "A Time for Choosing Speech, October 27, 1964," Ronald Reagan Presidential Library & Museum, https://www.reaganlibrary.gov/reagans/ronald-reagan/time-choosing-speech-october-27-1964.

39. Peniel E. Joseph, "From Ronald Reagan in Philadelphia, Miss., to Donald Trump in Tulsa, a Pattern of Racially Divisive Politics," *Washington Post*, June 20, 2020.

40. We use lowess-smoothing to track public opinion among rural and urban respondents across each year using the General Social Survey (GSS) place of residence variable.

41. David B. Danbom, *Born in the Country: A History of Rural America* (Baltimore, MD: Johns Hopkins University Press, 2017), 238.

42. Danbom, *Born in the Country.*

43. Ross Benes, *Rural Rebellion: How Nebraska Became a Republican Stronghold* (Lawrence: University Press of Kansas, 2021), 10

44. Benes, *Rural Rebellion*, 88.

45. Benes, *Rural Rebellion*, 88.

46. Jonathan Thompson, "The First Sagebrush Rebellion: What Sparked It and How It Ended," *High Country News*, January 14, 2016.

47. David F. Salisbury, "Sagebrush Rebels See Open Range in Reagan's Victory," *Christian Science Monitor*, November 18, 1980.

48. Salisbury, "Sagebrush Rebels See Open Range in Reagan's Victory."

49. Salisbury, "Sagebrush Rebels See Open Range in Reagan's Victory."

50. Morris P. Fiorina, with Samuel J. Abrams and Jeremy C. Pope, *Culture War? The Myth of a Polarized America* (Boston: Longman, 2011).

51. Fiorina, *Culture War?*

52. Quoted in Tim Alberta, "The Ideas Made It, But I Didn't," *Politico*, April 22, 2017, https://www.politico.com/magazine/story/2017/04/22/pat-buchanan-trump-president-history-profile-215042/.

53. Kim Phillips-Fein, "The Long Unraveling of the Republican Party," *The Atlantic*, September 6, 2022.

54. Calum Russell, "'Tongues Untied': Marlon Riggs' Pioneering Documentary," *Far Out*, February 25, 2022.

55. E. J. Dionne Jr., "Buchanan TV Spot Assails Arts Agency," *Washington Post*, February 27, 1992.

56. David Rodgers, "Maverick's Message: Buchanan Campaign Rides into Arizona with a Pledge to Defend Frontier," *Wall Street Journal*, February 23, 1996.

57. David Brooks, "The Modern Conservative," *Wall Street Journal*, February 15, 1996.

58. CBS News/New York Times, "CBS News/New York Times Poll: April National Poll" (Ithaca, NY: Roper Center for Public Opinion Research, Cornell University, 1992), data set, https://ropercenter.cornell.edu/ipoll/study/31091379.

59. NBC News/Wall Street Journal, "NBC News/Wall Street Journal Poll: 1992 Presidential Election and the Economy," Hart-Breglio Research Companies (Ithaca, NY: Roper Center for Public Opinion Research, Cornell University, 1992), data set, https://ropercenter.cornell.edu/ipoll/study/31094734.

60. Hans-Georg Betz, "Icons of Radical Right-Wing Populism: Pat Buchanan, the Political Horse Whisperer" (London: Carr Centre for Analysis of the Radical Right, September 2, 2019).

61. Thomas Frank, *What's the Matter with Kansas? How Conservatives Won the Heart of America* (New York: Metropolitan, 2004), 5–6.

62. Alberta, "The Ideas Made It, But I Didn't."

63. Gerald F. Seib, "Four Groups of Voters May Be Key to Election," *Wall Street Journal*, April 22, 2008.

64. "Peter Hart—2010 Elections and the Mood of America," University of California Television (UCTV), May 28, 2010, https://www.uctv.tv/shows/Peter-Hart-The-Mood-of-America-and-the-2010-Elections-18334.

65. NBC News/Wall Street Journal, "NBC News/WSJ Survey # 6002: Election 2000/ Internet Shopping," Hart-Teeter Research Companies (Ithaca, NY: Roper Center for Public Opinion Research, Cornell University, 1999), data set, https://ropercenter.cornell.edu/ipoll/study/31094794.

66. American National Election Studies, 2000 Times Series Study, https://electionstudies.org/data-center/2000-time-series-study/.

67. Sam Tanenhaus, "When Pat Buchanan Tried to Make America Great Again," *Esquire*, April 5, 2017.

68. See also Eyal Press, "The Voice of Economic Nationalism," *The Atlantic*, July 1998, 96–100, https://www.theatlantic.com/past/docs/issues/98jul/buchanan.htm.

69. William J. Clinton, "Remarks at the Signing Ceremony for the Supplemental Agreements to the North American Free Trade Agreement," September 14, 1993, https://www.presidency.ucsb.edu/documents/remarks-the-signing-ceremony-for-the-supplemental-agreements-the-north-american-free-trade.

70. Kristina Johnson and Samuel Fromartz, "NAFTA's 'Broken Promises': These Farmers Say They Got the Raw End of Trade Deal," *The Salt*, NPR, August 7, 2017.

71. "NAFTA's Legacy: Empty Promises for U.S. Farmers," Citizen.org, https://www.citizen.org/wp-content/uploads/nafta_factsheet_agriculture_may.pdf.

72. Johnson and Fromartz, "NAFTA's 'Broken Promises.'"

73. Jeff Faux, "NAFTA's Impact on U.S. Workers" (blog), Economic Policy Institute, Washington, D.C., December 9, 2013, https://www.epi.org/blog/naftas-impact-workers/.

74. Suzi Parker, "NAFTA's Small-Town Impact," *Christian Science Monitor*, September 9, 1999, https://www.csmonitor.com/1999/0909/p1s2.html.

75. "The Town Maytag Left Behind," CBS News, October 18, 2007, https://www.cbsnews.com/news/the-town-maytag-left-behind/.

76. "The Town Maytag Left Behind."

77. Seth C. McKee, "Rural Voters in Presidential Elections, 1992–2004," *The Forum* 5, no. 2 (2007): 000010220215408884154, https://doi.org/10.2202/1540-8884.1154.

78. "Spotted Owl Became Symbol in 1990s Controversy," *Seattle Times*, April 27, 2007, https://www.seattletimes.com/seattle-news/spotted-owl-became-symbol-in-1990s -controversy/.

79. David Firestone, "A New Voice for Winning Back Lost Democratic Voters," Opinion, *New York Times*, March 9, 2023, https://www.nytimes.com/2023/03/09/opinion/marie -gluesenkamp-perez-democratic-voters.html.

80. Tom Breen, "Bill Clinton Stops in West Virginia," Associated Press, March 6, 2008, http://usatoday30.usatoday.com/news/politics/2008-03-26-3170870511_x.htm.

81. Firestone, "A New Voice for Winning Back Lost Democratic Voters."

82. Nate Silver, "How Obama Really Won the Election," *Esquire*, June 28, 2022.

83. "Where Will Young Voters Impact the 2022 Elections?," CIRCLE (Center for Information & Research on Civic Learning and Engagement), 2022.

84. CBS News/New York Times, "CBS News/New York Times Poll: 2008 Presidential Election/Reverend Jeremiah Wright" (Ithaca, NY: Roper Center for Public Opinion Research, Cornell University, 2008), data set, https://ropercenter.cornell.edu/ipoll /study/31091543.

85. Howard Berkes, "Obama Made Inroads Into Rural Republican Base," NPR, November 8, 2008.

86. Berkes, "Obama Made Inroads into Rural Republican Base."

87. Bill Bishop, "Rural Support for McCain/Palin Grows Stronger," *Daily Yonder*, September 22, 2008.

88. Michael Falcone and Zachary Abrahamson, "Republican Base Still Wild About Sarah Palin," Reuters, September 29, 2009.

89. Ruben Navarrette, "Sarah Palin Understands Small-Town America," CNN, December 24, 2008.

90. Karl Vick and James V Grimaldi, "Palin's Family Always Held a Place in Her Politics," NBC News, September 7, 2008.

91. Katie Couric and Brian Goldsmith, "What Sarah Palin Saw Clearly," *The Atlantic*, October 8, 2018.

92. Frank Rich, "She Broke the G.O.P. and Now She Owns It," *New York Times*, July 11, 2009.

93. Timothy Shenk, "A Lost Manuscript Shows the Fire Barack Obama Couldn't Reveal on the Campaign Trail," *New York Times*, October 7, 2022.

94. Matthew Bigg and Nick Carey, "Protesters Disrupt Town-Hall Healthcare Talks," Reuters, August 8, 2009.

95. Theresa Davidson, "Symbolic Racism or Self-Interest? Comparing Rural and Urban Worries About Obamacare," *Open Journal of Social Sciences* 6, no.6 (June 2018): 210-24.

96. Liz Hamel and Bryan Wu, "The Health Care Views and Experiences of Rural Americans: Findings from the Kaiser Family Foundation/Washington Post Survey of Rural America— Findings," Kaiser Family Foundation, December 3, 2018.

97. "Tea Party Movement: Billionaire Koch Brothers Who Helped It Grow," *The Guardian*, October 13, 2010.

98. Brian Montopoli, "Tea Party Supporters: Who They Are and What They Believe," CBS News, December 14, 2012.

99. Robb Willer, Matthew Feinberg, and Rachel Wetts, "Threats to Racial Status Promote Tea Party Support Among White Americans," *SSRN*, May 4, 2016, http://dx.doi.org /10.2139/ssrn.2770186.

100. "Who Are the Tea Party Activists?," CNN, February 18, 2010.

101. Angie Maxwell, "Tea Party Distinguished by Racial Views and Fear of the Future," Diane D. Blair Center of Southern Politics & Society, University of Arkansas, 2010, https://blaircenter.uark.edu/polling-data-reports/2010-poll/tea-party/.

102. Bill Bishop, "One More Time: Rural Voters Didn't Desert Dems in 2008," *Daily Yonder*, May 31, 2018.

103. "Obama's 2008 Rural Appeal Will Be Put to the Test in November," NBC News, May 2, 2012, https://www.nbcnews.com/news/world/obamas-2008-rural-appeal-will -be-put-test-november-flna749000.

104. David Montgomery, "How the Urban-Rural Divide Shaped the Modern Congress," Bloomberg, November 5, 2018.

105. "Obama's 2008 Rural Appeal Will Be Put to the Test in November."

106. Marc Kovac, "During Ohio Stop, Trump Says He Will Win the State," *Times-Gazette*, October 28, 2016, https://www.times-gazette.com/story/news/2016/10/28/during-ohio-stop -trump-says/19086525007/.

107. Nicholas F. Jacobs and Sidney Milkis, "Our 'Undivided Support': Donald Trump, the Republican Party, and Executive-Centered Partisanship," in *Dynamics of American Democracy: Partisan Polarization, Political Competition, and Government Performance*, ed. Eric Patashnik and Wendy Schiller (Lawrence: University of Kansas Press, 2020).

108. "Transcript of Republican Debate in Miami, Full Text," March 15, 2016, https://www .cnn.com/2016/03/10/politics/republican-debate-transcript-full-text/index.html

109. Erica Etelson, Anthony Flaccavento, and Cody Lonning, "Can Democrats Succeed in Rural Areas? Part 2," Rural Urban Bridge Initiative, November 2022, https:// ruralurbanbridge.org/.

110. Data are calculated from the *New York Times* exit poll, "National Exit Polls: How Different Groups Voted," *New York Times*, November 3, 2020, https://www.nytimes .com/interactive/2020/11/03/us/elections/exit-polls-president.html.

111. Dan Balz, "Democrats Again Lament Their Weakness in Rural Areas, But They Don't Have an Answer to the Problem," *Washington Post*, November 6, 2021.

112. Associated Press, "Farmer Suicide Rate Swells in 1980's, Study Says," *New York Times*, October 14, 1991.

113. David Smith, "'She Paved the Way for Trump': Will Sarah Palin Stay in the Republican Spotlight?," *The Guardian*, February 13, 2022.

114. Patrice Taddonio, "'A Serial Liar': How Sarah Palin Ushered in the 'Post-Truth' Political Era in Which Trump Has Thrived," *PBS*, January 10, 2020.

115. Don Gonyea, "How Sarah Palin Paved the Way for Donald Trump," *NPR*, January 23, 2016.

116. Molly Ball, "How Republicans Lost the Farm," *The Atlantic*, January 7, 2014.

117.   Sarah Vowell, "A Plan B for Responsible Americans Living in Red States," *New York Times*, October 6, 2022.

118.   Thomas Frank, "How the Left Lost Its Heart," *Los Angeles Times*, July 18, 2004.

4. LISTENING TO RURAL AMERICANS

1.   Helmut Norpoth, "The American Voter in 1932: Evidence from a Confidential Survey," *PS: Political Science and Politics* 52, no. 1 (2019): 14–19.

2.   Norpoth, "The American Voter in 1932."

3.   Norpoth, "The American Voter in 1932."

4.   Andrew Gelman, *Red State, Blue State, Rich State, Poor State: Why Americans Vote the Way They Do* (Princeton, NJ: Princeton University Press, 2010).

5.   Jon Huang et al., "Election 2016: Exit Polls," *New York Times*, November 8, 2016.

6.   James G. Gimpel, Nathan Lovin, Bryant Moy, and Andrew Reeves, "The Urban–Rural Gulf in American Political Behavior," *Political Behavior* 42, no. 4 (2020): 1343–68.

7.   Robert Wuthnow, *The Left Behind: Decline and Rage in Small-Town America* (Princeton, NJ: Princeton University Press, 2019).

8.   Andre M. Perry, "A Memo to President-Elect Biden: Don't Coddle White Racial Anxieties" (Washington, D.C.: Brookings Institution, November 12, 2020), https://www.brookings.edu/blog/the-avenue/2020/11/12/a-memo-to-president-elect-biden-dont-coddle-white-racial-anxieties/.

9.   See also Hanna Love and Tracy Hadden Loh, "The 'Rural-Urban Divide' Furthers Myths About Race and Poverty—Concealing Effective Policy Solutions" (Washington, D.C.: Brookings, December 12, 2020), https://www.brookings.edu/blog/the-avenue/2020/12/08/the-rural-urban-divide-furthers-myths-about-race-and-poverty-concealing-effective-policy-solutions/.

10.   Gary King, "Why Context Should Not Count," *Political Geography* 15, no. 2 (1996): 159–64.

11.   Zoe Nemerever and Melissa Rogers, "Measuring the Rural Continuum in Political Science," *Political Analysis* 29, no. 3 (2021): 267–86, https://static1.squarespace.com/static/5d3e05f63e493d0001bd883e/t/60426cf76d71d9513771fd23/1614966008403/Nemerever+Rogers+2021.pdf.

12.   An analysis of respondent ZIP codes further suggests that our average rural respondent lived in a ZIP code that was 60 percent rural. For respondents living in a ZIP code that was majority rural, that number was 55 percent.

13.   James E. Campbell, Helmut Norpoth, Alan I. Abramowitz, Michael S. Lewis-Beck, Charles Tien, James E. Campbell, Robert S. Erikson, et al. "A Recap of the 2016 Election Forecasts," *PS: Political Science & Politics* 50, no. 2 (2017): 331–38, https://doi.org/10.1017/S1049096516002766.

14.   Scott Keeter et al., "Gauging the Impact of Growing Nonresponse on Estimates from a National RDD Telephone Survey," *Public Opinion Quarterly* 70, no. 5 (2006): 759–79, https://doi.org/10.1093/poq/nfl035.

15. Alexander Coppock and Oliver A. McClellan, "Validating the Demographic, Political, Psychological, and Experimental Results Obtained from a New Source of Online Survey Respondents," *Research and Politics* 6, no. 1 (2019), https://doi.org/10.1177/2053168018822174.

5. DOWN AND OUT IN RURAL AMERICA?

1. "Remembering Holden Brothers Farm Market," *Island Life NC*, accessed April 27, 2023, https://islandlifenc.com/holden-brothers-farm-market/.

2. Interview with Holden family members, not for attribution per interviewees' request.

3. Thomas Frank, *What's the Matter with Kansas? How Conservatives Won the Heart of America* (New York: Metropolitan, 2004), 7.

4. Census Tract 204.08, Brunswick County, North Carolina, https://data.ydr.com/census/total-population/total-population-change/census-tract-20408-brunswick-county-north-carolina/140-37019020408/.

5. Michael C. Dawson, *Behind the Mule: Race and Class in African-American Politics* (Princeton, NJ: Princeton University Press, 1994); Gabriel R. Sanchez and Natalie Masuoka, "Brown-Utility Heuristic? The Presence and Contributing Factors of Latino Linked Fate," *Hispanic Journal of Behavioral Sciences* 32, no. 4 (2010): 519–31; and Evelyn M. Simien, "Race, Gender, and Linked Fate," *Journal of Black Studies* 35, no. 5 (2005): 529–50.

6. Claudine Gay, Jennifer Hochschild, and Ariel White, "Americans' Belief in Linked Fate: Does the Measure Capture the Concept?," *Journal of Race, Ethnicity, and Politics* 1, no. 1 (2016): 117–44.

7. Edward Pessen, "Equality and Opportunity in America, 1800–1940," *Wilson Quarterly* (1976–) 1, no. 5 (Autumn 1977): 136.

8. Pessen, "Equality and Opportunity in America, 1800–1940."

9. Jeffrey G. Williamson and Peter Lindert, "Unequal Gains: American Growth and Inequality Since 1700" (VoxEU column, London: Centre for Economic Policy Research, June 16, 2016), https://cepr.org/voxeu/columns/unequal-gains-american-growth-and-inequality-1700.

10. David B. Danbom, *Born in the Country: A History of Rural America (Revisiting Rural America)*, 2nd ed. (JHUP, 2006), 63.

11. Danbom, *Born in the Country*, 73.

12. Danbom, *Born in the Country*, 121.

13. Danbom, *Born in the Country*, 146.

14. Sandy L. Maisel and Mark D. Brewer, *Parties and Elections in America: The Electoral Process*, 6th ed. (Lanham, MD: Rowman & Littlefield, 2011), 89.

15. Ronald Brownstein, "Can Trumpism Last Without Minority Voters?," *The Atlantic*, March 23, 2017.

16. "All Counties with Extreme Poverty in 2018 Were Rural (Nonmetro) Counties" (Washingon, D.C.: U.S. Economic Research Service, Department of Agriculture,

June 16, 2020), https://www.ers.usda.gov/data-products/chart-gallery/gallery/chart
-detail/?chartId=98593.

17.   Shiro Kuriwaki, "Cumulative CCES Common Content, version 7," data set, Harvard
Dataverse, https://doi.org/10.7910/DVN/II2DB6.

18.   William Hawk, "Expenditures of Urban and Rural Households in 2011," *Beyond the
Numbers* 2, no. 5 (2013), https://www.bls.gov/opub/btn/volume-2/expenditures-of-urban
-and-rural-households-in-2011.htm.

19.   Enrico Moretti, *The New Geography of Jobs* (New York: Houghton Mifflin Harcourt,
2012); Will Wilkinson, *The Density Divide: Urbanization, Polarization, and Populist
Backlash* (research paper, Washington, D.C.: Niskanen Center, 2019), https://www
.niskanencenter.org/wp-content/uploads/2019/09/Wilkinson-Density-Divide-Final
.pdf.

20.   "Regional Data: GDP and Personal Income," Bureau of Economic Analysis, https://
apps.bea.gov/itable/?ReqID=70&step=1&acrdn=5#eyJhcHBpZCI6NzAsInNoZXB
zIjpbMSwyNCwyOSwyNVosImRhdGEiOltbIlRhYmxlSWQiLCIiMDEiXS
xbIkNsYXNzaWZpY2FoW9uIiwiTkFJQ1MiXV19.

21.   We would guess that the gap between urban and rural America widens even more
if more granular data existed; neither the census nor the IRS provides geographic
estimates for incomes above $200,000 a year—or roughly three times the median
household income in 2020. For each decennial census, we identified the closest income
bracket reported to the community.

22.   Jennifer Van Allen and Brian Kevin, "Three Charts That Explain Maine's Surging
Real Estate Prices," *Down East*, March 2021, https://downeast.com/issues-politics
/welcome-to-the-wild-wild-world-of-maine-real-estate/.

23.   "Rural Education Levels Are Increasing, But Still Lag Behind Urban Areas," Economic
Research Service, U.S. Department of Agriculture, October 22, 2018, https://www.ers
.usda.gov/data-products/chart-gallery/gallery/chart-detail/?chartId=90366.

24.   Elizabeth A. Dobis et al., "Rural America at a Glance," *Economic Information Bulletin*
no. 230, Economic Research Service, U.S. Department of Agriculture, November 2021,
https://www.ers.usda.gov/webdocs/publications/102576/eib-230.pdf?v=8357.1.

25.   Patrick Gillespie, "Coal Miners Become Computer Coders," *CNN*, April 22, 2016,
https://money.cnn.com/2016/04/22/news/economy/coal-workers-computer-coders
/index.html.

26.   Michael J. White, "The Measurement of Spatial Segregation," *American Journal of
Sociology* 88, no. 5 (March 1983).

27.   The typical urban county in our data set contains 157 census tracts, while the typical
rural county has about 7; suburban counties (between 50.1 and 89.99 percent of the
population lives in an urban block) have, on average, 29 tracts. When adjusting for
population size, though, there are 0.0002 tracts per person in urban areas, whereas
there are 0.0004 tracts per person in rural counties. Although there are fewer tracts,
there are fewer people. Rural communities have more tracts per person, which indicates a more granular portrayal of neighborhoods and is likely to exacerbate the dissimilarity index calculations.

28. Gordon H. Hanson, "Economic and Political Consequences of Trade-Induced Manufacturing Decline," in *Meeting Globalization's Challenges: Policies to Make Trade Work for All*, ed. Luís Catão and Maurice Obstfeld (Princeton, NJ: Princeton University Press, 2019).

29. "Rural Economies Depend on Different Industries." Economic Research Service, U.S. Department of Agriculture, May 29, 2018, https://www.ers.usda.gov/data-products /chart-gallery/gallery/chart-detail/?chartId=89121.

30. "ERS Charts of Note," Economic Research Service, U.S. Department of Agriculture, https://www.ers.usda.gov/data-products/charts-of-note/charts-of-note/?page =5&topicId=2d26875b-d523-4e2c-bf40-5281a376d38d.

31. Katherine Eriksson, Katheryn Russ, Jay C. Shambaugh, and Minfei Xu, "Trade Shocks and the Shifting Landscape of U.S. Manufacturing" (Working Paper 25646, National Bureau of Economic Research, Cambridge, MA, March 2019), https://www.nber.org /papers/w25646. https://www.nber.org/system/files/working_papers/w25646/w25646.pdf.

32. Jess Bidgood, "A Paper Mill Goes Quiet, and the Community It Built Gropes for a Way Forward," *New York Times*, August 2, 2014, https://www.nytimes.com/2014/08/03/us /a-paper-mill-goes-quiet-and-the-community-it-built-gropes-for-a-way-forward .html.

33. Whit Richardson, "How Much Farther Can Millinocket Fall?," *Portland Press Herald*, updated August 21, 2014, https://www.pressherald.com/2014/08/17/how-much-further -can-millinocket-fall/.

34. J. Choi, I. Kuziemko, E. L. Washington, and G. Wright, "Local Economic and Political Effects of Trade Deals: Evidence from NAFTA" (Working Paper 29525, National Bureau of Economic Research, Cambridge, MA, November 29, 2021), https://www.nber.org /papers/w29525.

35. Elena Cristina Mitrea, Monika Mühlböck, and Julia Warmuth, "Extreme Pessimists? Expected Socioeconomic Downward Mobility and the Political Attitudes of Young Adults," *Political Behavior* 43 (2021): 785–811.

36. David Autor et al., "Importing Political Polarization? The Electoral Consequences of Rising Trade Exposure," *American Economic Review* 110, no. 10 (October 2020): 3139-183.

37. B. Kal Munis, "Us Over Here Versus Them Over There . . . Literally: Measuring Place Resentment in American Politics," *Political Behavior* 44 (2022): 1057–78; Munis, "Place, Candidate Roots, and Voter Preferences in an Age of Partisan Polarization: Observational and Experimental Evidence." *Political Geography* 85 (2021): 102345.

38. Nicholas F. Jacobs, "Economic Sectionalism, Executive-Centered Partisanship, and the Politics of the State and Local Tax Deduction," *Political Science Quarterly* 136, no. 2 (2021): 311–38.

39. Davis Autor and Melanie Wasserman, *Wayward Sons: The Emerging Gender Gap in Labor Markets and Education* (Washington, D.C.: Third Way, 2013).

40. Richard V. Reeves and Eleanor Krause, "Why Are Young, Educated Men Working Less?," Brookings Institution, blog, February 23, 2018), https://www.brookings.edu/blog/social -mobility-memos/2018/02/23/why-are-young-educated-men-working-less/.

41. Richard V. Reeves, *Of Boys and Men: Why the Modern Male Is Struggling, Why It Matters, and What to Do About It* (Washington, D.C.: Brookings Institution Press, 2022)

42. Mark Muro, Robert Maxim, and Jacob Whiton, *Automation and Artificial Intelligence: How Machines Are Affecting People and Places* (Washington, D.C.: Brookings Institution, January 24, 2019), https://www.brookings.edu/research/automation-and-artificial-intelligence-how-machines-affect-people-and-places/.

43. *An Examination of the 2016 Electorate, Based on Validated Voters* (Washington, D.C.: Pew Research Center, August 9, 2018), https://www.pewresearch.org/politics/2018/08/09/an-examination-of-the-2016-electorate-based-on-validated-voters/.

44. *An Examination of the 2016 Electorate, Based on Validated Voters.*

45. Ruth Igielnik, Scott Keeter, and Hannah Hartig, *Behind Biden's 2020 Victory* (Washington, D.C.: Pew Research Center, June 30, 2021), https://www.pewresearch.org/politics/2021/06/30/behind-bidens-2020-victory/.

46. Art Cullen, "Want to Know Why Democrats Lose Rural America?," *New York Times*, December 11, 2022.

47. Cullen, "Want to Know Why Democrats Lose Rural America?"

6. A WASTELAND OF ALIENATION?

1. Robert Wuthnow, *The Left Behind: Decline and Rage in Small-Town America* (Princeton, NJ: Princeton University Press, 2019).

2. Benjamin E. Sasse, *Them: Why We Hate Each Other—and How to Heal* (New York: St. Martin's, 2018), 28.

3. See also Cornelia Butler Flora and Jan L. Flora, *Rural Communities: Legacy and Change* (Boulder, CO: Westview, 2012).

4. A. Glendinning, M. Nuttal, L. Hendry, M. Kloeb, and S. Wood, "Rural Communities and Well-Being: A Good Place to Grow Up?," *Sociological Review* 51 (2003), 129–56.

5. Timothy P. Carney, *Alienated America: Why Some Places Thrive While Others Collapse* (New York: Harper, 2020), 12.

6. Carney, *Alienated America*, 13.

7. Carney, *Alienated America*, 288.

8. Carney, *Alienated America*, 95–97.

9. Arthur M. Schlesinger, "Biography of a Nation of Joiners," *American Historical Review* 50, no. 1 (1944): 1, https://doi.org/10.2307/1843565.

10. Schlesinger, "Biography of a Nation of Joiners," 6.

11. Ralph Louis Ketcham, *The Anti-Federalist Papers: The Constitutional Convention Debates* (New York: Signet Classics, 2003), 17.

12. George W. Pierson, *Tocqueville and Beaumont in America* (New York: Oxford University Press, 1938), 4.

13. Pierson, *Tocqueville and Beaumont in America.*

14. Schlesinger, "Biography of a Nation of Joiners," 10.

15. C. S. Fischer, "Changes in Leisure Activities, 1890–1940," *Journal of Social History* 27, no. 3 (1994): 455, https://doi.org/10.1353/jsh/27.3.453.

16. Gerald Gamm and Robert D. Putnam, "The Growth of Voluntary Associations in America, 1840–1940," *Journal of Interdisciplinary History* 29, no. 4 (1999): 533, https://doi.org/10.1162/002219599551804.

17. Gabriel A. Almond and Sidney Verba, *The Civic Culture: Political Attitudes and Democracy in Five Nations* (Princeton, NJ: Princeton University Press, 1963).

18. Nathan Dietz and Robert T. Grimm. Jr., "A Less Charitable Nation: The Decline of Volunteering and Giving in the United States," February 28, 2019, 2, https://cppp.usc.edu/wp-content/uploads/2019/03/Grimm-Robert-Dietz-and-Grimm_A-Less-Charitable-Nation_March-2019-USC-Conference-Paper.pdf.

19. Keon L. Gilbert, Sandra C. Quinn, Robert M. Goodman, James Butler, and John Wallace, "A Meta-Analysis of Social Capital and Health: A Case for Needed Research," *Journal of Health Psychology* 18, no. 11 (2013): 1385–99, https://doi.org/10.1177/1359105311435983.

20. Isabel V. Sawhill, *Social Capital: Why We Need It and How We Can Create More of It* (Washington, D.C.: Brookings Institution, July 2020), https://www.brookings.edu/wp-content/uploads/2020/07/Sawhill_Social-Capital_Final_07.16.2020.pdf.

21. Francis Fukuyama, *Trust: The Social Virtues and the Creation of Prosperity* (New York: Simon & Schuster, 1995).

22. Amy Fried and Douglas B. Harris, *At War with Government: How Conservatives Weaponized Distrust from Goldwater to Trump* (New York: Columbia University Press, 2021).

23. Alexandra Hudson, "*Bowling Alone* at Twenty," *National Affairs* (Fall 2020), https://www.nationalaffairs.com/publications/detail/bowling-alone-at-twenty.

24. Robert Putnam, *Bowling Alone: The Collapse and Revival of American Community* (New York: Simon & Schuster, 2000), 63.

25. Putnam, *Bowling Alone.*, 49.

26. Putnam, *Bowling Alone*, 72.

27. Putnam, *Bowling Alone*, 105.

28. Gallup, "Religion," accessed April 27, 2023, https://news.gallup.com/poll/1690/religion.aspx.

29. "The Space Between: Renewing the American Tradition of Civil Society," U.S. Congress Joint Economic Committee, December 18, 2019, https://www.jec.senate.gov/public/index.cfm/republicans/2019/12/opportunity-rightly-understood-rebuilding-civil-society-with-the-principle-of-subsidiarity.

30. Heidi Shierholz, *The Number of Workers Represented by a Union Held Steady in 2019, While Union Membership Fell* (Economic Policy Institute, Washington, D.C., January 22, 2020), https://www.epi.org/publication/2019-union-membership-data/.

31. Hudson, "*Bowling Alone* at Twenty."

32. Joint Economic Committee, "The Space Between."

33. Dietz and Grimm, "A Less Charitable Nation."

34. Eric Liu, "How Donald Trump Is Reviving American Democracy," *The Atlantic*, March 8, 2017), https://www.theatlantic.com/politics/archive/2017/03/how-donald-trump-is-reviving-our-democracy/518928/.

35. Claudia Deane and John Gramlich, "2020 Election Reveals Two Broad Voting Coalitions Fundamentally at Odds" (Washington, D.C.: Pew Research Center, Novmeber 6, 2020), https://www.pewresearch.org/fact-tank/2020/11/06/2020-election-reveals-two-broad-voting-coalitions-fundamentally-at-odds/.

36. Albert O. Hirschman, *Exit, Voice, and Loyalty: Responses to Decline in Firms, Organizations, and States* (Cambridge, MA: Harvard University Press, 1972).

37. Marc J. Heatherington, "The Political Relevance of Political Trust," *American Political Science Review* 92, no. 4 (1998), https://www.cambridge.org/core/journals/american-political-science-review/article/abs/political-relevance-of-political-trust/01A108C6CBF31F661CB9027497A8D638; Robert J. Boeckmann and Tom R. Tyler, "Trust, Respect, and the Psychology of Political Engagement," *Journal of Approved Social Psychology* 32, no. 10 (2002): 2067–88, https://onlinelibrary.wiley.com/doi/abs/10.1111/j.1559-1816.2002.tb02064.x.

38. Frederick Solt, "Economic Inequality and Democratic Political Engagement," *American Journal of Political Science* 52, no. 1 (2008): 48–60, https://onlinelibrary.wiley.com/doi/full/10.1111/j.1540-5907.2007.00298.x.

39. Steve Peoples, "Some Democrats in Rural Pennsylvania Fear Saying Their Party's Name: 'The Brand Is So Toxic,'" *Penn Live Patriot News*, February 18, 2022, https://www.pennlive.com/politics/2022/02/some-democrats-in-rural-pennsylvania-fear-saying-their-partys-name-the-brand-is-so-toxic.html; see also: Christopher Cadelago, "Barbershop Confrontations, Profane Signs, and Despair: Pro-Biden and Alone in Rural America," *Politico*, March 4, 2022, https://www.politico.com/news/magazine/2022/03/04/pennsylvania-rural-democrats-trump-neighbors-00008915.

40. J. D. Vance, *Hillbilly Elegy: A Memoir of a Family and Culture in Crisis* (New York: Harper, 2016).

41. Ivy Brashear, "Keep Your Elegy: The Appalachia I Know Is Very Much Alive," in *Appalachian Reckoning: A Region Responds to* Hillbilly Elegy, ed. Anthony Harkins and Meredith McCarroll (Morgantown: West Virginia University Press, 2019), 166.

42. Christopher Ingraham, "The Harmful, Popular Misconceptions About Rural America," *Washington Post*, January 3, 2020, https://www.washingtonpost.com/business/2020/01/03/five-myths-about-rural-america/.

43. "The Geography of Social Capital in America," U.S. Congress, Joint Economic Committee, April 11, 2018, https://www.jec.senate.gov/public/index.cfm/republicans/2018/4/the-geography-of-social-capital-in-america#toc-009-backlink.

44. CCES, 2020, https://dataverse.harvard.edu/dataset.xhtml?persistentId=doi%3A10.7910/DVN/E9N6PH.

45. "The Geography of Social Capital in America."

46. Elizabeth Dias and Ruth Graham, "The Growing Religious Fervor in the American Right: 'This Is a Jesus Movement,'" *New York Times*, updated April 11, 2022, https://www.nytimes.com/2022/04/06/us/christian-right-wing-politics.html.

47. Putnam, *Bowling Alone*, 159.

48. Charles Murray, *Coming Apart: The State of White America, 1960-2010* (New York: Crown Forum, 2012), 200.

49. Wuthnow, *The Left Behind*, 139.

50. Carney, *Alienated America*, 136

51. Robert D. Putnam and David E. Campbell, *American Grace: How Religion Divides and Unites Us* (New York: Simon & Schuster, 2012), 444.

52. Glenn C. Daman, "Why the Rural Church Matters," Lifeway Research, May 18, 2018, https://research.lifeway.com/2018/05/18/why-the-rural-church-matters/.

53. Pamela Riney-Kehrberg, *The Routledge History of Rural America* (New York: Routledge, 2018), 3.

54. Ray Waddle, "Faith Futures; An Interview with Mark Chaves," *Reflections* (Fall, 2009), https://reflections.yale.edu/article/how-firm-foundation-churches-face-future/faith-futures-interview-mark-chaves.

55. Tim Reid, "Banks Foreclosing on Churches in Record Numbers," Reuters, March 8, 2012, https://www.reuters.com/article/us-usa-housing-churches/banks-foreclosing-on-churches-in-record-numbers-idUSBRE82803120120309.

56. Reid, "Banks Foreclosing on Churches in Record Numbers."

57. Linda Lyons, "Communities of Faith," Gallup, February 11, 2003, https://news.gallup.com/poll/7756/communities-faith.aspx.

58. Joint Economic Committee, "The Space Between."

59. Paul Krugman, "Wonking Out: Facts, Feelings, and Rural Politics," *New York Times*, October 21, 2022.

60. Sanchir Avirmed, "Four Ways That Neighborhood Schools Strengthen Communities," Chicago Community Trust, August 7, 2017, https://www.cct.org/2017/08/four-ways-that-neighborhood-schools-strengthen-communities/.

61. "Published Data: Closed Schools," Wisconsin Department of Public Instruction, accessed April 27, 2023, https://dpi.wi.gov/cst/data-collections/school-directory/directory-data/published-data.

62. "Arkansas NCES Directory," Arkansas Department of Education Data Center, accessed April 27, 2023, https://adedata.arkansas.gov/nid/Home/School.

63. Craig Howley, "The Rural School Bus Ride in Five States," Rural School and Community Trust, August 20, 2001, https://www.ruraledu.org/user_uploads/file/Rural_School_Bus_Ride.pdf.

64. Aimee Howley and Craig Howley, "Rural School Busing,," ERIC Institute of Education Sciences, December 2001, https://eric.ed.gov/?q=Rural+School+Busing&id=ED459969.

65. Sam Dillon, "In Rural Utah, Students' School Day Stretches to 12 Hours (with 4 on the Bus)," *New York Times*, May 28, 2004, https://www.nytimes.com/2004/05/28/us/in-rural-utah-students-school-day-stretches-to-12-hours-with-4-on-the-bus.html.

66. Dillon, "In Rural Utah, Students' School Day Stretches to 12 Hours."

67. "School Consolidation Failed to Live Up to Its Promises," WVPB (West Virginia Public Broadcasting), November 6, 2015, https://www.wvpublic.org/news/2015-11-06/school-consolidation-failed-to-live-up-to-its-promises.

68. Robert Alley, "Pros & Cons of School Consolidation," *The Classroom*, updated May 17, 2019, https://www.theclassroom.com/pros-cons-school-consolidation-7931065.html.

69. Thomas B. Foster, "Decomposing American Immobility: Compositional and Rate Components of Interstate, Intrastate, and Intracounty Migration and Mobility Decline," *Demographic Research* 37 (2017): 1515-48.

70. We employed a manual, deductive process whereby variables were established in advance and values assigned to different responses. Two researchers would each code every response. When there was full agreement, they moved to the next response. When there was a disagreement, a third researcher was brought into the process to resolve the dispute.

71. More information about genism and LDA analysis can be found here: https://pypi.org /project/gensim/. In short, we used our list of words to generate two probability distributions: A probability distribution over topics for the entire list and a second probability distribution over words for each topic. The first distribution tells us, for the entire list, what proportion of the document belongs to each topic. This is often interpreted as the "topic composition" of the document. We report those percentages in the text. The second distribution tells you, for each topic, what the probability of each word is given that topic. This is often interpreted as the "word composition" of the topic. We manually selected words with high probabilities (>0.8) of appearing in that topic.

72. Vance, *Hillbilly Elegy*, 188.

73. Hannah Getahun, "Trump Acknowledged J. D. Vance's Past Comments Disparaging Him But Has 'Put That Aside,'" *Business Insider*, April 24, 2022.

74. William Vaillancourt, "J. D. Vance Repeatedly Cited Racism as Reason Trump Drew So Much Support in 2016," *Rolling Stone*, April 15, 2022.

75. "Democrats Rural Problems Are About More Than Just White Voters" (video), YouTube, posted by NBC News, May 1, 2022, https://www.youtube.com/watch?v =UH886ygdQUA.

76. "2022 Exit Polls," CNN, https://www.cnn.com/election/2022/exit-polls/ohio/senate/0; "Exit Polls," CNN Politics, https://www.cnn.com/election/2020/exit-polls/president/ohio.

7. CLINGING TO THEIR GUNS AND RELIGION?

1. Nick Brumfield, " 'Country Roads': How John Denver's Hit Became the World's Most Popular Song," *Expatalachians*, March 5, 2019.

2. Sid Smith and Chicago Tribune, " 'Nice' John Denver Has His Activist Side," *South Florida Sun Sentinel*, August 20, 1986, https://www.sun-sentinel.com/1986/08/20 /nice-john-denver-has-his-activist-side/.

3. Kate Daloz "How the Back-to-the-Land Movement Paved the Way for Bernie Sanders," *Rolling Stone*, April 19, 2016.

4. Daloz, "How the Back-to-the-Land Movement Paved the Way."

5. Jacob R. Brown et al., "The Increase in Partisan Segregation in the United States" (draft), Congress Files, January 17, 2022, http://congress-files.s3.amazonaws.com/2022 -07/Brown_Cantoni_Enos_Pons_Sartre%2520%25282022%2529_0.pdf.

6. Jose DelReal and Scott Clement, "Rural Divide," *Washington Post*, June 17, 2017, https://www.washingtonpost.com/graphics/2017/national/rural-america/.

7. Ed Pilkington, "Obama Angers Midwest Voters with Guns and Religion Remark," *The Guardian*, April 14, 2008.

8. Scott Ninneman, "When Bringing a Gun to School Was a Good Thing," Medium, October 18, 2019, https://medium.com/@SpeakingBipolar/when-bringing-a-gun-to-school-was-a-good-thing-50642171a203. Also see Charles C. W. Cooke, "Gun Clubs at School," *National Review*, January 21, 2013, https://www.nationalreview.com/2013/01/gun-clubs-school-charles-c-w-cooke/.

9. German Lopez, "Bernie Sanders's Record on Gun Control, Explained," *Vox*, March 4, 2019.

10. Noah S. Schwartz, "The Pen Is Mightier Than the AR-15," *Daily Yonder*, January 11, 2023.

11. Kim Parker, Juliana Horowitz, Anna Brown, Richard Fry, D'Vera Cohn, and Ruth Igielnik, "What Unites and Divides Urban, Suburban and Rural Communities," Pew Research Center, 2018, https://www.pewresearch.org/social-trends/2018/05/22/what-unites-and-divides-urban-suburban-and-rural-communities/.

12. "Database of Megachurches in the U.S.," Hartford Institute for Religion Research, accessed May 3, 2023, http://hirr.hartsem.edu/megachurch/database.html.

13. Thomas Frank, *What's the Matter with Kansas? How Conservatives Won the Heart of America* (New York: Metropolitan, 2004), 245.

14. Movement Advancement Project, *Where We Call Home: LGBT People in Rural America* (report, Movement Advancement Project, Boulder, CO, April 2019), https://www.lgbtmap.org/policy-and-issue-analysis/rural-lgbt.

15. Ryan Smith, "Women in Black, Veterans Fill Park for Rallies," *Meadville Tribune*, September 4, 2014.

16. Eric B. Hodges, "'Storming the Castle': Examining the Motivations of the Veterans Who Participated in the Capitol Riots," *Journal of Veterans Studies* 7, no. 3 (2021): 46–59.

17. Tim Murphy and Bill Bishop, "Largest Share of Army Recruits Come from Rural/Exurban America," *Daily Yonder*, March 3, 2009.

18. Steven C. Beda, "Analysis: Press Overplays 'Angry Rural Militia' Stories," *Daily Yonder*, October 30, 2018.

19. Jonathan Chait, "Why Liberals Like Compromise and Conservatives Hate It," *New Republic*, March 2, 2011, https://newrepublic.com/article/84630/why-liberals-compromise-and-conservatives-hate-it.

20. *Fewer Are Angry at Government, But Discontent Remains High* (report, Pew Research Center, Washington, D.C., March 3, 2011), https://www.pewresearch.org/politics/2011/03/03/fewer-are-angry-at-government-but-discontent-remains-high/.

21. H. Michael Crowson, Stephen J. Thoma, and Nita Hestevold, "Is Political Conservatism Synonymous with Authoritarianism?," *Journal of Social Psychology* 145, no. 5 (2005): 571–92, https://www.tandfonline.com/doi/abs/10.3200/SOCP.145.5.571-592?journalCode=vsoc20; Karen Stenner, "Authoritarianism and Conservatism: How They Differ and

When It Matters," in *The Authoritarian Dynamic* (Cambridge: Cambridge University Press, 2005), chap. 6.

22. Oscar Winberg, "Insult Politics: Donald Trump, Right-Wing Populism, and Incendiary Language," *European Journal of American Studies* 12, no. 2 (2017), https://journals.openedition.org/ejas/12132.

23. Patrick J. Egan, *Partisan Priorities: How Issue Ownership Drives and Distorts American Politics* (Cambridge: Cambridge University Press, 2013).

24. Arthur Lupia, "Shortcuts Versus Encyclopedias: Information and Voting Behavior in California Insurance Reform Elections," *American Political Science Review* 88, no. 1 (1994): 63–76, https://doi.org/10.2307/2944882.

25. Bruce Stokes, "Republicans, Especially Trump Supporters, See Free Trade Deals as Bad for the U.S." (report, Pew Research Center, Washington, D.C., March 31, 2016), https://www.pewresearch.org/fact-tank/2016/03/31/republicans-especially-trump-supporters-see-free-trade-deals-as-bad-for-u-s/.

26. Nicholas F. Jacobs and Sidney Milkis, "Our 'Undivided Support': Donald Trump, the Republican Party, and Executive-Centered Partisanship," in *Dynamics of American Democracy: Partisan Polarization, Political Competition and Government Performance*, ed. Eric Patashnik and Wendy Schiller (Lawrence: University Press of Kansas, 2020).

27. Oliver Milman, "'It's Got Nasty': The Battle to Build the U.S.'s Biggest Solar Farm," *The Guardian*, October 30, 2022, https://www.theguardian.com/environment/2022/oct/30/its-got-nasty-the-battle-to-build-the-uss-biggest-solar-power-farm.

28. "10 Reasons Industrial-Scale Solar Isn't Right for Agricultural-Rural Areas," Citizens for Responsible Solar, https://www.citizensforresponsiblesolar.org/10-reasons.

29. Annie R. Specht and Tracy Rutherford, "The Pastoral Fantasy on the Silver Screen: The Influence of Film on American Cultural Memory of the Agrarian Landscape," *Journal of Applied Communications* 99, no. 1 (2017).

30. Specht and Rutherford, "The Pastoral Fantasy on the Silver Screen."

31. Carl van Doren, *Contemporary American Novelists (1900–1920)* (New York: Macmillan, 1922; repr. ed., 1971).

32. Rachael Price, "Beyond 'Main Street': Small Towns in Post-'Revolt' American Literature" (Ph.D. diss., University of Arkansas, May 2016), https://scholarworks.uark.edu/cgi/viewcontent.cgi?article=2475&context=etd.

33. Price, "Beyond 'Main Street.'"

34. Price, "Beyond 'Main Street.'"

35. Thomas Halper and Douglas Muzzio, "It's a Wonderful Life: Representations of the Small Town in American Movies," *European Journal of American Studies* 6, no. 1 (2011).

36. Tiffany Brannan, "A Father's Day Treat: The Andy Hardy Film Series," *Epoch Times*, June 12, 2021.

37. Halper and Muzzio, "It's a Wonderful Life."

38. Ted Anthony, "Andy Griffith Evoked, Stylized Small-Town America," *San Diego Union-Tribune*, July 4, 2012.

39. Isabel Machado, "The Sunbelt South, The 1970s Masculinity Crisis, and the Emergence of the Redneck Nightmare Genre," *Study the South*, June 19, 2017.

40. As cited in Bill Ganzel, "Rural America in the Movies," Wessels Living History Farm, 2009, https://livinghistoryfarm.org/farmingin the70s/life_10.html.

41. Anthony Harkins, *Hillbilly: A Cultural History of an American Icon* (Oxford: Oxford University Press, 2004), 206.

42. Gregory Fulkerson and Alexander R. Thomas, eds., *Reimagining Rural: Urbanormative Portrayals of Rural Life* (Lanham, MD: Lexington, 2019), 55.

43. Ariel Miller, "The Construction of Southern Identity Through Reality TV: A Content Analysis of *Here Comes Honey Boo Boo, Duck Dynasty* and *Buckwild*," *Elon Journal of Undergraduate Research in Communications* 4, no. 2 (2013).

44. Miller, "The Construction of Southern Identity Through Reality TV."

45. Jeremy Egner, "'Ozark' on Netflix: This Lake Has Hidden Depths," *New York Times*, July 14, 2017.

46. Janet Dabbs, "'Ozark': Lake Folks Have A Love-Hate Relationship with Netflix Series About Their Hometown," *Lake Expo*, January 14, 2020.

47. Bobbie J. Sawyer, "Why the 1990s Are an Underrated Golden Age in Country Music," *Wide Open Country*, January 17, 2018.

48. Joseph P. Williams, "Behind the Music: Conservatives and Country Music's Complex History," *US News*, April 1, 2015.

49. Jeffrey M. Jones and Joseph Carroll, "Music, Cars, and the 2004 Election," Gallup, November 2, 2004.

50. Charlotta Mellander, Richard Florida, Peter J. Rentfrow, and Jeff Potter, "The Geography of Music Preferences," *Journal of Cultural Economics* 45 (2018): 593–618.

51. Mellander, Florida, Rentfrow, and Potter, "The Geography of Music Preferences." .

52. Michael Hendrix, "Why 2016 Came Down to Whole Foods vs. Cracker Barrel," Medium, November 10, 2016, https://medium.com/@michael_hendrix/why-2016-came-down-to-whole-foods-vs-cracker-barrel-4361cb9b1e5f.

53. Michael Solender, "NASCAR's Push to Broaden Its Appeal," *Business North Carolina*, April 27, 2021.

54. Helena B. Evich, "Revenge of the Rural Voter," *Politico*, November 13, 2016.

55. Quoted in Thomas B. Edsall, "The Resentment Fueling the Republican Party Is Not Coming from the Suburbs," Opinion, *New York Times*, January 25, 2023.

56. dyadmin, "In Reaction to Palin, Remember That 'Geography Matters,'" *Daily Yonder*, September 2, 2008.

57. Tiffany Verbeck, "It's Time to Write More Complex Rural Characters," Writing Cooperative, September 20, 2019.

58. You will find it at Penelope Taynt, "Hillbilly Moment—A Meaty Loaf!," YouTube, November 5, 2015, https://www.youtube.com/watch?v=v8Kojx-nqPc.

59. Jeffrey H. Anderson "Criminal Neglect," *City Journal*, October 4, 2022.

60. Tina Metzer, "Rural Entrepreneurs Turn Stereotypes on Their Head" (Ewing Marion Kauffman Foundation, Kansas City, MO, September 20, 2022), https://www.kauffman.org/currents/rural-entrepreneurs-challenge-stereotypes-ruralrise/.

61. Quoted in Isabel Machado, "The Sunbelt South, the 1970s Masculinity Crisis, and the Emergence of the Redneck Nightmare Genre," *Study the South*, June 19, 2017.

62. Quoted in Thomas B. Edsall, "'Lean into It. Lean into the Culture War,'" *New York Times*, July 14, 2021.

63. James Hibberd, "Holy Duck! A&E's 'Duck Dynasty' Return Shatters Cable Record," *Entertainment Weekly*, August 15, 2013.

64. Dante Chinni, "The Politics of Who Watches 'Duck Dynasty,'" *Wall Street Journal*, December 20, 2013.

65. Chuck Barney, "'Duck Dynasty': Why Is This Show so Popular?," *Mercury News*, March 27, 2013.

66. Barney, "'Duck Dynasty.'"

67. Daniel Luzer, "Duck Decoy," *Washington Monthly*, January 9, 2014.

68. Shannon E. M. O'Sullivan, "Playing 'Redneck': White Masculinity and Working-Class Performance on Duck Dynasty," *Popular Culture* 49, no. 2 (2016): 367–84.

69. Natalie Finn, "Duck Dynasty's Al and Lisa Robertson Memoir Bombshells: Drugs, Infidelity, and an Abortion at 17," *E! News*, January 9, 2015.

70. Luzer, "Duck Decoy."

71. Drew Magary, "What the Duck?," *GQ*, December 17, 2013.

72. Magary, "What the Duck?"

73. Steve Warren, "Phil Robertson on Abortion: 'It's Just Evil,' " CBN News, March 20, 2018, https://www1.cbn.com/cbnnews/entertainment/2018/march/phil-robertson-on-abortion-its-just-evil.

74. Heather Hollingsworth and John Hanna, "Kansas Recount Confirms Results in Favor of Abortion Rights," *AP News*, August 24, 2022.

75. Joe Belden, "A Deeper Look at the Kansas Vote on Abortion Protection," *Daily Yonder*, August 23, 2022.

8. IRREDEEMABLY RACIST?

1. Sean McElwee and Jason McDaniel, "Economic Anxiety Didn't Make People Vote Trump, Racism Did," *The Nation*, May 8, 2017.

2. Nikki McCann Ramirez, "Tennessee Dems Call Out 'Racial Dynamic' That Fueled Expulsion From House," *Rolling Stone*, April 6, 2023, https://www.rollingstone.com/politics/politics-news/tennessee-democrats-call-out-racial-dynamic-house-expulsion-1234711134/.

3. J. D. Tuccille, "Spat Among Tennessee Lawmakers Illustrates a National Urban-Rural Divide," Reason, April 12, 2023, https://reason.com/2023/04/12/spat-among-tennessee-lawmakers-illustrates-a-national-urban-rural-divide/.

4. "Creating More Inclusive Public Spaces: Structural Racism, Confederate Memorials, and Building for the Future," PRRI, September 28, 2022, https://www.prri.org/research/creating-more-inclusive-public-spaces-structural-racism-confederate-memorials-and-building-for-the-future/.

5. David A. Graham, "The United States of Confederate America," *The Atlantic*, October 4, 2022.

6.   Graham, "The United States of Confederate America."

7.   April Simpson, "Why Rural America Is Joining the Movement for Black Lives," Pew Trusts, updated June 12, 2020, https://www.pewtrusts.org/en/research-and-analysis /blogs/stateline/2020/06/12/why-rural-america-is-joining-the-movement-for-black -lives.

8.   Daniel T. Lichter et al., "National Estimates of Racial Segregation in Rural and Small-Town America," *Demography* 44, no. 3 (2007): 563–81.

9.   Katherine J. Cramer, *The Politics of Resentment* (Chicago: University of Chicago Press, 2016), 166.

10.   Matthew D. Nelsen and Christopher D. Petsko, "Race and White Rural Consciousness," *Perspectives on Politics* 19, no. 4 (2021): 1205–18.

11.   Cramer, *The Politics of Resentment*, 166.

12.   Paul M. Sniderman and Edward G. Carmines, *Reaching Beyond Race* (Cambridge, MA: Harvard University Press, 1999).

13.   P. J. Henry and David O. Sears, "The Symbolic Racism 2000 Scale," *Political Psychology* 23, no. 2 (2002): 253–83; Donald R. Kinder and David O. Sears, "Prejudice and Politics: Symbolic Racism Versus Racial Threats to the Good Life," *Journal of Personality and Social Psychology* 40, no. 3 (1981): 414–31.

14.   Donald R. Kinder and Lynn M. Sanders, *Divided by Color: Racial Politics and Democratic Ideals* (Chicago: University of Chicago Press, 1996).

15.   Tyler Monroe and Rob Savillo, "Fox News Has Attacked Black Lives Matter Over 400 Times in a 6-Month Period," Media Matters for America, May 26, 2021, https:// www.mediamatters.org/black-lives-matter/fox-news-has-attacked-black-lives -matter-over-400-times-6-month-period.

16.   "2020 George Floyd/Black Lives Matter Actions Map," Creosote Maps, accessed May 1, 2023, https://www.creosotemaps.com/blm2020/.

17.   Helen Kennedy, "Tea Party Express Leader Mark Williams Kicked Out Over 'Colored People' Letter," *New York Daily News*, July 18, 2010.

18.   Robb Willer, Matthew Feinberg, and Rachel Wetts, "Threats to Racial Status Promote Tea Party Support Among White Americans," *SSRN*, May 4, 2016, http://dx.doi.org /10.2139/ssrn.2770186.

19.   Angie Maxwell, "How Southern Racism Found a Home in the Tea Party," *Vox*, July 7, 2016, https://www.vox.com/2016/7/7/12118872/southern-racism-tea-party-trump.

20.   Christopher S. Parker and Matt A. Barreto, *Change They Can't Believe In: The Tea Party and Reactionary Politics in America* (Princeton, NJ: Princeton University Press, 2013), 8.

21.   Christopher S. Parker and Matt A. Barreto, "The Tea Party and Obamaphobia: Is the Hostility Real or Imagined?," in *Change They Can't Believe In: The Tea Party and Reactionary Politics in America* (Princeton, NJ: Princeton University Press, 2013), chap. 5.

22.   Willer, Feinberg, and Wetts, "Threats to Racial Status Promote Tea Party Support."

23.   Lawrence D. Bobo, "Prejudice as Group Position: Microfoundations of a Sociological Approach to Racism and Race Relations," *Journal of Social Issues* 55, no. 3 (1999): 445–72.

24.   Diana C. Mutz, "Status Threat, Not Economic Hardship, Explains the 2016 Presidential Vote," *PNAS* 115, no. 19 (2018): E4330–E4339, https://doi.org/10.1073/pnas.1718155115.

25.   Theda Skocpol and Vanessa Williamson, *The Tea Party and the Remaking of Republican Conservatism* (Oxford: Oxford University Press, 2016).

26.   Kevin Arceneaux and Stephen P. Nicholson, "Who Wants to Have a Tea Party? The Who, What, and Why of the Tea Party Movement," *PS: Political Science & Politics* 45, no. 4 (2012): 700–710.

27.   Jonathan Chait, "What Is the Tea Party?," *New Republic*, February 23, 2011, https://newrepublic.com/article/84061/what-the-tea-party.

28.   Martin Gilens, *Why Americans Hate Welfare: Race, Media, and the Politics of Antipoverty Policy* (Chicago: University of Chicago Press, 1999).

29.   Tali Mendelberg, *The Race Card: Campaign Strategy, Implicit Messages, and the Norm of Equality* (Princeton, NJ: Princeton University Press, 2001).

30.   Robert Wuthnow, *The Left Behind: Decline and Rage in Small-Town America* (Princeton, NJ: Princeton University Press, 2018), 152.

31.   Kinder and Sanders, *Divided by Color*.

32.   Paul M. Sniderman and Thomas Piazza, *The Scar of Race* (Cambridge, MA: Belknap Press of Harvard University Press, 2004).

33.   David O. Sears, Jim Sidanius, and Lawrence Bobo, *Racialized Politics: The Debate About Racism in America* (Chicago: University of Chicago Press, 2000).

34.   Eduardo Bonilla-Silva, *Racism Without Racists: Color-Blind Racism and the Persistence of Racial Inequality in the United States* (Lanham, MD: Rowman & Littlefield, 2010).

35.   Cindy D. Kam and Camille D. Burge, "Uncovering Reactions to the Racial Resentment Scale Across the Racial Divide," *Journal of Politics* 80, no. 1 (2018): 314–20, https://doi.org/10.1086/693907.

36.   Charles A. Gallagher, "Color-Blind Privilege: The Social and Political Functions of Erasing the Color Line in Post Race America," *Race, Gender & Class* 10, no. 4 (2003): 22–37.

37.   David C. Wilson and Darren W. Davis, "Reexamining Racial Resentment: Conceptualization and Content," *Annals of the American Academy of Political and Social Science* 634, no. 1 (2011): 117–33; Stanley Feldman and Leonie Huddy, "Racial Resentment and White Opposition to Race-Conscious Programs: Principles or Prejudice?," *American Journal of Political Science* 49, no. 1 (2005): 168–83.

38.   David O. Sears, Colette Van Laar, Mary Carrillo, and Rick Kosterman, "Is It Really Racism? The Origins of White Americans' Opposition to Race-Targeted Policies," *Public Opinion Quarterly* 61 (1997): 16–53.

39.   Paul M. Sniderman, Edward G. Carmines, Geoffrey C. Layman, and Michael Carter, "Beyond Race: Social Justice as a Race Neutral Ideal," *American Journal of Political Science* 40, no. 1 (1996): 33–55.

40.   James R. Kluegel and Eliot R. Smith, *Beliefs About Inequality: Americans' Views of What Is and What Ought to Be* (London: Taylor & Francis, 2017).

41.   Christopher M. Federico, "Race, Education, and Individualism Revisited," *Journal of Politics* 68, no. 3 (2006): 600–610; Christopher D. DeSante, "Working Twice as Hard to Get Half as Far: Race, Work Ethic, and America's Deserving Poor," *American Journal of Political Science* 57, no. 2 (2013): 342–56.

42. Herbert McClosky and John R. Zaller, *The American Ethos: Public Attitudes Toward Capitalism and Democracy* (Cambridge, MA: Harvard University Press, 1984); Richard A. Brody and Paul M. Sniderman, "From Life Space to Polling Place: The Relevance of Personal Concerns for Voting Behavior," *British Journal of Political Science* 7, no. 3 (1977): 337–60, https://doi.org/10.1017/s0007123400001022.

43. Kinder and Sanders, *Divided by Color*; McClosky and Zaller, *The American Ethos*.

44. Michaela Keck, "The 'Deep Story' of the White American South, or *Strangers in Their Own Land* (2016) by Arlie Russell Hochschild (Part I)," blog, *American Studies*, May 23, 2018, http://blog.asjournal.org/the-deep-story-of-the-white-american-south-or-strangers-in-their-own-land-2016-by-arlie-russell-hochschild-part-i/; Arlie Russell Hochschild, *Strangers in Their Own Land: Anger and Mourning on the American Right* (New York: New Press, 2016).

45. Timothy P. Carney, *Alienated America: Why Some Places Thrive While Others Collapse* (New York: Harper, 2019), 223.

46. Daniel T. Lichter and Kenneth M. Johnson, "A Demographic Lifeline? Immigration and Hispanic Population Growth in Rural America," *Population Research and Policy Review* 39, no. 5 (2020): 785–803, https://doi.org/10.1007/s11113-020-09605-8.

47. Sarah Melotte, "Parts of Rural America Are Adding Adult Population and Diversity, Census Shows," *Daily Yonder*, February 23, 2022, https://dailyyonder.com/parts-of-rural-america-are-adding-adult-population-and-diversity-census-shows/2022/02/23/.

48. Rogelio Saenz, "A Profile of Latinos in Rural America" (National Fact Sheet no. 10, Carsey Institute, University of New Hampshire, January 23, 2008), https://doi.org/10.34051/p/2020.36.

49. Alan Abramowitz and Jennifer McCoy, "United States: Racial Resentment, Negative Partisanship, and Polarization in Trump's America," *Annals of the American Academy of Political and Social Science* 681, no. 1 (2018): 137–56, https://doi.org/10.1177/0002716218811309.

50. Michael Hout and Christopher Maggio, "Immigration, Race, and Political Polarization," *Daedalus* 150, no. 2 (2021): 40–55, https://doi.org/10.1162/daed_a_01845.

51. Angela X. Ocampo, Sergio I. Garcia-Rios, and Angela E. Gutierrez, "*Háblame de tí*: Latino Mobilization, Group Dynamics, and Issue Prioritization in the 2020 Election," *The Forum: A Journal of Applied Research in Contemporary Politics* 18, no. 4 (2021): 531–58.

52. Barack Obama, "Remarks by the President at a Campaign Event in Roanoke, Virginia," July 13, 2012, https://obamawhitehouse.archives.gov/the-press-office/2012/07/13/remarks-president-campaign-event-roanoke-virginia.

53. Aaron Blake, "Obama's 'You Didn't Build That' Problem," *Washington Post*, July 18, 2012.

54. Andrew Cline, "What 'You Didn't Build That' Really Means—and Why Romney Can't Explain It," *The Atlantic*, August 10, 2012.

55. Callum Borchers, "In Roxbury, Romney Hits Obama's Business Message," *Boston Globe*, July 20, 2012.

56. Cline, "What 'You Didn't Build That' Really Means."

57. Perry Chiaramonte, "'You Didn't Build That': Small Biz Owners on the Brink Seethe Over Obama's Comments," *Fox News*, November 30, 2015, https://www.foxnews.com/us/you-didnt-build-that-small-biz-owners-on-the-brink-seethe-over-obamas-comments.

58. David Brooks, "The Party of Work," Opinion, *New York Times*, November 9, 2012, https://www.nytimes.com/2012/11/09/opinion/brooks-the-party-of-work.html.

59. Charles Abbott, "Obama, McCain Neck-and-neck for Rural Vote: Poll," *Reuters*, October 23, 2008.

60. Chloe Maxmin and Canyon Woodward, *Dirt Road Revival: How to Rebuild Rural Politics and Why Our Future Depends on It* (Boston: Beacon, 2022).

9. RADICALIZED BY FOX?

1. Morgan Lee, "New Mexico Prosecutor Says Republican-Led County Commission Must Certify Vote," updated June 16, 2022, https://www.abqjournal.com/2509028/new-mexico-prosecutor-says-gop-county-must-certify-vote.html.

2. Gino Spocchia, "Trump Shares Video of Cowboy Activist Saying 'The Only Good Democrat Is a Dead Democrat,'" *Independent* (UK), May 28, 2020.

3. Annie Gowen, "New Mexico County Certifies Election Results, Bowing to Court Order," *Washington Post*, June 17, 2022.

4. Susan Montoya Bryan and Morgan Lee, "Conspiracy Theories Fuel Anger as New Mexico Counties Try to Certify 2022 Primary Vote," *PBS*, June 17, 2022, https://www.pbs.org/newshour/politics/conspiracy-theories-fuel-anger-as-new-mexico-counties-try-to-certify-2022-primary-vote.

5. Gowen, "New Mexico County Certifies Election Results."

6. Bryan and Lee, "Conspiracy Theories Fuel Anger."

7. Bryan and Lee, "Conspiracy Theories Fuel Anger."

8. "Do You Live in a News Desert?," UNC Hussman School of Journalism and Media, https://www.usnewsdeserts.com/#viz1626105082044.

9. David Ardia et al., "Addressing the Decline of Local News, Rise of Platforms, and Spread of Mis- and Disinformation Online" (report, Center for Information, Technology, and Public Life, University of North Carolina at Chapel Hill, accessed May 4, 2023), https://citap.unc.edu/local-news-platforms-mis-disinformation.

10. Nicholas Lemann, "Margaret Sullivan on the Epidemic of News Deserts and Ghost Papers," Literary Hub, August 17, 2020, https://lithub.com/margaret-sullivan-on-the-epidemic-of-news-deserts-and-ghost-papers/.

11. Danny Hayes and Jennifer L. Lawless, *News Hole: The Demise of Local Journalism and Political Engagement* (Cambridge: Cambridge University Press, 2021), 20.

12. Hayes and Lawless, *News Hole*, 21.

13. Dan Pfeiffer, *Battling the Big Lie: How Fox, Facebook, and the MAGA Media Are Destroying America* (New York: Twelve, 2022), 136.

14. Penelope Muse Abernathy, "The Loss of Newspapers and Readers," in *The Expanding News Desert* (report, UNC Hussman School of Journalism and Media, 2018), https://www.usnewsdeserts.com/reports/expanding-news-desert/loss-of-local-news/loss-newspapers-readers/.

15. Katherine J. Cramer, *The Politics of Resentment: Rural Consciousness in Wisconsin and the Rise of Scott Walker* (Chicago: University of Chicago Press, 2016), 108.

16. Penny Abernathy, "The State of Local News 2022," Northwestern Local News Initiative, June 29, 2022, https://localnewsinitiative.northwestern.edu/research/state-of-local-news/report/.

17. Hayes and Lawless, *News Hole*, 39.

18. Pfeiffer, *Battling the Big Lie*, 141–142.

19. Lydia Saad, "Political News Receiving Heightened Public Attention," Gallup, November 16, 2021.

20. David Trilling, "How the Media's Coverage of Political Polarization Affects Voter Attitudes," Journalist's Resource, August 9, 2016, https://journalistsresource.org/politics-and-government/medias-coverage-political-polarization-affects-voter-attitudes/.

21. Jane Reuter, "A Brief History of Internet Service Providers," Viasat, August 13, 2019, https://news.viasat.com/blog/satellite-internet/a-brief-history-of-internet-service-providers.

22. Reuter, "A Brief History of Internet Service Providers."

23. Tom Wheeler, "Closing the Digital Divide in Rural America" (blog), U.S. Federal Communications Commission, November 20, 2014, https://www.fcc.gov/news-events/blog/2014/11/20/closing-digital-divide-rural-america.

24. Wheeler, "Closing the Digital Divide in Rural America."

25. John Busby, Julia Tanberk, and Tyler Cooper, *BroadbandNow Estimates Availability for All 50 States; Confirms That More than 42 Million Americans Do Not Have Access to Broadband* (report, BroadbandNow, Los Angeles, May 5, 2021).

26. "Biden-Harris Administration Announces $401 Million for High-Speed Internet Access in Rural Areas," news release, Rural Development, U.S. Department of Agriculture, July 28, 2022, https://www.rd.usda.gov/newsroom/news-release/biden-harris-administration-announces-401-million-high-speed-Internet-access-rural-areas.

27. Paul M. Barrett, Justin Hendrix, and J. Grant Sims, *Fueling the Fire: How Social Media Intensifies U.S. Political Polarization—and What Can Be Done About It?* (New York: Stern Center for Business and Human Rights, New York University, 2021).

28. Michael Rea, "Letter to the Editor: Rural Broadband Opens Floodgates to Conspiracy Theories," *Winchester Star*, May 16, 2022.

29. H. J. Mai, "Wisconsin's Midterm Results Could Determine Which Party Controls the U.S. Senate," NPR Morning Edition, November 7, 2022, https://www.npr.org/2022/11/07/1134513913/wisconsins-midterm-results-could-determine-which-party-controls-the-u-s-senate.

30. Matt Taibbi, *Hate Inc.: Why Today's Media Makes Us Despise One Another* (New York: OR Books, 2019), 40.

31. Kal Munis and Nicholas Jacobs, "Why Resentful Rural Americans Vote Republican," *Washington Post*, October 20, 2022.

32. Zella Hanson, " 'News for the Rich, White, and Blue': Nikki Usher on Her New Book and the State of American Journalism," *Duke Research Blog*, November 23, 2021.

33. Yanna Krupnikov and John Barry Ryan, *The Other Divide: Polarization and Disengagement in American Politics* (Cambridge: Cambridge University Press, 2022), 226.

34. Colleen McClain, "70 percent of U.S. Social Media Users Never or Rarely Post or Share About Political, Social Issues" (Pew Research Center, Washington, D.C., May 4, 2021), https://www.pewresearch.org/fact-tank/2021/05/04/70-of-u-s-social-media-users-never-or-rarely-post-or-share-about-political-social-issues/.

35. Ashley Kirzinger, Cailey Muñana, and Mollyann Brodie, "Vaccine Hesitancy in Rural America," KFF, January 7, 2021, https://www.kff.org/coronavirus-covid-19/poll-finding/vaccine-hesitancy-in-rural-america/.

36. Jan Hoffman and Erin Schaff, "Faith, Freedom, Fear: Rural America's Covid Vaccine Skeptics," *New York Times*, April 30, 2021.

37. Elaine Godfrey, "The Rural Pandemic Isn't Ending," *The Atlantic*, April 14, 2021.

38. Monica Potts, "Why Being Anti-Science Is Now Part of Many Rural Americans' Identity," FiveThirtyEight, April 25, 2022.

39. Tim Marema, "By the Numbers: Capitol Arrestees and Rural America," *Daily Yonder*, February 3, 2021.

40. Charely Locke, "How the $4 Trillion Flood of Covid Relief Is Funding the Future," *New York Times*, November 24, 2021.

41. Casey Parks, "The Tragedy of America's Rural Schools," *New York Times*, September 9, 2021.

42. Nicholas Casey, "For a City Already in a 'Death Spiral,' What's After Lockdown?," *New York Times*, May 13, 2020.

43. John G. Bullock, Alan S. Gerber, Seth J. Hill, and Gregory A. Huber, "Partisan Bias in Factual Beliefs About Politics," *Quarterly Journal of Political Science* 10, no. 4 (2015): 519–78; Markus Prior, Gaurav Sood, and Kabir Khanna, "You Cannot Be Serious: The Impact of Accuracy Incentives on Partisan Bias in Reports of Economic Perceptions," *Quarterly Journal of Political Science* 10, no. 4 (2015): 489–518.

44. Francis Fukuyama, *Trust: The Social Virtues and the Creation of Prosperity* (New York: Simon & Schuster, 1995).

45. Krupnikov and Ryan, *The Other Divide*, 54.

46. Krupnikov and Ryan, *The Other Divide*, 57.

47. Joshua A. Tucker et al., "From Liberation to Turmoil: Social Media and Democracy," *Journal of Democracy* 28, no. 4 (October 2017): 46–59.

48. Dan Hopkins, "All Politics Is National Because All Media Is National," FiveThirtyEight, June 6, 2018.

49. Nicholas Kristof, "The Daily Me," Opinion, *New York Times*, March 18, 2009.

50. Laila Lalami, "Does American 'Tribalism' End in a Compromise, or a Fight?," *New York Times*, June 26, 2018.

51.   Robert D. Putnam, *Bowling Alone: The Collapse and Revival of American Community* (New York: Simon & Schuster, 2000), 180.

52.   Putnam, *Bowling Alone*, 178.

10. PULLING IT ALL TOGETHER: FINDING THE RURAL VOTER

1.   Ariel Malka and Mark Adelman, "Expressive Survey Responding: A Closer Look at the Evidence and Its Implications for American Democracy," *Perspectives on Politics* (2022), 1–12, https://doi.org/10.1017/S1537592721004096.

2.   Nicholas F. Jacobs and B. Kal Munis, "Place-Based Resentment in Contemporary U.S. Elections: The Individual Sources of America's Urban-Rural Divide," *Political Research Quarterly* (September 7, 2022), https://doi.org/10.1177/10659129221124864

3.   Jacobs and Munis, "Place-Based Resentment."

11. BRIDGES ACROSS THE RURAL-URBAN DIVIDE

1.   Jane Jacobs, *The Death and Life of Great American Cities* (New York: Random House, 1961), 238.

2.   Nancy Krieger, Christian Testa, Jarvis T. Chen, William P. Hanage, and Alecia J. McGregor, "Relationship of Political Ideology of US Federal and State Elected Officials and Key COVID Pandemic Outcomes Following Vaccine Rollout to Adults: April 2021–March 2022," *The Lancet Regional Health: Americas* 16 (2022), https://doi.org/10.1016/j.lana.2022.100384.

3.   Lydia Saad, "Country Living Enjoys Renewed Appeal in U.S.," Gallup, January 5, 2021, https://news.gallup.com/poll/328268/country-living-enjoys-renewed-appeal.aspx.

4.   Wendell Berry, *The Art of the Commonplace: The Agrarian Essays* (Berkeley: Counterpoint, 2002).

5.   Bill Bishop, "Speak Your Piece: What's with This Dismissal of Rural America?," *Daily Yonder*, December 18, 2008, https://dailyyonder.com/speak-your-piece-whats-dismissal-rural-america/2008/12/18/.

6.   Michelle Goldberg, "Tyranny of the Minority," Opinion, *New York Times*, September 25, 2017, https://www.nytimes.com/2017/09/25/opinion/trump-electoral-college-minority.html.

7.   Sidney M. Milkis, *Political Parties and Constitutional Government: Remaking American Democracy* (Baltimore: Johns Hopkins University Press, 1999).

8.   "From John Adams to Jonathan Jackson, 2 October 1780," National Archives, Founders Online, https://founders.archives.gov/documents/Adams/06-10-02-0113.

9.   E. E. Schattschneider, *Party Government* (New York: Holt, Reinhart, and Winston, 1942), 33.

10. V. O. Key Jr., *Southern Politics in State and Nation* (Knoxville: University of Tennessee Press, 1984).

11. Richard Hofstadter, "Southern Politics, by V. O. Key Jr.," *Commentary*, April 1950, https://www.commentary.org/articles/richard-hofstadter/southern-politics-by-v-o-key-jr/.

12. Hofstadter, "Southern Politics, by V. O. Key Jr."

13. Hofstadter, "Southern Politics, by V. O. Key Jr."

14. John H. Aldrich, "Southern Parties in the State and Nation," *Journal of Politics* 3 (August 2000): 643–70.

15. "Roads," Huey Long: The Man, His Mission, and His Legacy, accessed May 6, 2023, https://www.hueylong.com/programs/roads.php.

16. Congressional Roll-Call Votes Database, Voteview, https://voteview.com/search/Congressional%20Roll-Call%20Votes%20Database/.

17. Jonathan Rodden, *Why Cities Lose: The Deep Roots of the Urban-Rural Political Divide* (New York: Basic Books, 2019).

18. Les Power, "Fox News' Obsession with Critical Race Theory, by the Numbers," Media Matters for America, June 15, 2021, https://www.mediamatters.org/fox-news/fox-news-obsession-critical-race-theory-numbers.

19. Stephen Neukam, "Marjorie Taylor Green Calls Again for 'a National Divorce,'" *The Hill*, February 20, 2023, https://thehill.com/homenews/house/3866590-marjorie-taylor-greene-calls-again-for-a-national-divorce/.

20. Alesha Doan, "Kansas' Vote to Maintain Abortion Access Shows the State Is Less Red Than Many Think," *USAPP–United States Politics and Policy* (blog), London School of Economics, September 8, 2022, https://blogs.lse.ac.uk/usappblog/2022/09/08/kansas-vote-to-maintain-abortion-access-shows-the-state-is-less-red-than-many-think/.

21. Docking Institute of Public Affairs, "Kansas Speaks: Fall 2021 Statewide Public Opinion Survey," February 2022, https://www.fhsu.edu/docking/Kansas-Speaks/2021-kansas-speaks-report-final_1.pdf.

22. Docking Institute of Public Affairs, "Kansas Speaks."

23. Mary Anne Glendon, *Rights Talk: The Impoverishment of Political Discourse* (New York: Free Press, 1991).

24. Adam Liptak, "Tea-ing Up the Constitution," *New York Times*, March 13, 2010, https://www.nytimes.com/2010/03/14/weekinreview/14liptak.html.

25. Tony Webster, "The Risky Shift Phenomenon: What Is It, Why Does It Occur and What Are the Implications for Outdoor Recreationists?," *Avalanche Journal Blog*, Canadian Avalanche Association, Winter 2005, https://www.avalancheassociation.ca/blogpost/1815963/354569/The-Risky-Shift-Phenomenon-What-Is-It-Why-Does-It-Occur-and-What-are-the-Implications-for-Outdoor-Recreationists.

26. Hofstadter, "Southern Politics, by V. O. Key Jr."

27. Frank Rich, "No Sympathy for the Hillbilly," Intelligencer, *New York* magazine, March 20, 2017, https://nymag.com/intelligencer/2017/03/frank-rich-no-sympathy-for-the-hillbilly.html.

28. Using an AI search engine, we used JSTOR data and found some 237 colleges or universities that offer areas of study in urban politics, but just 169 that offer the same for rural politics.

29. Lane Wendell Fischer, "Q&A: How to Support Rural Students Pursuing Higher Education," *Daily Yonder*, July 22, 2022, https://dailyyonder.com/qa-how-to-support -rural-students-pursuing-higher-education/2022/07/22/.

30. National Center for Education Statistics, "2.7. College Enrollment Rates," *Status of Education in Rural America*, June 2007, https://nces.ed.gov/pubs2007/ruraled/chapter2_7.asp.

31. Anne Dennon, "College Attendance Among Rural Students Takes a Dive," blog, *Best Colleges.com*, updated November 10, 2021, https://www.bestcolleges.com/blog /rural-students-college-enrollment-decline/.

32. Matthew Levendusky and Neil Malhotra, "Does Media Coverage of Partisan Polarization Affect Political Attitudes?," *Political Communication* 33, no. 2 (2015).

33. Nick Bowlin, "Joke's on Them: How Democrats Gave Up on Rural America," *The Guardian*, February 22, 2022, https://www.theguardian.com/us-news/2022/feb/22 /us-politics-rural-america.

34. Paul Waldman, "We've Been Told a Lie About Rural America," Opinion, *Washington Post*, October 28, 2022, https://www.washingtonpost.com/opinions/2022/10/28/lie-rural -americans-broadband-democrats/.

35. Jennifer Bradley and Bruce Katz, "Village Idiocy," *New Republic*, October 7, 2008, https://newrepublic.com/article/61563/village-idiocy.

36. Paul Krugman, "Working Out: Facts, Feelings, and Rural Politics," Opinion, *New York Times*, October 21, 2022, https://www.nytimes.com/2022/10/21/opinion/rural-america -politics.html.

37. Paul Krugman, "Can Anything Be Done to Assuage Rural Rage?," Opinion, *New York Times*, January 26, 2023, https://www.nytimes.com/2023/01/26/opinion/rural-voters -economy.html.

38. Claire Carlson, "What the *New York Times* Got Wrong About 'Rural Rage,'" *Daily Yonder*, February 2, 2023, https://dailyyonder.com/what-the-new-york-times-got -wrong-rural-rage/2023/02/02/.

39. Bowlin, "Joke's on Them."

40. Chris McGreal, "Democrat Tim Ryan Is Running Against His Own Party—It Could Help Him Win," *The Guardian*, November 7, 2022, https://www.theguardian.com /us-news/2022/nov/07/tim-ryan-ohio-senate-midterms-jd-vance.

41. McGreal, "Democrat Tim Ryan Is Running Against His Own Party."

42. David Firestone, "A New Voice for Winning Back Lost Democratic Voters," Opinion, *New York Times*, March 9, 2023, https://www.nytimes.com/2023/03/09/opinion/marie -gluesenkamp-perez-democratic-voters.html.

43. "Kent Is *Clearly Favored* to Win Washington's 3rd District," updated November 8, 2022, FiveThirtyEight 2022, https://projects.fivethirtyeight.com/2022-election-forecast/house /washington/3/.

44. Jim Brunner and David Gutman, "Democrat Marie Gluesenkamp Perez Defeats Republican Joe Kent in WA House Race," *Seattle Times*, updated November 14, 2022,

https://www.seattletimes.com/seattle-news/politics/democrat-marie-gluesenkamp
-perez-defeats-republican-joe-kent-in-wa-house-race/.

45. Firestone, "A New Voice for Winning Back Lost Democratic Voters."

46. Firestone, "A New Voice for Winning Back Lost Democratic Voters."

47. Robert Leonard, "Biden Has Already Done More for Rural America Than Trump Ever
Did," Opinion, *New York Times*, April 26, 2022, https://www.nytimes.com/2022/04/26
/opinion/biden-trump-democrats-rural-america.html.

48. Tony Pipa, "A Policy Renaissance Is Needed for Rural America to Thrive," Opinion,
New York Times, December 27, 2022, https://www.nytimes.com/2022/12/27/opinion
/rural-america-left-behind-places.html.

49. Ian Haney-Lopez, "The Racism at the Heart of the Reagan Presidency," *Salon*,
January 11, 2014, https://www.salon.com/2014/01/11/the_racism_at_the_heart_of_the
_reagan_presidency/.

50. Amanda Abrams, "How Outreach and Deep Canvassing Can Change Rural Politics,"
Yes! (magazine), November 22, 2021, https://www.yesmagazine.org/democracy/2021
/11/22/rural-politics-voters-outreach-canvassing.

51. Aaron Ross Coleman, "How Black People Really Feel About the Police, Explained,"
Vox, June 17, 2020, https://www.vox.com/2020/6/17/21292046/black-people-abolish
-defund-dismantle-police-george-floyd-breonna-taylor-black-lives-matter-protest.

52. Akilah Johnson, "Can Politics Kill You? Research Says the Answer Increasingly Is Yes,"
Washington Post, December 16, 2022, https://www.washingtonpost.com/health/2022
/12/16/politics-health-relationship/.

INDEX

Page numbers in *italics* represent figures or tables.

Abernathy, Penelope Muse, 328, 330
abortion, 102–3, 120, 259, 286, 391
ACA. *See* Affordable Care Act
ACLU. *See* American Civil Liberties Union
Adams, John, 386
A&E, 284–85
affective partisanship, 337
affirmative action, 102
Affordable Care Act (ACA), 126–27, 170, 299
Agnew, Spiro, 100
agrarian values, 73
agricultural consolidation, 88
agricultural economy: globalization and, 69; government measures controlling, 75; Jefferson and, 63; NAFTA and, 118; in post-Revolutionary War era, 61–62; specialization in, 87; trade politics and, 167
agricultural extension schools, 69
agricultural subsidies, 109
agricultural transition, 86–89
alcoholism, 271
Aldrich, John, 388
Alger, Horatio, 165

Alienated America (Carney), 204
alienation, 204, 235
Almanac of American Politics, The, 101
Almond, Gabriel, 207
Amanda Show, The (television show), 279
American Civil Liberties Union (ACLU), 74, 219
American Community Survey (2018), 156, 171, 183
American Conservative Union, 104
American exceptionalism, 362
American Farm Bureau Federation, 139
American Grace (Putnam and Campbell), 227
"American Intellectual Frontier, The" (Dewey), 80
American Loggers (television show), 275
American National Election Studies (ANES), 150, 289
American Nurses Association, 214
America Online (AOL), 335
Andy Griffith Show, The (television show), 273
Andy Hardy series, 272

ANES. *See* American National Election Studies

Anglo-Saxon supremacy movement, 76

Annals of the American Academy of Political and Social Science (journal), 303

anti-abortion policy, 391

anticosmopolitanism, 312–14, *313*, 320, 367, 378

antidemocracy, 65

anxiety, 163, 188–95; economic, 188, 190–94, *191*, 247, 318, 375; gender and perceptions of sources of, 197; place-based, *191*, 191–92, 194, *195*, 362, 366, 369; shared, 318

AOL. *See* America Online

Appalachian Reckoning (Brashear), 222

Apprentice, The (television show), 278

Arceneaux, Kevin, 300

Arnow, Pat, 274

ascriptivism, 288

Aspen Institute, 219

associational life, 212–13

Atlantic (magazine), 125, 167, 219; COVID-19 coverage, 343

authoritarianism, 267

Ax Men (television show), 275

back-to-the-land movement, 245

Bad Day at Black Rock (film), 272

Bakker, Jim, 104

balance of payments, 53–54, *54*, 398–99

Baltimore Evening Sun (newspaper), 79

Barreto, Matt, 299

Barrett, Bob, 312

bathroom bills, 259

Bauman, Samantha, 123

Bayer, Dan, 410–11

Bayh, Birch, 111

Benes, Ross, 109–10

Berry, Wendell, 383

Beverly Hillbillies, The (television show), 273, 286

Biden, Joe, 6–7, 9, 19, 131–33, 369–71, 401–3; "feeling thermometer" questions and, 210–12, *211*; Iowa and, 199; Palin debate with, 125; Pennsylvania and, 93–94; political engagement and, 219, 221; Rural Voter Model and, *370*; State of the Union address, 11; West Virginia and, 129

Big Sort, The (Bishop), 46

Bipartisan Infrastructure Law (2022), 336

Birth of a Nation (film), 76

birthright citizenship, 310, *311*

Bishop, Bill, 46, 383

Black Americans, 294–96, 298, 302, 378, 410; demographic shifts and, 300; Great Migration by, 74; hard work and perceptions of, 305–8; Juneteenth and, 288; polls and, 411; in rural electorate, 317–18; rural population changes and, 24; vaccine hesitancy and, 344

Black Lives Matter, 297

Blair Center for Southern Politics, 128

Blair Witch Project, The (film), 275

BLM. *See* Bureau of Land Management

Blob, The (film), 275

blocks (census), 34–37, 41; U.S. House districts and, 133–34

blue-collar jobs, 308–9; gender differences in, 196; losses in, 177, *178*, 179

Blue Wave of 2018, 6

Born in the Country (Danbom), 166

Boston Brahmins, 62

Bowlin, Nick, 397

Bowling Alone (Putnam), 212, 227

Bradley, Jennifer, 29

Brashear, Ivy, 222

Breckinridge, John C., 45

broadband, 335, 352, 398

Brooks, David, 115, 321

Brooks, Garth, 277

Brown, Sherrod, 243

Brownback, Sam, 391

Brownstein, Ron, 167

Brown v. Board of Education, 101, 103–4

Brunswick County, North Carolina, 159

Bryan, William Jennings, 71–72, 74, 79, 115

Buchanan, Pat, 98, 112–17, 120, 138
Buckwild (television show), 275
Bureau of Economic Analysis, 171
Bureau of Land Management (BLM), 110–11
Burge, Camille, 302
Burns, Ken, 277
Bush, George H. W., 112–14
Bush, George W., 116–17, 121, 123, 277
Buzzfeed, 342
Byler, David, 94

cable television, 356
Campbell, David, 227
Capra, Frank, 272
Carlson, Claire, 399–400
Carlson, Tucker, 9, 404
Carney, Timothy, 204, 222, 312
Carter, Jimmy, 7, 46, 89, 94, 103, 105, 122
Carvel, James, 93
Casey, Nicholas, 346
CBS/*New York Times* polls, 123
CCES. *See* Cooperative Congressional Election Study
census blocks, 34–37, 41; U.S. House districts and, 133–34
Census Bureau, 37, 159, 183, 419n22; relationship files, 133. *See also* American Community Survey
census tracts, 36, 183, 432n28
Chait, Jonathan, 301
Change They Can't Believe In (Parker and Barreto), 299
charitable contributions, 214
Chaves, Mark, 228
Chen, Jowei, 49
Chesney, Kenny, 278
Chicks, the, 277
child poverty, 184
Child Protective Services, 259
China, 268; manufacturing and, 130, 186–87; Trump and, 130
China shock, 186–88
Christian evangelicalism, 258

Christian fundamentalism, 76, 80
Christianity, 256–60; country music and, 278
Christian nationalism, 227
Christian right, 103–4
Church, Frank, 111
church attendance, 256–57
churches, 227–29
CINT, 156
cities, 28; Hamilton and, 64; Jefferson and, 63
Civic Culture (Almond and Verba), 207
civic culture, participant, 207–8
civic decline thesis, 216–18
civic disengagement, 358
civic engagement, 205, 219, 378; rural areas and, 225–26; trust and, 208
civic idealism, 28
civic life, 205
civic pride, 194, 247, 319–20, 366, 368
Civilian Conservation Corps, 83
civil rights, 91, 96
Civil Rights Act (1964), 100, 409
civil society, 204
Civil War, 67–69, 165–66, 207, 386
class, political behavior and, 167
Clean Air Act, 102
Clean Water Act, 102
Cleveland, Grover, 71
climate change, 352
Cline, Andrew, 321
Clinton, Bill, 117–22, 130
Clinton, Hillary, 6, 29, 121, 154, 250, 322, 384–85; ecological fallacy and, 144–47; economy and, 10, 144; Iowa and, 123; rural vote and, 130–31, 138
CNN, 340
CNN/Opinion Research Corp. surveys, 128
coal mining, 129–30
coded language, 301, 409
Colby College, 1
college, 379; information economy and, 196; rural areas and, 148; skepticism toward, 367; views on, *313, 314*

College Advising Corps, Rural Initiatives, 396

Collins, Susan, 176

Colored Farmers' National Alliance and Cooperative Union, The, 69

Columbia Journalism Review, 25

Comet Ping Pong Pizza, 327

Coming Apart (Murray), 227

commercialism, 65

Commission on Country Life, 73

communal values, 366

community cohesion, 234–41

community collapse, 216–17; rural churches and, 228

community connectedness, 218, 413

community engagement, 204, 214, *215, 218*

community grievance, 194

community institutions, 235

community organizations, 213

community structures, 202

community well-being, 365

commuting patterns, 36

competition: international trade and, 187; Jay Treaty and, 64; political, 385–93

composition effect, 8, 148–49, 413

CompuServe, 335

Confederate Flag, 298, 303–4

Confederate states, 386; Tea Party and, 128

Confederate symbols, 290

confidence intervals, 363

connectedness, 13, 203

conservative culture, 265

conservative reaction, 283; politics of, 99–105

conservative revolution, 90–92

conservative values, 265–70, *266*

conspiracism, 122, 367, 371

conspiracy theories, 327, 353

Constitutional Convention, 61

content analysis, 261

Cook, Charlie, 129

Cook County, Illinois, 57

Cook Political Report, 129

Coolidge, Calvin, 78

Cooperative Congressional Election Study (CCES), 168, *169*, 300

cosmopolitanism, 367

cottonseed oil, 69

Council on Foreign Relations, 105

counties, 26–27; census tracts and, 183; dissimilarity index and, 183–84; political statistics and, 37; population density measures of, 36; ruralness measures and, 36, 153–54; ruralness of, *38*

"Country Boy Can Survive, A" (song), 245

Country Life Movement, 73

country music, 277–78

Country Music (documentary), 277

"Country Roads" (song), 244–45

county agents, 75

county election commissions, 324–25

Couric, Katie, 125

covert racism, 292

COVID-19 pandemic, 92–93, 170, 214, 328, 355, 382, 412–13; media coverage of, 342–46; relief spending in, 345; Rural Rabble-Rousers and, 352; vaccination for, 343–44

Cracker Barrel, 278

Cramer, Kathy, 14–15, 291, 331, 397

crime levels, 226

critical race theory, 328, 390, 411

Cruz, Ted, 130

Cullen, Art, 199

cultural divides, 74, 91

cultural-generation gaps, 9

cultural issues, 121–22

cultural memory, 271

cultural perceptions, 248

cultural precarity, 363, 366, 374, 376

cultural wedge issues, 259

culture, 246, 319–20; conservative, 265; gaps in, 270; nonwhite rural residents and, 316–20

culture war, 104, 112, *113*

Culver, John, 111

cyberbalkanization, 358

Cyrus, Billy Ray, 277

Daily Yonder, 399

Danbom, David, 166

Danom, David, 69

Danville River Mill, 119

Darrow, Clarence, 74

Davenport, Marilyn, 299

Davis, Darren, 303

Davis, John W., 80–81

Daylight Savings Time (DST), 75–76

Death and Life of Great American Cities, The (Jacobs), 382

deeply engaged voters, 347–55, *354*, 409

Deliverance (film), 274

delocalization, of news, 341

democracy: community connections and, 208; competition and, 385–93; Jacksonian, 206; landownership and, 63; yeoman, 65

Democracy in America (Tocqueville), 165

Democratic National Committee, 393

Democratic National Convention of 1924, 80

Democratic National Convention of 2004, 126

Democratic Party: demographic groups and, *132*; factions in, 80; "feeling thermometer" questions and, *211*; grievance and, 372–74; New Deal and, 83–85; Populists and, 71; predicting support of, 372–74, *373*; rural areas and, 393–94; rural counties and Senate candidates from, 133, *134*; rural hostility to, 372; rural-urban divide and, 8; rural voters and, 66, *66*, 369–74, 398–401; showing up and, 393–95, 401; South and, 67–68, 78–79, 84–85, 89, 386–89; state legislatures and, 137

Democratic-Republican Party, 65, 67

demographic gaps, 8–9

demographic groups: conflating, 150; party importance of, *132*

demographic shifts: back-to-the-land movement and, 245; racial attitudes and, 300; Rural Voter Survey and, 310

Denver, John, 244–45

Department of Agriculture: Reagan on size of, 106; ruralness measures, 36

Department of Labor, 129

Dewey, John, 80

digital subscriber lines (DSL), 335

discrimination: hard work and overcoming, 308; impact of historical, 296, 306; individualism and, 302; past, *295*, 296, 298, 307–8; perceptions of, 294, *295*; racial, 290–91, 294, *295*, 301–2; structural features of, 302

disinformation, 353

dissimilarity index, *181*, 181–84

distrust, 202–4, 208; political, *211*, 211–12

divides, 59

Dixie Chicks, 277

Dixville Notch, New Hampshire, 31

Dobbs decision, 391

dog whistles, 301, 408

Doheny-Farina, Stephen, 358

Dominion, 326

Dondore, Dorothy Anne, 271

Douglas, Stephen A., 45

Down Home North Carolina, 410

Downs, Anthony, 388, 390

droughts, 82

drug abuse, *230*, 230–31

DSL. *See* digital subscriber lines

Duck Dynasty (television show), 139, 275, 284–86

Duffus, Mike, 119

Duke, David, 115

Dukes of Hazzard, The (television series), 29

Dust Bowl, 82

East Millinocket, Maine, 187

echo chamber phenomenon, 357–58

ecological fallacies, 144, 399

economic anxiety, 188, 247, 375; grievance and, 194; in rural communities, 190–92, *191*; shared, 318; in urban communities, *191*, 192–93

"Economic Anxiety Did Not Make People Vote for Trump, Racism Did," 289

economic decline, 162, 189, 250, 371

economic deprivation, 162–63; social solidarity and, 176–80

economic grievance, 292; nonwhite rural residents and, 316–20

economic growth: divides in, 74; partisanship and, 171; rural perceptions of, 162

economic indicators, 168–70, *169*

economic inequalities, 165–66, 174–76, *175*, 177

economic integration, 162, 180–85

economic mobility, 188–89, 375; gender and perceptions of, 197

economic opportunity, 165; racial differences in, 308; views toward other groups and, 309

Economic Opportunity Act (1964), 88

economic segregation, 183

Economic Theory of Democracy, The (Downs), 388

economic transitions, 179; China shock and, 186–88

economic vulnerability, 166

economic well-being, 365

Education Amendments (1972), 102

Egner, Jeremy, 276

election of 2020: certification of results, 324–25; political engagement and, 219–21, *220*; Trump claims about, 326; voter turnout in, 218

Electoral College, 44, 50–51, 53, 56, 60

electoral institutions, 60

"electric church" ministries, 104

electric lighting, 207

electrification, 83

electronic entertainment, 213

elite consensus, 98

Emerging Republican Majority, The (Phillips), 100

Endangered Species Act, 102

Enlarged Homestead Act (1909), 82

environmental movement, 110

Environmental Protection Agency (EPA), 120, 129

environmental protections, 120

EPA. *See* Environmental Protection Agency

Equal Employment Opportunity Commission, 102

Equal Rights Amendment (ERA), 104

Esquire (magazine), 122

eugenics, 76

evangelicals, 99–100, 103–4, 256–60, 363, 366, 368

Evans, Hiram, 77

evolution, 73

excise tax, 64

expertise: grievance and, 164, 317; local, 341; New Deal and, 91; views of, 98, *313*, 314, 367, 382

extremism, 357–58, 367, 392; ideological, 18; religious, 258; unequal institutions and, 50

Facebook, 200, 337, 358

Fairfax County, Virginia, 45, 47

Falwell, Jerry, 103–4

family life patterns, changing, 213

Farm Bankruptcy Act, 83

Farm Credit Administration, 83

Farmers' Alliance, 69, 207

"Farmers Declaration of Independence" (Patrons of Husbandry), 69

Fauci, Anthony, 18, *211*, 352; "feeling thermometer" questions and, 210, *211*

FDR. *See* Roosevelt, Franklin D.

Federal Communications Commission, 335

Federal Emergency Relief Administration, 81

federal government: balance of payments and, 53–55, *54*, 398–99; confidence in, 107–10, *108*; county agents and, 75; deeply engaged voters and, 350; formation of, 63; Hamilton and Jefferson debate over, 63–64; infrastructure investments, 55, 399; Johnson war on poverty and, 90–92; one-party systems and, 388; Reagan and, 103, 107, 109–10; rural land purchase lending by, 89; rural-urban continuum measures, 36; Southwest settlement, 82

"Federalist No. 10," 63, 386

Federal Land Policy and Management Act, 110

federal spending, 399; ruralness and, 53–55

Fey, Tina, 125

fiber optic lines, 335

film, 272, 274–75, 280

financial well-being, 189, 375

Finkenauer, Abby, 6

Fiorina, Mo, 112

First Great Migration, 74

fiscal conservatism, 10

Fischer, Claude, 207

"Fitter Families for Future Firesides" competitions, 76, 291

5G, 335

FiveThirtyEight.com, 343

Flaccavento, Anthony, 131

Flat Rock Church, 228

Fletcher, Tommy, 90

Floyd, George, 289, 291, 296, 298, 411

flyover country, 29; journalists and, 339

food stamps, 102

foreign policy, 105

Fourteenth Amendment, 325

Fox News, 2, 9–10, 210, 297, 326–27, 332, 351, 390

Frank, Thomas, 10, 140, 160–61, 285

free trade, 4, 109, 117

French and Indian War, 63

Frey, William, 8

Fukuyama, Francis, 208

Gallup, 157, 213, 277; on news consumption, 332–33; on rural religiosity, 229

Galston, Bill, 283

Gamble, James, 166

Gannett, 331

gap instinct, 32, 55

gay rights, 104

gender discrimination, 102

gender gap, 314–16, *315*; in partisanship, 198; Rural Voter Survey and, 198; in Trump support, 196, 198

General Social Survey (GSS), 107, *108*, 112, 151, 240; trust and, 209, *209*

genism, 438n71

Gensim library, 240

geographic mobility, 236

geography: comparisons based on, 25; group identity and, 13; as political fault line, 21; political institutions and, 49; racial attitudes and, 320; rural politics and, 49; wedge issues and, 11

"Geography of Social Capital in America, The" (Joint Economic Committee), 223

gerrymandering, 49, 389

Ghosting the News (Sullivan), 329

ghost newspapers, 329

Gideon, Sara, 176

Gimple, James, 279

Gingrich, Newt, 112, 117

Ginsberg, Ruth Bader, 49

"givers *versus* takers" argument, 283

giving rate, 214

Glendon, Mary Ann, 391

global economic interdependence, 210

globalization, 4, 10, 69, 150, 160, 177; China shock and, 186–88; gender differences in feelings about, 314

Gluesenkamp Perez, Marie, 120, 403–5

GoFundMe, 200

Goldberg, Michelle, 384

Golden, Jared, 404–7

Goldsmith, Brian, 125

Goldwater, Barry, 92–93, 102, 111

Gonyea, Don, 138

Gordon, Linda, 77

Gore, Al, 116, 120

government institutions: confidence in, 107–8, *108*; distrust in, 192, 203

Gowdy, Trey, 126

Grange. *See* Patrons of Husbandry

Great Agricultural Transition, 86–89

Great Betrayal, The (Buchanan), 117

Great Depression, 141–43, 167, 244–45; media during, 272

Great Migration, 74

Great Northern Paper Company, 187

Great Plains, 69; agricultural frontier expansion in, 166; open cattle markets and, 383

Great Recession, 110, 127, 138, 186, 299, 328–29; rural churches and, 228

Great Society, 88–89, 92, 102

Great Valleys and Prairies of Nebraska and the Northwest, The (Wilber), 82

Green Acres (television show), 273

Greenback Party, 70

Greenberg, Anna, 123

Greene, Marjorie Taylor, 263, 353, 390

Greenhouse, Linda, 103

Griffin, Couy, 325, 327

Griffith, Andy, 273

Griffith, G. H., 76

group consciousness, 365

grouped data, 31, 41

group identity, 12–16; rural identity and, 19–20

group-level data, 144

group position theory, 300

GSS. *See* General Social Survey

Guardian, The (newspaper), 397

gun control, 120, 255, 289–90; rights talk and, 392

gun culture, 247, 286

gun ownership, 249–56, 374

gun regulations, 251, *253*, 254

Guth, James, 104

Halloween (film), 275

Hamilton, Alexander, 56, 63–65, 67

hard money, 61

"hard work" questions, 304–9

Harkins, Anthony, 274–75

Harris, Kamala, 352

Hart, Peter, 116

Hart of Dixie (television show), 256, 276

Hatch, Orrin, 111

Hate Inc. (Taibbi), 340

Hayes, Danny, 329–30, 332

health insurance, *169*, 170, 184

Heclo, Hugh, 97

Hee Haw (television show), 273

Heitkamp, Heidi, 133

Here Comes Honey Boo Boo (television show), 275

Hickock, Lorena, 81

higher education, 396

Hill, Faith, 277

Hillbillies for Hire (television show), 275

Hillbilly (Harkins), 274

hillbilly culture, 241

Hillbilly Elegy (Vance), 7, 221, 402

"Hillbilly Moment–A Meaty Loaf!" (video), 279

Hills Have Eyes, The (film), 275

Hochschild, Arlie, 305

Hodges, Eric, 261

Hoff, Dena, 118

Hofstadter, Richard, 387, 393

Holden Farms Market, 158–62, 164

Homestead Act (1862), 69, 82, 207

homophily, 357

homophobia, 114

Hoover, Herbert, 141–42

Hopkins, Daniel, 356

horror films, 275, 280

Houser Poll, 142

housing segregation, 291

Hout, Michael, 310

"How the Left Lost Its Heart" (Frank), 140

Huckabee Sanders, Sarah, 11

Humbard, Rex, 104

Humphrey, Hubert, 100

hunting, 251, 254–55, 374

Hussein, Saddam, 122

Ice Road Truckers (television show), 275
identity: place membership and, 203; social community and, 202
ideological extremism, 18
ideological homogenization, 389, 392
If You Lived Here You'd Be Home by Now (Ingraham), 222
Illinois State Senate, 57
immigration, 160, 210, 309–12, *311*, 316, 367, 379
implicit prejudices, 302
income brackets, 432n21
income gap, 171
income inequality, 4
Increasingly United States, The (Hopkins), 356
individualism, 205, 304–5, 309; discrimination and, 302
industrialization, 32, 57, 65, 69
Industrial Revolution, 69, 73
information economy, 4; education and, 196; gender gaps and, 196; jobs and, 177, *178*, 179
Inglis, Bob, 126
Ingraham, Christopher, 222
Institute for Rural Journalism and Community Issues, 222
institutions: community, 235; confidence in government, 107–8, *108*; distrust in, 192, 202–3, 208; electoral, 60; extremism and unequal, 50; geography and political, 49; legitimacy crisis in, 49–50; in "real America" myth, 395–97
integration: dissimilarity index and, *181*, 181–84; economic, 180–85; measures of, 181
interest-based communities, 358
international economy: borders and, 34; rise of, 186
internet: media growth and, 356; news and, 334–38; partisan polarization and, 337; Rural Rabble-Rousers and, 355
internet connectivity, 334–38; mobile, 336; surveys and, 157

Iowa Caucus, 123, 199, 322
IPSOS, 156
isolation, 201, 205
It's a Wonderful Life (film), 272

Jackson, Alan, 277
Jackson, Jonathan, 386
Jacksonian democracy, 206
Jacobs, Jane, 382
January 6th Capitol insurrection, 50, 325, 344–45, *354*, 378
Jarmin, Gary, 104
Jay Treaty (1794), 64–65
J. David Houser and Associates, 142
Jefferson, Thomas, 19, 30, 44, 56, 63–65, 67
Jim Crow, 81, 85, 95, 409
job-training programs, 161
Johnson, Lyndon, 46, 88–91, 93, 122, 291
Johnson, Ron, 339
Joint Economic Committee, 223, 225
Juneteenth, 287–88

Kaiser Family Foundation, 127, 343–44
Kam, Cindy, 302
Kansans for Life, 391
Kansas: constitutional amendment referendum in, 391; cultural wedge issues and, 259
Katz, Bruce, 29
Katznelson, Ira, 85
Kelly, Megyn, 138
Kennebec County, Maine, 46, 48
Kennedy, John F., 122
Kent, Joe, 404
Kerry, John, 120, 123, 322
Key, V. O., Jr., 16, 387–88, 390, 393
Kincaid Act (1904), 82
Kinder, Don, 294
King, Stephen, 275
KKK. *See* Ku Klux Klan
Klan movement, 76–78, 291
Krugman, Paul, 53, 398–400

Krupnikov, Yanna, 341, 347, 350–51
Ku Klux Klan (KKK), 76–78, 115, 272

labor force participation, 171
Lalami, Laila, 357
Landon, Alf, 5, 142
landownership, democracy and, 63
Latent Dirichlet Allocation (LDA), 240,
    438n71
Latinos, 309–12, *311*, 379
Laucher, Marvin, 180
Law and Order (television show), 281
Lawless, Jennifer, 329–30, 332
LDA. *See* Latent Dirichlet Allocation
League for the Advancement of States Equal
    Rights, 111
League of Women Voters, 219
learned helplessness, 241
Lease, Mary Elizabeth, 70
Lee, Michael, 223, 235
Legend of Shelby the Swampman, The
    (television show), 275
Leonard, Robert, 407
LePage, Paul, 255
Lewis, Sinclair, 28, 271
LGBTQIA+ people, 259–60, 402
Life (magazine), 90
Life Below Zero (television show), 275
likely voter models, 154
Limbaugh, Rush, 210
Lincoln, Abraham, 67
Lincoln, Benjamin, 62
Lindert, Peter, 165
linked fate, 13–14, 164, 185, 365
literacy, 206
Literary Digest (magazine), 142
literature, 271
Little House on the Prairie, The (television
    series), 29, 245, 273
Liu, Eric, 219
Lobao, Linda, 87
localism, 205
local news, 326, 328–31, *334*, 341

local politics, 16
local television, 331
Long, Huey, 388
long decline supposition, 171
Louisiana Territory, 65
Lucid, 156
lyceum movement, 206

Madison, James, 63–64, 386
Maggio, Christopher, 310
Magnuson, Warren, 111
Mai, H. J., 339
Maine: Democrats and, 404–7; gun ownership
    and, 255; Kennebec County, 46, 48
Maines, Natalie, 277
Main Street (Lewis), 28, 271
Maloney, Brian, 321
manufacturing: China and, 130, 186–87; decline
    of, 162, 167, 196, 305, 403; Hamilton and,
    64; NAFTA and, 118–19, 130; rural America
    and, 24, 29, 186–87; Southeast and, 33
MarketWatch, 342
marriage equality, 255
Massachusetts: in post-Revolutionary
    War era, 62–63; Worcester County,
    153–54
mass entertainment: internet and, 336; rural
    culture in, 270–83
Mathews County, Virginia, 40–41
Matthews, Melvin, 228
Maytag, 119
McAdoo, William Gibbs, 80
McCain, John, 8, 121–22, 124, 322
McCaskill, Claire, 242
McConnell, Mitch, 127
McEntire, Reba, 277
McGovern, George, 6, 111
McKinley, William, 167
Meadville, Pennsylvania, 261
Mecklin, John, 77
media: changing landscape of, 326–27;
    country music, 277–78; COVID-19
    and, 342–46; cultural memory and,

271; expansion of, 355–56; in Great
Depression, 272; homogenization of, 357;
internet and, 334–38, 355–56; local news
decline, 326, 328–31; misrepresentation in,
327–28; nationalization of news, 210,
332–33, 353; new, 355–56; perceptions of
rural life portrayals, 281–83, 282; "real
America" myth and, 397; rural America
portrayals in news, 338–47, 343; rural
culture in, 270–83; social, 337, 355;
stereotypes and, 281
Media Cloud, 342
Media Matters, 297
media politics, 327
mediation, 339
Medicaid, 4
mega-churches, 257
Melnick, Shep, 102
Mencken, H. L., 79
meritocracy, 304, 308
Metropolitan Revolution, The (Katz and
Bradley), 29
Meyer, Katherine, 87
Michels, Tim, 339
micropolitan statistical areas, 36
migrant labor, 34
military service, 260–64, 265, 376
Milk, Harvey, 104
Millinocket, Maine, 187–88, 287–88
Mills, Janet, 255
mobile internet access, 336
mobility: economic, 188–89, 197, 375;
geographic, 236; social, 304
Mondale, Walter, 46–47
Monster.com, 280
Moonshiners (television show), 275
Morning Consult, 139
Moscone, George, 104
motivated reasoning, 348
Mount Vernon, Maine, 297, 352
Movement Advancement Project, 259
multivariate modeling, 360–61
Munis, Kal, 189, 340

Murray, Charles, 227
Mutz, Diana, 300
My Big Redneck Family (television show),
275
MySpace, 358

NAFTA. See North American Free Trade
Agreement
Nation, The (magazine), 289
National Endowment for the Arts, 114
nationalism, 260–64
nationalization: of news, 210, 353, 357; of
rural identity, 76, 96
nationalized news, 332–33
National Public Radio (NPR), 339, 342
National Rifle Association, 255–56
National Tea Party Federation, 299. See also
Tea Party
nativism, 137
Navarette, Ruben, Jr., 124
Negroponte, Nicholas, 355
Nemerever, Zoe, 153
New Deal, 5, 80–86, 88, 91–92, 100, 135, 167
New Hampshire Union Leader (newspaper),
330
Newlin, Matt, 396
new media, 355–56
news: COVID-19 and, 342–46; decline of
local, 326, 328–31, 341; delocalization of,
341; echo chamber phenomenon and,
357; engagement with, 334; expansion of,
355–56; homogenization of, 357; internet
and, 334–38; nationalization of, 210,
332–33, 353, 357; primary sources of, 337;
rural America portrayals in, 338–47, 343;
rural sources of, 327
News for the Rich, White, and Blue (Usher),
341
newspapers, 206; advertising revenue and,
329–30; ghost, 329; rural politics stories
ion, 340; subscriptions to, 334
Newton, Iowa, 119
New York (magazine), 395

New York Times (newspaper), 50, 93, 342, 345, 347, 398, 407; COVID-19 coverage, 343; *Ozark* review in, 276; Scopes trial coverage by, 74

Nicholson, Stephen, 300

Nickelodeon, 279

Nixon, Richard, 91–92, 100–102, 112, 167, 409; southern strategy and, 292

nonwhite rural residents, 4; grievance, culture, and social capital and, 316–20

Norpoth, Helmut, 142

North American Free Trade Agreement (NAFTA), 109, 117–19, 121, 130, 186, 210, 268; ghost towns and, 162

Northern Exposure (television show), 276

Northwestern University/Medill Local News Initiative, 331

"No Sympathy for the Hillbilly" (Rich), 395

Novak, Robert, 99

NPR. *See* National Public Radio

Nwanevu, Osita, 50

Obama, Barack, 8, 120–29, 135, 139, 249–50, 252, 355, 411; economic concerns and, 126; local media and, 332; Tea Party and, 299–300, 392; Trump and, 122, 289; "you didn't build that" comment, 320–22

Obamacare, 110. *See also* Affordable Care Act

Obamaphobia, 299–300

Occupational Safety and Health Administration, 102

Office of Management and Budget, ruralness measures, 36

offshoring, 177

Oklahoma! (film), 272

Oliver, Maggie Toulouse, 326

one-party systems, 386–88, 390–91

online surveys, 155, 157

On Target (Schwartz), 255

opioid abuse, 231

Oswego, New York, 45–47

Otero County, New Mexico, 324, 326–27

Our Town (Wilder), 271

overrepresentation, 27, 49, 52, 56

Ozark (television show), 276–77

Palin, Sarah, 121, 124–26, 138–39, 264

Parker, Christopher, 299

participant civic culture, 207–8

partisan polarization, 99; internet usage and, 337; rural America press coverage and, 346

partisan press, 206

partisanship, 160, 247; affective, 337; economic correlates to, 171; gender gap in, 198; gun ownership and, 252–54, *253*; internet usage and, 337; rural, 20–21, 97–98

partisan sorting, 389

party competition, 385–93; lack of, 386–88; spatial modeling framework of, 388

Party Down South (television show), 275

patriotism, 260–64, *262*, 286, 362–63, 366, 368; in country music, 278

Patrons of Husbandry (Grange), 69, 71, 207

Pearson, Justin J., 290

Pelosi, Nancy, 243, 404

penny press, 206

People's Party (Populist Party), 70–71

Perot, Ross, 118, 120

Perry, Andre M., 150

persistent poverty, 179

personal well-being, 362; economic grievance and, 194

Petticoat Junction (television show), 273

Pew Research Center, 11, 218; on broadband access, 336; on religious attitudes, 256

Peyton Place (film), 272

Pfeiffer, Dan, 332

Phenix City Story, The (film), 272

Philadelphia, Pennsylvania, 30

Phillips, Kevin, 100, 138

Pipa, Tony, 408

Pizzagate, 327

place-based anxiety, *191*, 191–92, 194, *195*, 362, 366, 369, 371 place-based communities, 358

place-based grievance, 192–94, *195*, 247, 362, 366, 375

place-based solidarity, 163–64

polarization, 46, 99

police brutality, 296

police reform, 297

policy framing: covert racism and, 292; progressives in rural America and, 407

political behaviors: class and, 167; connecting with candidates and, 402; quantifying, 360

political distrust, *211*, 211–12

political engagement, 218; gaps in, 348

political extremism, 367

political identity, 25; averages and, 361; rural-urban divide and, 381

political institutions: geography and, 49; liberal politics and, 393

political journalism, 338–47

political party competition, 385–93

political radicalization, 18

Politico, 8, 342

polling data: Black Americans and, 411; geography and, 151; political journalism and, 341; on Tea Party, 128; voter sentiment and, 142

pop culture, 248

population density, 419n22; ruralness and, 39–40, *40*

populism, 3–4; Buchanan and, 115; elitism replaced by, 268; Palin and, 126; right-wing, 268; rural politics in aftermath of, 72–79

Populist movements, 62, 68, 70–72, 167

Populist Party. *See* People's Party

poverty, 250, 388; child, 184; community types and exposure to, *185*; Johnson war on, 90–92; persistent, 179; rural, 81–82, 90, 159, 162, 168; urban, 162, 171

power: of association, 206; one-party systems and, 387; of rural voters, 95–96; Senate and distribution of, 50, 53

Prairie and the Making of Middle America, The (Dondore), 271

presidential primaries: Buchanan and, 114–15; Iowa and, 199; Trump and, 130

primary elections: certification of, 324–26; lack of party competition and, 388–91; Trump endorsements and, 242

private militias, *262*, 378

Procter, William, 166

Program in Agrarian Studies, 396

Progressive Movement, 207

Prohibition, 77, 80, 142–43

protectionism, 187

Proud Boys, 289

PRRI. *See* Public Religion Research Institute

public education, 74

Public Religion Research Institute (PRRI), 290

public schools, 206, 378

public services, 4

Putin, Vladimir, 331

Putnam, Robert, 212–14, 216, 227, 235, 357–58, 383

Q-Anon, 18

Quarry, The (video game), 280

racial animosity, 359

racial attitudes, 302–3, 368; changes in, 410–11; demographic shifts and, 300; geography and, 320; hard work and, 304–9

racial discrimination, 290–91, 301–2; perceptions of, 294, *295*

racial equality, 408–9

racial identifications, 294

racial justice, 297

racial politics, 320

racial prejudice, 294, 368–69

racial relations, 76, 288

racial resentment, 194, 293, 305, 360–62, 371–72; hard work and, 306–8, *307*; measuring, 294–96, *295*, 300–302, 305

racial stereotyping, 369, 411

racism, 114, 292, 316–17, 368; beliefs and, 294; coded language and, 301, 409; implicit prejudices and, 302; rural consciousness and, 291; rural voters and, 408–12; structural, 290; symbolic, 294, 296, 298, 300, 303, 316; Tea Party and, 299, 301; Trump and, 289, 291

Rea, Michael, 337–38

Reagan, Ronald, 7, 46, 48, 92, 102–6, 108–13, 167, 409; on Department of Agriculture, 106; distrust toward government and, 98; federal government and, 103, 107, 109–10; NAFTA and, 117; presidential campaign start, 107; southern strategy and, 292

"real America" myth, 98, 106–11, 137, 188, 202, 385; institutions in, 395–97

reality shows, 275

Reconstruction, 71, 76, 386

regional politics, 71

Reimagining Rural Policy Initiative, 408

religion, 256–60, 257; rural voter model and, 376–77; social capital and, 227–29

religious divides, 21

religious extremism, 258

religious schools, segregation and, 103

replacement theory, 353, 354

representation: geographic schemes of, 49; overrepresentation, 27, 49, 52, 56; in state legislatures, 56; U.S. Senate and, 51–52, 56

republican movement, 64–65

Republican Party: demographic groups and, 132; first candidates run by, 66–67; in post-Civil War era, 71–72; rural area dominance by, 389; small towns and, 124; state legislatures and, 137; "two Americas" rhetoric and, 121

resentment, 163

Resettlement Agency, 83

Revolutionary War, 61, 165

Revolution of 1800, 67

Rich, Frank, 126, 395

"Rich and Miserable" (song), 278

Riggs, Marlon, 114

rights talk, 391–92

right-wing populism, 268

Riney-Kehrberg, Pamela, 228

risky shift phenomenon, 392

Roaring Twenties, 74, 76

Robb Elementary School shooting. See Uvalde, Texas, school shooting

Roberts, Oral, 104

Robertson, Alan, 139

Robertson, Pat, 104

Robertson, Phil, 285–86

Rodden, Jonathan, 49, 389

Roe v. Wade, 102–3

Rogers, David, 115

Rogers, Melissa, 153

Romney, Mitt, 8, 321–22

Roosevelt, Franklin D. (FDR), 5, 46, 79, 81, 90–91, 141–44, 167

Roosevelt, Theodore, 73

Roper Center, 151

Rosenberg, Nathan, 88

Rosling, Hans, 32

Ross, Edward Alsworth, 73

Rossi, Leslie, 340

Rossiter, Clinton, 167

rural: conflating with other demographics, 150; difficulties in defining, 25–27, 30

rural America, 22, 38; assumptions about, 24; church attendance rates in, 256–58; community cohesion in, 234–41; conservative values and, 265–70, 266; COVID-19 vaccination and, 343–44; creating better images of, 355–58; cultural perceptions of, 248; descriptions of community, 239, 239–40; differences in areas of, 32–33; distrust in, 203; drug abuse and, 230, 230–31; economic anxiety in, 190–92, 191; economic changes and, 4, 177; economic inequality in, 174–76, 175; economic integration and, 180–85; ethnicities of, 24; expansion of, 69; gender differences in economic perceptions, 197; gross domestic production in, 171–74, *173*; group identity of, 12–16; gun ownership and, 249–56, *253*; hometown residence and, 236; hostility toward Democratic Party in, 372; interconnectedness with, 400; manufacturing and, 186–87; measurement challenges and, 26–27; media on, 29, *343*; news media engagement, *334*; news media portrayals of, 338–47; patriotism and, 260–64, *262*; place-based grievance in, 191–92, *193*; political engagement in, 220, 220–21; politics of "hard work" in, 299–304; pop culture and, 248; progressives and, 402–8, 410; public policy debates and, 268–70, *269*; public services in, 4; race and racism in, 293–98; religious beliefs and practices in, 256–58, *257*; sense of place and, 13–16; social capital in, 212–26, *226*, 234, 238; social engagement in, *215*, 216–17, 221–26; trust declines and, 382; unification of, 61; urban America need of, 382–83; views of community in, 236–37, *237*, 238, *238*

Rural America Survey, 223, 247; on anticosmopolitanism, 312–14, *313*; on immigration attitudes, 309–12, *311*; women and gender questions, 314–16, *315*

rural areas: civic engagement and, 225–26; college and, 148; crime levels in, 226; federal spending and, 399; internet access and, 157, 334–38; 1920 census on, 78; overrepresentation of, 49, 56; persistent poverty levels in, 179; U.S. Senate voting advantage for, 50, *51*, 52

rural bias, 56–57

Rural College Student Experience, The (podcast), 396

rural communities: connectedness and, 203; COVID-19 and, 382; economic thinking and shared sense of place, 182; identity and, 202; ideological homogenization in, 389; inequality in, 400; stereotypes about, 234–35

rural consciousness, 14, 291

rural counties, 36–37; Census Bureau measurement of, 419n22; census tracts in, 183, 432n28; missing from census estimates, 419n23; U.S. Senate and, 133, *134*

rural culture, 246, 249, 292, 319–20, 362; in mass entertainment, 270–83; southernification of, 290

rural decline, 159

rural development, 396

rural economy, 171–72, *172*, 189, 318; current state of, 168–76; energy economy and, 383; gender similarities in perceptions of, 197; global economic depression and, 81–82; historical, 165–67; media coverage on, 346; schools' place in, 231–33; World War I and, 75

Rural Electrification Administration, 83

rural grievance, 163–64, 185, 188–95, *193*, 384; Democratic Party and, 372–74; left-leaning politics and, 395; nonwhite rural residents and, 316–20

rural identity, 12–16, 19–20, 106, 318, 363, 368; development of, 246; economic deprivation and, 163; nationalization of, 76, 96; politicians exploiting, 384; rural-urban divide and, 364–65; white and nonwhite, 318–19, *319*

Rural Initiatives, 396

rural land use, 270

rural life: film depictions of, 272, 274–75; literary depictions of, 271; perceptions of media portrayals of, 281–83, *282*; television depictions of, 272–77

ruralness, 26–28; balance of payments and, 53–54, *54*; block density and, 35; counties by, *38*; defining in negative, 33–34; federal spending and, 53–55; historical measure of, 30–31; measures of, 36–43, 152–54; median household incomes and, 179; population density and, 39–40, *40*; state size and, 51–52; U.S. House districts and, 133, *134*; U.S. Senate and, 133, *133* rural partisanship, 20–21, 97–98

rural politics, 171, 241–43; conservative revolution and, 90–92; demographic parts of, 99; geography and, 49; grievance importance to, 164; impact of, 48–55; local politics and, 16; media distortions of, 328; research approach to, 17–22; sectionalism and, 68, 68, 72

rural poverty, 81–82, 159, 162, 168, 250; Johnson and, 90

rural pride, 241–43

Rural Rabble-Rousers, 347–55, 357, 367–68, 385, 409

rural realignment thesis, 85–86, 86

rural reality shows, 275

Rural Rebellion (Benes), 109

rural resentment, 14–15

rural schools, 227, 229–30, 230, 231–34; media coverage on, 346

rural sitcoms, 276

Rural Sociological Society, 396

Rural-Urban Commuting Area, 36

rural-urban divide, 3, 143; in aftermath of populism (1896-1932), 72–79; charting, 380; composition effects and, 148–49; COVID-19 and, 412; Democratic Party and, 8; early Republic, Civil War, and agrarian unrest (1824-1912), 67–72; engagement differences and, 348; foundations of (1760-1824), 61–67; Great Agricultural Transition (1960-1980), 86–89; gun ownership and, 251; media use of, 397; New Deal and rural realignment (1932-1960), 80–86; political history and, 5–12; political identity and, 381; politicians exploiting, 384; racism questions and, 296; reconsidering, 56–58; religious attitudes and, 256; rural identity and, 364–65; Trump and, 6–11

Rural Voter Model, 216, 362–65, 364, 368; Biden and, 370; questions used in, 374–79; Trump and, 370

rural voters, 12, 59–60, 359; composition effects and, 148; creation of, 97–98, 106–11; deeply engaged, 347–55, 349, 409; Democratic Party and, 66, 66, 369–74, 398–401; economic self-interest and, 160–61; emergence of, 137–40; FDR and, 83; identity and, 95–96; importance of, 49; Nixon and, 101; overrepresentation and, 49; Populists and, 70–71; power of, 95–96; predictive model of, 360–68; prior survey research of, 150–51; racism and, 408–12; survey subjects and topics for, 150–57

Rural Voter Survey, 5, 22, 98, 128, 149, 151, 154; anxiety and, 188; on conservative values, 266, 267–68; deeply engaged voters and, 347–55, 349, 354; demographic distribution of, 152; drug abuse and crime attitudes, 230, 230–31; economic mobility questions, 189; "feeling thermometer" questions in, 210–12, 211; gender gaps and, 196–98; mobile phone use and, 157; on news consumption, 331; on public policy debates, 268–70, 269; race questions in, 293–98, 295, 297; racial attitudes and "hard work" questions, 304–9, 307; on religious beliefs and practices, 256–58, 257, 259; on school engagement, 230; social capital and, 214; social engagement and, 215; survey panels and, 155–56; voter model questions, 374–79

rural voting patterns, 20, 152; homogenization of, 393; measuring in past, 43–48; in postwar period, 86

rustic literature, 271

Ryan, John Barry, 341, 347, 350–51

Ryan, Tim, 242–43, 402–3

Sagebrush Rebellion, 110–11

San Bernardino County, California, 39

Sanders, Bernie, 255

Sanders, Lynn, 294

San Francisco Chronicle (newspaper), 342

Sasse, Ben, 201

Satterwhite, Emily, 283

Saturday Night Live (television show), 124–25

Saunders, Elizabeth, 71

Sawhill, Isabel, 208

Schitt's Creek (television show), 276

Schlafly, Phyllis, 103

Schlesinger, Arthur, 205

school closures, 232–33

school consolidation, 233–34

school shootings, 251–52

Schwartz, Noah, 255

Schwebach, Ryan, 326

Scopes, John, 73–74, 79

Second Amendment, 392

sectionalism, 68, *68*, 72, 76

segregation, 85, 89; economic, 183; housing, 291; religious schools and, 103

Seib, Gerald, 116

sense of place, 13–16, 366; economic thinking and, 182

shared fate, 196–98, 243, 359, 413

Shays, Daniel, 61–63

Sheboygan, Wisconsin, 339

Shelterbelt Project, 83

shifting baseline problem, 26, 30, 50

Siegel, Reva, 103

silent majority, 101

Silver, Nate, 49

Simmons, William Joseph, 76

Sinclair Broadcast Group, 331

sitcoms, 276

small-scale manufacturing, NAFTA and, 118–19

small-state minimums, 57

small states, 51–52; policy imbalances and, 57

small towns, 124; connectedness and, 203

smartphones, 157, 336

Smith, Al, 45, 80

social bonds, 204

social capital, 203, 366, 377, 383; churches and, 227–29; measuring, 217–18; nonwhite rural residents and, 316–20; in rural America, 212–26, *226*, 234, 238; Rural Voter Survey and, 214; schools and, 229–31; trust and, 208; in urban America, 226; Vance on, 242

social capital index, 223, *224*

Social Capital Project, 226

social community, identity and, 202

social contract, 102

social distancing, 382

social divisions, 95

social engagement, 203, 221–26; by area type, *215*; generational change and, 216–17, *217*; levels of, 212–13; Rural Voter Survey and, 214, *215*; schools and, 229

social inequality, 292

social issues, 123

social media, 337, 355

social mobility, 304

social solidarity, economic deprivation and, 176–80

social trust, 203, 208; declines in, 209, *209*

Sokolove, Michael, 93–94

solar fields, *269*, 270

Solid South, 95, 135–36, 386–87, 389

Something Wicked This Way Comes (film), 275

Source, The, 335

southernification, 290

Southern Politics in State and Nation (Key), 387, 393

southern rural reality shows, 275

southern strategy, 292

spatial modeling framework, 388

special education, 232

Special Supplemental Nutrition Program for Women, Infants, and Children, 102

specie, 61

Splendor in the Grass (film), 272

state capitals, 57

state house districts, 57

state legislatures: Democratic Party and, 137; population equality in representation in, 57; Republican Party and, 137 stay laws, 62

stereotypes, 339, 369, 411; dangers of, 283–86

Stevens, Ted, 111

Stewart, Jon, 122

Storm Lake Times (newspaper), 199

Storm Warning (film), 272

Strangers in Their Own Land (Hochschild), 305

structural racism, 290

Stucki, Bryce, 88

suburban America: conservative values and, *266*; drug abuse and, *230*; economic anxiety in, *191*, 192; gun ownership and, 250–51, *253*; news media engagement, *334*; patriotism and, *262*, *263*; place-based grievance in, 192, *193*; political engagement in, 220, *220*; public policy debates and, *269*; religious beliefs and practices in, *257*; schools and, *230*; social engagement in, *215*, 216; views of community in, *237*, *237*, *238*, *238*

suburban counties: census tracts in, 432n28; economic deprivation and, 184; populations of, *43*; Southern state populations and, *67*, *86*

Sullivan, Margaret, 329

Supreme Court, 49, 57, 103; public opinions of, 107

survey panels, 155–56

survey response rates, 155

Sutton, Willy, 101

Swamp People (television show), 275

symbolic groups status model, 300

symbolic racism, 294, 296, 298, 300, 303, 316

Symms, Steven, 111

systemic barriers, 411

Taibbi, Matt, 340

teachers: guns and, 252, *253*; rural schools and, 232, 234

Tea Party, 127–28, 305, 355, 392; Obama and, 299–300; racism and, 299, 301

tech economy, 177

telephone surveys, response rates and, 155

television, 213; local, 331; rural life depictions in, 272–77; rural politics stories on, 340

television evangelists, 104

tender laws, 62

Tennessee Valley Authority, 83

Texas Chainsaw Massacre (film), 275

text classification, 240

Them (Withnow), 201

Thompson, David, 234

Title IX, 102

Tocqueville, Alexis de, 165, 206

Tongues Untied (documentary), 114

topic composition, 438n71

Torrance, County, New Mexico, 325

trade wars, 268–69

transcontinental railroad, 69

transportation aid, 57

travel, 312–13, *313*

traveling rural ministers, 228

Truman, Harry, 122

Trump, Donald, 1–4, 24, 143–51, 167, 170, 369–72, 409–10; abortion vote and, 286; birther conspiracism and, 122; Buchanan and, 99, 116; China and, 130, 268–69; civic engagement and, 219; coal mining and, 130–31; conservatism and, 98; consumer differences and, 278; COVID-19 and, 412; downballot impacts of, 95–96, 99; election manipulation claims, 326; evangelicals and, 258; gender gap in voters for, 196, 198; immigration and, 309–10, 312; Iowa and, 199; media and, 341–42; Obama and, 122, 289; Palin and, 138–39; Pennsylvania and, 93–94; political engagement and, 219, 221; populism and, 268; primary election endorsements by, 242; racism and, 289, 291; rural America press coverage and, 25, 346; rural partisanship and, 133; Rural Rabble-Rousers and, 155, 351; rural resentment and, 14; rural-urban divide and, 6–11; Rural Voter Model and, *370*;

rural voters and, 402; Sinclair and, 331; trade wars and, 268; on urban crime, 231; Vance and, 241–43

Trump House, 340, 347

trust: civic engagement and, 208; declines in, 202–3, 209, *209*, 382; importance of, 205–12; social, 203, 208; social capital and, 208. *See also* distrust

Trust (Fukuyama), 208

Tuccile, J. D., 290

Turner, Frederick Jackson, 70

TWA flight 847 hijacking, 105

Twain, Shania, 277

Twitter, 337

"two Americas" rhetoric, 121

two-party system, 386; spatial modeling framework of competition and, 388

2020 Census, 419n22

Uberti, David, 25

uncivil discourse, 351

unemployment rates, *169*, 170

unions, 214

"Unite the Right" rally, 289

universalism, 304

urban America: church attendance rates in, 257–58; conservative values and, *266*; descriptions of community, 240–41; drug abuse and, *230*; economic anxiety in, *191*, 192–93; economic inequality in, 174–76, *175*; gender differences in economic perceptions, 197; gross domestic production in, 171–74, *173*; gun ownership and, 250–51, *253*; identifying, 365; interconnectedness with, *400*; media representations of, 281; news media engagement, *334*; patriotism and, *262*; place-based grievance in, 192–93, *193*; political engagement in, 220, *220*; public policy debates and, *269*; religious beliefs and practices in, *257*, 257–58; rural America needed by, 382–83; schools and, *230*; social capital in, 226;

social engagement in, *215*, 216; views of community in, 237, *237*, 238, *238*

urban areas: affluence concentration in, 174; block density and, 35; crime levels in, 226; dissimilarity index and, 184; ideological homogenization in, 389; inequality in, 401; 1920 census on, 78

urban counties: Census Bureau measurement of, 419n22; census tracts in, 183, 432n28

urban culture, 246

urban economies, 171–72, *172*

Urban Influence Codes, 36

urbanization, 20, 28; back-to-the-land movement and, 245

urbanized blocks, 37, 41

urban poverty, 162, 171

U.S. Census: American Community Survey of 2018, 156; blocks system, 34–35; of 1920, 78; rural area definitions by, 34

U.S. Constitution: rural-urban split and, 61, 63; Tea Party and, 392

Usher, Nikki, 341

U.S. House of Representatives, 57; census blocks and districts for, 133–34; percentage rural districts and control of, *406*, 406–7; ruralness of districts, 133, *134*

U.S. Senate, 56; rural area voting advantages for, 50, *51*, 52; rural counties and, 133, *134*

Uvalde, Texas, school shooting, 251–52, 255

vaccine hesitancy, 344

vaccines, 343–44, 382

Vance, J. D., 7–8, 149, 202, 221–23, 241–43, 402

Verba, Sidney, 207

Verbeck, Tiffany, 279

Vietnam syndrome, 105

Vietnam War, 262, 264

Virgin River (television show), 256, 276

virtual communities, 358

visual media, rural politics stories in, 340

voluntary associations, 206

volunteering, 214

voting machines, 326–27

voting patterns: homogenization of, 393; measuring in past, 43–48; predicting, 360

voting rights, 65

Wabash County, Indiana, 41–42

Waldman, Paul, 398

Walker, Scott, 14–15

Wallace, George, 89, 100

Wall Street Journal (newspaper), 115

Walmart, 119

Waltons, The (television series), 244–45, 273

War of 1812, 165

Washington, George, 62–64, 206, 386

Washington Monthly, 285

Washington Post (newspaper), 222, 340, 342, 398

wastelands of alienation thesis, 235

Waterville, Maine, 1–2, 380

Watt, James, 111

Webster, Charles, 124

wedge issues, 259, 292

Welch, Edgar, 327

What's the Matter with Kansas? (Frank), 10, 160

Whiskey Rebellion, 64

whiteness, 150; politics of "hard work" and, 299–304

white supremacy, 289, 298

Whole Foods Market, 278

Wilber, Charles Dana, 82

Wilder, Thornton, 271

Williams, Hank, Jr., 245–46, 283

Williams, Mark, 299

Williamson, Jeffrey, 165

Willkie, Wendell, 167

Wilson, David, 303

Wilson, Woodrow, 80

windshield surveys, 235

wireless networks, 335

women, 314–16, *315*

"Wonking Out" (newsletter), 399

Worcester County, Massachusetts, 153–54

work associations, 214

working-class voters, 167

working from home, 214

Works Progress Administration, 83

World Trade Organization (WTO), 186

World War I, 74–76

Wright, Jeremiah, 123

Wrong Turn (film), 275

WTO. *See* World Trade Organization

Wuthnow, Robert, 201, 227, 301–2

Wuthnow, Thomas, 149

yeoman democracy, 65

YouGov, 156–57

Youth Conservation Corps, 88

YouTube, 337

zombie news outlets, 329

www.ingramcontent.com/pod-product-compliance
Ingram Content Group UK Ltd.
Pitfield, Milton Keynes, MK11 3LW, UK
UKHW031421060325
455916UK00004B/123